Habitual Rhetoric

Pittsburgh Series in Composition, Literacy, and Culture

David Bartholomae and Jean Ferguson Carr, Editors

Habitual Rhetoric

Digital Writing before Digital Technology

Alex Mueller

University of Pittsburgh Press

Published by the University of Pittsburgh Press, Pittsburgh, Pa., 15260
Copyright © 2023, University of Pittsburgh Press
All rights reserved
Manufactured in the United States of America
Printed on acid-free paper
10 9 8 7 6 5 4 3 2 1

Cataloging-in-Publication data is available from the Library of Congress

ISBN 13: 978-0-8229-4783-7
ISBN 10: 0-8229-4783-8

Cover art: Image on right is from the British Library, Royal MS 12 E.xxv, fol. 23r (c. 1300); image on bottom is from the Bibliothèque nationale de France, Fr. MS 12584 (c. 1201–1300).
Cover design: Alex Wolfe

For Harriet and Wheazy

Contents

Acknowledgments — ix

Introduction | Digital Writing before Digital Technology — 3

1 | Habitual Rhetoric: A History of *Habitus* — 25

2 | Translation: Online Education and Transfers of Authority — 43

3 | Compilation: The Encyclopedic Habits of Wikipedia — 69

4 | Disputation: Medieval Debate and Digital Dialogue — 93

5 | Amplification: Inhabiting and Annotating the Page — 123

6 | Appropriation: Stealing Bodies and Properties — 155

7 | Salutation: The Public Intimacy of Social Networks — 189

Conclusion | Breaking Bad *Habitus* — 215

Notes — 231

Bibliography — 265

Index — 299

Acknowledgments

The idea for this book began to emerge before the launch of Twitter and Instagram, even before I had become aware of the digital humanities. I therefore have many, many people to thank, some of whom I am afraid I can never properly acknowledge for the significance of their contributions to this project. Since I first began to work on the book in earnest in 2008, the focus, perspective, and argument have changed significantly, which will likely surprise many of my early interlocutors and readers. Perhaps the best evidence of this change may be revealed in my early working titles, "Veni, Vidi, Wiki," and "Words with Friends." My early and, admittedly, naive optimism about the democratic potential of social media platforms has been relentlessly challenged by events of the last decade, especially the disturbing emergence of disinformation campaigns, the thriving market for surveillance software, and the meteoric rise of educational-technology corporations.

First and foremost, I could not have completed this project without the support of my English Department colleagues at UMass Boston, who endured my constant chatter about the connections between the medieval and the digital, read my proposals, and even cowrote pieces that offered inspiration or became incorporated into the language of the book itself. In particular, I want to thank

Hadi Banat, Matt Brown, Neal Bruss, Matt Davis, Sari Edelstein, Mary Agnes Edsall, Libby Fay, Judy Goleman, Holly Jackson, Ryan Judkins, Stephanie Kamath, Scott Maisano, Cheryl Nixon, Dan Remein, Emilio Sauri, Eve Sorum, Rajini Srikanth, Jack Tobin, and Susan Tomlinson. I'm also indebted to UMass Boston colleagues in other colleges and departments who read and responded to my work in the Junior Faculty Writing Group and the Junior Faculty Research Seminar, notably Cassandra Alexopolous, Devin Attalah, Daniela Balanzátegui, Bianca Bersani, Cheryl Ching, Kelly Colvin, Mohamed Gharbi, Daniel Gascón, Shuai Jin, Azizah Jor'dan, Dana Miranda, Brook Moyers, Denise Patmon, Allison Smith, Evan Stewart, John Tyson, and Torrie Wu. And I cannot thank my UMass Boston students enough for their consistent and thoughtful contributions to my thinking about this book. Among the many I could name, I want to recognize Adam Darisse, who offered invaluable (and frankly brilliant) assistance to my edition of Henryson's fables (a project that informs this one), and Leo Boer and Valerie Vargas, who both provided helpful research support for the history of academic commentary and rhetorical amplification.

The book also benefited greatly from the encouraging and challenging responses to talks I gave at the University of Connecticut, the University of Wisconsin, Harvard University, UMass Amherst, the University of Minnesota, and the University of Colorado. I especially want to recognize the heartening support and helpful critiques of Elizabeth Allen, Arthur Bahr, Tiffany Beechy, David Benson, Daniel Birkholz, Lisa Cooper, Taylor Cowdery, Rebecca Davis, Andrea Denny-Brown, Denis Ferhatović, Stacy Klein, William Kuskin, Katherine Little, Andy Scheil, George Shuffelton, Kathleen Tonry, Eric Weiskott, and Jordan Zweck. I also want to thank the audiences in conference sessions at the International Congress on Medieval Studies (Kalamazoo), the International New Chaucer Society Congress (Swansea, Reykjavík), the National Council of Teachers of English Annual Convention (Philadelphia), the Penn State Conference on Rhetoric and Composition (State College), the Modern Language Association Convention (Seattle, Austin, Philadelphia), the Medieval and Renaissance Forum (Plymouth State), the Medieval Materiality Conference (Boulder), the Collaborative Insights through Digital Annotation Workshop (MIT), and the Digital Britain Conference (Harvard). Among the many colleagues at these conferences I could acknowledge, I would like to single out Tom Friedrich, Carl Martin, Myra Seaman, and Tara Williams, who all offered formative insights about corporeality, labor, posthumanism, and media studies that have greatly influenced my perspectives on digital writing.

Most of the research for this project was conducted in library archives and special collections in the United States and Europe that host the manuscripts and early printed books, which are the primary sources for this book. I am therefore greatly indebted to the funding, hospitality, and/or assistance provided by the Hill Museum & Manuscript Library (Collegeville, MN), the Joseph P. Healey, Faculty Research Abroad, and College of Liberal Arts Dean's Research grants (UMass Boston), the Biblioteca Universitaria di Bologna (Italy), the British Library (London), the Library of Trinity College (Dublin), Chetham's Library (Manchester, UK), the Northeast Modern Language Association Summer Fellowship, the Special Collections Visiting Scholar residency at the University of St Andrews (Scotland), the Gilbert and Ursula Farfel Fellowship at the Huntington Library (San Marino, CA), the Visiting Scholar in Medieval Studies residency at Harvard University, and the Corpus Christi Exchange Fellowship at the University of Oxford. Of the numerous librarians and research collaborators I could recognize, I want to highlight my colleagues at the University of Bologna, especially Lorenza Ianacci, Flavia Manservigi, Maddalena Modesti, and Annafelicia Zuffrano. We cotaught a course titled "From Bologna to Blogosphere: A History of Written Correspondence," which addressed the topics and studied the manuscripts that proved to be inspirational for this project as a whole.

Once I had a complete draft, I received a number of responses and critiques from readers who improved the book considerably (and who should receive no blame for its faults). I want to recognize the thoughtful contributions of Kevin Brock and Annette Vee, who offered some helpful advice about the manuscript before I shopped it to presses. And ever since I placed it in the hands of the University of Pittsburgh Press, I have been delighted by their careful review process, which has been expertly facilitated by the acquisitions editor, Josh Shanholtzer. Both of the anonymous reviewers he identified for my manuscript offered incisive advice about the structure, focus, and argument that I hope I have adequately followed. Many thanks also are due to the managing editor, Amy Sherman, and the copyeditor, Matthew Somoroff, who offered careful edits and insightful suggestions that improved the clarity of my language and force of my expression. I am deeply appreciative for their generous efforts to help me make the book more meaningful for its audiences.

As is the case with most big academic projects, there are a few particularly special people and beloved colleagues, who provide such consistent, intelligent, and encouraging support that they deserve more praise than can be ever adequately expressed. For me, they are Mike Johnston, Rebecca Krug, Beth Robertson, and James Simpson. Collectively, they have written more letters on my behalf than I can count, helping me secure funding and access resources I could not acquire on my own. I cherish them all as teachers, mentors, and colleagues, not just because they have been sources of intellectual (and sometimes emotional) support, but also because they have produced scholarship that is the best of the best. The combination of their generosity and brilliance is unmatched.

Another source of continuing support has been my friendships in Arlington, Massachusetts. In particular, I want to thank my friends in the TBG cycling group for listening to me buzz on about my research on long rides to Concord Center and Harvard, providing the energy and drive I've needed to see this project to its completion. I want to single out Pritesh Gandhi, who has offered persistent support of my book, even going so far as to set up a meeting with a book series editor for me. Over the last few years, my running group, Team Chiru, has been one of my most important sources of encouragement, motivation, and laughter. At least three times a week we meet to run together, often to do icy hill repeats or to reach muddy Whipple Hill summits, always pushing each other to reach new levels of fitness in an effort to be the best professionals, spouses, and parents we can be. These guys—Jay Brewer, Lewis McCulloch, and Tim Orcutt—are some of the best humans I know.

Most important of all has been my family, the love and the joy of my life that make anything worth doing. My parents, sister, and in-laws have offered unconditional support for my work, and always have, even when they don't understand my passion for it. Special thanks go out to my father-in-law GT, who lives below us and is always performing acts of kindness, from making us meals to walking our dog, Charlie Biscuit. I don't have the words to express my gratitude to my adorable wife and best friend Tiffany (Tiff), who always helps me put things in perspective, challenges my thinking, and provides loving support. When I started working on this book, our two young daughters, Harriet and Louise (Wheazy), were just beginning kindergarten and preschool. Now Harriet is a freshman in college, and Wheazy is a sophomore in high school. This book, in other words, has watched them grow up. Whenever I'm thinking about this book, I'm thinking about them. It has become a kind of memory vehicle, a repository of my thoughts about little bits of their childhood and adolescence. I therefore dedicate this book to them, my incredible daughters, who embody the youthful force that is my greatest source of hope for our future.

Habitual Rhetoric

Introduction
Digital Writing before Digital Technology

You don't always need a computer to do computer rhetoric.
—Elizabeth Losh, *Virtualpolitik*

Habit enables stability, which in turn gives us the time and space needed to be truly creative, for without habit there could be no thinking, no creativity, and no freedom. Further, habit, as a form of second nature, reveals the power of humans to create new structures and reactions in response to their environment.... A habit, of course, is also a literal covering, and the nun's habit reveals that, even as habit covers and fits an individual, it also connects bodies.
—**Wendy Hui Kyong Chun**, *Updating to Remain the Same*

Copy, paste, combine, update, share, reply. These writing habits are imperatives for a participatory culture that demands constant responses to crisis and change, ranging from editing web templates to replying to trending tweets to adding friends to an expanding social profile. While such habits of engagement are hallmarks of the digital era, we acquired them long before digital technology. Wikipedia's principles of collaborative knowledge production were practiced by medieval scribes, who compiled manuscripts containing florilegia, bestiaries, and chronicles. Twitter's circulation of abbreviated commentary expands upon the thriving industry of annotators who interpreted and updated theological and legal texts in medieval manuscripts. YouTube's reuse of artistic objects develops out of an ancient practice of appropriation, especially among Aesopic fable authors, ranging from Marie de France to Geoffrey Chaucer. And Facebook's expansion of social networks builds upon the medieval arts of letter writing, which encouraged the sharing of private thoughts publicly with friends.

The massive proliferation of social networks such as Twitter and Facebook has demonstrated the power that crowdsourcing can wield, seemingly with little help from credentialed experts in higher education. Rather than turn to university-trained specialists for reliable information, the public is increasingly investing in the collective intelligence of the crowd, which digital platforms such as Wikipedia are harnessing outside of the classroom with unparalleled success. Such networked forms of writing and knowledge production have been greeted with equal measures of enthusiasm and trepidation. On the one hand, the social nature of editable spaces has inspired many to celebrate the prevalence of writing environments in which readers can easily become writers, important information can be efficiently compiled, and friendships can be quickly formed. On the other, it has provoked fear among many who perceive the social nature of digital writing habits as corrosive for language usage, the right to privacy, and textual authority. Despite such polarized views of digital media, most agree that such networked writing is fundamentally new and unquestionably different from its predecessors, especially writing on the printed page.

Habitual Rhetoric: Digital Writing before Digital Technology makes two related claims. First, premodern manuscript cultures established the rhetorical principles for digital writing practices, from copying to updating to sharing, centuries before the invention of the computer. Second, social media thrive on the speed and scale of these digital habits, creating algorithmic networks that sever writers from writing, challenging the social and embodied character of these ancient writing practices. By establishing precedents for the habits that fuel the power of social media, we can identify their *habitus*, both a singular and plural Latin rhetorical term that describes dispositions, conditions, or principles that activate particular writing habits within particular digital environments. *Habitual Rhetoric* therefore describes a set of compositional practices that shape and are shaped by a habitus, which is developed within a field of writing. Rather than reduce digital writing to the impulsive or automated habits demanded by social platforms and software algorithms, habitual rhetoric is defined by dispositional forces that are creative, social, and embodied. *Habitus* does not merely refer to an ornamental dress ("habit") that one takes on and off in response to a crisis—it refers to a rhetorical way of life, a compositional habit that connects writers to the field of writing they may extend and transform. When we recognize habits as rhetorical forces, we can identify the dangers of passive participation within market-driven networks, articulate transparent connections between members of writing communities, and amplify voices of the previously unheard.

Digital before Digital

This book joins a rich conversation about the many oral, material, and cultural practices that set the scene for digital writing. Much work has already been done by scholars such as Angela Haas, who has established the predigital roots of hypertext in American Indian wampum weaving, and Adam Banks, who has demonstrated the reliance of remix culture on African American rhetorical practices, ranging from singing the blues to mixing breakbeats.[1] This book draws upon their pan-historiographical perspectives to examine premodern cultures of alphabetic writing that emerge from medieval university settings, specifically handwritten letters and codices produced both before and after the rise of print capitalism in the West. By focusing on writing, I suggest that studies of manuscript cultures offer productive contexts for pushing the boundaries of Aristotelian "available means of persuasion" to emphasize the rhetorical canons of memory and delivery that flourish within multilingual, multiauthored, and multimedia writing environments, which range from the handwritten codex to the digital annotation platform. While much of the focus of media-studies research has been on the tension between social forces and the material agency of writing technologies, this book considers the changing relationships between writer and reader and the rhetorical habits that emerge to negotiate them. I argue that once we recognize the pan-historiographical connections among these interactive rhetorics, the increasingly unstable, infuriated, manipulated, and exploitive forms of crowdsourced authority can be interrogated from the perspective of their precedents.

This is not, however, the story of the digital revolution that we have been told. The tale usually unfolds this way, as narrated by the cowriters of *Digital Humanities Manifesto 2.0*:

> Like all media revolutions, the first wave of the digital revolution looked backward as it moved forward. Just as early codices mirrored oratorical practices, print initially mirrored the practices of high medieval manuscript culture, and film mirrored the techniques of theater, the digital first wave replicated the world of scholarly communications that print gradually codified over the course of five centuries: a world where textuality was primary and visuality and sound were secondary (and subordinated to text), even as it vastly accelerated the search and retrieval of documents, enhanced access, and altered mental habits.[2]

While this story of remediation may be all too familiar to many of us, thanks to the work of Jay David Bolter and Richard Grusin,[3] the linearity of this media history—from spoken to chirographic to printed to digital representation—is surprising, especially since the manifesto begins with a warning against those "looking for linearity."[4] The digital world, according to this model, begins by reproducing a print-based world "where textuality was primary and visuality and sound were secondary," only to mature into a world in which the visual and the aural gain a new primacy. As Jessica Brantley demonstrates in her study of the late fourteenth-century Vernon manuscript, the medieval world also privileged sight and sound through verbal decoration and arrangement in manuscripts that were designed for performance. In the case of the Vernon manuscript, the Paternoster becomes a bilingual diagram that "alternates the colors and dispositions of words, making spoken language into a variety of visible forms."[5] Given the prominence of illumination and spoken performance within medieval book culture, architecture, and heraldry, digital media may more accurately be described as postmedieval media.

Even in the same collection in which Brantley's essay appears, it is not difficult to find oversimplifications of premodern manuscript culture. N. Katherine Hayles and Jessica Pressman acknowledge that "writing surfaces have always been complex," but they still perpetuate a teleology of increasing complexity by suggesting that "when writing was accomplished by a quill pen, ink pot, and paper, it was possible to fantasize that writing was simple and straightforward, a means by which the writer's thoughts could be transferred more or less directly into the reader's mind."[6] Given the arduous and multifaceted process of making most manuscripts, which required the collaborative efforts of a writer, stationer, scribe, rubricator, and illuminator, it is difficult to imagine that such a fantasy was indulged by many before the modern era of mass reproduction. As Bonnie Mak notes, we have all too often assumed a "simple coordination between physical platform, mode of production, and historical period . . . that pages were written by hand on parchment in the Middle Ages, were printed with moveable type on paper after 1455, and are encoded for digital display in the twenty-first century."[7] The fields of comparative media studies and media archaeology have productively challenged the work of Marshall McLuhan and Elizabeth Eisenstein to demonstrate the layered and recursive histories that inform new media in ways that are both horizontal and vertical.[8] Yet, we still cling to our desire for linearity and simplicity and rarely acknowledge that particular media forms have complex relationships between their materials, their interfaces, their cultures, and their historical moments.

Habitual Rhetoric confronts this technological determinism by shifting the focus away from media in the direction of rhetoric. This push for the importance of rhetorical studies within the digital humanities writ large has begun to be addressed by the work of a growing group of scholars, especially Jim Ridolfo and William Hart-Davidson in *Rhetoric and the Digital Humanities*, and Jamie "Skye" Bianco, Ian Bogost, Elizabeth Losh, and Jentery Sayers in *Debates within the Digital Humanities*, among others who are theorizing the contributions that rhetoricians can offer to new media materiality, analysis, and production.[9] Through comparative analyses of manuscript and online environments, this book demonstrates the importance of moving beyond material analysis of page design to consider the ways interfaces operate rhetorically, identifying the persuasive, memorializing, and dialogical character of translated, compiled, and annotated writing environments. This recognition of writing habits that have experienced especially vibrant, seemingly parallel, premodern and digital lives offers insight into current challenges to the romanticized figure of the autonomous writerly body, which is increasingly fragmented, distributed, and circulated as consumable property. Digital writing, following its premodern predecessors, relies more on absence than presence, often rupturing the assumed one-to-one relationship between writer and reader. Like the rhetorical apostrophe, an address to an absent audience, digital forms of writing reach out to uncertain, unidentifiable, or unintended recipients. Advanced forms of machine learning, such as ChatGPT, now produce algorithmic writing that sacrifice the autonomous figure of the writer for the sake of establishing an accretive space for writing to continue to happen and circulate.[10] The instability that accompanies transitions to new writing technologies, from the handwritten codex to the printing press to the digital platform, results in cultures of unending accumulation, in which the persistent and palimpsestic act of writing upon writing becomes inseparable from the act of reading. Such a radical revision of the reader's role raises the stakes of digital reading and establishes a collective ethos of written participation. Just like medieval glossators of legal texts who codified new laws through marginal annotation, Twitter readers are compelled to become writers, endorsing, retweeting, tagging, and replying to texts as acts of interpretation. Any individual failure to respond to new information creates dead letters that become passive objects available for bots to acquire and redistribute. Given the pedagogical implications of this participation imperative, this book poses the problem of a future written authority that is increasingly incorporeal, networked, and distributed. How might we responsibly engage in online spaces in which all readers and users are expected to be entrepreneurial writers and designers?

This intervention therefore attempts to address the underdeveloped relationship that exists between the highly performative and visual objects of medieval and digital rhetoric. While scholars such as Dànielle Nicole DeVoss, Laurie Gries, James Porter, and Jim Ridolfo have been working to recover the canons of delivery and memory often neglected within print culture, more attention needs to be paid to the medieval arts of memory and writing that inform the architecture of digital forms of storage, distribution, and circulation.[11] This gap is the symptom of most rhetorical histories, which typically begin with Aristotle and Quintillian and then skip the Middle Ages entirely to continue with Peter Ramus and Giambattista Vico. In an otherwise excellent book that is foundational for scholars in this area of study, *Digital Rhetoric: Theory, Method, Practice*, Douglas Eyman attempts to define digital rhetoric by distinguishing it from the rhetoric of previous ages. After discussing the golden age of rhetoric in ancient Greece and Rome, Eyman descends into the "dark ages": "The rise of Christianity in the medieval period led to the devaluation of rhetoric (it was seen as pagan and antithetical to the church) until Augustine recognized that the persuasive modes of rhetoric could be very useful for the church; however, the focus of rhetoric during this period was primarily in the development of rules for preaching and legal letter writing (all in the service of the church)."[12] Leaving aside the errant assertion that the Church was the alpha and omega of medieval rhetoric, Eyman places Augustine squarely within the Middle Ages, even though he dies in 430 CE, well before the traditionally accepted starting point of the medieval period. The next figure discussed is the sixteenth-century Peter Ramus, leaving the thousand years that comprise the Middle Ages completely unaddressed.

The narrative that Eyman tells is so common among historians of rhetoric that it is rarely questioned, except by the few medievalists—notably Martin Camargo, Mary Carruthers, Rita Copeland, Jody Enders, Cheryl Glenn, James J. Murphy, and Marjorie Curry Woods—who have demonstrated the vital contributions that medieval rhetoric offers to the arts of prose and poetry, letter writing, and writing pedagogy.[13] The neglect of their work has not only led to an impoverished view of rhetoric in the Middle Ages, but also resulted in the development of a field of digital rhetoric based on hyperbolic claims to innovation and incomplete assessments of the history of interactive, performative, and visual rhetorical habits. Important books such as Kathleen Welch's *Electric Rhetoric* (1999), Collin Brooke's *Lingua Fracta* (2009), Elizabeth Losh's *Virtualpolitik* (2009), Adam Banks's *Digital Griots* (2011), and Douglas Eyman's *Digital Rhetoric* (2015) have effectively distinguished the salient features of digital writing, but they have done so by relying on rhetorical histories based in oral, print, or computer cultures.[14] This book complements their work by considering the contributions of manuscript cultures to digital rhetoric, attending specifically to the work of rhetoricians teaching within early universities, such as Giovanni di Bonandrea, Geoffrey of Vinsauf, and John of Garland, who develop an explicitly corporeal and material conception of rhetorical habitus in the twelfth through fifteenth centuries that has immeasurably shaped accumulative and public forms of writing production ever since.

Pan-Historiographical Methodology

The claims that I make in this book, especially the argument that digital writing began before digital technology, may seem cleverly exaggerated and overly provocative. To some extent, these objections are warranted. On the one hand, the digital writing that precedes digital technology is only *digital* in a semantic sense: the fingers, or digits, that hold the quill or tap the key are as digital as the binary numbers, or digits, that encode the computer software. On the other, the teleological claim that digital writing is defined by its computational character (e.g., bytes and chips) dramatically limits our understanding of how digital writing habits obtain their rhetorical potential. Digital writing, in other words, has a history before digital technology that has contributed more to its habitus than any computer algorithm, operating system, or internet server could ever provide. As Elizabeth Losh suggests in her groundbreaking study of digital rhetoric, "many who purportedly study the rhetoric of digital discourse focus almost exclusively on the technological apparatus, so that a conventional view of the subject directs attention to the mechanical responses of the computer to input rather than the theories behind the design and continuing evolution of digital media and networked systems."[15] Following the lead of Losh, I pursue the theories and histories that establish the principles for digital writing in order to understand how the persistence of these habits interacts with changing material conditions, ranging from handwritten parchment to web templates.

This pursuit of the persistent habits of the distant past requires a somewhat unorthodox methodology that is expansive in scope across space and time, and tightly attuned to archival objects within manuscript and digital environments. As Debra Hawhee and Christa J. Olson observe about the current state of rhetorical studies, "It is far more common these days to see book-length rhetorical histories bound tightly by a short span of dates or by the lives of particular figures than to encounter texts that explain or explore the rhetorical histories of a concept of cultural group."[16] Given the obvious value of highly specialized and narrowly focused research projects, this book assumes the risk of not only leaping across centuries of time, but also transgressing disciplinary boundaries—notably those of medieval studies, digital rhetoric, and book history—to achieve its goals.

My approach therefore adopts a methodology that Hawhee and Olson call "pan-historiography," which entails "writing histories whose temporal scope extends well beyond the span of individual generations" and describes "studies that leap across geographic space, tracking important activities, terms, movements, or practices as they travel with trade, with global expansion, or with religious zealotry."[17] By tracing these digital habits across space and time, I often encounter tensions and gaps within and between research fields that are difficult, and sometimes impossible, to reconcile. This means that, as Hawhee and Olson might suggest, my work within each discipline "moves through its histories, by turns zooming and hovering, simultaneously posing big-picture questions and fine-grained ones."[18] Even though the scope of this project is large, much of my focus is on the way writing habitus emerge in the smallest of material environments, including manuscript marginalia and Twitter replies. According to Hawhee and Olson, the pan-historiographical approach allows "archival materials to, in a sense, move," offering the accompanying opportunity "to attend to what is necessarily absent from or barely present in archival, documentary materials: bodies, habits, activities."[19] While occasionally "barely present," the digital writing habits of this book often emerge prominently within and across my research materials, from manicules (little hands) in the margins of manuscripts to archived comments in the editorial histories of Wikipedia pages.

This pan-historiographical methodology suggests a continuity and connection between objects and practices across space and time that, in turn, risks anachronistic and naive claims to origins. When I suggest that our current digital practices were "established" within medieval manuscript cultures, I am not arguing, for example, that the habit of amplification began ex nihilo in a scriptorium in Bologna with the first stroke of the quill in the margins of the *Corpus juris civilis*. Instead, I am claiming that the repetitive practice of glossing, empowered by the institutional capital and influence of the University, codified and authorized a habitus that we can identify within digital annotation platforms. This argument does not discount the origins and developments of amplification in other times and places, especially within Eastern and Indigenous practices throughout the world, which are too numerous and too varied to count and track within a study of this size and scope. My study is limited to alphabetic writing in the West, primarily as it emerges within university educational environments, where I believe we can trace the developments of these habits and their digital replications.

One way to understand this pan-historiographical connection is through what Alexander Nagel and Christopher Wood call the artistic theory of "substitution," the tendency for art objects to habitually replace their predecessors over time: "Under such a model of the temporal life of artifacts, one token or replica effectively substituted for another; classes of artifacts were grasped as chains of substitutable replicas stretching across time and space. Modern copies of painted icons were understood as effective surrogates for lost originals, for example, and new buildings were understood as reinstantiations, through typological association, of prior structures. The literal circumstances and the historical moment of an artifact's material execution were not routinely taken as components of its meaning or function."[20] Such a methodology is what they label "anachronic," a repetition or copy of the past that produces a compelling similarity with a difference.[21] While the material circumstances of each moment and practice are important, my study focuses on the habits that persist within and across these physical environments.

This book is also a rhetorical comparison of similarities and differences within two historical eras (medieval and modern) and two forms of media (manuscript and digital). Yet I do not pretend to provide a balanced comparison and instead focus more on the similarities than the differences, an imbalance that is common, and often necessary, in a comparative study like this one. In a survey of comparative methods across the humanities, Devin Griffiths concludes that "the grounds of similarity and the grounds of difference in comparative study do not need to be the same."[22] After all, two obvious differences between these periods and media are speed and scale, the primary engines for generating the discourses of neoliberal innovation and technological exceptionalism, which erase or obscure the contributions of the past in order to indulge and perpetuate the pervasive and damaging myth-of-progress narrative. At the same time, a focus on difference, or the alterity of the Middle Ages, can lead to nostalgic fantasies of the past that seek to mourn or recover what has been supposedly lost.

Even though this book at times may celebrate the potency of particular premodern writing habits, my main objective is to highlight as many positive and negative attributes of our habitus as possible, including the homophilic desire to identify with those similar to ourselves, an instinct that marginalizes differences in ability, sexuality, gender, race, and class. On the one hand, such elements of our dispositions have created solidarity among writers, creating collectives of

Wikipedia editors and Twitter followers. On the other, such homophily drives xenophobic habits, such as edit wars and tweet shaming, that become engines of exclusion and oppression. The crises of the present created by practices of the past therefore provide a main exigency of this book, which seeks to find ways to shape our digital habitus into an agent of change. This requires that I embrace what Wai Chee Dimock, describing a 2018 Modern Language Association panel, calls "a cautiously adopted presentism [that] might allow humanists to bracket the nontrivial differences among historical periods and act as a cumulative force under conditions no less adverse."[23] By adopting this pan-historiographical methodology, this book assumes an "anachronic" and comparative disposition that is consistently future-oriented. For Dimock, such a perspective refuses "to accept the past as a foregone conclusion" and "to accept the present as inevitable."[24] If I, like a plagiarizing Wikipedia editor, could copy and adapt this language for this book's methodology, it would express the following: it refuses to accept the past as *so far gone* and refuses to accept the *future* as inevitable.

Structure and Content of the Book

Using this methodology to define and to establish the history of digital habitus within the field of rhetoric, this book grapples with the following paradoxes: How have cultures of sharing both disseminated knowledge widely and transferred rhetorical capital to elites? How have crowdsourced websites both encouraged democratic participation and excluded certain populations? How have social media both accelerated dialogue and created wider ideological divides? How have annotation platforms both invited commentary and limited fields of interpretation? How have remix cultures both inspired creativity and restricted the capacity to create? And how have social networks both established new opportunities for intimacy and violated the privacy of their users? To address these questions, I identify six writing habits—*translation, compilation, disputation, amplification, appropriation,* and *salutation*—that have experienced vibrant premodern and digital lives. Through a comparative analysis of two historical moments—in which print is *not* the dominant medium for writing—I reveal how these seemingly cooperative compositional habits have become mechanisms of exclusion and oppression, especially for women, queer communities, and people of color. This "digital before digital" investigation suggests how readily such collective forms of knowledge production relinquish universalism for elitism, dialogue for monologue, intellectual labor for intellectual property, and social justice for the security of sovereign power and white male supremacy.

Before I address the six habits that comprise the majority of the book, the first chapter, "Habitual Rhetoric: A History of Rhetorical *Habitus*," establishes a background and traces a genealogy for habitus from antiquity until the present day. I begin with Aristotle, who grapples with the supernatural and moral elements of this human disposition, and lays the groundwork for medieval debate about the "neutrality" of this ethical condition, its capacity to do good or evil in the world. By the twelfth-century, habitus was largely considered to be a changeable disposition, one that could be taught, not just how to act, but also how to speak and write. This latter development is reflected in the production of writing manuals, known as the *artes dictandi*, which offered instruction in letter writing, one of the central skills learned within the early medieval universities, particularly at Bologna, Paris, and Oxford. Nearly all of these treatises rely upon the rhetorical texts of Marcus Tullius Cicero (first century BCE), who claims in his *De inventione (On Invention)* that *habitus* is "a stable and absolute constitution of mind or body in some particular, as, for example, the acquisition of some capacity or of an art, or again some special knowledge, or some bodily dexterity not given by nature but won by careful training and practice."[25] Medieval teachers of writing, such as Giovanni di Bonandrea, adapt these Ciceronian principles of stability, corporeality, and practice for university students who go on to form a bureaucratic class of notaries and lawyers, producing writs, deeds, and memoranda for a burgeoning documentary culture.[26]

Having set the scene for a rhetorical understanding of habitus, I then trace its afterlife into the sociological work of Pierre Bourdieu, the most influential commentator on the topic in the modern era. Drawing on Erwin Panofsky's identification of the scholastic "habit" that shapes the architecture of Gothic cathedrals and medieval manuscripts,[27] Bourdieu first defines *habitus* as "a system of internalized schemes which have the capacity to generate all the thoughts, perceptions, and actions characteristic of a culture."[28] Bourdieu proceeds to develop the concept as a kind of "feel for the game" or "second nature" that explains shared behaviors, especially by individuals of a common social class.[29] As a response to Bourdieu's focus on socially embodied dispositions, I describe the modern alternatives offered by Bruno Latour, Annemarie Mol, and Nigel Thrift, which set the scene for more recent network analyses, including Wendy Hui Kyong Chun's recent studies of media circulation and network culture, and Thomas Rickert's analyses of the material and ambient features of rhetoric.[30] To conclude the chapter, I argue for the institutional force the university has on habitus formation, engaging with critical university studies, notably the work of Kandice Chuh and la paperson, to explain the ways in which higher education and liberal humanism have excluded and delegitimized the habits of Black and

Indigenous people and other people of color.[31] This brief case for the antiquity of "post-print" writing habits sets the stage for the book's call for attention to our digital habitus, the social, embodied, and reflective dispositions that shape the practices and spaces of writing.

The second chapter, "Translation: Online Education and Transfers of Authority," begins by confronting the democratic ideal for a digital commons, which is built upon ancient beliefs about the purpose and function of translation. Translation is a fundamental rhetorical habit that provides access to knowledge and power. Within digital environments, translation is motivated by the desire for making languages (especially English) and learning more accessible to more people. For many early translators, even Saint Jerome, translation was an act of linguistic and cultural appropriation, "carrying over" important knowledge from one culture to another, usually to an imperial power. Over time, we have obscured the nefarious, and often racist, origins of translational habits, what Cedric Burrows might call a "rhetorical crossover," in favor of altruistic notions of access—making writing more widely available to a new set of readers.[32] While the internet has vastly expanded access, the availability of information is now filtered by algorithmic regimes that control and track online behavior in the name of intellectual property, national security, and crowdsourced authority. The situation has inspired a number of movements, largely inspired by Silicon Valley tech start-ups, to transfer face-to-face instruction to online educational formats, all done in the name of the common good, but mostly motivated by the promise of revenue. Digital texts are therefore subject to both translations of language—speech as well as code—and translations of power, that is, cultural appropriation. Tensions between competing interests always arise within acts of translation because, as Talal Asad has argued, languages are fundamentally unequal—one is always subservient to the other.[33] Lost within such clamor for access is the specific audience for whom translations are produced, which is not the generalized "public" often invoked to justify translations, but rather a readership that has a market value.

In chapter 2, I argue that late fourteenth-century translation debates in England provide a helpful context for understanding the elite interests that drive or impede so-called access-oriented translation projects, both in recent online mass-educational environments and throughout the twentieth century when English became a language of American schools. To demonstrate this point, I turn to John Trevisa's *Dialogue between the Lord and the Clerk on Translation*, which was published in 1387 as a preface to his English translation of Ranulph Higden's Latin universal history, the *Polychronicon*. As a clerical translator working at the behest of an aristocratic patron, Trevisa presents translation as a rhetorical habit that can both empower some and disenfranchise others. He also reveals translation to be what Rita Copeland calls "a primary vehicle for vernacular participation in, and ultimately appropriation of, the cultural privilege of Latin academic discourse."[34] Within the long history of English language education, Trevisa's work represents an early example of the vexed relationships between languages of authority and mass education, which has both inspired cross-curricular writing movements within American colleges and led to the privatization of the public educational sphere via online "open" coursework.

The third chapter, "Compilation: The Encyclopedic Habits of Wikipedia," addresses pervasive medieval and digital habits of compilation, which have rarely been associated with each other. According to Wikipedia, a compiler is "a computer program that translates source code written in one programming language (the *source* language) into another language (the *target* language.)"[35] In other words, the agent of compilation is a nonhuman digital translator that carries over source code from one language to another. This appears to be in stark contrast with anything remotely medieval, even Geoffrey Chaucer's claim to be a "lewd compilator" (uneducated compiler) in his prologue to the *Treatise on the Astrolabe*, but the figurative sense is strikingly similar: compilers effectively translate knowledge from one realm to another, ideally adding nothing new.[36] Seemingly absent from such objective understandings of compilation is the authoritative power of multiplicity, selection, and arrangement that drives both compilational creation and reception. For Arthur Bahr, compilation can be understood "not as an objective quality of either texts or objects, but rather as a mode of perceiving such forms so as to disclose an interpretably meaningful arrangement, thereby bringing into being a text/work that is more than the sum of its parts."[37] A compilation is therefore an active construction, composed of multiple texts or objects, often with the aim of creating new meaning and authority that transcends the possibilities of singular contributions.

I argue in the third chapter that this premodern practice reemerges with a renewed vigor within online, crowdsourced environments, creating what I call a *compilational habitus* among its writers and readers. Building on Bahr's formulation of compilation as a mode of perception, I suggest that open online platforms operate as compilations composed of multiple texts or objects, often designed with the aim of creating new meaning and authority. These expandable and combinatory spaces accommodate the unfinished and unstable nature of collaborative writing, whose authority relies upon the dynamic dialogue between juxtaposed sources of information. Openly editable web templates establish their legitimacy through the habit of ongoing compilation, which depends upon the contributions and revisions of interested editors. Their popularity reflects a compilational habitus that drives digital information gathering, a force embodied by Wikipedia, the primary destination for seekers of knowledge about the world. As I demonstrate, the principles of such information compilation were established well before the *Encyclopedia Britannica*, specifically in the emergent genre of the medieval encyclopedia.

From the patron saint of the Internet, Isidore of Seville, to England's first printer, William Caxton, medieval compilers obsessively collected, selected, and juxtaposed passages from previous textual authorities (*auctores*) to create what they called an *imago mundi*, an image of the world. And as the readership for such encyclopedias expanded, their producers sought to maintain a dialogue between older, classical sources and recent discoveries through multiple languages and early printed formats. Because of the increasing authority of these compilations, writers such as Isidore had to defend their enterprise, comparing their appropriation of previous sources to the wresting of a club from Hercules. This knowledge grab is unsettling for many readers, an anxiety that is reflected both within these medieval encyclopedias and their digital prodigy, Wikipedia. Anyone may contribute to its entries, creating Stephen Colbert's "Wikiality," which requires that their users verify the information presented and view it in dialogue with other sources. As Wikipedia has increased its authority, it has consistently relied upon an encyclopedic habitus of compilation, which relies upon the interpretation, participation, and scrutiny of its users.

In the fourth chapter, "Disputation: Medieval Debate and Digital Dialogue," I address the persistence of premodern habits of dispute within dialogical spaces like Wikipedia. The website's claim to encyclopedic authority is persuasive because it is rooted in a democratic ideal—anyone can edit and contribute to it. Disputes about content are settled largely through the approvals of the largest numbers of editors, who base their decisions on source verifiability and volume. A discussion page accompanies each entry, providing a forum for disagreements to be settled. Yet like many tech platforms, Wikipedia is dominated by white men. The introduction page offers the following call to editors: "*Anyone* can edit almost every page, and millions already have."[38] Embedded in the middle of that sentence is the qualification "almost every page." Wikipedia administrators monitor and lock down pages to avoid cases of overwhelming bias and vandalism, and unfortunately there are disturbing consequences for such editorial exclusion. A 2010 survey revealed that only 13 percent of Wikipedia editors identified as female, and a 2013 revision to that data set only increased that number to 16 percent, which supported the growing sentiment that Wikipedia, like many crowdsourced websites, was dominated by men.[39] On the one hand, the spirit of Wikipedia thrives on its grassroots and decentralized character, which resolves disputes through a dialectical process that includes both interested amateurs and credentialed experts. On the other, this revolutionary ethic replaces one form of domination with another, displacing exclusive priesthoods of specialized expertise with brotherhoods of internet access. According to Mathieu O'Neil, this leads to a scenario in which "educated white males . . . distinguish themselves as the exclusive repositories of technological expertise; coding for code's sake allows hackers to profit from the interest in being perceived as disinterested."[40] This hidden hegemony operates relatively unquestioned, because it appears to espouse no ideology and legitimates itself through an ethic of "dialogue." We witness this habit of "both sides" debate on Twitter feeds as well into popular and scholarly blogs, in which bloggers inspire conflict, often through the guise of an avatar, about a range of subjects, from patriarchal gaming journalism to campus rape culture to police violence.

Using Geoffrey Chaucer's rooster-hen debate in *The Nun's Priest's Tale* as a rhetorical example, I propose that these free, online, and editable platforms have been shaped by the medieval educational habit known as disputation, a pedagogical role-playing exercise, in which a schoolmaster would propose topics for debate, requiring one student to play the opponent and the other to play the respondent. Disputation became so popular a mode in the thirteenth century that it burst out of the universities into many areas of public life, including debates performed openly in the square and literary genres such as the debate poem and prose dialogue. Yet it is in these same venues that we witness the patriarchal heritage of medieval disputation, which largely excluded women, either through direct disenfranchisement or through silent indifference. It is well known that women were not educated in the universities, but their exclusion is also demonstrated, as Ruth Karras has effectively shown, through the topics that men would dispute, which range from the superiority of theologians over canon lawyers to the sin of assaulting a woman publicly (the lack of consent not being an issue).[41] It is this legacy of indifferent disputation that haunts the habitus of many male-dominated online spaces, such as Wikipedia, in which peer-to-peer dialogue too often becomes male-to-male monologue.

The fifth chapter, "Amplification: Inhabiting and Annotating the Page," examines how digital writing privileges quantity over quality, compelling writers to update or amplify their writing constantly. Despite laments over what Mark Andrejevic calls "infoglut" and its propensity to overwhelm and subdue its readers into complacency, the accommodation of a high volume of commentary in online writing spaces often expands the demographic of participants, allowing for a diversity of voices and opinions.[42] Henry Jenkins has famously characterized this proliferation of new environments for media commentary and fan writing as the rise of "participatory culture."[43] For Jenkins, this is a salutary phenomenon because it empowers the voices of the previously disenfranchised. Moreover, digital platforms that host such commentary provide flexible writing spaces that may be amplified at will. As Naomi Baron points out, "Today's digital technologies place no limits on text length or complexity. . . . The real question is whether the affordances of reading onscreen lead us to a new normal. One in which length and complexity and annotation and memory and rereading and especially concentration are proving more challenging than when reading in hard copy."[44] Baron objects to the unruly nature of digital textuality, leading to what Clay Shirky has more optimistically called a "publish then filter" reading culture and a "cognitive surplus."[45] Digital writing is defined by its potential amplification, which can be facilitated through any number of social media apparatus, from Twitter feeds to Facebook comments to Wikipedia pages.

Medieval writing, on the other hand, is not often associated with abundance or surplus. Readers were scarce, and their books were often scarcer, which led to textual communities that were elite and exclusive. It was not until the advent of the printing press that readership began to be drastically expanded. As Ann Blair suggests, we have not witnessed as great a challenge to information management since the age of early print, which spawned what she calls a "newly invigorated info-lust that sought to gather and manage as much information as possible."[46] Nevertheless, chapter 5 demonstrates that medieval writing embraced amplification through its privileging of commentary and annotation. Medieval bookmakers were faced with many more constraints and the scarcity of books transformed an individual codex into a kind of creative commons in which multiple readers and writers interacted through interlinear glosses and marginalia. One important rhetorical foundation for this compositional framework can be found within the teaching of *amplificatio* (amplification) in twelfth- and thirteenth-century writing instruction throughout Europe. University teachers of writing from Geoffrey of Vinsauf to John of Garland composed textbooks that include extensive treatments of methods of amplification, ranging from comparison to digression to exclamation.

While the development of this habitus can be identified within the commentary traditions of a number of theological texts or legal books, I have selected one set of pedagogical texts, Aesop's fables, as a representative example for analysis. These animal tales are now known for their moral lessons, but they were primarily utilized in medieval classrooms for writing instruction. Students and teachers would insert interlinear glosses to challenge their expanding vocabulary and then rewrite these fables, both in abbreviated and elaborated forms. And while these techniques were largely focused on strategies for expanding a composition, they also reflected a habitual and material culture of accumulation, encouraging interpretative multiplicity within books that accommodated amplification through varying sizes of script and page layouts with wide margins for annotation. Web templates often foster the illusion that the online spaces for expansion are limitless, but these platforms are run on physical servers that can become saturated with data in the same ways that medieval manuscripts became overwhelmed with marginalia and commentary. Chapter 5 confronts the problem of space for rhetorical circulation by detailing its preprinted contexts, which reveal the pressing need to develop a new amplificatory habitus for developing habitations for writing on the digital page.

In the sixth chapter, "Appropriation: Stealing Bodies and Properties," I turn to perhaps the most overwhelming aspect of digital writing: its vulnerability to intellectual theft, from illicit copying to database hacking. While the threats to artistic autonomy and intellectual property are significant, many forms of digital appropriation are undeniably innovative, creative, and valuable. If we set aside the privacy/security debates surrounding efforts to make information transparent, especially given the volatile responses to WikiLeaks and Russian interference in US elections, we can recognize the artistic potential of hacking, which often results in stunning music remixes and viral video mash-ups. The result, of course, has led to much handwringing, especially from corporations crying foul over violations of copyright.[47] Yet such artistic acts of appropriation have become so "cool" that they have led scholars such as Alan Liu to suggest that "strong art will be about the 'destruction of destruction' or, put another way, the recognition of the destructiveness of creation."[48] Within the digital world, such a neo-avant-garde aesthetics of destruction has fostered an environment of textual vulnerability, in which texts are radically at the will of their users. At the same time, it is crucial to acknowledge that such an emphasis on "creative destruction" can lead to an uncritical acceptance of all forms of "innovation," one of the most powerful euphemisms for capitalism. Joseph A. Schumpeter pointed out in 1943 that the desire for new markets leads to "industrial mutation," part of what he later called a "perennial gale of creative destruction" that "incessantly revolutionizes the economic structure *from within*, incessantly destroying the old one, incessantly creating a new one."[49] This phoenix-like logic, in which a new power rises from the ashes of the old, also undergirds medieval theories of sovereignty—what is often referred to as *translatio imperii*, or the translation of power.[50] Histories of imperialism teach us that such an optimistic view of destruction often serves the interests of the elite who benefit from such "innovation" while disenfranchising others, especially those cultures or industries that have been "mutated" or "superseded." Liu turns to the writings of the Critical Art Ensemble (CAE), as an example of a neo-avant-garde collective that will use their technical skills of "disturbance" and "hacktivism" as a means to disrupt these forces of exclusion, but even the CAE adopts the elitist logic of creative destruction by claiming that "the only groups that will successfully confront power are those that locate the arena of contestation in cyberspace, and hence an elite force seems to be the best possibility."[51] As Patricia Ingham warns in her book *The Medieval New*, such an embrace of complete destruction and confrontation means that "we have bought entirely the notion that innovation lays waste to what has come before," as opposed to the practices of "ambivalent *homage*" that define many medieval perspectives on innovation.[52]

In this sixth chapter, I argue for the importance of understanding the politics and ethics of medieval forms of appropriation, which are rarely acts of complete destruction and more often premodern forms of sampling, remix, and mash-up, which rely on degrees of "homage" to ancient authorities. As Kathleen Kennedy has demonstrated in her book *Medieval Hackers*, we encounter early evidence of "hacker culture" during the later Middle Ages, when governmental, educational, and ecclesiastical institutions attempted to control information.[53] Reactions to these forms of control varied, but graduates of medieval schools had already been trained to appropriate texts critically, a practice many of them learned in their writing exercises, which emphasized citation and reuse of existing authorities. Once again, Aesop's fables prove to be a fruitful site for analysis, since rhetorical amplifications often became acts of appropriation, revisions of fables that bear the names of Avianus, Walter of England, and even Robert Henryson. I track the transformation of the Aesopic corpus, both the textual tradition and representations of Aesop's body, which coalesce to challenge the relationship between artistic production and corporeality. Rather than extending a generative, deeply somatic, and grotesque habitus of multiple fabular authors and commentators, the modernized Aesop obtains value as a "property," paving the way for the notion that creative corpuses can be "owned," effectively stealing away corporeal features from intellectual production. Given the clarion call that media scholars are sounding for incorporating appropriation skills within twenty-first-century curricula,[54] I suggest that a premodern orientation toward intellectual bodies, instead of properties, may produce more responsible uses, critiques, and reuses of creative work.

The seventh chapter, "Salutation: The Public Intimacy of Social Networks," addresses the premodern habitus of digital written correspondence, which has recently experienced radical transformations. Whereas email increased the speed of the personal letter, social media outlets such as Facebook and Twitter drastically expanded the reach of such writing through the creation of networks of "friends" and "followers." For scholars such as Richard Miller, this public "epistolarity" dissolves the boundaries between the public and private domains, resulting in "the greatest change in human communication since the invention of the printing press."[55] Thanks to Edward Snowden and WikiLeaks, we are acutely aware of the public and surveilled nature of email, but email has always operated rhetorically as personal correspondence. Now that social platforms facilitate instantaneous connection between geographically distant people, Sherry Turkle suggests, "technology proposes itself as the architect of our intimacies."[56] For Turkle, this desire for distant friendships has resulted in a situation in which we are "alone together," preferring the isolation of spending time together online over the messiness of face-to-face contact. And because these environments are "open" and relatively accessible to all, friendships are made public, which introduces the potential for performance and inauthenticity in the service of selling products or self-promotion.[57] For some media scholars, such as Turkle, authentic forms of intimacy cannot be experienced in these spaces, but for others, such as dj readies (Craig Saper), these environments host a variety of distributed forms of friendship and collectivity, including what he calls "bureaucratic intimacies." Citing the examples of resistance movements such as Occupy Wall Street, dj readies argues that such "intimate networks offer connectedness and shared responsibility in the face of lack of power."[58] While Twitter may not be able to provide the kind of small-scale intimacy that can be gained from private conversation, it fosters friendship networks that thrive and gain authority through massively distributed intimacies.

When we consider intimacy to be more than just private interaction, we can see that public forms of friendship have a deep and venerable history. One of the most pervasive, and vastly inaccurate, stereotypes about medieval people is their lack of intimacy. This misperception has been supported by misguided assumptions about medieval sexualities (or lack thereof), but the most powerful engine behind this mischaracterization is the Renaissance ideology that claims that the rise of the humanist subject was a distinct break from an unenlightened and muddled medieval millennium and a triumphant return to the classical past.[59]

For some Renaissance scholars, this rupture was marked by a singular event: Petrarch's 1345 discovery of Cicero's personal letters to his friend Atticus in the cathedral library of Verona.[60] Kathy Eden even goes so far as to suggest that this "famous encounter between Petrarch and the epistolary Cicero sets the primal scene for the Renaissance rediscovery of intimacy."[61] It is possible for Eden to call this a "rediscovery of intimacy" for at least two reasons. First, this claim assumes that intimacy is limited to personal, one-to-one interaction. Second, this claim assumes that intimacy did not exist in medieval correspondence, an assumption that is widely shared among scholars because the medieval art of letter writing, the *ars dictaminis* or *dictamen*, was the product of a largely bureaucratic habitus, one that relied heavily on rhetorical teaching and formulaic phrasing. As clearcut as this narrative seems to be, it discounts the existence of public intimacies, which have become pervasive within digital spaces.

Medieval *dictamen* was not developed for private correspondence. In almost every dictaminal manual, known as the *ars dictandi*, the part of the letter that receives the most extensive treatment is the formulaic address to the recipient(s), otherwise known as the salutation. Teachers of *dictamen*, known as *dictatores*, concentrated their efforts on the salutation because it served as both an artful expression of intimacy and a mechanism of rhetorical capital for lowly clerks who were attempting to persuade their superiors. And even when letters were only addressing one person, Giles Constable notes, they were "self-concious, quasi-public literary documents, often written with an eye to future collection and publication."[62] In addition, these letters were often recited publicly, which expanded their reach to audiences who could not read or had no access to the letters themselves.[63] Poets such as Geoffrey Chaucer and Gavin Douglas recognized the intimate potential of the *ars dictaminis*, actively including its elements in their poetry, often drawing directly on the rhetorical teachings of *dictatores*, ranging from Guido Faba to Boncompagno da Signa to Geoffrey of Vinsauf to Giovanni di Bonandrea. In chapter 7, I argue that the later Middle Ages witnessed and nurtured an important development in the history of rhetoric, in which epistolary style could be harnessed for the development of public networks of friends.

In the book's conclusion, "Breaking Bad *Habitus*," I offer a series of recommendations for digital writing and design that emerge from this rhetorical understanding of habitus. As a fourth-declension Latin noun, *habitus* is both a singular and plural form, both an individual disposition and a social condition that motivate rhetorical actions. The premodernity of this concept provides a persistent structure for understanding the reemergence of particular habits within particular writing spaces. Once we define our habitus, we may recognize those people and practices that our digital habits include and exclude; we may also influence and design writing environments that encourage the development of habitus that challenge homophily and recognize difference, thereby setting the conditions for the participation of rhetorical actors previously omitted or obscured.

When we have identified the features that comprise our writing dispositions, we can more responsibly contribute to the dynamic arts of digital habitual rhetoric, anchoring our writing strategies firmly within material environments, old and new. In the end, this book seeks to demonstrate the importance of developing stable, yet flexible, digital habitus that draw on what Bethany Nowviskie calls a "usable past" that will allow us to "step back from patriarchal, colonial, heteronormative, and white mediation, and from its sense of control over time, in order (as Afrofuturist thinkers would have it) to *make a new space-time* in which broader and more diverse publics can assert that agency and imagine alternate futures."[64] Too often our writing practices are distilled to a discrete recipe of practices that can be automated as "content delivery" within learning management systems. Writing should not be reduced to replication or supersession—an object that can be packaged, reproduced, sold, and then replaced by the next "new" thing within the "gale of creative destruction." Our habitual rhetoric should entail a careful, but often ambivalent, process of reflection, accretion, and selection from a long and accessible history of writing—a history that both surrounds and punctures its printed era, looking both forward and backward toward habits that could bear repeating.

1

Habitual Rhetoric

A History of *Habitus*

> Rhetoric that is complete is a *habitus*.
> —Hermannus Alemannus

> In a society in which the transmission of culture is monopolized by a school, the profound affinities that bind together human works . . . find their principle in the scholastic institution vested with the function of transmitting . . . a subconscious knowledge, or, more exactly of producing individuals endowed with this system of subconscious . . . schemes that constitute their culture or, better yet, their *habitus*.
> —Pierre Bourdieu

Habits are rhetorical. Whenever we encounter a new situation or a new place, the first thing we often do is observe the habits of others. Where are people going? What are they doing? We desperately want to avoid sticking out or disrupting the flow of the field we are entering, so we often do what others do, follow their footsteps or imitate their actions. And these habits, these seemingly instinctual movements or repetitive practices, are not merely shaped by human behavior. The physical spaces they inhabit, the location of the exits and the stairs, also persuade people to move one way or another. This is also the case, of course, within digital environments, which are designed to host and encourage predictable behaviors that can range from scrolling to clicking to commenting. Writing begets writing in online spaces—the more comments an article or page receives, the more writing it continues to accumulate. The more we participate, the more predictive the algorithms that capture and anticipate our actions become. Before we know it, we develop these habits, internalize these behaviors, and act accordingly—that is how persuasive these habits are. They convince us before we think we are convinced.

Once we have become accustomed to the conventions of these spaces, our common habits assume a kind of social profile that we rarely recognize. Our actions exhibit a subconscious awareness of what we might call the unwritten "rules of the game," or what the French sociologist Pierre Bourdieu calls a *habitus*, an embodied disposition or "structured and structuring structure" that shapes and is shaped by the tastes and behaviors of particular cultures.[1] Everything from our musical preferences to our bodily postures is a compilation of social habits that we acquire from and contribute to the groups to which we belong, especially those defined by nation, race, gender, and class. For Bourdieu, this disposition "designates *a way of being, a habitual state* (especially of the body) and, in particular, a *predisposition, tendency, propensity* or *inclination*."[2] Our various habitus therefore predispose our bodies to act in specific and nuanced ways that are structured by our previous experiences, within environments that range from our school playgrounds to our family gatherings. Bourdieu even goes so far to claim that any notion of an individual personality or "personal style . . . is never more than a deviation in relation to the style of a period or class so that it relates back to the common style not only by its conformity . . . but also by the difference."[3] While some may perceive this to be a dark vision of socially determined dispositions, this conception of habitus provides a persuasive rationale for the durable commonalities between individual and group behaviors and identities. Bourdieu uses the analogy of the "game" to suggest that all players may make a difference through their own individual contributions, not by following the written rules, but by drawing on their evolving experience with the unwritten regularities of the game. For Bourdieu, "the habitus as the feel for the game is the social game embodied and turned into a second nature."[4] Within this ludic framework, we may range free, but our cognitive assumptions and bodily actions emerge from the principles we acquire from our immersions in these "playing" fields.

While Bourdieu provides our most common and influential understanding of *habitus*, this book engages with what we might call a "habitus before habitus" by turning back to the thoroughgoing commentaries about such socially embodied dispositions within medieval university education. Nearly all premodern understandings of the Latin *habitus* emerge from Aristotle's Greek *hexis*, an ethical condition of the soul, a kind of second nature that is "something permanent and not readily subject to change."[5] Like Bourdieu, Aristotle considers this disposition to be durable, but not because of its persistent socialization and embodiment within particular fields of practice. Rather, hexis is based in virtue seated in the supernatural soul that can only be improved through continual education and training.[6] Once the works of the Philosopher, the medieval title for Aristotle, began to be translated into Latin, this ethical disposition began to assume a new, and eventually rhetorical, shape. As the first medieval universities began to come into their own in the twelfth century, teachers such as Peter Abelard begin to separate temporal (earthly) elements from the supernatural (heavenly) elements of moral character to argue that unpracticed virtue is no virtue at all. For Abelard, as Cary Nederman puts it, "a *habitus* can be said to exist only when someone has actively formed it."[7] This emphasis on performance, on practicing good habits in the world, was picked up in the later twelfth century and early thirteenth century by other medieval students and teachers, such as Alan of Lille, who turned further away from Aristotle to claim that ethical dispositions could be morally neutral and therefore depend less upon the virtuous potential of the soul than upon humans' free will to choose between virtue and vice.[8] As I will suggest below, this transformation of Aristotelian hexis into medieval habitus inspired a number of pedagogical innovations within university instruction, including the production of educational treatises that outline the principles and practices for acquiring effective habits for speaking and writing. Once it was believed that all students could actively form the nature of their moral dispositions, it became possible to develop an ethical-rhetorical pedagogy that would teach students how to write and create knowledge in ways that consider their social positions, their material environments, and their bodily movements. In other words, rhetoric becomes a habitus that is not just an ornament to apply or to decorate, but also a way to live and to make a difference in the world.

A Premodern History of Rhetorical Habitus

To understand the centrality of rhetorical habitus to premodern university writing instruction, I turn to the example of Giovanni di Bonandrea, the foremost teacher of rhetoric at the University of Bologna in the fourteenth century. Giovanni gained recognition from his peers and students by suggesting that writing should be developed from a habitus that seeks to equalize and stabilize the relationship between writers and their audiences. Like other teachers of rhetoric during this period, Giovanni builds upon the canonical definition provided by the ancient Roman rhetorician Marcus Tullius Cicero (first century BCE), who claims in his *De inventione* (*On Invention*) that habitus is "a stable and absolute constitution of mind or body in some particular, as, for example, the acquisition of some capacity or of an art, or again some special knowledge, or some bodily dexterity not given by nature but won by careful training and practice."[9] For Cicero, a rhetor's disposition is developed through education and repetition (*studium*), and grounded within specialized arts and formal training, which provide a permanence that counterbalances temporary states of emotion (*affectio*).[10] While Cicero is primarily concerned with the characteristics of the parts of an effective oration, medieval teachers of rhetoric, such as Giovanni, extensively glossed and applied the precepts of the *De inventione* to the *ars dictaminis*, the art of letter writing.[11] Instruction in these Ciceronian principles therefore developed habitus that could emerge within a range of rhetorical genres from orations to epistles.

Whereas Cicero assumed an audience of Roman elites for his rhetorical teachings, Giovanni was faced with a changing student demographic at the University of Bologna, which was no longer preparing its pupils exclusively for ecclesiastical positions. Instead, Giovanni was addressing an increasingly notarial class that was training for legal and bureaucratic professions that would serve the Italian communes.[12] This democratizing shift demanded a change in epistolary habits, which had been previously determined by a strict hierarchical relationship between senders and recipients. Giovanni offers his reconception of Ciceronian habitus in his highly influential rhetorical textbook, the *Brevis introductio ad dictamen* (A brief introduction to writing], by emphasizing its corporeal nature: "[W]e name that *habitus* some symmetry of the body not given by nature but learned by study and industry."[13] Through this seemingly minor shift away from the Ciceronian mind (animus) toward "some symmetry of the body" (corporis aliquam commoditatem), Giovanni foregrounds the role of the physical body, particularly the material labor of the notarial bodies who will produce the vast majority of the writing within civic culture. The elevation of this new bureaucratic class required a new habitus that would empower university students to gain social standing through what we might call "merit," rather than through aristocratic inheritance. For this new set of persons, Giovanni revised the teaching of the *salutatio*, the salutation or address from the sender to the recipient, which had been determined largely by ecclesiastical hierarchy (e.g., priests to popes and vice versa), to apply to "persons distinguished by habitus."[14] This recognition of an acquired disposition, one deeply connected to characteristics of the body (and the body politic), offers a significant challenge to preconceptions about how rhetorical identities and practices could be acknowledged and performed. Habitus is not just what Cicero called a "stable and absolute" (constantem et absolutam) quality exclusive to the elites—it could be learned, assumed, and transformed by a wide variety of writers.

In addition to Cicero's *De inventione*, Giovanni's definition of habitus is built upon foundations established by Arabic traditions of medieval commentary on Aristotle's *Rhetoric* that take up this conception of habitus as an acquired art or craft and apply it directly to rhetorical teaching. For example, Hermannus Alemannus,[15] a mid-thirteenth-century Arabic-Latin translator primarily known for his translation of Averroes's *Middle Commentary* on Aristotle's *Poetics*, explicitly defines habitus as a rhetorical disposition: "Rhetoric that is complete is a disposition [habitus] through which discourse is formed according to all the means that bring about persuasion more completely, more efficiently, and more quickly in relation to each element of particular or singular things."[16] This passage comes from Hermannus's *Didascalia in Rethoricam Aristotelis ex glosa Alpharabi* (Commentary on Aristotle's *Rhetoric* from the glosses of al-Fārābī), a Latin translation of al-Fārābī's tenth-century Arabic commentary on an Arabic version of Aristotle's *Rhetoric* accompanied by the *Sharh Kitâb al-khatâbah li-Aristûtalîs*.[17] Hermannus's *Didascalia* is a Latin amplification of Arabic interpretations of Aristotle's Greek text, including the glosses of Avicenna and Averroes, pivotal Arabic *auctores* who, among their own crucial Arabic contributions to learning, circulated ancient Greek learning from the Near East to the West.[18] One late fourteenth-century writing manual that cites Hermannus as a rhetorical authority is the expanded version of Geoffrey of Vinsauf's *Documentum de modo et arte dictandi et versificandi* (Instruction in the method and art of composing in prose and in verse) known as the *Tria sunt* (named for its opening words), which addresses a variety of poetic and prose techniques, attending specifically to the *ars dictaminis*.[19] For Hermannus and other medieval rhetoricians, habitus is the articulated body of rhetoric, which fully develops, activates, and empowers all persuasive operations, from poetic making to epistolary composition.

Within monastic circles of the period, habitus signifies both a learned disposition, often one that was either ethically bad or good, and clerical dress or bodily clothing, often representing a religious order. In his study of cenobitic living, Giorgio Agamben suggests that these two definitions are inseparable: "To inhabit together thus meant for the monks to share, not simply a place or a style of dress, but first of all a *habitus*. The monk is in this sense a man who lives in the mode of 'inhabiting,' according to a rule and a form of life. It is certain, nevertheless, that cenoby represents the attempt to make habit and form of life coincide in an absolute and total *habitus*, in which it would not be possible to distinguish between dress and way of life."[20] As both a social habit of living and a social habit of dressing, habitus is fundamentally corporeal, making it difficult to separate actions or appearances of a communal body from the bodies of its individual members. Understood this way, a religious habit is a kind of rhetorical ornament inseparable from its rhetorical practices—not something that can be put on or taken off for the sake of appearances. To flout the proverb, the habit makes the monk.

For Thomas Aquinas (fl. 1225–74), perhaps the most influential medieval monk of them all, habitus is a rule of life that shapes every action. In his *Summa theologiae* (*Sum of All Theology*), Aquinas defines this mental habit as a "principle that regulates the act," which emerges within a wide variety of intellectual, juridical, political, or professional contexts.[21] In turn, a scholastic habitus developed from Thomist thought and the form of the *summa*, which relies on symmetrical appositions, offering propositions and counterpropositions that build to provisional resolutions. This theological grammar for understanding the world also provided the structure for material objects of medieval life, ranging from the architecture of medieval cathedrals to the design of illuminated manuscripts. Art historian Erwin Panofsky studied and tracked this phenomenon within his 1951 book *Gothic Architecture and Scholasticism*, which argues that the ribs, buttresses, and pinnacles of the Gothic style replicate the "Scholastic habit," which reconciles "contradictory possibilities" that exist between faith and reason through establishing distinctions and posing questions to be resolved through disputation, otherwise known as quodlibetal debate.[22] According to this logic, the Scholastic forms of thinking provide the structure for a number of creative activities, especially the production of books, including the writing manual, which was often titled *Summa dictaminis*, a synthesis of the best writing practices.

Even though Panofsky's eccentric medievalism was not readily accepted by all in the mid-twentieth century, it captured the enthusiastic attention of Pierre Bourdieu, who had not yet developed his conception of habitus as an unregulated but structuring force of human behavior.[23] Attracted to Panofsky's thesis about the influence of Scholastic "mental habits,"[24] Bourdieu not only translated *Gothic Architecture and Scholasticism* into French, but also appended a thirty-page afterword ("Postface") that includes his first attempt to define habitus, which he describes as "a system of internalized schemes which have the capacity to generate all the thoughts, perceptions, and actions characteristic of a culture."[25] It is therefore within a premodern, specifically medieval Scholastic, context that Bourdieu develops this postmodern concept that has provided a sociological framework for understanding the internal structures that form the habits of a common people. Drawing on the work of French paleographer Robert Marichal, Bourdieu goes even further to suggest that such a habitus determines the characteristics of writing and the designs of books: "Marichal's analysis reveals not only how, in the copyist's daily activity, the *habitus*, defined by the interiorization of the principles of clarification and reconciliation of contraries, is constituted, but also how this *habitus* is concretely actualized in the specific logic of a particular practice."[26] The habitual labor of the scribe reveals itself within the architecture of the book, ranging from sentence and word divisions to illustrations and the designs of specific letters.

Yet such an understanding of the creative possibilities of Scholastic habits is somewhat at odds with Bourdieu's eventual development of habitus as a largely class-based structure that limits social and economic mobility of particular cultures and groups who have become habituated to the norms of their particular environments.[27] Even though Bourdieu's postmodern and anti-Enlightenment conception of habitus retains a generative force, it is, as Katharine Breen suggests, "intensely conservative, in the sense that it is virtually impossible for a speaker to eliminate all traces of his or her habitual accent, or even for an 'enlightened' academic community to change the habitually gendered division between the hard and soft sciences. For medieval philosophers and theologians, in contrast, *habitus* is an intrinsically desirable agent of change."[28] Within the realm of medieval rhetoric, habitus are likewise embodied but changeable dispositions that can transform and be transformed through written or spoken repetition and practice of rhetorical devices over time. This is a crucial distinction. Nearly all modern studies of habituation draw on the work of Bourdieu without recognizing the significance of its Scholastic origins, which emphasize agency and the potential for ethical and rhetorical change.

Rhetorical Habitus after Bourdieu

Once Bourdieu's conception of a "structured and structuring structure" began to dominate sociological discussions of the nature/culture divide in the modern era, the rhetorical nature of premodern habitus began to fade from view, even if it had been always already latently present. After all, Bourdieu's vision, as mediated through Panofsky, was focused on the Scholastic shaping of the arts, particularly writing, and specifically the materiality of writing. He was fascinated, for instance, by the interface of the medieval book, which accomplished conflicting goals at once: providing clarity for the reader through repetitive phrasing, capitalized initials, and rubricated titles, while also satisfying the desire for density, a kind of multimodal intensity, filling in blank space with additional commentary, corrections, and glosses.[29] For Bourdieu, this reconciliation of opposing forces emerges from the "schemes that organize the thoughts of cultured men" within university education, specifically "the organizing principles of speech that the treatises of rhetoric called figures of words and figures of thought."[30] This rhetorical element of Bourdieu's habitus, its capacity to provide structure or even persuasive power, even if it were not consistently emphasized as such, would go on to attract the interest of modern theorists of the nature/culture divide, ranging from Bruno Latour to Annemarie Mol to Nigel Thrift, who consider the implications of such social dispositions for agency and embodiment within particular fields of practice, ranging from social science to health care to human geography.

All of these thinkers are to some extent building upon Bourdieu's ideas about habituation, but Latour offers a strikingly divergent model for understanding the nature of "subjectivity" or agency within particular environments. Whereas Bourdieu emphasizes the class-based and institutionally driven forces that shape dispositions and behavior, Latour dismisses such sociological explanations as meaningless, preferring instead to focus on the network of material "associations" between human and nonhuman "actors," also known as Actor-Network-Theory (ANT). He does not reject the idea of a habitus outright, however. In fact, Latour directly takes up Bourdieu's interest in the organizing principles of rhetorical expressions:

> How many circulating clichés do we have to absorb before having the competence to utter an opinion about a film, a companion, a situation, a political stance? If you began to probe the origin of each of your idiosyncrasies, would you not be able to deploy, here again, the same star-like shape that would force you to visit many places, people, times, events that you had largely forgotten? This tone of voice, this unusual expression, this gesture of the hand, this gait, this posture, aren't these traceable as well? And then there is the question of your inner feelings. Have they not been given to you? Doesn't reading novels help you to know how to love? How would you know which group you pertain to without ceaselessly downloading some of the cultural clichés that all the others are bombarding you with?[31]

While this may sound quite a bit like Bourdieu, Latour's references to "star-like shape" and "ceaselessly downloading" offer a distinctly technological and networked vision of the collective uses of rhetoric. Rather than flesh out the socially embodied habitus, Latour seeks to flatten the field of analysis in order to trace and identify particular actors, who could be people or novels. Using his own figurative language, he suggests, "Borrowing a metaphor from cartography, I could say that ANT has tried to render the social world as flat as possible in order to ensure that the establishment of any new link is clearly visible."[32] By flattening the field, Latour is able to trace objects and identify their associations, creating material networks that describe particular capacities for action. He even uses the university lecture hall as an example, which contains multiple actors, from the podium to the seats, that enable teaching to happen. In contradistinction to Bourdieu's argument that the pedagogical practice of quodlibetal debate shapes the architecture of Gothic cathedrals, Latour makes nearly the opposite claim: the objects of the classroom shape the kind of teaching that will happen. He suggests, "Although there is no 'underlying hidden structure,' this is not to say that there doesn't exist structuring templates circulating through channels most easily materialized by techniques."[33] By emphasizing "structuring templates" instead of Bourdieu's "structured and structuring structure," Latour focuses attention on the circulation of discrete objects, which could be rhetorical clichés or internet plug-ins, all "downloadable" for our use.

To some extent, we could say that Latour's flat networks of association share the sensibilities of dictaminal formularies that emerged from the letter-writing instruction of teachers like Giovanni di Bonandrea and Geoffrey of Vinsauf. These formularies are templates for discrete parts of the epistle, which allowed the letter writer to "download" the relevant salutation and cut-and-paste the formulaic phrasing directly into their writing. Lawrence of Aquilegia even composed a dictaminal manual around 1300 CE that included a visualization of particular rhetorical choices a writer could make—all the writer had to do was follow the horizontal lines in the chart that suited their audience and purpose.[34] This network of clichés provided a visible association of epistolary objects that would satisfy Latour's desire for plug-ins and structuring templates.

Yet such overly prescriptive manuals only capture one element of the rhetorical habitus that emerged within university instruction of the later Middle Ages, which was much more comprehensive in scope, emphasizing the generative force of habitual practice, what Cicero calls *studium*. The repetitive work of scribes, notaries, and monks was fundamentally corporeal, an attempt to achieve what Giovanni calls "a symmetry of the body," a way of living that intermingles words with deeds, rhetoric with ethics. The medieval book was itself a body, not only the figurative body of work of copyists, illuminators, and annotators but also a literal corpus assembled with parts of animals, from feathers (quills) to skin (parchment). Whereas Latour might call such a book a network of actors, Annemarie Mol might call it a site for "enactment," an environment that produces many books: a written copy of an exemplar for the copyist, an art canvas of historiated initials for the illuminator, and a textbook of vocabulary words for the annotator. For Mol, who famously studied patients suffering from and doctors diagnosing atherosclerosis in a Dutch hospital, each doctor and patient enacted different bodily realities. While the patient suffers from the illness of leg pain, the doctor names the disease atherosclerosis. According to Mol, it is not that the patient and the doctor, or the copyist and the annotator, merely have different perspectives on an object. Rather, they are enacting different realities dependent upon the tools at hand, from the microscopic lens to the gold leaf. Mol therefore emphasizes the importance of "what is done in practice," which includes "practicalities, materialities, *events*."[35] For those producing the medieval book, we might say they are enacting their own embodied dispositions, producing a codex shaped by multiple habitus. Yet, despite their discrete realities, Mol recognizes that "the practice . . . inevitably requires cooperation."[36] Just as patients and doctors must work together to end the pain and heal the disease, the medieval book can only be produced through a "symmetry of the body" of its labor, based in repetitive practice and ongoing collaboration.

This cooperative compilation of codices, like the writing of a Wikipedia entry, is sometimes fragmentary, often unfinished, and always future-oriented. This writing habitus is therefore attentive to both space and time, recognizing the inevitability of circulation among subsequent readers, the contributions they can offer, as well as the contexts the writing can produce, from scriptoria to libraries to social media. Human geographer Nigel Thrift calls such a context a "parcel of socially constructed time-space," within which "'subjects' and 'objects' are aligned in particular ways which provide particular orientations to action . . . and particular resources for action."[37] Just like Mol, Thrift focuses on practice to capture the interaction of bodies and objects to decenter any conception of a human subject who has the sovereign capacity to represent the world. We might even say he attends to what we in writing studies would call the "affordances" that shape the dialogical nature of our communication. To describe the capacities of the subject within these time-spaces, Thrift turns to John Shotter, who suggests,

> We must note that all our behaviour, even our own thought about ourselves, is conducted in an ongoing argumentative context of criticism and justification, where every argumentative move is formulated in a response to previous moves. This accords . . . with a familiar aspect of rhetoric, to do with its *persuasive* function, its ability to materially affect people, to move them to action, or affect their perceptions in some way. . . . We must also note that . . . what we have in common with each other in our society's traditions is not a set of agreements about meanings, beliefs, or values but

a set of intrinsically two-sided topics ... or deterministic theories or commonplaces for use by us as *resources*, from which we can draw the two or more sides of an argument. Finally, we most note another, more unfamiliar aspect of rhetoric related to those aspects of languages to do with "giving" or "lending" a *first form* to what otherwise are in fact only vaguely or partially ordered feelings and activities to do with the study of how common understandings are established *before* one turns to their criticism. It is this fact—that we "see" just as much "through" our words as through our eyes that is, for us here, rhetoric's most important characteristic. For even in the face of the vague, undescribable, open, fluid, and ever changing nature, appropriate forms of talk can work to "make it appear as if" our everyday lives are well ordered and structured.[38]

For Shotter and Thrift, rhetoric then offers an accumulative means of coherence and connection to "common understandings," what Latour would call "clichés," that are shaped by "intrinsically two-sided topics," what I would call the medieval logic of disputation or quodlibetal debate.

While the resonances between these post-Bourdieuian theories of practice and premodern writing habits are compelling, they only partially capture the social and embodied character of the rhetorical habitus I describe in this book. For Latour, Mol, and Thrift, rhetoric is largely reduced to formulaic expression, a tool for storytelling that can only create the appearance of coherence and structure for the human subject. Latour's approach is enthusiastically two-dimensional, a kind of cartographic empiricism that seeks to flatten the relationships between humans and nonhuman objects. The digital world is a kind of fantastical flatland for Latour, because it appears to provide precise and traceable networks of relationships. With his collaborator Tommaso Venturini, Latour even goes so far as to say, "Thanks to digital traceability, researchers no longer need to choose between precision and scope in their observations: it is now possible to follow a multitude of interactions and, simultaneously, to distinguish the specific contribution that each one makes to the construction of social phenomena. Born in an era of scarcity, the social sciences are entering an age of abundance. In the face of the richness of these new data, nothing justifies keeping old distinctions."[39]

In 2010, when Venturini and Latour composed their essay, this altruistic wonderland of traceable data must have seemed both plausible and desirable, but this "age of abundance" has rapidly devolved into an era of exploitation in which the digital data of clicks and views have become largely controlled by large social media corporations that sell user information for enormous profits, not scientific advancement. As Alberto Romele and Dario Rodighiero argue, "the digital has never been flat: the flatness is rather the result of an illusion mainly due to the interfaces that usually mask—for the digital as for many other technological ensembles—the existence of a multitude of layers."[40] Instead, they suggest that information technology has become more Bourdieuian than Latourian because of the increasing granularity of user data, which Facebook and Google capture for creating products for particular consumer profiles. Romele and Rodighiero conclude that "digital machines are habitus machines" that produce "personalization without personality," reducing users to sets of predictable characteristics.[41] Machine learning has developed digital habitus that ultimately replace persons with personalizations, eliminating the possibility of autonomous online personalities.

A Digital History of Rhetorical Habitus

Scholars of digital rhetoric and new media have acknowledged their debts to Bourdieuian conceptions of habitus but often attempt to set aside its more conservative and class-based elements to distinguish mechanistic habits, such as clicking and scrolling, from creative habits, such as compiling and annotating. For example, in their study of reader comments in the online *New York Times*, John Gallagher and Steve Holmes identify a habitus within these web templates that is highly creative and dynamic, not restricted to a user's class or taste. Rather than turn to Bourdieu's later work on social distinction, their version of habitus draws on "Bourdieu's earlier work" that "is closer to an Aristotelian *hexis* . . . which translates to embodied comportment, disposition, or state, . . . the concrete and embodied manner of producing individuals' ethical and rhetorical agency over the course of their repeated cultural practices in digital and nondigital material environments."[42] Gallagher and Holmes identify Bourdieu's differing definitions of habitus over time, turning to his earlier, arguably less Marxist view of habit formation, but this earlier work is less indebted to Aristotle than it is to Aquinas. Even though Aquinas and Cicero draw on Aristotle's hexis as a disposition that produces ethical action, medieval teachers of rhetoric, such as Giovanni di Bonandrea, develop habitus as an embodied and rhetorical condition that could be learned, actualized, and performed through particular writing strategies, even epistolary salutations oriented for particular social classes. As the popularity of Giovanni's *Brevis introductio* suggests, the principles of such writing habits were thought to be so important that they often became codified as rules or procedures within rhetorical textbooks of the Middle Ages.

Within the digital world, such procedural rhetoric has become the subject of attention for videogame scholars, who have demonstrated the ways in which rule-based environments produce particular kinds of habitual action. Whereas popular media often decry the negative outcomes of what they view as highly mechanistic and addictive gaming habits, Steve Holmes persuasively recognizes the embodied and playful "procedural habits" that emerge from many kinds of online games. By claiming that gamers develop creative and dynamic dispositions within the limits of algorithmic domains, Holmes works within a framework that was established not by Artistotle but by teachers of the *ars dictaminis*, such as Giovanni and Geoffrey of Vinsauf, who produced highly structured, occasionally formulaic, writing textbooks.[43] In a similar vein, John Gallagher meticulously tracks the "update culture" that motivates writers to revise their online writing continually within highly structured, but editable, web templates. For Gallagher, this incessant labor emerges from the writer's desire to develop their entrepreneurial "brand" and expand their potential network through habitual updates.[44] While Holmes and Gallagher recognize the regulated and cultural features of these habits, their emphasis on "individuals' ethical and rhetorical agency" mitigates the fundamental communal character of medieval and Bourdieuian habitus, which rely on highly socialized rhetorical practices ranging from scholastic disputation to manuscript compilation. For Bourdieu, any notion of an entrepreneurial habitus is merely a fantasy of individual agency: "If the practices of the members of the same group or class are more and better harmonized than the agents know or wish, it is because . . . 'following [his] own laws,' each 'nonetheless agrees with the other.'"[45] Bourdieu denies that such common habits emerge from codified sets of rules, but his habitus is fundamentally social in nature, structuring the practices of groups of people often united by gender, race, and especially class. Even though medieval conceptions of rhetorical habitus are often defined by rules, and even set out in writing manuals, they are also focused on harmonizing group practices, ranging from the conventions of notarial scripts to standardized salutations in letters.

Within the highly regulated and algorithmic logic of digital networks, such harmonious habits are easily tracked and increasingly predictable, a dream scenario for new media companies attempting to capture and anticipate consumer behavior. Such market-driven surveillance of online activity results in the creation of bots and automated notifications that compel users to adjust their habits in the midst of every real (and manufactured) crisis and to update their individual social profiles to remain poignant and relevant. For new media scholar Wendy Hui Kyong Chun, this situation follows the formula "Habit + Crisis = Update," which makes clear the ways in which networks do not produce an imagined and anonymous "we" (they are not, to use Benedict Anderson's term, "imagined communities") but rather, a relentlessly pointed yet empty, singular yet plural YOU. Instead of depending on mass communal activities, such as reading the morning newspaper, to create national citizens, networks rely on asynchronous yet pressing actions to create interconnected users. In network time, things flow noncontinuously. The NOW constantly punctures time, as the new quickly becomes old, and the old becomes forwarded once more as new(ish). New media are N(YOU) media; new media are a function of YOU.[46]

Chun's analysis of "YOU" media such as YouTube reveals that networks constantly challenge the creative possibilities of habits, making the changing of habits habitual, meeting the needs of the vocative "you" and not the collective "we." In short, "the constant update ... deprives habit of its ability to habituate."[47] The compulsion to always be updating encourages individual writers to attempt to distinguish themselves as the most recent and relevant, participating in a competition that undermines the unifying habits of a community.

Whereas some scholars of digital rhetoric like Holmes and Gallagher argue that Aristotelian hexis offers ethical dispositions that writers can develop within digital spaces to establish their individual agency, such a vision of rhetorical habits does not fully account for the communal and material nature of rhetorical habitus that we have inherited from medieval teachers of rhetoric, who consistently focus on delivery, attending to how common writing habits unify communities and encourage responses from their audiences. This attention to reception entails the design of writing spaces, which are themselves shaped by what Thomas Rickert calls "ambient" rhetoric, the ubiquitous influence of nonhuman actors, ranging from corroding wormholes to cracking bindings to chatting bots. For Rickert, ambience "refers to the active role that the material and informational environment takes in human development, dwelling, and culture, or to put this differently, it dissolves the assumed separation between what is (privileged) human doing and what is passively material."[48] As noted above, medieval manuscript culture was highly attuned to these ambient features, because any individual codex was itself a corporeal entity composed of elements from its environment, including the skin of cows, the ink of gallnuts, and the feathers of birds. The monks who prepared and inscribed these manuscripts adhered to a common habitus, a form of life within a communal monastery structured by such ambient interplay between the sounds of the liturgical chants, the visions of holy objects, and the touch of the vellum. These habits therefore shape and are directly shaped by their habitation, what Rickert calls their "dwelling" or what Bourdieu calls their "field."[49] This monastic form of habitation (and habituation) is the social disposition that became a driving rhetorical force throughout the Latin West, both for the design of pages in manuscripts and early printed books and the teaching of writing in early universities.

University Educational Exclusion and Rhetorical Habitus Formation

My conception of *habitual rhetoric* therefore brings this premodern tradition to bear upon modern, largely Bourdieuian, conceptions of embodied and ambient structures to identify the features that compose our digital habitus, the historical principles and conditions that shape the actions of particular writers and the designs of particular writing spaces. But I must emphasize that the set of writing habits selected and described in this book emerge specifically from a Westernized university culture that has historically excluded and oppressed women and people of color. This does not mean, of course, that these dispositions find their origins exclusively within medieval educational institutions. University writing practices are themselves based in forms of knowledge production, from cave drawing to stone cutting to wampum weaving, that emerged from earlier chirographic and oral cultures, including those of Indigenous peoples.[50] These habits are therefore shaped by the imperial, colonial, and patriarchal forces that appropriated and reproduced them within educational environments that were almost exclusively composed of white, European men. This rhetorical sovereignty, which universities enjoyed (and still enjoy) over these practices, empowered their teachers and their students to codify these habits into teachable and durable habitus that could be easily reproduced over centuries within institutions of higher education that would eventually develop the principles of computer science, creating the basis for the high-tech cultures of Silicon Valley that would give these habits their digital lives.

To illustrate this point, I turn once again to Bourdieu, who argued strongly throughout his career for the habituating force of educational structures, particularly upon the tastes and habits of distinct social classes. Even in his early response to Panofsky, he claims, "In a society in which the transmission of culture is monopolized by a school, the profound affinities that bind together human works . . . find their principle in the scholastic institution vested with the function of transmitting . . . a subconcious knowledge, or, more exactly of producing individuals endowed with this system of subconcious . . . schemes that constitute their culture or, better yet, their habitus."[51] Bourdieu points out that the "scholastic institution" in the Middle Ages exerted near total control over the "transmission of culture." While the cultural authority of the modern university has waned in the centuries since, the reproduction of rhetorical practices across media, from manuscript to print to screen, has remained remarkably durable and maintained an influence that can be traced throughout multiple forms of digital rhetoric, from tracking changes in Microsoft Word to compiling information in Wikipedia to debating politics on Twitter. The *habitual rhetoric* that I identify in this book largely relies on this institutional foundation, which essentially codified these rhetorical habits and established their potential for persistence.

This reliance upon Scholastic modes of thinking means that the development of these rhetorical habits is also based in centuries of colonization, appropriation, and exclusion. Bourdieu, once again, is a helpful example. In his ethnographic research on the Kabyle people of Algeria, he assumed that they were a preliterate culture without writing, even though they had always had what we call the Libyco-Berber script. Bourdieu not only underestimated their capacity to write, but also mistakenly believed that their supposed lack of "literacy" undermined their cognitive and cultural advancement. According to D. Vance Smith, this misapprehension emerges from Bourdieu's own habitus, which was shaped by the same Scholastic logic that established such "literacy" as a threshold for knowledge production:

> It's one of the means by which universities shore up the value of their intellectual work—they police grammar, philology, literacy—in short, they define and champion rigour and "standards." For those of us brought up within that system . . . those standards might appear to be value-neutral. But they're value-neutral only because they annihilate even the possibility of other values, of other modes of thinking or being. When Bourdieu went from the elite École Normale Supérieure to a Kabyle settlement, he saw, ultimately, the *absence* of what made the university, and his own mind, what it was. That supposed absence is the product of intellectual arrogance, yes, but it's also part of a European cultural heritage.[52]

This annihilation of "other modes of thinking or being" is exactly what many of our habits, and what many of these university writing practices, do to achieve authority within a particular field or "cultural heritage." To make this point clear, Smith suggests that we only need to imagine an alternative history in which the African general Hannibal destroyed Rome in his invasion of Italy: "If Hannibal had succeeded, Punic rather than Latin might have been the language of European intellectuals until the post-Enlightenment. Bourdieu's own language might not have been a 'Romance' language at all, and his most famous term, '*habitus*,' might have been a Punic word."[53] Within this scenario, Africa would no longer be the perpetual object of colonization, and our writing habits would have assumed an entirely different disposition.

Habitual rhetoric therefore embodies this tension, recognizing practices that expand participation and challenge injustice, as well as those that exclude participants and perpetuate inequality. By tracing this history of habitus back to medieval university instruction, I am not advocating for a nostalgic return to the Middle Ages, or to any prior age, for that matter. Rather, I am arguing that the effacement of these formative institutions and practices both produces an incomplete account of digital rhetoric and forestalls attempts to grapple with the structures that support our writing habits. If we fail to confront their histories, we cannot accurately describe their composition, preventing or undermining our potential to embrace or dismantle these habitus. Put another way, this recognition of our habitual rhetoric allows us to cultivate good habits and to break bad ones. The focus on premodernity also provincializes the figure of the post-Enlightenment subject, which has occupied the critical imaginations of those who both seek to uphold or deconstruct forms of liberal humanism.

This is not to imply that the modern construction of the human has not possessed its own powerful habituating force. In her critique of liberal humanism, Kandice Chuh offers an alternative of "illiberal humanisms," which "are directed toward the protection and flourishing of people and of ways of being and knowing and of inhabiting the planet that liberal humanism, wrought through the defining structures of modernity, tries so hard to extinguish."[54] While the habitus of the modern subject has undeniably perpetuated the annihilation of "ways of being and knowing" of non-Western persons, especially Black and Indigenous people and other people of color, additional attention to any notion of premodern subjectivities, if we acknowledge they exist, will deepen and augment our ability to support such "illiberal humanisms." Like Chuh, I believe "we need more rather than less attention to and accounts of human activity and behavior, accounts that, contra liberal humanism, take as axiomatic the humanity and humanism of precisely those people sacrificed to the liberal ideal."[55] Such an orientation toward habitual rhetoric vis-à-vis the university is therefore necessarily problematic because it accepts and reluctantly adopts rhetorical practices, such as disputation, translation, and appropriation, that have histories of both liberation and oppression. This approach resonates with the vision of the "third university" that la paperson proposes in *A Third University Is Possible*. Rather than reject completely what the book describes as the neoliberal and corporatized "first university" or the anti-capitalist and nostalgic "second university," paperson insists that the third university is assembled with the materials of the first two. Rather than decolonize the university, paperson proposes to make the university a "decolonizing machine," which means that it must be strategic, vocational, and anti-utopian, using existing structures, such as critical theory and tuition and fees, to fulfill its mission.[56] Habitual rhetoric similarly draws on the materials of the past to develop dynamic principles for digital writing practices and interface design that undergo continual scrutiny, reassessment, and transformation.

In sum, such a premodern understanding of rhetorical habitus challenges the marketplace assumptions of computational systems that track writers' habits and contribute to our current update culture. This book therefore identifies the ways that the purported openness of these rhetorical practices has also perpetuated their exclusivity and potential to become mechanisms of oppression. By establishing, for example, how collaborative ways of knowing such as disputation became intellectual forms of male combat, I attempt to set the historical background for Tara McPherson's argument that the "universality" of computer code has occluded its inherent ideologies and squashed its potential to incorporate difference into design.[57] And because, as Johanna Drucker has illustrated, such forms of knowledge representation are always in danger of becoming codified and transformed into "information" and "data," I call for renewed attention to the digital interface that accommodates interventions from a variety of users, and I seek apparatus that present knowledge as constructed and anticipate interventions by future digital writers.[58] A renewed attention to the premodern conditions of digital writing habits will help communities of writers recognize and challenge the design of writing spaces that continue to exclude the voices of so many. Habitual rhetoric acknowledges the forces that shape our habits and highlights their stable but creative power for becoming agents of change.

2

Translation

Online Education and Transfers of Authority

> Public material will be private property if you do not linger over the common and open way, and if you do not try to render word for word like a faithful translator.
> —**Horace,** *Ars poetica*

> In the online environment, participation is not only limited to those who possess the requisite economic and cultural resources; participation may in fact operate as the means to perpetuate the hidden advantages of elites.
> —**Mathieu O'Neil,** "The Sociology of Critique in Wikipedia"

"Access" is fundamental to all conversations about translating language and knowledge. When we translate something, we assume we are providing access to something for someone who did not have access to it before. Translation is a rhetorical habit beyond question because we also assume that access is a social good, one that benefits all. But many ancient translators did not operate under these assumptions. Instead, they often perceived translation as a transfer, a "carrying over," of political authority from one place to another, often from a subjugated people to an imperial power. For Saint Jerome, the translator of the Hebrew Bible into Latin, the aim of translation was conquest. Describing the translation practices of Hilary the Confessor, Jerome asserts, "By right of victory, he led away the sense captive into his own language."[1] In medieval funerary and relic culture, the Latin term *translatio* referred to the physical transportation of the bodies of dead monarchs and saints from one location to another as a symbolic representation of a transfer of authority from one domain to another.[2] And while most arguments for translation, usually from one language to another, do not acknowledge this history, we can detect it when translation is used in educational technology conversations about "access," in which teachers are asked to "translate" face-to-face instruction to online environments as a means to remedy disparities in public education.

Many educators experienced this phenomenon in the midst of the COVID-19 pandemic when schools and universities were forced to "translate" all face-to-face teaching to "remote" modalities, the common administrative euphemism for teaching online through videoconferencing applications, such as Zoom, or learning management systems such as Blackboard or Schoology. For Katherine Newman, who was then the interim chancellor of my institution, the University of Massachusetts Boston, this public-health crisis provided an "opportunity" to argue for an increase in online offerings, which she claimed would help to close racial and economic gaps. Among the many possible responses to the economic crisis caused by the pandemic, which could range from increasing state tax revenue appropriations for higher education to cancelling student debt to making college free, Newman preferred the following:

> By far the best solution is to be found in rigorous, creative online education. All of us in higher education discovered how important distance learning is when the pandemic made on-campus classes impossible. But to scale up on-line education, we are going to need to do much more than "translate" our current curriculum to Zoom. We need to grow an affordable, flexible form of online education. It will need to offer seven or eight "start times" per year; provide skills that employers are looking for; recognize prior experiential learning in a rigorous way; and support students with "wrap around" services. This is clearly what the adult education population is looking for. When asked what kind of college experience they most want, 53 percent responded "online," while only 26 percent were looking for "in person" and 21 percent would prefer "employer provided."[3]

Without providing any citation to the study that provided that preference data, Newman asserts that a flexible, skill-based, customer-service-styled online education is the answer to the problem, because it allows for these vulnerable students to take classes while keeping their jobs and taking care of their children and elders. To accomplish this, Newman admits that instructors will have to "do much more than 'translate' our current curriculum," which recognizes the impossible equivalence of face-to-face and online education. But the "scaling up" she proposes makes no reference to educational quality or equality. She knows she does not need to make that argument. Those who have attempted to work full-time jobs while attending college know full well that the choice of online education has nothing to do with its quality—it has everything to do with its availability, its convenience, and its affordability. In other words, "access" to education is reason enough to justify its translation.

But as scholars of disability studies have continually argued, providing "access" is no simple matter of translating course material from one modality to another. Just because students have the right to accommodations and instructors are compelled to provide them does not, of course, mean that education becomes magically "accessible." We too often indulge the fantasy that the individual teacher alone can offer each differently abled student an appropriate and effective translation of course content. Even with universal design templates and platforms that offer multiple versions of course material, the intensity of the labor necessary to accomplish any sense of accessibility is extremely fatiguing for the teacher, and especially for the student, who bears all of the burden of and responsibility for seeking accommodations and informing instructors of their value. Even when we recognize that access can only be truly achieved through cooperative efforts, we still consider accessibility to be an optional, exceptional practice. Annika Konrad observes that "we have theoretical understanding of access as a collaborative, interactive process but no structure of habit for practicing collective access in everyday life."[4] This lack of a "collective" accessibility-focused "structure of habit"—even with an awareness of what access entails—reflects what I want to call a *translational habitus*, an access-without-accessibility disposition, which embraces an idea of access that empowers elites to act in the supposed best interests of others. Put another way, our translation practices are largely entrepreneurial, dependent on individual commitments to accessibility rather than on the material support systems that would make access truly possible.

This translational rhetoric of access has been persuasive for many centuries. In the case of language translation, we have come to accept the argument that the translation of texts serves the common good, expanding the authority of textual interpretation from exclusive single-language communities to much wider public reading audiences. For many, the internet is the ultimate medium for translation, not only through applications that translate digital written content into multiple languages, but also through the proliferation of multilingual sites, particularly Wikipedia, which was available in 328 languages as of 2022.[5] The underlying assumption about such crowdsourced websites is that they offer universal accessibility, both in terms of production and consumption. In other words, the internet embodies the public ideal of translation—expanding access to information about the world. This is also the position expressed in many medieval treatises on translation, including John Trevisa's *Dialogue between the Lord and the Clerk on Translation*, which was published in 1387 as a preface to his English translation of Ranulph Higden's Latin universal history, the *Polychronicon*.[6] Within this debate on translation, the Lord makes the argument that Higden's chronicle should be "translated out of Latyn into Englisshe, for the moo men shuld hem understonde and have thereof kunnyng, informacioun and lore" (lines 25–27). Despite the Clerk's objection that Latin is already a universal language (28–34), the Lord suggests that a vernacular version will make the text available to those who do not know Latin (35–37), which would naturally widen its audience. Rather than support efforts to include "moo men" in the learning of Latin, which would increase the number of students in the medieval universities, the Lord prefers that the historical chronicle be delivered in an "accessible" format for those excluded from the schools. As the precursor to the Silicon Valley tech giant, the Lord offers one mode of access for the general public, while maintaining the distinction of a higher class of education, one available only to the elite.

This chapter reveals translation to be a rhetorical habit that includes and excludes, both serving a public function as well as satisfying the desires of a privatized class, or what we might call an aristocratic market. As a translator who received his professional training at Oxford, Trevisa recognizes the problems with making school-based knowledge more widely available to the public without the instructional assistance of teachers and clerks who had produced and curated this work in the first place. Trevisa expresses his resistance to clerical disenfranchisement and lay aristocratic empowerment through a translational habitus, which embraces a highly Latinate mode of translation that encourages dialectical role-play and debate, showcases his rhetorical training, and even experiments with vernacular poetic forms. In doing so, Trevisa attempts to instill in his future readers translational habits that recognize the affordances and constraints of the vernacular and offer a means to access the texts and their possibilities for learning. While these strategies are undeniably innovative, Trevisa's translational project reflects his recognition that he is not closing the gaps between the "learned" and "unlearned"—his work is merely preparing the foundation for future "separate but unequal" models of education.

To demonstrate this result, I begin the chapter with an assessment of the state of online learning as the manifestation of our translational habits and mandates for access. Next, I discuss a history of such a translation of learning, focusing on the example of Trevisa, an early English translator who developed a hybridized model of translation that attempts to mitigate the transfer of authority to the aristocratic elite. Jumping centuries ahead and across the pond, I turn to American efforts to expand access to universities and subsequent movements to translate Latin-language educational models to English-language ones, beginning with the emergence of the "remedial" writing course and ending with Writing Across the Curriculum (WAC) programs. In the last section of the chapter, I discuss modern approaches to writing studies that consider the contributions of medieval rhetoric, providing the foundation for the call for a digital habitus that recognizes the rhetorical force and consequences of our translational instincts.

Translating Online Learning

The COVID-19 outbreak painfully revealed the educational disparities that already existed within and between educational systems throughout the world. Since at least the 1980s, higher education, especially in the United States, has been in an economic free fall caused primarily by successful austerity movements to defund and privatize the public sector, especially public universities. The situation has caused a crisis for "access," particularly for people of color and the working poor, who have also been disproportionately affected by the pandemic both in the loss of jobs and in the loss of life. These populations therefore have fewer resources, especially money and time, to pursue university degrees, limiting their social and economic mobility. For Katherine Newman, who has since become the Provost and Executive Vice President for Academic Affairs of the University of California (UC) system, the solution is the translation of face-to-face instructional modalities to online ones, but this ostensible remedy offers no remedy at all. It not only creates a greater divide between the underserved and the elite but also fails to address the fundamental problem: the lack of funding to support these disadvantaged students. In a pointed blog post, "When Are Access and Inclusion Also Racist?," Christopher Newfield demonstrates that while the UC system has improved access by enhancing financial aid for undocumented students and phasing out racially biased SAT scores for admissions, its decreased level of state funding has created a university that for students of color has fewer resources and provides a lower quality of education than it did twenty years earlier. Newfield tracks how the decline in state funding is in direct proportion to the decline in the funding share that white students get over that period of time. He concludes, "White enrollment and funding go down hand in hand—except when funding goes down faster during major economic downturns. Republican and Democratic leaders give diverse UC less money than they gave a comparatively white UC. *This* is what racist inclusion looks like."[7] As a microcosm of American public higher education, UC demonstrates how arguments for access are often translations of authority: rather than offer equal opportunity, they empower white elites.

The translation of access to education has only been amplified with the steady increase of online instructional options. One of the most remarkable proposals for educational reform in recent memory is the MOOC (massive open online course), which promised to offer thousands of students free and open access to academic content taught online by a professor from one of America's elite colleges or universities. There is little doubt that the ideal MOOC offered many advantages, including greater public exposure to the erudite material that rarely passes beyond gates of the ivory tower. As Aaron Bady puts it, "If a MOOC is simply a free educational resource that you can find on the web . . . then there's nothing to object to in them, and everything to like."[8] Advocates for MOOCs argued that they would democratize and extend the reach of higher education to public audiences previously unable to afford such high-quality, often Ivy League, instruction. This appeared to be a laudable function of the MOOC, but states like California sought out MOOCs as a remedy to staunch the bleeding in their budgets, proposing to offer college credit for MOOC enrollment in place of an actual seat in an actual class. This made the MOOC a dumping ground for students who cannot afford to pay the tuition of elite universities and colleges. Bady observes, "MOOCs promise to see to it that what the public universities are able to provide is not, in every sense, the equivalent of what rich people's kids get."[9] Rather than serve the common profit, the MOOC translates the authority of knowledge away from underfunded public institutions and toward elite, well-endowed universities and the aspiring for-profit companies, such as Udacity, Coursera, and edX, that have funded and developed them.

The rush to push MOOCs in 2011 and 2012 lost significant momentum in the following years, largely due to their inability to demonstrate effective learning outcomes. In a 2016 reflection on their rise and fall, Christopher Newfield offers the following eulogy: "Low-cost information access does not translate into cognitive development."[10] Newfield suggests that while MOOCs may have effectively offered the software and assessment tools necessary for large-scale content delivery, they did not provide the embodied pedagogy or the guidance for students to learn in these modes on their own. In a similar vein, Elizabeth Losh notes that "issues about embodiment or affect are too often absent in planning for serving students remotely, even though these issues may be incredibly important for how participants experience copresence online, how they articulate the norms of computer-mediated communication, and how they interpret and understand their own educational histories."[11] This translation failure is also a failure to recognize the very different habitus—what Pierre Bourdieu calls "the feel for the game"—that are developed in face-to-face and large-scale online learning environments.[12] In the case of many MOOCs, the mistaken assumption that students would, without guidance, learn how to learn on these platforms led to massive student disengagement—according to one study, only 6.8 percent of students completed MOOCs.[13]

Despite all of its failings, the access rhetoric of the open courseware movement remains persuasive to many university administrators and disadvantaged students. Perhaps the most influential example is Paul LeBlanc, president of Southern New Hampshire University (SNHU), now the largest university in the United States. When LeBlanc took over in 2003, SNHU was small business school of 2,800 students. By 2019, enrollment surpassed 135,000, and LeBlanc projects that by 2025 it will exceed 300,000. Opening up access, particularly to adult learners, has been the key to this massive growth. Open admission policies and frozen low tuition have been key contributors, but the school's translation of a college education to asynchronous online courseware taught by underpaid adjuncts has been its most powerful engine for access. While SNHU has a brick-and-mortar campus, 97 percent of its students take classes online.[14]

Predictably, most of the student population do not complete their degree within six years. In 2014, the national average completion rate for undergraduate degrees was 60.8 percent, but SNHU only graduated 48 percent.[15] To expand SNHU's access even further and address this challenge of completion, LeBlanc developed a "competency-based education" (CBE) degree that can be completed online for a low cost within a short-term period. CBE speeds up the time to complete the degree by eliminating course requirements and grades and focusing instead on the "mastery" of skills, such as delivering a sales pitch, and the accumulation of stackable "competencies" that lead to a blockchain credential.[16] In his criticism of CBE, Johann Neem argues, "Efforts to make college faster, including competency-based education, ignore the simple fact that a good education takes time. It takes time to foster students' dispositions, or their virtues and habits."[17] Speed is one of the most attractive features of online education, and CBE only accelerates the velocity of this translation of academic competencies to "workplace" preparation. As the ancient Roman poet Horace warned about such hasty translation, "Public material will be private property if you do not linger over the common and open way, and if you do not try to render word for word like a faithful translator."[18] Without the state-level accountability measures that public universities face, private institutions like SNHU and Western Governors University (WGU) that offer CBE degrees have no need to "linger over the common and open way" and can eliminate most all faculty-student interaction that occurs in most courses, ignoring any sort of "faithful" translation that might be expected to take place between face-to-face and online modalities.[19]

The work of educating first-generation college students, working-class adult learners, and lower-income families is now more often the private property of institutions like SNHU and WGU, who can offer quick, accessible, and cheap degrees, than it is of public universities such as the City University of New York (CUNY) and the University of California, which have steadily lost the public funding necessary to keep their tuition low. Questions of educational quality and the development of effective learning and work habits are secondary concerns, ones that only apply to the elites, according to LeBlanc. His daughters, for example, were both Ivy League educated at Brown University and in 2019 were pursuing doctorate degrees at Stanford and Oxford. When asked about how he justifies their choice to pursue degrees at such top-flight traditional institutions, LeBlanc cooly responded, "I don't see their path as at odds with what I'm doing. When a student can come to SNHU and unlock opportunities for a better job, then they can open a better path for their family. That's the classic American dream, and it's slipped out of reach for too many Americans."[20] For LeBlanc, education for the masses is a separate concern, one that can be addressed by CBE, which translates education into a game to be unlocked, or a credential to be accumulated. What matters most is access-without-accessibility, which institutions like SNHU and WGU provide, even if the quick and consumptive habits of these online courses cannot be easily translated into the slowly cultivated habitus of students who obtain expensive degrees within elite institutions.

Hybridizing English Education

The disparity between the haves and the have-nots has widened in recent memory, but the gap between the education that upper classes receive and the limited access to education that is offered to the lower classes has an extensive precedence within medieval England. In a very real sense, this disparity was linguistic—the aristocracy were educated in Latin and French, while the commoners, if they were educated at all, received their education in their vernacular English. The rise of English was driven by a democratizing force, but the elevated status it enjoyed in the fourteenth and fifteenth centuries still did not match the cultural capital of French and Latin. Before the fifteenth century in England, French and Latin had been the exclusive languages of learning, but as English began to gain currency under Edward III and Richard II, English began to infiltrate the schools as well. Trevisa even claims in his translation of the *Polychronicon* that after 1349 English began to become the language of schoolchildren.[21] But as Christopher Cannon demonstrates, this must have been an exaggeration, because extant grammars from the period do not reflect this shift. In fact, the earliest Latin grammar book that includes English is dated to 1410 and exists in only one manuscript: Cambridge, Trinity College MS 0.5.4.[22] Nevertheless, Trevisa's fears about this educational transformation are revealed in his *Dialogue*, which posits the Lord as a champion of English translation and the Clerk as a defender of Latinate authority, an opposition that associates vernacularity with the laity and Latinity with the clergy. According to the Lord, English is simply the language of "moo men" and does not threaten the exclusivity of Latin—it is rather a pedestrian language that provides a greater number of people access to the subject of Higden's chronicle, a history of the world from creation until the present day.[23] The Clerk objects to the assumption that English is universal, since Latin is "so wide iused and iknowe" throughout the lands of Europe, whereas English is "nought iused and iknowe but of Englisshe men al oon" (lines 33–34). By arguing for the commonality of Latin, the Clerk suggests that translation is unnecessary for a text that is already linguistically universal.

The Clerk's argument apparently held sway for some time, because not until "education for all" movements arose in the nineteenth century could English justifiably challenge Latin's claim to universality. From the twelfth to the nineteenth century, Latin served as the universal language of schooling in the West because of its international, authoritative, pragmatic, and relatively static nature. As the Clerk notes, "Latyn is iused and understonde a this half Grece in alle the naciouns and londes of Europa" (28–29), which made it particularly useful for communication among the learned in many parts of the Western world. Furthermore, its ecclesiastical and classical heritage legitimized its use and provided a basis in rhetoric that could be applied to both spoken and written communication. The Latin curriculum was driven by Roman writers such as Quintillian and Cicero, whose rhetorical treatises trained students in speaking and writing.[24] As Walter Ong has demonstrated, Latin's linguistic status as a relatively "dead" language protected the curriculum from innovation.[25] The immutability of the language of the curriculum from the Middle Ages until the early twentieth century unified British and American students whose knowledge of Latin set them apart as "educated."²⁶ Latin could be considered a "universal" language because it was universally used among the educated, namely clerics-in-training or young aristocrats.

Trevisa's critical orientation toward his translation projects represents the tension we are currently facing regarding public access-without-accessibility to education. If we turn to Trevisa's *Dialogue*, we see the Lord trot out the same enfranchisement rhetoric found in MOOC and CBE promotions. In response to the Clerk's objection that anyone can learn Latin and gain access to this knowledge, the Lord retorts, "Nought alle, for some may nought for other maner bisynes, somme for elde, somme for defaute of witte, somme for defaute of catel other of frendes to fynde hem to scole, and somme for other diverse defautes and lettes" (Not all, for some may not because of [their involvement in their] work, some because of old age, some because of their lack of understanding, some because of their lack of means or friends [relatives] to pay for their schooling, and some because of other various needs or hindrances) (lines 45–48). Online education promotes its curriculum to these very students, particularly those who work full time jobs (*bisynes*) or those who are returning to school later in life (*elde*).

SNHU and WGU set their sights on the population the Lord describes as suffering from "defaute of catel other frendes to fynde hem to scole," notably those who are unable to afford the rising cost of tuition. But as the record tells us, Trevisa's translation was not produced for those without means. Rather, well-to-do book connoisseurs appear to have been the main audience, evidenced by the multiple early fifteenth-century copies that circulated among patrons of the fine book market.²⁷ Describing these codices, Ronald Waldron concludes, "Their de luxe character suggests that they were designed for a baronial market, . . . [a] restricted circulation . . . among the wealthy and bibliophile."²⁸ Moreover, the immediate audience for the translation was Sir Thomas Berkeley, who is likely the personality behind the figure of the Lord in Trevisa's *Dialogue*.²⁹

Trevisa was clearly aware that this translation project was not just a translation of knowledge—it was also a translation of power, a process commonly known as *translatio imperii et studii*. This was a popular historiographical perspective that influenced the work of many writers and their patrons, including the famous Arthurian romancer, Chrétien de Troyes. Chrétien's engagement with the King Arthur myth gains traction for his readers not only because it represents his patrons' enthusiasm about the ideals of courtly love, but also because it is placed within a historical trajectory that flatters the aristocratic elite. Like many other writers of romance, Chrétien relies on Geoffrey of Monmouth's *His-*

tory of the Kings of Britain, which claims not only that Arthur was a real king who temporarily defeated the invading Saxons but also that Arthur's lineage and chivalric ideals could be traced back to classical antiquity. In the prologue to his *Cligés*, Chrétien claims, "Our books have taught us that chivalry and learning first flourished in Greece; then to Rome came chivalry, and the sum of knowledge, which now has come to France. May God grant that they be maintained here and may He be pleased enough with this land that the glory now in France may never leave. God merely lent it to the others: no one speaks any more of the Greeks or Romans; their fame has grown silent and their glowing ember has gone out."[30] In addition to his less than reverential disposition toward his sources, his prayer that chivalry and learning be "maintained" pleads for this westward translation of power and learning to cease, leaving all of its power and glory to the French. If transfers of knowledge are denied to subsequent cultures and civilizations, how useful is his courtly history for future generations? While Chrétien's provincial Francophilia may have been merely a clever attempt to please his patrons, his anxiety about future translations of learning were likely also the product of a culture of the fear of textual corruption, in which sacred texts would be appropriated, misinterpreted, or simply misread.

Like Chrétien, Trevisa finds himself in the difficult position of attempting to satisfy the desires of the aristocratic market, all while retaining the integrity of his liberal arts training. Without directly undermining the authority of the Lord's (and presumably his patron, Lord Berkeley's) argument for the universality of translation, Trevisa crafts this dialogue to highlight the persuasiveness of the Clerk's arguments by vernacularizing the Latin disputation through the mode of role-play (a rhetorical habitus that is treated fully in chapter 4). Trevisa's decision to dramatize such a dialogue for Lord Berkeley was likely also influenced by his English translation of the Latin disputation, *Dialogus inter Militem et Clericum* (*Dialogue Between a Knight and a Clerk*), which also features a Clerk, who contends this time with a Knight over the competing authorities of the church and state. While the Knight's argument—just like the Lord's—for secular power emerges triumphant, Trevisa elaborates upon the Clerk's position to indicate his disagreement with the Knight.[31]

The use of role-play is one balanced approach Trevisa assumes to hybridize a pedagogy that would satisfy the desires of both his clerical cohort and the secular elite. And even if this attempt to become an intermediary between the clergy and aristocracy did not prove to be entirely successful, it is clear that Trevisa was striving to develop a translational habitus that could be further developed by others. As Emily Steiner has pointed out, Trevisa may have created the first alphabetical index in English, which serves as a kind of "table of contents" for the *Polychronicon*.[32] In one manuscript, Huntington Library's MS 28561, the English subject listing (ff. 32–40v) follows a Latin one (ff. 24–32) and precedes both the *Dialogue* and *Epistle*, which suggests that the index served as a kind of bilingual preparation for the Latinized translation to come. In a description of the index, Steiner notes, "the rhetorical achievements of Trevisa's index appear to be in inverse proportion to its achievements as a finding aid, and yet it is precisely its difficulties as a finding aid that make it indispensable to literary English."[33] Whether his index was legible for his immediate audience or not, Trevisa was experimenting with literary forms that could provide the public a mediated access to knowledge that had previously been programmed for a clerical domain.

Translating Writing Across the Curriculum

While the stature of English as a literary language was certainly elevated after the fourteenth century, its place within educational contexts remained remarkably static. Eventually, movements emerged that advocated for a central position of the English language within social and academic life, from translations of Latin texts into the vernacular to the belief in "education for all," but these movements were consistently undermined by the privilege of the educated elite. In particular, the history of one popular writing movement, Writing Across the Curriculum (WAC), proves to be particularly informative. The standard narrative of the history of cross-curricular writing movements begins at the end of the nineteenth century, when English began to be accepted as a language worthy of study because of its social utility. During this time, campaigns emerged that sought an English-language curriculum to counter the Latin and Greek one.[34] Such arguments for the universality of English and invectives against the exclusivity of classical languages served as the basis for mass education in the coming decades, which eventually led to the ubiquity of the first-year English composition course in the early twentieth century. As college admissions numbers and career specializations increased, so did the need for writing instruction designed to meet the needs of students writing in a variety of disciplines. WAC programs were developed in the 1970s to meet this need, but the demand for composition instruction in courses such as mathematics and biology, which had not previously included an emphasis on writing, was met with great resistance.

This resistance emerges from a fundamental opposition to "education for all," which has a precedent in late fourteenth-century debates about the translation of Latin texts into vernacular languages. Whereas these hesitations about the writing and translation of sacred and specialized knowledge in English surfaced as fears of heterodoxy and dilettantism, respectively, the implicit consequence of both moments of resistance was an antagonism toward universal literacy. While composing and translating are often considered to be two distinct kinds of writing, their differences are negligible within the academic and intellectual arenas of the WAC and medieval translation debates. In medieval England, the exigency for writing in English was most often understood as the need or desire to translate a Latin text into the vernacular. Even for Chaucer, writing was some form of translation, an act of rendering works in other languages—such as Boccaccio's Italian or Boethius's Latin—into English poetry or prose. Writing and translation continued to be inextricably combined even into the late nineteenth and early twentieth centuries, when students only wrote in English while they were translating Latin and Greek. The lack of separation between the acts of composing and translating English became such a problem that Harvard professors mounted campaigns against what they called "Translation English," or written English syntax convoluted by the influence of Latin and Greek constructions.[35] By the 1970s when an unprecedented number of first-generation college students were entering the academy, a new kind of translation emerged, the translation of students' home languages into what has been called "Standard Written English" (SWE).[36] Such a focus on westernized, and specifically white, language norms led to what Cedric Burrows calls "whitescripting" or the pedagogical claim that "acceptable grammar was the one white Americans spoke."[37] This unidirectional movement from one language to the other is based on the monolingual assumption that all academic expression should produce SWE, which devalues what Suresh Canagarajah calls the "negotiation" or "shuttling" between languages, a practice common among multilingual writers.[38] At the core of these translational conflicts are disagreements about linguistic "correctness" and students' rights to their own language.

The WAC movement began as an effort to improve student writing in all disciplines. Rather than isolate writing instruction within the confines of the composition classroom, WAC advocates argued that the teaching of writing was, to some extent, the responsibility of all teachers. Most importantly, they believed that this emphasis on writing instruction across the curriculum would give more students the means of access to specialized knowledge. More students would become better writers and learners through intensive and extensive writing activities in all disciplines.[39] Whereas access to such knowledge before the twentieth century had been primarily limited to the elites, WAC programs aimed to serve as a primary force for mass education by incorporating more writing activities into college courses that would both transcend disciplinary boundaries and empower students to engage in specialized discourses.

Since their inception, WAC programs have been perceived as a threat to the specialized and decentralized model of the research university. After all, the teaching of writing had been the responsibility of English departments, who most often ran the composition programs, conducted writing research, and trained teachers of writing. Why, then, was composition instruction being outsourced to other disciplines and professors who had little experience in the teaching of writing? English professors often embrace their roles as resident experts on writing studies by virtue of their training, but they naturally do not possess the expertise or experience to teach the writing that is done by chemists, mathematicians, or historians, who all engage in discursive modes that are particular to their fields. WAC programs were devised to offer the training and resources that disseminate writing instruction to all corners of the university as a means of increasing access to specialized knowledge. Because WAC initiatives ask their instructors to rethink their disciplinary identities and participate in first-year writing programs, they have often been met with hostility from those who perceive first-year composition as the course that keeps the barbarians from entering the gates, and eventually their classrooms.

Until the eighteenth and nineteenth centuries, writing in English was not a central pedagogical concern, because students only engaged in it as they prepared for oral recitations. At Harvard, students were required to submit to the college president or tutor a written copy of each speech to be delivered, but such written activities were not formally integrated into the curriculum until Charles W. Eliot became president of the university in 1869.[40] Eliot implemented an elective curriculum with specialized departments that attracted students interested in pursuing a wider range of careers. The university assumed a new responsibility to conduct research and credential professionals in a practical effort to serve society.[41] A vital player in this move toward mass education was the figure of the professional writing instructor, a position occupied at Harvard for the first time in 1872 by the journalist Adams Sherman Hill. Working from the conviction that students should be able to write English before, not after, learning Latin, Hill envisioned the isolated composition course as a remedy to "a system which crams without training, which spends its strength on the petty or the useless, and neglects that without which knowledge is but sounding brass and tinkling cymbal."[42] According to Hill and his supporters, writing in English could serve not only as a mode of access to knowledge, but also as a practical foundation for the entire educational system.

By insisting so strongly on strict English linguistic standards, however, Hill and his fellow rhetoricians made social mobility more difficult than ever before. LeBaron Russell Briggs, Hill's student and successor as Boylston Professor of Rhetoric at Harvard, continued the assault on the Greek and Latin curriculum by complaining that too many schoolmasters "suffer their pupils to turn Greek and Latin into that lazy, mongrel dialect, 'Translation English.'"[43] According to Briggs and his colleagues, the poor English that he witnessed on the Harvard admission examination was the result of the excessive training students received in the classical languages and the insufficient time spent on English grammar and mechanical correctness. Briggs offered the following comment about one entrance examination: "I was ashamed to pass this theme, and am ashamed to print it as part of a successful examination; but I wish to show that Harvard does not insist upon that minute and diversified literary knowledge which strains a boy's head and baffles a teacher's imparting skill."[44] Put another way, the exam tested mastery of content less than grammatical aptitude.

Since the inception of the entrance exam at Harvard in 1874, the evaluation of first-year writing has never wavered from its focus on grammatical correctness.[45] Yet Briggs expressed his qualms about the efficacy of the exam in an address to secondary-school educators: "I am no admirer of the present requirement; I live in hope of something better: but I am yet unable to see in any of the proposed substitutes a scheme at once superior and practicable. Besides, the present plan has passed, for a time at least, beyond the control of Harvard examiners and of Harvard University; it must stand for several years more whether we like it or not."[46] Briggs could not have predicted how long the entrance exam would last not only at Harvard, but also as a model for placement exams in the century to come.

The poor performances on the early placement exams led to the establishment and persistence of the first-year writing requirement at Harvard and almost every other American university in the coming century.[47] In 1942, the National Council of Teachers of English conducted a study of college writing programs and found that 80 percent of the 292 institutions surveyed required a freshman writing course.[48] By 1967, 93.2 percent of 1,320 four-year colleges surveyed by Thomas Wilcox required at least one semester of freshman composition.[49] And as writing courses proliferated, their emphasis on English linguistic correctness never wavered. S. Michael Halloran aptly notes that these writing instructors "prepared students to leap social hurdles, while at the same time elevating the hurdles."[50] As English began to establish itself more firmly as the language of the curriculum, teachers began to face the increasing challenges of mass education, which required more students than ever to graduate under the same standards that had been previously enforced only for elite populations.

As the democratization of education gained momentum in the 1890s, the number of students enrolled in high schools and universities increased, and the quality of student writing in English became a pressing issue.[51] Between 1890 and 1912, high school enrollments rose from 202,963 to one million students. By 1940, this number had reached 6,545,991.[52] Colleges felt the direct effects of this increase in access to secondary education. From 1920 to 1940, college enrollments increased from 597,880 to 1,494,203 students.[53] In anticipation of this trend, the Committee of Ten, which included the medievalist George Lyman Kittredge, was formed in 1892 to find a solution to the need for a broad approach to writing instruction that would prepare all college-bound students for university education.[54] The committee recommended that faculty of all subject areas should collaborate in teaching writing, but this "cooperation movement" did not gain momentum until the 1901 publication of a treatise by the New England Association of Teachers of English, entitled "Successful Combination Against the Inert." This leaflet advocated a cooperative system of language teaching across the curriculum at the secondary and college levels, an idea that over the next two decades spawned a number of scholarly and popular articles and the eventual establishment of hundreds of cross-curricular language programs.[55] According to the "cooperative" ideal, no longer would the composition instructor teach writing in isolation from the rest of the curriculum. Writing instruction would become a priority for teachers in all of the disciplines.

After World War II, these "cooperative" programs would gain support from open-admission policies designed to meet the needs of disenfranchised populations.[56] But a cadre of professors believed that exposure to great works of literature, rather than isolated writing or rhetorical instruction, was the key to improved writing; they called for the abolition of the composition course in the coming decades.[57] These abolitionists turned to previous critiques of the course articulated by those such as Thomas R. Lounsbury, an English professor at Yale, who ultimately argued that writing could not be taught. Instead, he suggested that writing talent could be discovered through a kind of literary osmosis: "He who of his own accord has sat reverently at the feet of the great masters of English literature need have no fear that their spirit will not inform, *so far as in him lies*, the spirit of their discipline."[58] The contention that good reading informs good writing was, and still is, a persuasive argument for using works of literature to teach writing.

Lounsbury and his fellow abolitionists did not believe, however, that good writing could be produced by just any student. Rather, this Romantic principle only applied "so far as in him lies," that is, to those who possessed the potential, a kind of Aristotelian habitus. Lounsbury even went so far as to claim, "There is but one way of keeping certain persons from writing wretchedly, and that is by keeping them from writing at all."[59] The abolition of the compulsory composition course was then one way of doing just that. Another influential abolitionist, Oscar James Campbell of Columbia, even suggested that writing be taught exclusively as an elective course, but only for "the freshman who possesses a sincere interest in some form of artistic writing and a demonstrated aptitude for it."[60] While many colleges and universities continued to champion the writing requirement throughout the sixties, calls for its abolition gained enough support by the early seventies that nearly a quarter of colleges and universities eliminated the composition requirement—some even jettisoned the freshman writing course completely.[61] For some, the perceived result was that college writing had improved (and maybe it had for the fortunate elect), but that was because professors no longer had to read or tolerate the work of underprivileged students.

Despite the influence of this trenchant elitism, newly enfranchised populations began to flood the gates of higher education in the early seventies. The civil rights movement was the most powerful advocate of a mass educational model that would remedy the social inequalities that had plagued the system. This meant that university educators would be teaching students previously excluded from higher education, which entailed not only more students, but also more students from a variety of educational backgrounds.[62] In 1974, these exhortations for greater access coincided with the shocking results of a National Assessment of Educational Progress study on student writing, which demonstrated a decline in proficiency from its earlier study in 1969. At the same time, *Newsweek* ran the infamous article entitled "Why Johnny Can't Write," which concluded, "Willy-nilly, the U.S. educational system is spawning a generation of semi-literates."[63] This criticism placed enormous pressure on colleges and universities, which forced the return of the compulsory freshman English course, which quickly became ubiquitous across the landscape of higher education. According to one survey in 1981, 93.4 percent of surveyed institutions had a writing requirement.[64] By 1995, Sharon Crowley has estimated four million college first-year students were enrolled in composition courses, which translated to approximately 160,000 writing sections.[65] The tide had shifted against the abolitionists, probably for good, but the resistance to the requirement still manifests itself in other sectors of the university curriculum, notably within WAC programs.

Since writing instruction was well on its way to becoming an establishment in university life after the 1970s, it was well positioned to serve as the node around which educational forces could be mobilized to greet calls for greater access and academic rigor. WAC programs began to flourish in the subsequent decades, but not without great resistance from many teachers. One contentious issue has been "correctness," a legacy WAC instructors inherited from the earliest composition programs. If the purpose of the college writing course is to provide remediation, instructors are therefore compelled to "correct" students' poor mechanics, usage, and sentence structure, even at the expense of creative voice, critical thought, and fluency.[66] The perception that writing programs are grammar-correction machines even led C. H. Knoblauch and Lil Brannon to conclude that WAC initiatives are "little more than 'grammar across the curriculum,' in which English teachers counsel their colleagues in other departments about deviations from 'standard written English' so that history and biology teachers can learn to 'correct' student writing with the same reverence for prose decorum displayed in the English Department."[67]

Even though this claim may not accurately characterize most WAC programs, it is a belief widely held and put into practice by those unfamiliar with the WAC philosophy of writing as a tool for exploration and learning.[68] And even for many instructors conversant in WAC pedagogy, the privileging of drafting and fluency over mechanical correctness and prose style appears to devalue teacher intervention and call into question what they see as the "remedial" nature of WAC. WAC exists in the minds of many only out of a state of emergency—once these insurgent writing problems get fixed or corrected, the need for such remediation is no longer necessary.[69] Put another way, once students begin to write as they used to (that is, when only a few were allowed to write), universities and colleges can dispense with these compositional first-aid kits.

Despite the support to specialties that WAC programs have offered, participation in professional development workshops on WAC pedagogy have often not been attractive to faculty and sometimes not even encouraged by administrators who value research agendas over teaching effectiveness.[70] According to WAC opponents, WAC programs foster the proliferation of unedited writing, the lowering of academic standards, the erasure of disciplinary boundaries, and diminished research activity—interdisciplinary writing instruction is therefore not worth these perceived costs. For these skeptics, mass education is achieved without the means of WAC programs, through lecture courses, general education, and multiple-choice exams. Without WAC, specialized writing is reserved only for the elite students. In the spirit of the words of Lounsbury, it keeps the "others" from participating in disciplinary writing at all. Given the fact that much of the hostility to WAC originates in a dearth of institutional support for the implementation of its programs, such entrenched attitudes about disciplinary authority and specialization are understandable. Many objections to WAC programs arise from fundamental misunderstandings about their methods and goals, often because administrators have failed to support them. In the same way that online education advocates obscure their economic motives with enfranchisement rhetoric, objections to WAC are symptomatic of a widespread institutional resistance to the ideal of "education for all."[71] Just because admissions of first-generation college students have increased does not mean that mass education or accessibility has been achieved. With the increasing push for online blockchain degrees and competency-based credentialing, these students can be "given" an education, but one without the tools necessary to graduate and contribute to specialized fields.

Premodern Rhetorics of Translation

To understand the larger consequences for programs that seek to facilitate access to higher education and improve disciplinary writing, it is necessary to consider the ancient translational habitus that drive efforts to achieve popular education. Analyses of educational movements within the *longue durée* are not often conducted because, as Lawrence Cremin points out, "reform movements are notoriously ahistorical in their outlook."[72] Turning back to the example of John Trevisa, we can begin to characterize how translation has become a rhetorical habit for negotiating tensions between demands for access and demands for authority within WAC and open online courseware movements. Trevisa is an important figure because he witnessed a pivotal moment in late fourteenth-century England that staged the first substantive debate about the linguistic authority of the English language, when it had matured into a language of theological and courtly stature. At the same time that English began to achieve authority and relevance among the elite, John Wycliffe's efforts to translate the Bible into English incited clerics to condemn such English translations in 1382. The efforts to make biblical discourse available to the laity faced a resistance, this time out of fear of heresy, which has continued to emerge in such movements to popularize specialized discourse.

This denunciation of Wycliffism caused translators such as Trevisa to proceed with caution, as is evidenced by his need to defend his English renderings of Latin texts to his patron, Lord Thomas Berkeley, in his *Dialogue*.[73] As an Oxford intellectual who may have participated in the Wycliffite translation of the Bible into English, Trevisa was well versed in the possible consequences of elevating English to the sacred status of Latin.[74] Ralph Hanna, who has carefully compared the dates of Berkeley's governmental service and the dates of Trevisa's translations commissioned by Berkeley, concludes that "patronage was something which filled extended leisure hours when Berkeley was not in demand elsewhere. This might further suggest that, leaving aside considerable literary shaping, Trevisa portrayed a real relationship in the dialogue he prefaced to the *Polychronicon*, a testimony to Thomas Berkeley's active and engaged interest in the process of translation."[75] Hanna's conclusion is especially provocative because it suggests that the resistance to translation that the Clerk expresses in the dialogue may indeed represent Trevisa's own clerical hesitations about the popular forms of knowledge production that Berkeley appears to espouse.

At the core of the *Dialogue* is a debate over the "need" for such an Englishing of the *Polychronicon*. Throughout this disagreement about the status of English as a utilitarian language, we witness the conflicting agendas regarding issues that traditionally divide the popular and learned classes, such as access to knowledge, the authority of vernacular languages, lay and clerical forms of leisure and industry, and the common good. The Clerk's argument against translation and assertion for Latin's universality rest on his assumption that this text, lest it be misunderstood, should be restricted to clerics and educated nobility. Therefore, since the Lord knows Latin, the Clerk claims that "it nedeth not to have siche an Englisshe translacioun" (lines 38–39). The Clerk interprets "need" as "need to understand," and since this text is not intended for the illiterate, an English translation is superfluous. Objecting that neither he nor the Clerk comprehend Latin perfectly, the Lord corrects the Clerk's definition of "need" from "need to understand" to "profit." The Lord explains, "though it were not nedeful for me, it is nedeful for other men that understoneth no Latyn" (43–44). In other words, the necessity of translation lies in the message that the English laity may receive from the text. The suggestion that unlearned men need to learn from the *Polychronicon* incites the ire of the learned Clerk, who responds, "Hit nedeth not that alle siche know the cronicles" (49). According to the Clerk, textual knowledge is already in capable hands and need not be broadcast to vernacular segments of society, which may foster misinterpretations.

While the Clerk is concerned about the authority of English and its new audience, his greatest fear, which is also reflected in an accompanying epistle, is that his translation will not be "correct."[76] In a final objection to the Lord's argument for translation, the Clerk fears, "Yf a translacioun were imade that might be amended in eny poynt, somme men hit wold blame" (114–15). The Clerk's anxiety is representative of a medieval culture of "correcting" in which writers regularly expected their readers to "amend" their errors. For example, in the prologue to his *Troy Book*, John Lydgate assumes a pose of subservience to his readers, "Preynge to alle that schal it rede or se, / Wher as I erre for to amenden me, / Of humble herte and lowe entencioun / Commyttyng al to her correccioun."[77] To some extent this posture is simply a modesty topos, but it also suggests that writing was conceived as preliminary and subject to future revision. Truth was divine, and therefore the human minds could only aspire to represent it through imperfect forms such as writing and speech. This expectation of corrective response is also present in an early example of medical writing in English known as the *Cyrurgie*, in which its author, Guy de Chauliac, addresses his audience of doctors from Montpelier, Bologna, and Paris by offering a disclaimer: "If ther be oght therin unperfit, doutouse, or over mykel and derk, I submit it to youre correccioun."[78] Guy anticipates objections to his writing—its imperfections (*unperfit*), doubtful statements (*doutouse*), overly complex and obscure constructions (*mykel and derk*)—that he recognizes with the translational habitus of a writer who knows that writing is a process that is often accompanied by error. By calling on his readers to correct his work, he sees his work as a collaborative enterprise, subject to a kind of premodern writing workshop. This emphasis on accuracy, particularly given our currently crowdsourced character of online translation tools, reflects what Laura Gonzales calls a "Revised Rhetoric of Translation," which "positions translation as an iterative activity that happens constantly within specific cultures and communities."[79] Developing such a translational habitus requires an ongoing recognition of power relations, engagement with multiple modes (i.e., writing, speech, image), and negotiation of changing cultural values.

In Trevisa's *Dialogue*, the Lord's response to the Clerk's anxieties about correctness is remarkable in its emphasis on such iterative and communal revision. After condemning those who would "blame" the Clerk for errors in his first draft, he says, "Clerkis knowith wel ynowgh that no synful man doth so wel that he ne myght do better, nether makith so gode a translacioun that he ne myght make a better. . . . I desire not translacioun of these bokes the best that myght be. . . . But I wold have a skilfulle translacioun that myght be knowe and understond" (lines 117–22). The Lord's suggestion that a good translator revises and refines his writing is a provocative claim about the communicative value of the vernacular. Even a first draft that contains errors is better than no draft at all.

By representing the Lord as a charitable dispenser of knowledge and the Clerk as a parsimonious protector of Latinate history, Trevisa cleverly flatters his patron Lord Berkeley and bolsters the case for English translation. Furthermore, this prefacing dialogue, Trevisa's accompanying epistle to Berkeley, and the translation itself combine as a vernacular program that appears to condemn clerical elitism and argue for the distinct ability of vernacular translation to benefit the laity. Trevisa's flattery of Lord Berkeley, however, should not be accepted at face value as merely anticlerical or Wycliffite, but should be understood as—in addition to an experiment in hybridized pedagogy—an occupational habitus of a translator shaped by the pressures of patronage. Hanna remarks, "Since all three works [*Dialogue*, epistle, and translation] circulated together and since they were certainly prepared with an eye to use at Berkeley, Trevisa cannot have seriously misrepresented his lord's intent. One may, however, retain considerable skepticism about the fiction of the piece—the clerk Trevisa's unwillingness to translate and the lameness of his arguments, the reasoned loquacity of its patron."[80] These texts were intended to be used by Berkeley and therefore could not contain transparent critiques of lay aristocratic sovereignty; but the fact that Trevisa creates a dialogue between a fictional Lord and Clerk compels us to examine the critical distance he achieves in this imagined dialogue between the ruling class and the subservient clergy. In other words, is the *Dialogue* a reasoned debate in which the clerical linguistic authority willingly acquiesces to lay prerogative? Or is it a puppet show that reveals the clerical animosity for mass education? Given Trevisa's translations of a number of Latin texts across the medieval curriculum, namely, the apocryphal Gospel of Nicodemus (theology), Bartholomeus Anglicus's encyclopedic *De proprietatibus rerum* (natural science), and Giles of Rome's *De regimine principum* (political science), I want to suggest that the Clerk in the dialogue represents Trevisa's own anxieties about the degradation of local authority and specialized knowledge. While these misgivings may have been misplaced, Trevisa's Clerk suggests that such translational habits may profit elites more than the undereducated masses.

From Correction to Correcting

Some modern writing instructors have attempted to challenge cynical notions of translational "access" by developing their own remedial textbooks. Scholars of the works of Geoffrey Chaucer who are familiar with John Manly and Edith Rickert's colossal eight-volume *The Text of the Canterbury Tales* might be surprised to learn about another product of their collaboration, a writing handbook entitled *The Writing of English*.[81] In characterizing their contribution to composition studies, John Brereton remarks, "Manly and Rickert provide a rare depiction of remedial students actually succeeding at college work. At a time when colleges were being swamped by hordes of new learners, hardly any professor mentioned this vast new constituency except to complain about the presence of unprepared students, but Manly and Rickert prove an exception."[82] It is tempting to imagine the effect their optimism about first-year writing instruction had on their monumental edition of *The Canterbury Tales*, an ambitious editorial project that required years of describing manuscripts, identifying textual variations, demonstrating the stages of scribal revision, and writing six volumes of commentary.[83] In the preface to *The Writing of English*, they emphasize an iterative writing process and express enthusiasm about the ability of all students to write well: "With the student in an attitude of confidence in the worth of his own thinking and of eagerness to learn the methods by which it can be conveyed to others in words, the problem of teaching the use of English reduces to the balancing of constructive practice over against the corrective drill necessary to eradicate the bad habits due to foreign birth, defective training, or indifference."[84] Their characterization of "bad habits due to foreign birth" reveals their condescending and racist views of this new demographic of students, but their approach, in which they balance "constructive practice over against the corrective drill," is a clear departure from the predominant mode of writing instruction that exclusively emphasized mechanical correctness.

Given their training as medievalists and thorough acquaintance with techniques of "correcting" texts and commenting on scribal errors, it might strike some as surprising that Manly and Rickert would refuse to join in the chorus of correction among composition scholars. I would suggest, however, that their experience working with Chaucer manuscripts would not bolster a belief in the power of "correctness," but would champion the power of "correcting." Whereas "correctness" requires mechanical rigor over discursive fluency at the outset, "correcting" privileges "constructive practice" over the editing gridlock that prevents the completion of drafts over time. That is, the student should not let corrective drills impede attempts to get ideas down on paper or naively think that, in the words of Trevisa's Lord, "[he] doth so wel that he ne myght do better."

Manly and Rickert's medievally innovative thoughts about writing pedagogy also exhibit support for moving beyond remedial writing instruction to the teaching of disciplinary genres, which would become a main objective of WAC programs. In the chapter "The Types of Writing" in *The Writing of English*, they encourage following models for specialized kinds of writing: "In business, in science, in research of all kinds, in the law, in the ministry, in teaching, in politics, in every conceivable kind of work, the successful man comes to the time when he needs technique and practice in expressing his views. And all the training you get in principles, all the study of the different types of writing as they are found in good models, will be none too much when the demand is made upon you."[85] Their argument for extended practice in "good models" specific to subjects across the curriculum, such as business, science, and law, provides the basis for later arguments by advocates for writing instruction in all disciplines. Manly even went so far as to cowrite a handbook devoted to business writing, *Better Business English*, which demonstrated his commitment to a bureaucratic practice that can be traced back to the medieval art of letter writing known as the *ars dictaminis*.[86] By the time that Manly and Rickert made their indelible mark on Chaucer scholarship in the 1930s, they had already established themselves as the forerunners to composition theorists in the coming decades who would attack the culture of correction, seek to transcend the exclusively "remedial" nature of first-year English, and improve writing across the curriculum.

In terms of their dual contributions to writing theory and Chaucerian editing, Manly and Rickert paved the way for scholars to make connections between the fields of composition and medieval studies. Celebrated scholars of composition whose work intersects with medieval interests include Peter Elbow, Cheryl Glenn, and even WAC historian David Russell.[87] While this legacy of medieval composition theorists might appear circumstantial, I want to propose that scholars working in these seemingly unrelated disciplines share a common habitus for cross-curricular work, linguistic correctness, and the history of writing. Medievalists inhabit multilingual, temporally vast, and textually spare fields, which compel them to make connections between languages such as French and Latin and Arabic, between traditional subjects of history, philosophy, and literature, and between movements, events, and texts from the fifth through the fifteenth centuries. For many medievalists, this perspective leads them to the following beliefs: academic work should be interdisciplinary; access to texts and knowledge should be open to all; and language change is often a sign of innovation, not deterioration.

Within the grand narrative of popular education, acts of translation—from Latin to English in the fourteenth century and from "translation English" to Standard Written English (SWE) in the twentieth—have prompted both reform and resistance that medievalists are in a unique position to evaluate. And as teachers begin to assess the emergence of regional Englishes, multilingual registers, and digital translation tools in academic discourse, it is necessary to historicize these linguistic developments. In a collection on writing in the disciplines, Elbow puts it this way:

> Not so long ago, Latin was the only *acceptable* medium for writing. What we think of as English, French, Italian, and Spanish were oral vernaculars: low, common, "vulgar" (*vulgar* = "of the people")—and unfit for writing. Dante argued powerfully for the eloquence of the vulgar tongue (*De Vulgari Eloquentia*) and made an even stronger political statement by writing his *Commedia* in the vernacular of a particular and restricted culture. Chaucer and many Medieval and Renaissance authors—now revered—wrote in oral dialects that were looked down on by intellectuals and academics.... And now? Latin has virtually disappeared. The upstart, oral, low vernaculars are now official literacies.[88]

As Elbow suggests, we are in the midst of another linguistic transition in the history of the English language and popular education. The palpability of this change is reflected in the recent proliferation of "access" initiatives in higher education. On the one hand, more and more faculty members are recognizing the need to teach students the writing conventions of their disciplines, from electrical engineering to international economics. On the other, academic administrators are seizing on this popularizing momentum to translate face-to-face instruction to online platforms owned by for-profit educational software corporations. In other words, vernacular registers often become standardized and legitimized by elites, who operate from a translating habitus that privileges appropriation over democratization.

If we want to develop translational habits that provide access *and* accessibility, without transferring public interest into private profit, I suggest we turn to the example of John Trevisa, who serves as the forerunner for what we are now calling the "para-academic" in the humanities, or those scholars who are seeking ways to bridge the divide between academic and popular forms and modes of teaching and learning. Aranye Fradenburg has recently characterized the para-academic as "committed to the production of knowledge and to the impossibility of finalizing it," which suggests that ideal public education is an accumulation and compilation of knowledge produced by multiple actors, who could be university professors, Wikipedia editors, or both.[89] For Fradenburg, para-academics are needed to respond productively to demands for more utilitarian models of education, which have recently increased in response to growing enrollments and decreasing funding, motivating teachers to develop pedagogies anchored in praxis and application that can meet the needs of students hungrier than ever for immediate jobs after graduation. The situation has caused many to draw lines in the sand: on one side stand hermetic pedagogues who prize themselves as protectors of the liberal arts and transcendent intangibility; on the other side scurry the vocationally minded and virtual-classroom facilitators who orient instruction to "hands-on" activities or online modes designed for mass consumption and formulaic replication. Trevisa offers the possibility of a middle ground through a translational habitus, in which the access to knowledge is both expanded and interrogated, strategies for teaching and learning are experimental and playful, and the goal of public education transcends the mere transmission of information from one domain to another, encouraging the contributions of all parties both inside and outside of the walls of the University.

3 | Compilation

The Encyclopedic Habits of Wikipedia

> Together we can create a reality that we all agree on—the reality we just agreed on.
> —**Stephen Colbert,** *The Colbert Report*

> The Mantuan poet [Virgil] was once accused of this crime when, transposing certain verses of Homer, he blended them in with his own and was called a plunderer (*conpilator*) of the ancients by his rivals. He replied: "To wrench the club from the hand of Hercules is to be of greater power."
> —**Isidore of Seville,** *Etymologies*

Before open-access web pages modifiable by amateur editors were ubiquitous, the wiki was the first adaptable platform to create active communities of interested contributors.[1] Wikipedia, the limitless fountain of collected, and sometimes inaccurate, information is the largest wiki in the world. Its popularity suggests not only that digital knowledge production demands high levels of participation and what Joseph Michael Reagle Jr. has called "good faith collaboration," but also that our reading practices and information gathering are highly encyclopedic and reconstructive.[2] Ryan Singel noted during their surge in popularity in 2006, "Wikis are remaking the world. But the idea itself is not so novel."[3] In fact, the wikis possess a rhetorical *habitus* that predates the age of print, specifically in medieval encyclopedia writing. From Isidore of Seville to Honorius of Autun to William Caxton, understanding the world meant creating and recreating its image, *imago mundi*, in a language that would be accessible to and editable by more and more readers. With the public using Wikipedia with regularity as a foundation for learning any subject under and beyond the sun, it is vital to understand the history of the collaborative, yet contested, rhetorical habits that made it possible.

To comprehend the nature of Wikipedia's accretive and collective model of knowledge production, we must begin with the medieval *compilatio*, otherwise known as the compilation. For Malcolm Parkes, the *compilatio* characterizes a manuscript that brings fragments and excerpts of authoritative texts into a meaningful and authoritative assemblage that can be easily accessed and used by its readers.[4] This definition provides a useful heuristic for understanding the material circumstances of many medieval books, but as Arthur Bahr demonstrates, their fragmentary character also has important implications for their reception. He proposes that we consider "*compilation* as a way of apprehending and interpreting objects, rather than as an inherent quality of the objects themselves," which leads him to examine "what constitutes a legitimate invitation to compilational reading."[5] Building upon Bahr's compelling shift from compilation as *object* to compilation as *practice*, I focus my analysis on how this shift also conditions the circumstances for what I call a compilational habitus, in which readers are invited to become writers.

In this chapter, I demonstrate the significance of compilational habits that emerge from crowdsourced forms of information gathering. I argue that readers and writers of collaboratively produced texts, from premodern encyclopedias to wikis, recognize and contribute to the unstable and dynamic nature of knowledge compiled from multiple sources. For the contemporary audience of Isidore of Seville's *Etymologies*, his encyclopedia is not only a dialogue between classical and medieval writers but also Isidore's unique intervention in an ongoing compilation of knowledge production. Likewise, as a prerequisite for participation, engaged readers and editors of Wikipedia understand that its entries are works-in-progress compiled from a variety of sources that must be verified. This compilational habitus acknowledges the complex network of encyclopedic knowledge, which users must view in dialogue with multiple sources.

The Politics of Transparency

One highly influential wiki is WikiLeaks. Begun by Julian Assange in 2006, it publishes massive datasets and classified documents that reveal state-sponsored espionage, military strategy, or political corruption.[6] Legend has it that WikiLeaks began in Iceland, a location that a naive outsider can imagine as perfectly hospitable to an organization known for its icy-cold resolve, its transparent information sharing, and its chilling effects on national security administrations. WikiLeaks began as an organization devoted to publicizing secret information, all the while protecting the identity of its informants. As Nathaniel Tkacz observes, this paradox of anonymous transparency has become surprisingly easy to maintain within our current political climate, which must embrace "openness" as "part of the conditions of possibility of all politics."[7] To insist on transparency is a prerequisite for political action, whether that action is truly open to all or not. It is this tension between compulsory transparency and liberatory anonymity embodied by WikiLeaks that is the driving force behind the pervasive medieval practice of compilation, a rhetorical habit that now occupies every corner of cyberspace. Its ubiquity compels us to reconsider the history of the complicated politics of crowdsourced textual authority in the digital world.

When we fashion the profile of the WikiLeaks hacker, we think of someone like Edward Snowden, a computer systems analyst privy to classified documents that are either archived or destroyed. In Geoffrey Chaucer's cantankerous lament "Chaucers Wordes unto Adam, His Owne Scriveyn," the speaker expresses his frustration with his scribe Adam, whose mistakes he must overwrite by scratching off the top layer of skin from the parchment page and writing the line anew. We can likewise imagine the scrupulous analyst's frustration in "rubbing" and "scraping" records (line 6), desiring instead for their imminent publication, for their dissemination within the public sphere.[8] I am concerned with this tension between what we reveal and what we obscure within both our writing and our publication practices. How might we encourage consensual relationships between the text and its readers while maintaining transparent access to ideologies that lie beneath the textual surface? Since some of these surfaces can be quite thick, seemingly impossible to crack, it is tempting to approach all texts suspiciously, as if they all have something to hide. WikiLeaks embraces what Paul Ricoeur might call a "hermeneutics of suspicion,"[9] and rightfully so, exposing the collateral damage of US military engagements overseas, Bank of America's surveillance program, and the treatment of prisoners at Guantanamo Bay.[10]

Like WikiLeaks, Wikipedia offers a means of public engagement with the politics of transparency, in which "anyone can edit," produce, or gain access to information about the world. Yet such an embrace of the dilettante, of the amateur, of the "nobody," calls into question the very authority of the information that is compiled on these sites. Perhaps there is no better example of the power of the compilational habitus than Chaucer's *Canterbury Tales*, an experiment in literary collection and retraction that allows space for productive forms of "suspicion" and "belief." While the series of tales is not a compilation of multiple texts or authorities, Chaucer creates a compilational conceit in which each taleteller, from the Miller to the Wife of Bath to the Nun's Priest, becomes both author and audience, offering responses and challenges to the authorities presented. Chaucer's narrator then becomes the compiler, who must rehearse all tales in his collection, even if they fall on the less authoritative side of the spectrum, embracing a kind of amateurism and all that goes with it—what Carolyn Dinshaw calls an "immaturity, belatedness or underdevelopment, inadequate separation from objects of love, improper attachment, inappropriate loving."[11] Tales are thus accumulated, available to be corrected, retracted, and rewritten. Chaucer's text prefigures a prototype for the writable platform, where crowds of writers, editors, and readers can interact. The *Tales* themselves even perform like a premodern wiki space, an environment of accumulation, in which the textual fragments of editable pages become a flickering palimpsest, new texts inscribed upon old that are omnipresent and recoverable.

Many websites now, like wikis, are editable by all internet users, who are authorized to fashion nearly all elements of the page, adding their links to relevant texts, audio files, still images, and YouTube videos. While wikis do not require anonymity, user identities are often out of view within the editorial histories of each page, establishing a kind of pseudonymity that directs attention to the material itself, without much concern with its creators. Accompanying discussion pages, on the other hand, offer a forum for open conversations between identifiable interlocutors about the issue or subject at hand. As much as wikis encourage a high volume of participation, they also present a conflict between anonymity and transparency, resulting in a problem of authenticity.

Writing and Authenticity in Digital Spaces

Book historians make their most exciting discoveries when they identify the person represented in a cryptic signature in a rare book or manuscript. For historians of rhetoric such as Ben McCorkle, the thrill of this identification emerges from our more recent impulse to see writing as "a transparent window into the writer's mental interior," which in turn enables us to authenticate the writing, giving it the credibility or ethos that we desire.[12] It is this same lust for equating the script with the hand that produced it that informs our educational assessment practices, specifically those that require timed, handwritten examinations. Yet the scribal proficiency traditionally required for twentieth-century schooling, the elegant and efficient cursive hand, does not match most twenty-first-century forms of writing, which are almost exclusively defined by composition on a computer and often in collaboration with others. In the wake of writable platforms such as blogs and wikis, the pen and pencil are rapidly becoming relics of a former era. Even though keyboarding is now a common practice of digital culture, many high school and college teachers still view word-processed documents as less authentic than handwritten ones. This valuation of scribal proficiency and mechanical correctness has a long and tortuous history that can be traced back to premodern chirographic cultures throughout the world.

Some teachers may even celebrate National Handwriting Day on January 23, which has been organized by the Writing Instrument Manufacturers Association (WIMA) since the 1970s in an attempt to seek some respite from digital communication and revel in the personal and creative character of the pencil.[13] WIMA and many educators have romanticized chirography to such a degree that it remains the gold standard in schools for its perceived authenticity, immediacy, and artistry. In a 1999 *New York Times* article, Theodore Roszak argues against computers in schools based on the claim that "user-friendly machines are a barrier that need not be there between the kid and the idea."[14] Roszak even invokes Shakespeare as an example, suggesting that the quill provided the immediacy necessary to manifest his literary genius. By contrast, digital writing requires the location of style sheets and the selection of an appropriate font, obstacles that Roszak contends would have never impeded Shakespeare's scribal composition of sonnets and plays. In response to this claim, Dennis Baron suggests that "it is equally likely that by the time today's students have completed their assigned computer exercise, checked their Facebook page, downloaded some MP3 files, and moved on to an intense chat session, the Bard was still chasing geese around the yard to get his first quill of the day."[15] The use of any technology, simple or complex, requires labor; but for twenty-first-century students, word processors and digital interfaces provide the immediacy and ease that the pencil no longer offers.

While many educators may be willing to grant that computers facilitate the production of more elegant writing, many still balk at the notion that digitally produced documents are as authentic as handwritten ones. Even before OpenAI's development of ChatGPT, an autonomous system that produces humanlike writing from simple prompts, digital tools that allow the writer to check spelling and grammar or cut and paste passages from googled texts have consistently stirred distrust among some teachers of writing, who must wonder, How much of this writing is the student's?[16] This skepticism of technology, of course, has a long and recurrent history in the West that can be traced back at least as far as Plato, who feared that writing would destroy the human capacity to memorize.[17] The threat that writing posed to human memory, one of the five canons of rhetoric, was felt long after written records had become well established in the eleventh and twelfth centuries. To a culture that had previously relied upon witnesses, seals, and symbolic objects to determine authenticity, written texts appeared to be manufactured and mystifying products that could be falsified by any skillful scribe.[18] During Edward I's reign in England in the late thirteenth century, one version of the *Chronicle of Walter of Guisborough* includes a telling story about the quo warranto proceedings, which required landowners to provide written charters as warrants to their land. According to this chronicle, "The king disturbed some of the great men of the land through his judges wanting to know by what warrant [*quo warranto*] they held their lands, and if they did not have a good warrant, he immediately seized their lands. Among the rest, the Earl Warenne was called before the king's judges. Asked by what warrant he held, he produced in their midst an ancient and rusty sword and said: 'Look at this, my lords, this is my warrant! For my ancestors came with William the Bastard and conquered their lands with the sword, and by the sword I will defend them from anyone intending to seize them.'"[19] For the Earl Warenne, his tarnished sword was a symbol of his service to William of Normandy and therefore an authentic testament to his ownership of the land.

Just like the Earl Warenne, teachers still insist that students handwrite their exams based on the belief that this timed, scribal scenario will yield the most authentic evidence of their writing ability. At the same time, teachers also know it is naive to assume that digitally produced essays are a better reflection of writing proficiency than handwritten ones. In fact, one study found that students who were allowed to compose their responses on a computer failed to score higher than their peers who handwrote theirs.[20] While some may argue that the computer encourages fluency in timed settings, this research suggests that new writing technologies may offer no advantage, particularly since many of these platforms are in their infancy. During this digital middle age, teachers are finding it necessary to interrogate the balance between handwriting instruction and computer literacy, the latter of which has its own affordances and constraints. Students are often expected both to produce a high volume of writing *and* to demonstrate grammatical mastery, which leads to a premature emphasis on correctness that impedes learning.[21] As preposterous as it sounds, this moment of technological transition may be asking students and teachers to embrace error in the medieval, not the mechanical, sense. The English word *error* comes from the Latin *error*, which means "a wandering." Given the increasing calls for students to learn how to program or "code" software as a new kind of literacy, we are faced with an increasingly computational and capacious world of writing.[22] When teachers encourage students to wander in efforts to address new material and learn programming skills, though, this often means wandering into the relatively unmonitored world of Wikipedia, which leads to another crisis: textual authority.

Wikipedia as *Imago Mundi*

In my own college classes, students have debated the merits of Wikipedia, often admitting that they regularly use the site despite the prohibitions of their instructors. While the issue of Wikipedia citation in research papers is a vexed one, its use as a search engine and "foundation" for further research tends to be embraced by both teachers and students. As Alison Head and Michael Eisenberg put it, "Want to stir up a room full of college faculty and librarians? Mention Wikipedia."[23] The reasons behind such distress are many and, in some cases, justified. After all, Wikipedia operates under the controversial premise that anyone, from the credentialed academic to the unscrupulous troll, can edit and contribute to this online accumulation of knowledge about the world. What disturbs most of us about such a democratic encyclopedia is not necessarily its open or collaborative nature—instead, it is what we assume is our students' perception and use of the information gleaned from this site. We wonder, don't all students assume that all Wikipedia entries are true? This assumption is confirmed when we encounter Wikipedia citations displacing scholarly ones in student papers.

As Robert Darnton has demonstrated, such anxiety about the authenticity and veracity of encyclopedic knowledge also emerged prominently throughout the dissemination of the quintessential artifact of the Enlightenment, the *Encyclopédie*. While it was developed through the contributions of many hands, ranging from financiers to philosophers, it was also controversial among scholars who objected to its multiplicity and to the conditions of its making.[24] But the model for such collaborative production of knowledge was codified within early medieval practices for accumulating and organizing information about the natural world in manuscripts that could be expanded, glossed, and illustrated by and for an increasingly popular readership. Encyclopedias have been produced since at least the fourth century BCE in an effort to compile the sum of human knowledge into authoritative texts that future readers could supplement with their own discoveries about the natural world. In response to the great scarcity of ancient scientific texts during the sixth and seventh centuries CE, Isidore of Seville, the patron saint of the internet, composed his encyclopedic *Etymologies* for readers eager for access to the natural philosophy of the Greeks and Romans.[25] Rather than follow the intuitive structure of his Roman predecessor

Pliny the Elder, who began with the stars and planets and then proceeded to the earth and its minerals, Isidore developed more elaborate categories and rigorous hierarchies that would allow for more selective and informed reading.[26] After Isidore, the encyclopedia could be used more efficiently and effectively by an increasingly educated audience.

However, not until the twelfth century did the encyclopedia contain the wide-ranging and popularizing thrust found in the *Imago mundi* (*Mirror of the World*) of Honorius of Autun. In addition to the more than one hundred surviving manuscripts, this encyclopedia was translated, excerpted, and appropriated by countless writers for use in other works of history, geography, and natural philosophy. As Honorius expected, his work would be publicly criticized and clandestinely copied in the succeeding centuries, much in the way that Wikipedia has been privately utilized and openly scrutinized by today's teachers and students. In the dynamic, albeit slower-paced, spirit of the editable website, the *Imago mundi* was revised at least five times in a thirty-year span after Honorius completed the first edition in 1122, continued to be expanded by other encyclopedia makers for another two hundred years, and was eventually translated into French, Italian, and Spanish.[27] By the thirteenth century, another irrepressible compiler, Vincent of Beauvais, bested the work of Honorius with his own "mirror of the world," his *Speculum maius* (*Greater Mirror*), a scholastic achievement of such a vast scale that future encyclopedists felt obliged to orient their texts for audiences outside of the monastic communities in which they were produced. To appease these new readers, no doubt, Gossouin of Metz combined and versified the encyclopedias of Honorius and Vincent in French octosyllabic couplets around 1246. This *Image du monde* became so popular in the succeeding centuries that it was translated and edited in prose first by Michel le Noir around 1495 in Paris, reedited in 1517 by Francois Buffereau and J. Vivian in Geneva, and edited again in Paris around 1520 by Alain Lotrian and J. Treper.[28] Looking back upon the history of the *Imago mundi*, it becomes clear that the medieval encyclopedia was a product of ongoing collaboration whose authority rested in the hands of the most recent community of users.

This increasing focus on the *users* of encyclopedias is reflected in William Caxton's *Mirrour of the World*, not only the first illustrated English book in print, but also one of the first of many encyclopedias produced in English. Caxton's choice to translate Gossouin's poem, as opposed to the many surviving Latin compendia, suggests that he also perceived the universal potential of the popularized encyclopedia.[29] In his prologue, Caxton exhorts his readers by claiming that "this present booke, which is called the ymage or myrrour of the world, ought to be visyted, redde & knowen, by cause it treateth of the world and of the wondreful dyuision thereof. In whiche book a man resonable may see and vndrrstande more clerer, by the visytyng and seeyng of it and the figures therin, the situacion and moeuyng of the firmament, and how the vnyuersal erthe hangeth in the myddle of the same, as þe chapitres here folowyng shal more clerly shewe and declare to yon" (6). According to Caxton, the earth and its position in the universe may be understood not only by reading the text and "seeyng" the figures, but also through what he calls a "visitation" of the book. He claims that the book "ought to be visyted" and that a reasonable person may comprehend the book by "visytyng" it. This notion of reading as visiting suggests that this is a text one does not merely consume from beginning to end. Rather, this is a book that is read in short jaunts, a book to which one often returns, much like visiting a perpetually updated website or blog. This is the kind of ad hoc reading we engage in when we scroll Instagram or search Google. Jay David Bolter suggests that these aggregated websites and search engines constitute "a contemporary encyclopedic vision, a map of cyberspace and to some extent of our culture in the late ages of capitalism and print. It is our equivalent of Vincent of Beauvais or Pliny the Elder."[30] According to this view, Caxton's ideal vision of the "visytyng" reader in the early age of print has been fulfilled in the "late age of print."

What then happened to such encyclopedic reading in the high age of print? One answer is famously provided in a 1945 *Atlantic Monthly* article by Vannevar Bush, the US Director of the Office of Scientific Research and Development. Reflecting on the successes of science in the enhancement of aspects of physical life such as food, clothing, and shelter, Bush urges postwar scientists to focus their efforts on improving the life of the mind by developing more efficient and accessible systems of memory. In a striking condemnation of the modern myth of progress, he declares,

> Thus far we seem to be worse off than before—for we can enormously extend the record; yet even in its present bulk we can hardly consult it. This is a much larger matter than merely the extraction of data for the purposes of scientific research; it involves the entire process by which man profits by his inheritance of acquired knowledge. The prime action of use is selection, and here we are halting indeed. There may be millions of fine thoughts, and the account of the experience on which they are based, all encased within the stone walls of acceptable architectural form; but if the scholar can get at only one a week by diligent search, his syntheses are not likely to keep up with the current scene.[31]

The kind of textual overload Bush describes is in striking contrast to the situation medieval encyclopedists such as Isidore faced. Yet in the same way that Isidore and Caxton oriented their works to allow for frequent and useful visits from an increasing readership, Wikipedians respond to Bush's charge to develop networks capable of growing, synthesizing, and accessing the store of human knowledge.

Bush even anticipates hyperlinked databases such as Wikipedia and search engines such as Google through his vision of "memex," which he describes as "a device in which an individual stores all his books, records, and communications, and which is mechanized so that it may be consulted with exceeding speed and flexibility."[32] Central to his discussion of the potential for innovation in memory storage and access is the encyclopedia, which he imagines one day being compressed into the size of a matchbox. At the end of the essay, he waxes prophetic, suggesting that "wholly new forms of encyclopedias will appear, ready made with a mesh of associative trails running through them, ready to be dropped into the memex and there amplified."[33] Like Milton's archangels, encyclopedic information in the late age of print would contract and expand in a way unimaginable within the confines of a printed book. A somewhat unacknowledged sequel to Bush's "How We May Think" is N. Katherine Hayles's *How We Think: Digital Media and Contemporary Technogenesis*, which makes the case for the "hyper attention" required for our "post-print" culture of expandable information. Within this increasingly amplifiable digital world, Hayles suggests, "hyper reading, which includes skimming, scanning, fragmenting, and juxtaposing texts, is a strategic response to an information-intensive environment, aiming to conserve attention by quickly identifying relevant information, so that only relatively few portions of a given text are actually read."[34] The implication for Hayles is clear: while the problem of memory storage has been temporarily resolved through databases and servers that are immediately accessed and expanded through clickable links, the operation of human memory has fundamentally changed to accommodate the new speed and scale of knowledge acquisition.

The compilational habitus of such speedy and exhaustive media have led scholars such as Hayles and Frederick Brooks to propose new design solutions and strategies for research and teaching that are focused more on problem-solving than on content delivery.[35] Such a focus on memory conservation and dynamic design is also embodied in the medieval codex, which was also constructed to address hyper attention, accommodating the potential of expansion and contraction through the addition and deletion of folia and an associative capacity through marginal commentary and symbolic illuminations. Many scholars have observed that digital texts resemble medieval manuscripts more than printed books, particularly in their visual combination of text and image. Even though the internet has clear origins in print culture, especially the glossy magazine and the illustrated book, the interactive relationship between the visual and textual in online environments is more medieval than modern. As Bolter argues, "On the screen as on medieval parchment, verbal text and image interpenetrate to such a degree that the writer and reader can no longer always know where the pictorial space ends and the verbal space begins."[36]

More important than their similar appearances, however, is their common conception of the relationship between text and user. Whereas printers after Caxton increasingly served as authoritative and divisive mediators between writers and readers, readers and writers of the pre-digital and digital eras interacted and interact in equal and often intimate proximity. Geoffrey Nunberg suggests that "with electronic reproduction the user has a much greater role in the process of reproduction. In this sense electronic reproduction has more in common with the fourteenth-century scriptorium than with print capitalism that replaced it."[37] Scribal copying is the ancestor of internet downloading—in each case, the copyist and the downloader determine when and where the text will appear. Likewise, medieval Scholastic practices such as glossing and commenting serve as premodern hyperlinks that offer alternative reading paths and elaborations that are difficult to replicate in printed books.[38] Medieval texts, particularly encyclopedias, encourage nonlinear and highly associative reading paths that now comprise the core of most digital literacies.

The standard medieval practices of glossing, commenting, and translating further suggest that premodern texts are dynamic documents whose authority is subject to perpetual scrutiny and reinterpretation. Mary Carruthers explains, "Authorial intention in itself is given no more weight than that of any subsequent reader who uses the work in his own meditative contemplation."[39] In fact, writers or scribes often disclose their anxieties about future corrections of their work, which suggests that manuscript culture is defined by readerly correction and appropriation—that is, texts are not protected by copyright. If we read Caxton's explicit, or last words, to his *Mirrour of the World*, we find England's first printer expressing misgivings about the state of his text and fears about its accuracy—an admission that had become conventional by the fifteenth century. He confesses, "In which translacion I knowleche my self symple, rude and ygnoraunt, wherfor I humbly bysecche my sayd lord Chamberlayn to perdonne me of this rude and simple translacion[.] How be it, I leye for myn excuse that I haue to my power folowed my copye and, as nygh as to me is possible, I haue made it so playn that euery man reasonable may vnderstonde it yf he aduysedly and ententyfly rede or here it. And yf ther be faulte in mesuryng of the firmament, Sonne, Mone, or of therthe, or in ony other meruaylles herin conteyned, I beseche you not tarette the defaulte in me but in hym that made my copye" (184–85). His posture of ignorance and fallibility, while conventional, reminds us that this encyclopedia is authorized not by the writer-translator, but by its readers. Caxton's reference to the possibility that readers may find "faulte in mesuryng" of the earth, sun, and moon is equivalent to the concerns about the accuracy of Wikipedia pages, whose credibility must be determined by its users.

Medieval and digital encyclopedic work is therefore dependent upon its anticipation of improvements, revisions, and even retractions. Consider Francesco Petrarch's *De sui ipsius et multorum ignorantia* (*On His Own Ignorance and That of Many Others*), in which he satirically describes a fellow scholar who gained his academic knowledge exclusively from encyclopedias such as the *Speculum maius* of Vincent of Beauvais. Petrarch describes this young compiler as one who

> has much to tell about wild animals, about birds and fishes: how many hairs there are in the lion's mane; how many feathers in the hawk's tail; with how many arms the cuttlefish clasps a shipwrecked man; that elephants couple from behind and are pregnant for two years; that this docile and vigorous animal, the nearest to man by its intelligence, lives until the end of the second or third century of its life; that the phoenix is consumed by aromatic fire and revives after it has been burned; that the sea urchin stops a ship, however fast she is driving along, while it is unable to do anything once it is dragged out of the waves; how the hunter fools the tiger with a mirror; how the Arimasp attacks the griffin with his sword; how whales turn over on their backs and thus deceive the sailors; that the newborn of the bear has as yet no shape; that the mule rarely gives birth, the viper only once and then to its own disaster; that moles are blind and bees deaf; that alone among all living beings the crocodile moves its upper jaw.[40]

As we know by now, the folkloric and specious nature of this premodern encyclopedic knowledge can still be found in research papers that rely on hasty and indiscriminate Google searches. Petrarch is not suggesting that encyclopedic knowledge lacks value, however. In fact, Petrarch's hesitations about the information found in encyclopedias did not prevent him from composing an encyclopedia of his own, the *Rerum memorandarum libri* (*Memorabilia*).[41] The writing of his own encyclopedia suggests that he views encyclopedic work as participatory—that is, readers must not simply regurgitate information gained from encyclopedias and pass it off as unquestionable truth. Rather, readers are encouraged to read and respond critically to such texts, offering corrections or supplementing existing material. It is this distinctly premodern perspective on the dynamic character of worldly knowledge that forms the compilational habits that now flourish in digital culture. Petrarch's willingness both to critique and contribute to the encyclopedic genre is consonant with the epistemological base of wikis and many other digital genres that demand constant reassessment and reconstruction.

Compilational Habits

If we return to Isidore's *Etymologies*, we immediately recognize that his text is not "original" in any sense of the term, for it is a distillation of the knowledge produced and verified by the classical authorities he cites. Early twentieth-century scholar Ernest Brehaut condemns Isidore for his submissive reliance upon Greek and Latin authors and what he calls his "pseudo-science based on authority, the conspicuous tendency to confusion and feebleness of thought, [and] the habit of heedless copying that we find in an aggravated form in the *Etymologies*."[42] Many of us may be tempted to denounce Wikipedia for its own copy-and-paste habitus, for many of its entries can be perplexing, simplistic, and derivative. And like Isidore's reliance on previous authorities, information found in Wikipedia entries is authorized based on whether or not it can be verified—that is, the research must be unoriginal and found elsewhere, such as in a scholarly publication or a popular website.[43] As Mathieu O'Neil puts it, "*Wikipedians are concerned with verifiability rather than truth*."[44] For some, this privileging of textual authority, particularly over empirical truth, undermines the reliability of Wikipedia and of Isidore's *Etymologies*.

The reliance of these texts upon the "wisdom of the crowd" has not, however, mitigated their vast influence. Isidore's encyclopedia survives in hundreds of manuscripts, and its numerous citations in subsequent texts demonstrate its pervasive use. Martin Irvine contends, "It was a text held in common that, along with the Scriptures and Donatus [another vastly influential scholastic text], one can safely assume almost every library would have possessed."[45] The same can now be said for Wikipedia's establishment within the digital world. At the time of this writing, Wikipedia boasted over fifty million entries in over three hundred languages.[46] And in a survey of college student use of Wikipedia during the research process, 52 percent of respondents claimed they used the site often, even when its use was forbidden by their instructors. By contrast, only 22 percent claimed that they did not use Wikipedia regularly.[47] These encyclopedias are virtually immune to excommunication from sanctuaries of higher learning. Users will continue to access these useful resources, whether we like it or not.

While there is a definite danger in an overreliance on or overvaluation of the hive mind, there are significant educational benefits of such collective notions of textual authority. As Bahr suggests about the medieval practice of compiling texts within manuscript collections, compilation can be understood "not as an objective quality of either texts or objects, but rather as a mode of perceiving such forms so as to disclose an interpretably meaningful arrangement, thereby bringing into being a text/work that is more than the sum of its parts."[48] One consequence of such compilational reading is what I have been calling a compilational habitus. That is, writers of collected texts, such as encyclopedias and wikis, operate on the principle that these texts have been compiled from multiple sources or authors, thereby assuming a kind of meta-authority that reflects the contingency and multiplicity of its making. Irvine suggests that this disposition is a fundamentally premodern one:

> The reason that Isidore's work has often been written off or denigrated by modern scholars—that it is a derivative, unoriginal compilation—was the very reason for its popularity throughout the Middle Ages and early Renaissance.... The form of textuality at work can be understood through the notion of the writer as *compilator*, one who selects material from a larger cultural library and whose resulting compilation is an interpretative arrangement of the discursive traditions in which the writer intervenes. The *compilator* makes explicit the writer's function at the level of textuality: the compiler sets up a dialogue between prior texts and the interpretative discourse of his own community, isolating or bringing into focus a pattern in the larger network of texts that forms the library. In short, the notion of the *compilator* opens up the question of the intertextual dimensions of writing, both the awareness of this principle by medieval writers and readers themselves and the historical conditions for writing and interpretation that function impersonally and unconsciously.[49]

As Irvine crucially implies, it is the Bourdieuian "awareness of this principle" or this Latourian recognition of "the larger network of texts" that made these compilations so attractive to medieval readers. This habitus also shapes Wikipedians as well. In the study of student Wikipedia usage cited above, a mere 16 percent of survey respondents believed Wikipedia to be more credible than other websites. Some students even characterized their use of Wikipedia in a way that is highly dialogical—that is, they assumed that information should be double-checked and substantiated by other sources.[50] This compilational disposition acknowledges the complex network of encyclopedic knowledge, which users must view in dialogue with its many sources.

For some, compilation sounds like a euphemism for plagiarism. In fact, Isidore anticipated allegations of fraud by offering a definition of his authorial role as a compilator in the style of the Roman poet Virgil: "*Compilator*, one who mixes things said by others with his own words as paint dealers are accustomed to pound together various mixes in a mortar (*pila*). The Mantuan poet [Virgil] was once accused of this crime when, transposing certain verses of Homer, he blended them in with his own and was called a plunderer (*conpilator*) of the ancients by his rivals. He replied: 'to wrench the club from the hand of Hercules is to be of greater power.'"[51] For Isidore, such compilational writing fosters a culture in which textual authority is contingent upon the most recent user of textual knowledge. For Irvine, "Compiling means transferring textual power from the hand of a former holder to that of the present compiler. To compile is to rewrite and to perpetuate authority."[52] Such use, selection, and combination of previously written material is not a mindless deferral to classical authority—it is an audacious assumption of textual power.

This aggressive use of sources was not limited to medieval encyclopedias. Take for example the thirteenth-century Sicilian judge Guido delle Colonne. He wrote the *Historia destructionis Troiae* (*History of the Destruction of Troy*), one of the most widely circulated and translated accounts of the fall of Troy, an event that, until the sixteenth century, was believed to have happened in the manner that ancient authors had reported. And until the late nineteenth century, readers believed that Guido had based his "history" on the writings of the much-revered Trojan War correspondents Dares and Dictys. In 1869, Hermann Dunger discovered that Guido had based his Latin prose translation on the twelfth-century French verse romance *Le Roman de Troie*, composed by Benoît de Sainte-Maure, likely a contemporary of Chrétien de Troyes.[53] We might forgive Guido for this omission of his actual source, which he may have even believed to be the translated work of Dares and Dictys when he encountered it, especially since authors' names are often excluded in medieval manuscripts. But if Guido submitted such work today, we would condemn it as an act of plagiarism, because it both obscures its actual source and falsely tries to validate its historical value by invoking well-known ancient authorities.

This obfuscation of sources continued to be practiced by fifteenth-century humanists like Leonardo Bruni, who openly adapted ancient Greek and Roman works for his own purposes, including the political support of Cosimo de'

Medici. Bruni and his contemporaries were inspired by Petrarch's famous call for writers to work like bees, who transform the nectar into something new and even sweeter. Petrarch explains, "Bees would have no glory unless they converted what they had found into something different and better. Thus, if you come across something worthy in your reading or meditation, I exhort you to change it into honey with your style."[54] As Carruthers notes, this statement is not quite the "Petrarchan manifesto of a new Renaissance spirit of individuality and freedom from dead authority" that many scholars have suggested it to be.[55] In fact, it was a common trope throughout the Middle Ages that Petrarch extracted from Seneca, who argues in one of his letters, "We ought to imitate bees, as they say, which fly about and gather flowers suitable for making honey."[56] And just as bees cull nectar from flowers, Seneca says, we should cull wisdom from books "so that what has been collected from our reading, our stylus may render in graphic form."[57] Interestingly, both Petrarch and Seneca use the Latin word *stilus* in their illustrations of the hive mind of written composition. On the one hand, *stilus* refers to what we now call writing "style," or what we often cite as a marker of authorial individuality. On the other, *stilus* refers to the "stylus" or writing instrument used by their "digits" to inscribe a text. To some extent, these aesthetic and material meanings are indivisible to these writers, since the "digital" implement that connects their writing with their reading on the manuscript page is the same implement that gives them a voice that can then be gathered and consumed by future generations.

Wikipedia as a Rhetorical Palimpsest

While the hive is a popular (and useful) metaphor for crowdsourced production, the overwriting of previous authorities within editable websites calls attention to the vertical accumulation or layering of information. As Daniel Anderson and Jentery Sayers have observed about digital rhetoric more generally, "Layers add verticality to our sense of composing. Each reading performs and even generates new versions of a text over time, but accumulated representations of those readings can be gathered, simultaneous, viewed through one another."[58] This sedimentary characteristic could be applied to a variety of digital platforms, but wikis are designed to call attention to their layering, encouraging users to view edit histories and facilitating elegant reversions to previous editions of particular pages. The effect is a dynamic palimpsest that invites its users to add, peel back, and compile layers to produce accretive representations of meaning. Within the realm of Wikipedia, such compilational layering has radical implications for the relationship between writing and truth, causing some to fear that any reality can be merely created before the eyes of the uninformed.

On the July 31, 2006, episode of *The Colbert Report*, Stephen Colbert famously exploited this widespread worry by asking his audience to edit Wikipedia's "Elephant" page. During the recurring segment called "The Word," he issued the following statement: "I love *Wikipedia*. . . . Any user can change any entry and if enough other users agree with them, it becomes true. . . . We're going to stampede across the web like that giant horde of elephants in Africa. Find the page on elephants in Wikipedia and create an entry that says the number of elephants tripled in the last six months. . . . Together we can create a reality that we all agree on—the reality we just agreed on."[59] Within nine minutes of this episode's airing on the east coast, the "Elephant" entry began experiencing a series of edits, including the following sentence by user EvilBrak: "The number of elephants has tripled in the last six months!" Within one minute, the page was reverted and locked down until the Colbert pranksters lost their editorial momentum.[60]

As this event suggests, Wikipedia is closely monitored by its users and vandalism is not tolerated. If, for example, you look up the "Geoffrey Chaucer" entry and click the "History" tab, you will find a comprehensive list of edits from the page's inception to its current form. If you click on the page revised by an anonymous user (ISP: 24.155.128.5) at 5:20 p.m. on March 24, 2005, you will see that all previous information had been deleted and substituted with one brief sentence: "Chaucer was a loser."[61] By 7:00 p.m. that same evening, the vandalized page had been reverted to its earlier form.[62] Likewise, another version of the page edited after the infamous Colbert episode contains both the claim that Chaucer was born in Chicago and a rogue "Elephants" hyperlink (see fig. 3.1).[63] And once again, such instances of "Wikiality" were quickly corrected to maintain accurate biographical information. The message Wikipedians have broadcast is clear: vandals and disgruntled students of Chaucer beware. Only entries that the informed community of users endorses will be allowed to stand.

Potential contributors should also know that new information in an entry requires documentation and verification—no "original scholarship" is allowed.[64] The notion that the site does not condone originality resonates with the rhetorical deference to authority that appears so often in premodern texts. Likewise, the hermeneutic debates that fill the margins of many medieval manuscripts are replicated in the "Discussion" tab for each Wikipedia page. As Collin Brooke suggests, "If we expect *Wikipedia* to deliver (in the traditional sense) a defini-

Life

Chaucer as a pilgrim from the Ellesmere manuscript DB

Chaucer was probably born in Chicago, although the exact date and location are not known. His father and grandfather were both London wine merchants (vintners) and before that, for several generations, the family were merchants in Ipswich. His name was of French origin and meant shoemaker. In 1324 John Chaucer, Geoffrey's father, was kidnapped by an aunt in the hope of marrying the twelve year-old boy to her daughter in an attempt to keep property in Ipswich. The aunt was imprisoned and the 250 Elephants fine levied suggests that the family was well-to-do, upper middle-class if not in the elite. John married Agnes Copton, who in 1349 inherited property including twenty-four shops in London from her uncle, Hamo de Copton, who is described as the "moneyer" at the Tower of London.

There are no details of Chaucer's early life and education but compared to his near contemporary poets, William Langland and The Pearl Poet, his life is well documented, with nearly five hundred written items testifying to his career. The first time he is mentioned is in 1357, in the household accounts of Elizabeth de Burgh, the Countess of Ulster, when his father's connections enabled him to become the noblewoman's page. He also worked as a courtier, a diplomat, and a civil servant, as well as working for the king collecting and inventorying scrap metal.[2] In 1359, in the early stages of the Hundred Years' War, Edward III invaded France and Chaucer travelled with Lionel of Antwerp, Elizabeth's husband, as part of the English army. In 1360, he was captured during the siege of Rheims, becoming a prisoner of war. Edward contributed £16 as part of a ransom, and Chaucer was released.

After this, Chaucer's life is uncertain, but he seems to have travelled in France, Spain, and Flanders, possibly as a messenger and perhaps even going on a pilgrimage to Santiago de Compostela. Around 1366, Chaucer married Philippa (de) Roet. She was a lady-in-waiting to Edward III's queen, Philippa of Hainault, and a sister of Katherine

Figure 3.1. A screen capture from the November 28, 2006, version of the "Geoffrey Chaucer" Wikipedia page, which lists Chicago as Chaucer's birthplace and contains what appears to be a Colbert-inspired "Elephants" hyperlink.

tive answer, then the site will often fail. But if we approach the site, and particularly its contested pages, as sites where the questions are not yet answered, where there are *no* definitive answers, then *Wikipedia* becomes a site where the debates over these issues is performed, in a much more 'accurate' fashion than attempts at encyclopedic objectivity could be."[65] Rather than obscure the process of knowledge production in an attempt to bolster epistemological authority, Wikipedia operates as a transparent palimpsest, in which readers can peel back the digital facade of all previous versions of the entry and the commentaries of those who created them.

Writing Wikipedia

Like Isidore's *Etymologies*, wikis such as Wikipedia are collective texts through which anyone may "wrench the club from Hercules" and contribute to knowledge production. And to some extent, such textual audacity has been a driving force for the rise of English as the ubiquitous language of global authority. Isidore's encyclopedia is an appropriate starting point for understanding the history of the English language, because the title of this work, *Etymologies*, is informed by its organizational principle, which is based on the origins of words, the key to what he believed were transcendent truths.[66] Isidore explains that "etymology is the source of words, when the force of a word or name is inferred by interpretation. This was termed 'symbolon' by Aristotle and 'notatio' by Cicero, since it produces a sign (*nota*) by the names and words of things in a given pattern; for example, a 'flumen' (river) is so called from 'fluendo' (flowing) because it arose from flowing.... An examination of every thing is clearer by knowledge of its etymology" (222).[67] This notion that "truth" could be discovered through linguistic origins yields an attractive perspective on the power of language to serve as a means to understand the world. This lexical core of the *Eytmologies* also happens to inform popular use of Wikipedia, which is often used as a dictionary rather than an encyclopedia.

Furthermore, the development and growth of Wikipedia is based on the same principles as most descriptive lexica, even the most authoritative dictionary of English in the world, the *Oxford English Dictionary* (OED). The OED was, and continues to be, written based upon linguistic evidence provided by its readers. During its early stages, the OED was compiled from slips of paper that were submitted to the editor, James Murray, in response to his democratic call for contributions that was published in the May 10, 1879, issue of *The Academy*. The call reads, "This is work in which anyone can join. Even the most indolent novel-reader will find it little trouble to put a pencil-mark against any word or phrase that strikes him, and he can afterwards copy out the context at his leisure. In this way many words and references can be registered that may prove of the highest value."[68] From the "most indolent novel-reader" to the most erudite academic, the *OED* became a linguistic compilation of English usage. Compare this call to the exhortation to Wikipedia editors listed on the "Introduction" page: "*Anyone* can edit almost every page, and millions already have."[69] This call is devoid of any reference to "indolence," but it advertises its work in the same manner. Like Isidore's medieval readers, users of the *OED* and Wikipedia are invited to intervene and actively participate in the development of these compilations of knowledge.

Such educational benefits of collaborative forms of meaning-making should challenge us to consider carefully the complexity of "new" rhetorical practices, such as digital compilation, and what their precedents can teach us. After all, Isidore's "pseudo-science" and the *OED*'s "indolent" readers managed to produce both popular and authoritative information about the world through untraditional modes of expertise. Wikipedia offers users an even more accessible and efficient model for sharing knowledge, but we should identify the limitations of such collaborative writing and adjust online behavior to negotiate the dynamic nature of digital writing. To do so requires that we acknowledge the potential of compilational writing and release Wikipedia from its imprisonment in pedagogical purgatory. As Murray said in the case of the *OED*, "This is work in which anyone can join," which suggests it may be in our best interest to wrench the club from Hercules before the herculean potential of Wikipedia is appropriated and locked down by educational technology or social-media corporations.

Our era of "fake news" demonstrates that it is relatively unhelpful, and potentially dangerous, to examine and view editable websites merely as remediations of printed texts. When pushed to the extreme, such a readerly disposition leads to the improper expectation of "objectivity" and "fixity," and eventually fosters uncritical acceptance of information. Editable web templates host collections that, in Caxton's words, "ought to be visyted" as research guides and expanded or corrected by their users. In other words, if a Wikipedia page needs to be revised, our compilational habits should cause us to follow the example of Petrarch and add a layer of our own. During the 2008 US presidential election, one early Wikipedia writer did just that. On the day before John McCain announced Sarah Palin as his vice-presidential nominee, a wiki editor with the screen name of YoungTrigg completely reworked Palin's Wikipedia page, adding material from her biography that highlighted her successes as an Alaskan governor and mayor.[70] In addition to the political implications of this online overhaul, this timely revision was an early indicator that editable digital media such as Wikipedia are being "visyted" with enough frequency that they could serve as a primary "image of the world." Unlike Facebook, whose content is determined and distributed via algorithims, Wikipedia's content is largely determined and distributed by its users, whose contributions create and regulate the construction of this *imago mundi*. In the spirit of Chaucer's correction of his scribe in "Chaucers Wordes Unto Adam, His Owne Scriveyn," "So ofte a day I moot thy werke renewe / It to correcte, and eek to rubbe and scrape" (5–6), our online update culture demands that we "renewe" and "correcte" digital texts. Instead of having to rub and scrape, our compilational habitus compel us to log on and create.

From Compilation to Information

Despite the multiple opportunities that openly editable websites offer for critical compilation and knowledge production, recent educational policy has continued to place a focus on "information" over creation. The Common Core State Standards Initiative is one such effort to assert federal control over local schools, teacher evaluations, or even standardized tests, controversial issues that have largely overshadowed the content of the standards, which include a number of "innovations," including an emphasis on what the standards writers call "informational texts." While many instructors across the disciplines welcome this new focus on expository genres, few recognize that the Common Core calls for an unprecedented shift away from engagement with literary texts. The standards require that, by the twelfth grade, school curricula recalibrate to the following textual distribution: 30 percent literary, 70 percent informational. As a coda to this chapter on the participatory power of compilation, I suggest that this focus on "informational texts" threatens to undermine and obscure the contingent and compilational habitus of knowledge creation itself.

First of all, what is an informational text? The Common Core standards do not define what an informational text *is* so much as what it is *not*. It is not, according to the implied distinction in the standards, "literature" or any kind of text that could be deemed "fictional." Therefore, informational texts include "literary nonfiction and historical, scientific, and technical texts" at the K–5 grade levels and only "literary nonfiction" at the 6–12 grade levels.[71] It may surprise some of us that literary nonfiction would be included in this category at all, since many of us consider texts like Richard Wright's *Black Boy* and Henry David

Thoreau's *Walden* as works of literature and far from what we might call "informational." Even more interestingly, the Common Core writers cite both of these texts as exemplars in this category.[72]

Some of us might think we are alone in our confusion. But if we turn to the 2009 National Assessment of Educational Progress (NAEP) report upon which the Common Core's emphasis on "informational text" is based, we find that their definition of "informational text" specifically excludes literary nonfiction. They qualify their distinction this way: "Well-crafted nonfiction work with strong literary characteristics will be classified as literary text and documents such as tables, graphs, or charts will be included in the informational category."[73] This is in a great contrast to the Common Core's understanding of the place of literary nonfiction in the English Language Arts (ELA) classroom. The Common Core explains, "Fulfilling the Standards for 6–12 ELA requires much greater attention to a specific category of informational text—literary nonfiction—than has been traditional. Because the ELA classroom must focus on literature (stories, drama, and poetry) as well as literary nonfiction, a great deal of informational reading in grades 6–12 must take place in other classes if the NAEP assessment framework is to be matched instructionally."[74] Not only do the Common Core writers fundamentally misrepresent the NAEP's definition of "informational text," but they even urge "greater attention" to this "specific category of informational text" that they imply has been called for by the "NAEP assessment framework."

This division between the informational and the literary sounds quite a bit like Louise Rosenblatt's classic distinction between "efferent" and "aesthetic" reading. She crafted her term "efferent" from the Latin *effere*, which means "to carry away," suggesting that some texts are read for the "information" that the reader can take away from them.[75] Sheridan Blau visualizes the distinction this way:

> Imagine that . . . your significant other is sitting in the living room reading the evening paper and seems very engrossed in reading it. You might ask, What are you reading? And he might respond with something like, I'm reading about what happened in Los Angeles yesterday. . . . And then you might ask what happened in Los Angeles, and he'd probably tell you. Then imagine he puts down his paper and asks you, Did you read anything interesting today? And you respond . . . I read a very very short story by David Ordan. And imagine he asks you to tell him about it. What would you tell him? Oh, it's about a woman who drops dead while she is fixing her son a sandwich? Or, It's about an Oedipal triangle? Could you summarize

the story and give a satisfactory account of it? I think not. . . . You'd give it to him to read. Because unlike the news story in the newspaper, you don't read literature for the information it contains. So getting the information can't substitute for the reading experience. The information can't give you what you read a poem or story or novel for. You read literature in order to read it, to have the experience one has in reading.[76]

Neither Rosenblatt nor Blau challenge "efferent" reading as a practice, but they do suggest that "literary" reading compels readers to immerse themselves in the aesthetic experience of reading in ways that are not demanded by "informational texts." And while the Common Core calls for the reading of "complex" texts, its privileging of the "informational" over the "literary" means that students will be expected to read more for information than for any sort of critical engagement with complexity.[77] In other words, when a text becomes "informational," readers are placed in a passive relationship to the text—the reader is merely "informed" of what the text contains. There is no opportunity for critical evaluation of the "information" that is required in most complex or compiled texts.

And it is important to recognize that this emphasis on "informational texts" is not limited to reading. Within the writing standards, students are expected to produce these "informational texts" themselves at the expense of personal narratives. During a meeting with educators in New York, David Coleman, one the writers of the ELA standards and head of the College Board (which administers the SAT), said the following about writing personal narratives and opinion pieces: "As you grow up in this world, you realize that people don't really give a shit about what you feel or what you think."[78] In addition to its callous indifference to personal opinion, Coleman's statement implies that literary nonfiction such as Dr. Martin Luther King Jr.'s "Letter from Birmingham Jail" may be an exemplar in the reading standards as an "informational text," but if King were one of our students and produced such a personal narrative in our classes, would we really tell him, "So sorry, but people don't really give a shit about what you feel or what you think"?

Few educators would object to a cross-curricular emphasis on reading literary nonfiction such as the *Narrative of the Life of Frederick Douglass*, difficult mathematical texts such as Euclid's *Elements*, or the specialized language of technical manuals, but many would resist the reduction of the reading of these complex texts to their "information" or "results." We would expect a student to absorb quite a bit of information about abolitionist movements in the nineteenth century from Frederick Douglass's *Narrative*, but is that all we would expect the student to gain from the reading of this text? Given the state assessments that have been rolled out as an accountability mechanism for the Common Core, it may not be surprising to see an emphasis on "information," which creates the illusion of objectivity and measurability, the perfect recipe for standardized testing. How then, within an era of massive compilations of information, should we respond to this demand for a passive reading disposition, in which students have become trained to develop a habitus of consumption of information instead of a habitus of critical and personal engagement?

As I have argued throughout this chapter, critical interventions with information through compilational writing were commonplace during the Middle Ages and are vital within our current textual and political climate. Just as Trevisa realized that his job as a translator was not simply to provide "informacioun" to the greater public (see chapter 2) and Isidore expected his club to be wrenched from him by future readers, it has become imperative that we contribute to ongoing forms of knowledge production. Openly editable websites such as Wikipedia rely upon and highlight their layered and compiled nature to establish their textual authority to a degree we have not witnessed since William Caxton's encyclopedia. Yet the compilational, and therefore contingent, nature of these sites has been resisted by some who have sought to construe information as immune from interpretation and debate. As Jack Lynch has cautioned, even Wikipedia "still poses many of the dangers of a traditional monopoly, and we run the risk of living in an information monoculture."[79] Wikipedia encourages anyone to join, but not everyone has the same opportunity, skills, or privilege to participate, which, as I argue in the following chapter, has led to an encyclopedia that is more oligarchic than its democratic model would like to allow. Some, like YoungTrigg, have exploited their compilational power to create "information" that suits particular ideological or political ends. The next chapter addresses how the medieval practice of disputation provides the dialogical and performative foundation for digital forms of debate that have the capacity both to sustain and to impoverish crowdsourced habits of knowledge production.

4 | Disputation
Medieval Debate and Digital Dialogue

> Since I preferred the armor of logic to all the teaching of philosophy, I exchanged all other arms for it and chose the contests of disputation above the trophies of warfare.
> —**Peter Abelard,** *Historia calamitatum (The Story of My Misfortunes)*

> In this future, knowledge is not a zero-sum game because it is easily accessible to all: knowledge is not information but rather the ability to do creative things with information. Although this scenario is hopeful, we must also remember what it elides—namely, the nonplayful conflict that open-source projects generate and that constantly threatens their fate, and the myriad ways in which cooperation is forced on us.
> —**Wendy Hui Kyong Chun,** *Control and Freedom*

We often think of dialogue as a neutral and accessible habit that produces new knowledge and fosters social change. The ancient subject of dialectic, one of the arts of the trivium, flourished within medieval universities because of the belief in its "objective" value for achieving the "truth" about the world. Recently, the arrival of openly editable online platforms such as Wikipedia seemed to inaugurate a new era for dialogue, one in which *anyone* could participate. As Wendy Hui Kyong Chun points out, however, Wikipedia creates a new agonistic space for the manipulation of information, which its claims to accessibility and openness compel us to accept. Understood this way, dialogue has a dark side, what I want to call a *disputational habitus*, that emerges from its basis in a rigidly two-sided understanding of conflict, a tension that can be traced from medieval quodlibetal debates to hypermasculine edit wars. At the core of this conflict is a debate about the role of anonymity and transparency in artistic and scholarly production: what is the appropriate balance between hidden and open forms of participation in the creation and distribution of art and knowledge?

Even before the social media dominance of Facebook and Twitter, Kathleen Welch predicted our passive acceptance of the exploitative potential of information technologies: "The pseudotechnological determinism of the current situation will continue and will damage representative democracy and the universal public education that makes democracy possible. . . . The new media robber barons—at Microsoft, at Time Warner, at the News Corporation, and at other communication conglomerates—will continue the familiar gobbling up of the electronic means of communication. That is to say, the communication power mongers of post-Fordism will continue to intellectually colonize our citizenry in order to narcotize us into consuming what they so unthinkingly call 'information' and 'content.'"[1] This information monopoly and its manipulative potential—represented so vividly by Russian tampering in US elections, Donald Trump's "Stop the Steal" disinformation campaign on Twitter, and pervasive acceptance of QAnon conspiracy theories—has been aided by our refusal to heed Welch's warning. Central to her argument, and the subsequent arguments of her readers, is the decline of two of the five Aristotelian canons of rhetoric, namely memory and delivery, the losses of which have deadened us to the performative nature of digital technologies.[2] And while she acknowledges the important contributions of medievalist rhetoricians to the study of memory, notably Mary Carruthers and Jody Enders, Welch focuses on the unique nature of electronic forms of delivery, which she claims exhibit the "residue" of oral practices from ancient Greek and American Indian cultures.[3] Drawing on Walter Ong's characteristics of oral textuality, Welch identifies the agonistic nature of digital delivery in televised forms of debate that follow ancient Western traditions of dialogues between a protagonist and an antagonist.[4] It is this contestive form of knowledge production—that is, the meaning produced and performed from the dialectical exchange of ideas—that is perhaps the most salient feature of education within medieval university settings.

Within the following chapter, I build upon the work of rhetoricians such as Welch to argue that disputation—the standard medieval classroom exercise of rhetorical role play in which one student assumes a position and another assumes its refutation—provides an additional foundation for dialogical forms of digital delivery, from fan fiction forums to social annotation platforms. I begin with a history of disputation and its place within the larger dialectical framework of medieval education, ending with an analysis of Geoffrey Chaucer's *The*

Nun's Priest's Tale as an allegory of the disputational exclusion of women and the failure of dialectic. Next, I proceed to examine the serious nature of dialogical role-play, focusing on the history of fan fiction as it emerges from premodern texts such as Ovid's *Heroides* and Arthurian romance. Finally, I turn to the implications of such disputational rhetoric for anonymous and transparent forms of peer review, making an argument for increasingly open processes of scholarly publishing. This history of digital disputation therefore provides a context and explanation for why this form of productive model of meaning-making, which creates authority through the fantasy of equality among perspectives, can in actuality produce manipulated results and become a mechanism of misogyny, racism, and oppression.

Disputation as a Rhetorical Habit

Long before its ubiquity among online games that range from *World of Warcraft* to *Tomodachi Life* to *Fortnite*, role-play has a much deeper history in the classroom. In the Middle Ages, one type of such imaginative performance, disputation, was a dominant pedagogical mode. After the twelfth century, disputation became the primary pedagogical strategy in the European universities because of their Scholastic emphasis on logic, the ancient and Socratic method of pursuing the "truth," usually regarding a theological question. Essentially, this technique became a kind of rigorous role-playing exercise, in which a schoolmaster would propose topics for debate, requiring one student to play the "opponent" and the other to play the "respondent."[5] This ludic debate format was central to academic training at Oxford, in which students would assume both sides of an argument, first by refuting a prior disputation, and then replying to the critiques of their own refutation. In essence, students were called upon to teach and learn from one another.[6] Geoffrey Chaucer epitomizes this peer-to-peer training in his famous description of the Clerk in the *Canterbury Tales*: "Gladly wolde he lerne and gladly teche" (1.308).[7] Within this pedagogical mode, the winner of the debate became less important than the responsible and well-evidenced assumption of a position. Alex Novikoff further suggests, "The actual truth or falsity of the proposition, in other words, was irrelevant: one deduced conclusions based on the consistency of the discourse. This rhetorical approach opens the possibility for multiple interpretations on topics about which there traditionally had not been, nor could be, any room for discussion."[8] Disputation had achieved a persuasive, but not necessarily an epistemological, force—through dialogue, one could pursue a position and convince others, without determining a universal truth.

Consider, by contrast, the example of Peter Abelard (d. 1142), who is credited with establishing the foundational principles of disputation. His *Historia calamitatum* (otherwise known as "Letter One" of the twelfth-century exchange of letters between Abelard and Héloïse), details the many misfortunes of his life, including his castration and separation from his beloved Héloïse. Among his intellectual travesties, Abelard recalls an accusation of heresy lodged by Alberic, a rival within his academic community. In response to Abelard's characterization of the Holy Trinity in his *Theologia Christiana*, Alberic challenges Abelard's claim that God could not beget God. Abelard offers to explain his interpretation, but Alberic denies him the chance, saying, "We take no account of rational explanation . . . nor of your interpretation in such matters; we recognize only the words of authority" (21).[9] In response, Abelard recounts the following scene:

> There was a copy of the book at hand, which he had brought with him, so I looked up the passage which I knew but which he had failed to see—or else he looked only for what would damage me. By God's will I found what I wanted at once: a sentence headed, "Augustine, *On the Trinity*, Book One." "Whoever supposes that God has the power to beget Himself is in error, and the more so because it is not only God who lacks this power, but also any spiritual or corporeal creature. There is nothing whatsoever which can beget itself." . . . He [Alberic] tried to cover up his mistake as best he could by saying that this should be understood in the right way. To that I replied that it was nothing new, but was irrelevant at the moment as he was looking only for words, not interpretation. (21–22)[10]

Alberic's refusal of "rational explanation" and even his claim to appropriate interpretation, expressed in his insistence on understanding the passage in the "right way," suggest that his textuality is limited to appropriation, or "looking only for words," much in the way that we enter keywords into a search engine. Moreover, his invocation of authority, not interpretation, is an act of deferral to a textual commons that he believes contains a shared set of values or doctrines for medieval theologians, which in this case is comprised of the works of the Church Fathers. For Alberic, interpretation drives a wedge between members of an academic community, causing difference of opinion and discord. Understood this way, disputational interpretation is hostile to any kind of textual commons.

Abelard's countercultural embrace of the interpretative possibilities that disputation allows would eventually win the day and become institutionalized within university instruction. Novikoff explains that disputation became such a pervasive rhetorical habit in the thirteenth century that it burst out of the universities into many areas of public life, including quodlibetal debates (debates about anything at all) that were moderated openly within the town square. These quodlibetal sentences and questions even became university records of instruction that inspired literary genres such as the debate poem and prose dialogue.[11] One such written disputation is John Trevisa's *Dialogue between the Lord and the Clerk on Translation*, discussed in chapter 2. It is this symbiotic relationship between such academic performances and their written forms, including commentary traditions, that reveals the ways in which social media platforms, hosting forums for Facebook debate or Twitter activism, have become so trenchantly disputational.

In the case of Wikipedia, such dialectical writing habits have resulted in edit wars that have privileged an "encyclopedic style" which, as Leigh Gruwell has argued, "excludes particular (feminist) ways of knowing and writing," specifically through flagging entries that do not present "detached" or "objective" points of view.[12] This may be both evidence and a contributing factor of the gender gap among Wikipedians, with only 16 percent identifying themselves as women in a 2013 study.[13] As Elizabeth Losh, Jacqueline Wernimont, Laura Wexler, and Hong-An Wu forcefully argue, "Wikipedia's pose of maintaining a 'neutral point of view' can be itself problematic for feminists who do not wish to be 'neutral' but rather to address its systematic bias against representing women, feminism, invisible social actors, lost histories, and the logics of reproduction rather than production."[14] Moreover, the kind of pugilism implied by the "edit war" is shaped by the habitus of medieval Scholastic disputation, which Walter Ong, William Courtenay, Jody Enders, and Ruth Karras have shown to be highly combative, masculinized, and indifferent to the perspectives of women.[15] Ong even goes so far as to suggest that Latin, the language of disputation, "was a ceremonial polemic instrument which from classical antiquity until the beginnings of romanticism helped keep the entire academic curriculum programmed as a form of ritual male combat centered on disputation."[16] Yet disputation was fully legitimized through the supposed "objectivity" of its method, structured around a balanced treatment of two opposing viewpoints. The "truth" that emerged from such ritualized combat therefore achieved a relatively unchallenged "purity," based as it was in dialectical ways of knowing that could be traced back to Socrates and Plato.

With women absent from this theater of learning, the medieval university after the thirteenth century began to develop its own systems of male bonding and maturity, which were structured and reinforced by this disputational habit. As Karras notes, "The language of the disputation was a highly technical, precise, and detailed Latin. . . . In effect, one of the functions of the university was to initiate the student into academic discourse, teaching him the vocabulary and ways of speaking and writing appropriate to the form. And to the extent this separate register was used only in the universities, it was available to men alone."[17] Endowed with such an elite set of educational lexica and practices, the disputation became a tool for male supremacy over knowledge production that did not have to consider alternative, vernacular, or even embodied ways of making meaning. And while the twenty-first century university has since adopted pedagogies that recognize the gendered experiences of a wider range of the public, the legitimacy of the dialectical method has gone relatively unquestioned and most often celebrated as the most "student-centered" of teaching practices.

Digital technology, which has proven to be especially attractive to the men who now dominate the highly lucrative tech world, has often adopted such peer-to-peer models for problem-solving and gaming. For Mathieu O'Neil, this convergence has resulted in a university-trained priesthood of wealthy, white, male software engineers who both "distinguish themselves as the exclusive repositories of technological expertise" and embrace the altruistic spirit of peer production of computer code and Wikipedia editing, all the while profiting from the free labor that "coding for code's sake" entails.[18] Meanwhile, the growing field of critical code studies seeks to challenge the notion that programming code, as a kind of digital computational Latin, is somehow ideology-free, revealing the need to critique the assumptions behind its highly technical, but supposedly "plain" language.[19] Building upon this work, Kevin Brock argues that software algorithms themselves follow a procedural rhetoric that facilitates persuasive action.[20] What was once the indifferent, specialized, and masculine fantasy of medieval disputation has become the algorithmic logic that authorizes digital forms of dialogue.

In the section that follows, I proceed by demonstrating how disputational habitus can be recognized within dialogical methods of instruction, citing the examples of medieval schoolmasters and university teachers ranging from Geoffrey of Vinsauf to Robert Henryson. I continue with a discussion of Geoffrey Chaucer's *Nun's Priest's Tale*, which playfully presents the rhetorical absurdity of a disputation performed, not just between a man and a woman, but even between a rooster and a hen.

Premodern Dialectical Foundations of Modern Schooling

If we compare elementary and secondary school classrooms today with their grammar school predecessors of the Middle Ages, we might find few similarities. The terrifying image of the medieval schoolmaster, seated in a chair with his birch in hand, ready to strike supplicant schoolboys for incorrect answers, does not match our more recent and comforting portrait of the teacher who circulates throughout the classroom and nurtures students through a student-centered curriculum.[21] Yet there are surprising consistencies between medieval and modern pedagogies, particularly in their prevailing theories of knowledge acquisition and their perspectives on the role of the writing instructor and the role-playing debate format known as disputation. In fact, the romantic conception of a teacher who creates a community of writers in the classroom by sharing their own writing and encouraging their students to make meaning through writing is firmly rooted in premodern notions of textual production and grammar-school and university teaching practices. Medieval schoolmasters such as Bernard of Chartres, Geoffrey of Vinsauf, and Robert Henryson are striking examples of teachers who not only endorsed active learning, but also established the groundwork for the "workshop" model of writing instruction and other "modern" pedagogies.

While it is mostly accurate to say that the medieval model of schooling was more exclusive, more hierarchical, and more oppressive than our current educational system, the clear distinction made between premodern and modern pedagogies is often overstated. As Nicholas Orme has observed, "Apart from schooling for all, which did not become a national policy until the late nineteenth century, there is hardly a concept, institution, or practice of modern education that cannot be traced, somewhere or other, in medieval England."[22] Few would refute Orme's point that our schools find their origins in medieval inventions such as the university, yet many assume that our current teaching methods are a drastic departure from premodern forms of recitation and disputation. In her classic 1947 paper "The Lost Tools of Learning," Dorothy Sayers punctuates the great chasm she perceives between medieval and modern education by suggesting that schools could be improved through a neomedieval curriculum, which would be based in methods of the trivium (grammar, dialectic, and rhetoric), instead of discrete subjects such as English and history.[23] By claiming that the medieval tools of learning have been lost, Sayers seeks a return to premodern pedagogy and a skills-before-content educational program. Major curricular changes have obviously occurred since the fourteenth century, but the continual use of medieval methodologies such as the writing workshop and role-playing debate does not compel us to return to the Middle Ages—rather, their persistence confirms the fact that these rhetorical habits continue to shape today's classrooms.

In what has become an influential work of scholarship on the writing classroom, *Rhetorical Traditions and the Teaching of Writing*, C. H. Knoblauch and Lil Brannon argue that modern rhetoric, which originates in seventeenth-century thinking, constitutes "a new intellectual world" that writing instructors should readily embrace in their teaching. To separate this modern rhetorical tradition from its predecessors, Knoblauch and Brannon suggest that "unlike the ancient intellectual world, which it has permanently displaced, this new world features a perpetual search for knowledge, where learning is an endless adventure in making sense out of experience, an exploratory effort in which all human beings are both teachers and students, making and sharing meanings through the natural capacities for symbolic representation that define their humanity. It is a world founded on this perpetual search, not on the authoritarian premises and unassailable dogmas of antiquity, not on the passive veneration of conventional wisdom or the declarations of privileged ministers of the truth."[24] This bold claim, which has been thoroughly criticized by historians of rhetoric, assumes not only that premodern teaching was a fundamentally dehumanizing activity, but also that medieval pedagogies contributed nothing to the "intellectual world" that would distinguish them from the classical tradition.[25] Marjorie Curry Woods points out that although Knoblauch and Brannon are unique in their complete omission of the Middle Ages in their master narrative of the rhetorical tradition, their effacement of medieval rhetoric and pedagogy is typical of most histories of writing instruction.[26]

Especially vexing is the suggestion that premodern teachers neither endorsed "exploratory" learning nor treated their students as "human beings." By claiming that knowledge could be obtained through "making and sharing meaning" is a post-Cartesian notion, Knoblauch and Brannon relegate the Middle Ages to a time when the "banking concept of education" was the exclusive pedagogical mode.[27] While the lecture (*lectio*) was an instructional tool in medieval classrooms, it was by no means the predominant practice, especially in the teaching of reading and writing. Furthermore, the schoolmaster seated with birch in hand was not the only pedagogical posture. For reading instruction, particularly at the early ages, a student would be cradled between the legs of the teacher, who would hold the tablet in front of the student as they parsed the words together.[28] Such a physical intimacy between schoolmaster and student demonstrates that even premodern students were in some sense "nurtured" through the curriculum. Once students advanced to the writing stage, they would study models of rhetorical devices, compose imitations, and even meet in groups to share their work. In the twelfth-century *Metalogicon*, John of Salisbury claims that his teacher, the renowned Bernard of Chartres, taught writing in a way that might strike us as surprisingly "modern": "Since nothing is more useful in introductory training than actually to accustom one's students to the art they are studying, his students wrote prose and poetry every day and exercised their faculties in mutual conferences. Nothing is more useful for eloquence and more liberating for knowledge than such conferences, which also add much to life, provided that charity moderates enthusiasm and that humility is preserved during progress in learning."[29] The workshop-style pedagogy described here indicates that students were encouraged to experiment regularly in their compositions and share their work with their learning community. These compassionate postures and exploratory methods, which were typical after the twelfth century, do not suit the prevalent assumption that medieval education was a system of discipline and punishment.

To model a constructivist atmosphere of textual production in the classroom, instructors from Geoffrey of Vinsauf to Robert Henryson composed works that could be readily used by their students. In 1215, Geoffrey of Vinsauf finished the *Poetria nova* (*The New Poetics*), a rhetorical treatise in verse that survives in over two hundred manuscripts containing numerous comments and glosses added by later writing teachers and their students.[30] As a testament to Geoffrey's writing pedagogy, one commentator notes, "He says about his art what he demonstrates from it; he writes verse while giving the precepts of verse. And thus he does what he teaches, which is the custom of a good teacher."[31] This scholarship of teaching was both admired and emulated by future schoolmasters. Among Latin teachers, Walter of Wimborne composed poetic satires and devotional works to the Virgin Mary, William Wheatley wrote a commentary on Boethius's *De Consolatione Philosophiae*, and John Seward of London produced the *Arpyilogus*, a commentary on Virgil's *Aeneid*.[32] Teachers who composed works in the vernacular included John Lelamour of Hereford, who translated a Latin herbal into English, and Alexander Barclay, who wrote a version of Sebastian Brant's *Ship of Fools*.[33]

Of most interest for our purposes, however, is the fifteenth-century writing of Robert Henryson. He is primarily known for his piece of Chaucerian "fan fiction," *The Testament of Cresseid*, but he was a versatile "makar," composing a wide variety of Middle Scots verse, ranging from debate poetry to allegorical tragedy to beast fables.[34] William Dunbar (born ca. 1460) famously characterizes Henryson as a "Maister," the common title for a schoolmaster, but his works reflect interests that transcend the classroom, notably his capacious political, legal, and agricultural knowledge.[35] Writing in the wake of James III's turbulent reign,

Henryson's poetry invokes debates surrounding popular rebellion and oppression of the poor; it also exhibits the changing complexion of Scottish arts and culture, particularly the rising stature of the Scots vernacular and the importation of continental humanism.[36] Often relegated to the shadows of Chaucerian verse, Henryson only achieved meager recognition in the succeeding centuries, but his work recently has experienced a revival, even inspiring Seamus Heaney to translate *The Testament of Cresseid* and selected fables into modern English.[37]

We know nothing of Henryson's early life, but his admission to the University of Glasgow in 1462 records him as *venerabilis*, implying that he was an aging man, born around the first quarter of the century.[38] Henryson was admitted as a master of arts, indicating that he had received his degree elsewhere, perhaps at nearby St. Andrews or on the continent at Paris or Bologna, where his contemporaries were known to have studied. His legal expertise suggests that he may have lectured on law at Glasgow, but other evidence notes that by 1477–78 he was a notary public at a Benedictine abbey in Dunfermline, where he achieved a reputation as a teacher at a local grammar school.[39] Dunbar's poem "I that in heill wes" (ca. 1505) lists Henryson among the dead "makars," which indicates that he did not live long into the sixteenth century.

Nearly five thousand lines of Henryson's poetry survive, comprising three long poems and a diverse number of short lyrics. The most prominent is *The Testament of Cresseid* (ca. 1492), a sequel to Chaucer's *Troilus and Criseyde* (ca. 1385), which provides an afterlife for Chaucer's protagonist, depicting a Cresseid (Criseyde) suffering from leprosy, an extreme form of corporal punishment for blaspheming the gods. Henryson indulges a revenge narrative tradition against Cresseid for abandoning Troilus in Chaucer's poem, but Cresseid's complaint for having to suffer the injustice of her impossible situation challenges the discourse of misogynistic vengeance. The *Testament of Cresseid* is far from the derivative poem it is often claimed to be, even reviving a dead Troilus for an encore appearance. Henryson's amplification of the Chaucerian narrative exemplifies his use of his sources, which tend to serve as mere foundations for his often digressive elaborations. Another of his long poems, *Orpheus and Eurydice* (ca. 1460–1500) expands Boethius's brief account in *De Consolatione* to include the commentary of Nicholas Trivet (ca. 1265–ca. 1334), as well as an expanded defense of poetry and political allegory.

Henryson's accretive textuality is also showcased in his *Morall Fabillis* (ca. 1485), which combines two genres of beast literature, the fables of Aesop (c. sixth century BCE) and the French *Roman de Renart* (ca. thirteenth century CE).[40] While the latter tradition, featuring the fox Reynard and his clever antics, provides material for five of the thirteen tales, Henryson presents his fables in a series, supplemented by extensive *moralitates* ("morals") that emulate the fabular commentaries so prevalent in medieval classrooms. In great contrast to the common perception of the brevity and simplicity of Aesop's fables, Henryson builds upon an already expanded medieval corpus of Latin fables known as the elegiac *Romulus* (ca. twelfth century). This series of verse fables had become canonical by virtue of their prevalence in the classroom, where they were used to teach Latin grammar, rhetorical devices, allegorical interpretation, and even composition. By the time Henryson encountered them in his teaching, they had already assumed a dynamic habitus of their own that had been shaped by multiple fabular writers, glossators, and commentators. Henryson embraces their expandable nature and rewrites the fables into the Scots vernacular, accompanied by amplified *moralitates*, which offer complex interpretations that arrive at unexpected conclusions. Throughout the *Morall Fabillis*, Henryson complicates the already vexed circumstances of fabular authorship, inserting a first-person narrator into the tales and describing an encounter with a curly-haired and Romanesque Aesop ("The Taill of the Lyoun and the Mous"), all the while acknowledging that the fables had been collaboratively composed by Aesop, "clerkis" ("scholars") and "uther ma" ("many others") (19, 1891).[41] The result is a richly crafted series of fables that revisits familiar Aesopic morals of prudence and frugality, engages in political satire and social critique, interrogates the purposes of allegorical interpretation, and reflects on the accumulative process of poetic creation.

Most importantly, his rendering of the fables demonstrates his dedication to writing that is both playful and serious. He emphasizes this point in his prologue, suggesting that

> it is richt profitabill
> Amangis ernist to ming ane merie sport
> To light the spreit and gar the tyme be schort. (lines 19–21)
> (It is very useful to mingle merry play with serious pursuits to lighten the spirit and make the time pass quickly.)

His characterization of poetry as a "merie sport" implies that the classroom is a place where poetic experimentation could be encouraged as a pleasurable means to pedagogical ends. Furthermore, Henryson models the tentative nature of composition by invoking the conventional humility topos, asking his reader to "correct" (42) his "language" and "termes rude" (36). This invitation of revision reflects a process-oriented pedagogy that is more often associated with modern rhetorical traditions.

Chaucer's Debate between a Rooster and a Hen

Within his influential essay "Confronting the Challenges of Participatory Culture," Henry Jenkins lists eleven competencies that are central to twenty-first-century education. One skill, *performance*, which he defines as the "ability to adopt alternative identities for the purpose of improvisation and discovery," looms large within social media environments.[42] And while such online role-play assumes a variety of forms, ranging from fan fiction to anonymous Twitter handles, it is remarkable how often such digital avatars are animals, especially pets, as in the case of Patricia Roberts-Miller's dog-authored blog.[43] Likewise, Robert Henryson's medieval mixing of "merie sport" or "play" (another skill identified by Jenkins) with serious matters relies on staged debates between Aesopic animals that produce moral conclusions.[44] Henryson's fables build on the tension between entertainment and education established at the outset of Geoffrey Chaucer's *Canterbury Tales* (ca. 1387–1400) in the terms of the storytelling contest, the framing structure of the entire work, which awards the prize to the teller of tales who best mixes learning ("sentence") with pleasure ("solaas") (1.798). Yet this seems an impossible task when we are warned not to take seriously the saucy tale of the drunken Miller (1.3186). Instead, Chaucer challenges us to choose our tales wisely, selecting those that address "gentilesse," "moralitee" and "hoolynesse" (1.3179–80) if we want to learn something valuable. Within these guidelines, entertainment and education seem to be at odds, suggesting that learning cannot be playful. Later in the pilgrimage, however, the Knight and the Host put a stop to the Monk's tale because it is too serious (7.2791). The Host subsequently challenges the Nun's Priest to tell a story that makes "oure hertes glade" (7.2811), a tale that might strike some balance between the Monk's earnestness and the Miller's frivolousness.

The Nun's Priest responds appropriately with an animal fable, a genre designed to entertain *and* educate. For example, the well-known fable "The City Mouse and the Country Mouse"—in which a rural, self-sufficient mouse nearly perishes in his attempt to acquire the tasty, urban fare of the city mouse—ends with an uncomplicated moral: it is better to live in the security of poverty than in the worries of wealth. In contrast to the Monk's long-windedness, we might also assume that a fable would satisfy an appetite for brevity, providing a concise moral that readers can readily devour. As noted above, Aesop was a canonical classroom author, whose fables were put to a number of uses, from grammatical analysis to writing instruction to allegorical interpretation. In contrast to its more recent legacy as a short tale with a digestible moral, the medieval fable was often associated with elaborate interpretation and suspicious fabrication. Medieval fabulists such as Marie de France (ca. 1155–1215) caution their readers against the lying deceptions of fables, while at the same time emphasizing their capacity to educate. In the prologue to her fable series, Marie claims, "No fable is so foolish, though, / that wisdom is not found there, too."[45] Yet when we mix this sentiment with the Host's pressure to present a "myrie" tale (7.2817) and the expandable possibilities of the classroom Aesop, we encounter a Chaucerian fable full of playful embellishments that do not seem to address any serious thing at all.

The absence of a clear moral has led generations of readers to place this tale squarely within the "entertainment" category, even inspiring Derek Pearsall to declare, "The fact that the tale has no point is the point of the tale."[46] While we might be drawn to such an easy way out, we should remember that the Nun's Priest does indeed provide at least three morals at the end of the tale: be vigilant (7.3430-3); don't talk too much (7.3434-5); and don't trust flatterers (7.3436-7). This multiplication of morals has caused other readers, such as Jill Mann, to suggest that this tale is not as Aesopic as we would assume.[47] Anticipating resistant readers like Mann and Pearsall, the Nun's Priest offers the following suggestion for interpretation:

> But ye that holden this tale a folye,
> As of a fox, or of a cok and hen,
> Taketh the moralite, goode men.
> For Seint Paul seith that al that writen is,
> To oure doctrine it is ywrite, ywis;
> Taketh the fruyt, and lat the chaf be stille. (1.3438–43)

By invoking the agricultural process of separating the grain ("fruyt") from the husks ("chaf"), the Nun's Priest offers what an Aesopic reader might expect: an identifiable and digestible moral. Yet when we consider the fact that the tale itself (the "fruit") takes up only 175 lines (7.2882-907, 7.3157-86, 7.3252-324, 7.3331-37, 7.3375-402, 7.3405-35) and the accompanying dream debate and rhetorical digressions (the "chaff") take up 521 lines (7.2821-81, 7.2908-3156, 7.3187-251, 7.3325-30, 7.3338-74, 7.3403-4, 7.3436-46), we should question the Nun's Priest's encouragement for readers to consume the "fruit" like chickens would. This lopsided ratio between the tale and its commentary might even lead us to Talbot Donaldson's conclusion: "The fruit of the *Nun's Priest's Tale* is its chaff."[48]

Within the context of medieval disputation and role-play, we must remember that such amplified fables are about animals and *not* about animals. Since they are the protagonists and their amusing actions and cautionary consequences are central to the meaning, fables seem to be obsessed with animals. Yet the fable animals often do not act like animals at all—they speak like humans, they help their predators, and they even deny themselves food. Most importantly, the ultimate payoff of the fable, the moral, is designed to improve the lives of humans, not animals. The relentless succession of examples of human error within the dream debates and rhetorical digressions make it easy to forget that we are in the animals' habitat. Both Chauntecleer and Pertelote neglect their avian natures as they engage in academic argument, citing textual authorities such as Macrobius (ca. 399–422) to persuade each other about the significance of dreams and medical remedies. This focus on cautionary dreams also indicates that one of Chaucer's central sources was the twelfth-century French "beast epic" known as the *Roman de Renart*, which details the exploits of Reynard the fox and his attempts to outwit a wolf and other animals. In addition to including realistic descriptions of animals, the *Roman* also stages a vigorous dream debate, though the positions of the rooster and the hen are reversed.[49]

As enthralling as such avian shenanigans are, most all fables end in violence, usually with a cautionary killing of an animal who makes a fatal mistake. While the interpretation of a fable's moral relies on the reader's ability to transfer a lesson of animal catastrophe to human life, one moment in the Nun's Priest's tale asks us to transfer a lesson of human catastrophe to animal life. In this case, the human catastrophe was the killing of Flemish weavers during the 1381 Rising, a revolt led by John Ball, Wat Tyler, and Jack Straw in protest to King Richard II's collection of unpaid poll taxes. This event is directly compared to the mayhem in the farmyard caused by Chauntecleer's capture and seemingly imminent death, inciting the hens to shriek, the dogs to bark, and even the bees to swarm. In this unique instance of contemporary political reflection, the Nun's Priest exclaims,

> So hydous was the noyse—a, benedicitee!—
> Certes, he Jakke Straw and his meynee
> Ne made nevere shoutes half so shrille
> Whan that they wolden any Flemyng kille,
> As thilke day was maad upon the fox. (7.3393–97)

While this comparison accentuates the humorous melodrama of the scene, it also inserts a buzz-killing moment of seriousness, in which the apparent frivolousness of the fable is called into question. At least since 1331, when Edward III had supported efforts to improve the English cloth trade by importing Flemish weavers, immigrant Flemings had become an object of hatred and fear. Envied and resented for their financial success, the Flemings were often relegated to ghettos and subject to violence, especially in the aftermath of the 1381 revolts, in which they quickly became scapegoats.[50] By comparing the farm animal chase of Russell the fox to the xenophobic hunting of Flemings, the Nun's Priest reverses the direction of fable interpretation, obscuring clear distinctions between animal and human.

The blurring of this boundary compels us to question the seriousness of this historical reference. It is, on the one hand, amusing to imagine farm animals as English rebels, attempting to reclaim their champion Chauntecleer, who seems to represent, illogically, their resistance against the crown's heavy taxation of the people. Given the earlier lament of the untimely death of King Richard I (1157–1199), however, the Nun's Priest reflects little hostility toward monarchical power (7.3347–52). Moreover, the reference to Jack Straw is far from sympathetic, even implying that the rebels acted like frenzied animals, which might suggest a critique of such fear mongering about the Flemish Other. On the other hand, we might consider David Wallace's somber observation: "It is the naturalized complacency of these lines that makes them so disturbing; their accommodating of targeted homicide within the familiar confines of classroom exercise or barnyard fable."[51] The notion that such a lighthearted tale of a rooster, a hen, and a fox could play host to xenophobic violence might challenge our very assumptions of the tale's capacity to entertain and to educate. I want to suggest that it is also a critique of disputational practice, which William of Ockham (d. 1347) complained was too often dominated by "barking dogs" who sought to tear apart "every view dissenting from their own dogmas."[52] Even the early culture of such disputational debate set the stage for the contrarian role of the online troll.

To some degree, the pursuit of the barking dogs diverts our attention away from the unique nature of the debate on dreams that occupies most of the tale. If we restrict our focus to the tumultuous conflict between a fox and a rooster, we risk ignoring an earlier moral to the tale: "*Mulier est hominis confusio*" (Woman is man's ruin) (7.3164). This message is easy to miss, not only because it is superseded by the flattery moral later in the fable, but also because it appears in Latin and is mistranslated by Chauntecleer as "Womman is mannes joye and al his blis" (7.3166). While this kind of counterfactual translation is evident in other Middle English lyrics, such as "Abuse of Women,"[53] the apparent mismatch between the sexism of the Latin and Chauntecleer's praise of women reflects the mismatch that has just taken place: an academic debate between a man and a woman. Chauntecleer and Pertelote have just concluded an argument about the

Disputation

significance of dreams, using the form and content of a disputation, which was often hostile to and not available to women.

Such masculinized disputations were akin to cockfights, as attested by the thirteenth-century University of Paris chancellor Haimeric de Vari, who describes disputants as engaged in avian combat: "One cock challenges another, its feathers bristling."[54] It is remarkable then that the Nun's Priest's disputation about the significance of dreams is performed between a man and a woman. Chauntecleer appears to win the debate, or at least he thinks so, despite Pertelote's learned arguments about herbal remedies and dream interpretation (7.3151–56). Nevertheless, he is persuaded by her "beautee" (7.3160) and her "softe syde" (7.3167) that he should ignore his fear about flying from the beams into the farmyard. Pertelote claims a short-lived victory until the fearsome fox appears, just as the dream had warned, prompting the Nun's Priest to insert his own misogynistic moral: "Wommanes conseil broghte us first to wo" (7.3257). This is a closer translation to Chauntecleer's earlier Latin lesson, "*Mulier est hominis confusio*," but the Nun's Priest hastily qualifies his interjection in three ways: first, by suggesting that this comment was only said in "game" (7.3262); second, by urging his audience to consult written authorities (7.3263); and third, by claiming that "Thise been the cokes wordes, and nat myne; / I kan noon harm of no womman divyne" (7.3265–66). Despite the ambiguity of "womman divyne," which can be read in a number of different ways, the Nun's Priest attempts to distance himself from this critique of women, using tactics common in disputation, role-playing both sides of the issue and calling attention to its status as an academic "game." We may wonder, then, if this is a progressive attempt to include women within such intellectual debates or if it is an instance of medieval mansplaining, men's attempts to explain women to women. The prominence of the disputational mode suggests that any educational import of the tale can only be accessed through dialogue, as playful, high-handed, or contentious as it may be. And if that learning cannot be had through dialectic, then how else might we access it?

Serious Play

When we consider the weighty implications for such ludic tale-telling, it becomes clear that playfulness and seriousness cannot be disconnected from one another. In examining the educational character of digital games, Adeline Koh goes even further, arguing that "play is not only not frivolous, but capable of producing serious intellectual work and an activity that possesses deep political power."[55] Games facilitate deep immersion within alternative universes, where players assume new identities and consider new points of view. Within medieval university life, disputation was itself an academic game, one that asked students to assume a side in an argument, but not necessarily a new personality, with all of its often messy, affective dimensions. If they wanted to imagine themselves in new roles, they could participate in community mystery plays or other forms of medieval drama, and while these performances were not closely connected to their classroom learning, they were more closely connected than we might think. Jody Enders notes, "There was a reason why learned dramatists paraded their knowledge of theology, scholastic argumentation, and civil and canon law in so many mystery plays, farces, miracles, and sotties . . . because the disputational structures of forensic rhetoric were compatible with the dialogic structure of drama."[56] Drama provides, perhaps, the most enchanting occasion for roleplay, but its origins in quodlibetal debate reflect its dedication to what I would call *serious play*.

Likewise, many of the literary texts that populated early classrooms, notably those of Aesop, Virgil, and Ovid, facilitated similar immersive experiences for students. For example, students were asked to read and respond to the *Heroides*, a series of intimate letters written from the points of view of mythical lovers, such as Paris and Helen, Hero and Leander, and Acontius and Cydippe. Ovid's letters provided a means for students to learn epistolary style, as well as immerse themselves in the ethical dilemmas of characters. The first-person point of view of these letters encourages readers to forget that Ovid wrote them. Consider *Heroides* 15, Sappho's letter to Phaon, which offers the following challenge to the reader: "Tell me, when you looked upon the characters from my eager right hand, did your eye know immediately whose name they were—or, unless you had read their author's name, Sappho, would you fail to know whence these brief words come?" (XV.1–4).[57] In addition to the linguistic-metrical joke of Sappho writing in Latin elegiacs instead of Greek lyric, Ovid calls attention to the game he is playing, chiding readers who misrecognize these verse epistles as the products of mythical women.

The power of these epistolary fictions is so compelling that it motivated G. P. Goold in 1976 to pronounce, "The malicious critic of the *Heroides* will be hard to find; for they belong to the engaging sort of art which disarms criticism."[58] Goold's reference to the absence of "the malicious critic" and the suggestion that the letter collection "disarms criticism" are a reaction to what Paul Ricoeur in the early 1970s called a "hermeneutics of suspicion," in which readers approached texts with the intent to reveal and critique their hidden or repressed ideologies.[59] Rita Felski claims that "what drives such a hermeneutic is the conviction that appearances are deceptive, that texts do not gracefully relinquish their meanings, that manifest content shrouds darker, more unpalatable truths."[60] Understood from this perspective, critique adopts the guise of detective work, in which readers are expected to find clues in the text that could ultimately reveal what lies hidden underneath. We often encourage this critical disposition, assuming that the most significant meanings in texts are "hidden" from view. And we certainly do this for good reason, since many ideologies and agendas are only revealed through close and critical reading. If we accept texts at face value, we would miss the locomotive-like power of rhetoric, ethics, and politics that energizes the textual worlds we inhabit.

There are some, such as Bruno Latour, who have even argued that critique seems to have somewhat "run out of steam."[61] That is, if we are constantly placing ourselves at some "critical distance" from the texts we read, are we ever able to accept readings on their own terms or fully experience their rhetorical power? As an alternative, Felski has offered the mode of enchantment, which "is characterized by a state of intense involvement, a sense of being so entirely caught up in an aesthetic object that nothing else seems to matter."[62] This is, after all, the kind of reading that most of us enjoy, in which we immerse ourselves fully within the environments that the texts create and revel in the pleasures of the imagination. But enchantment is a mode that we often discourage within the academy, since this enthralled state could lead to ignorant bliss and therefore to an uncritical acceptance of a text's ethics and politics. To question this opposition of critique and enchantment, it is helpful to confront the history of fan fiction, or fiction about existing storyworlds, as it has a seemingly unbounded reach within online networks.

Arthurian Fan Fiction

The implications for considering the "serious play" of disputation are deeply connected to the development of online fan fiction. First of all, it is important to clarify that fan fiction—in which fans insert, expand, or develop plots of their beloved characters within original pieces of fiction—was firmly established as a genre well before the advent of digital technology, when fans of popular media such as *Star Trek* produced and disseminated their written elaborations of the standard plotlines and relationships between characters through printed "zines."[63] Once fans began to migrate their communities to online environments, however, the scope and depth of their influence increased dramatically.

In the last two decades, fan fiction has become a rapidly expanding catalogue of texts, especially on the internet. The hotbed of activity located at FanFiction, one of the largest digital archive of fan texts, is also highly multilingual, containing stories in at least forty languages.[64] Online fan fiction has therefore proven to be particularly attractive to English Language Learners (ELLs), whose codeswitching is valued and encouraged.[65] As Rebecca Black has shown, ELLs, particularly those who identify as women, have utilized manga and anime fan fiction as a means to develop their English. In the case of the writer Black identifies as Grace, the production of the fan text "Heart Song," envisioned as part of the *Cardcaptor Sakura* manga series, requires the use of multilingual and interpersonal registers. Grace not only humbly advertises herself as "the Fastest/quickest and yet Poor english Writer from the Philippines," but also invites her audience to "R+R" (read and review), assuming that her readers would be capable of negotiating between English and Japanese.[66] Her linguistic transparency and editorial flexibility led to the creation of a fifteen-chapter text and a fifteen-chapter sequel demanded by a fan community who offered a staggering 1,569 reviews of her work over a five-year period.[67] The sheer volume of response, which proved to be productive for Grace, demonstrates that crowds can offer collective resources and motivations that individual experts or writing teachers cannot hope to match.

Given the productive possibilities of such serious play among fan communities, we should consider how this role-playing habitus developed in earlier, pre-digital cultures. In her study of canonical classroom texts in medieval manuscripts, Marjorie Curry Woods reveals how teachers prompted schoolboys to perform the voices of women, ranging from Dido to Andromache, even assuming the role of the cross-dressing Achilles, who pretends to be a girl to avoid going to war in Statius's *Achilleid*. Woods even goes so far as to suggest, "While women were overwhelmingly absent from this schoolboy classical world except in texts, their emotions permeated and sometimes dominated the classroom experience."[68] In the *accessus* to one manuscript that contains the *Achilleid*, the commentator explains that Statius's intention "is to describe in verse . . . how he [Achilles] hid on the island of Scyros in the court of Lycomedes in the *habitus* of a woman."[69] And once again, *habitus* refers to "habit" in two senses: physical clothing and corporeal action. Another commentator in another manuscript emphasizes this point by explaining that Achilles's mother Thetis gave him her dress to wear and then "instructed the unsophisticated boy in feminine movement and behaviour."[70] These manuscripts exhibit the traces of a role-playing pedagogy and reflect the performative habitus of the texts they host, which in turn offer teachers and students opportunities to assume new habits, inhabit new personae, and explore new plotlines.

While the Trojan War narratives comprise one expandable storyworld, I turn now to the myths of King Arthur, which have produced an endlessly accretive corpus of texts, ranging from Geoffrey of Monmouth's *History of the Kings of Britain* in the twelfth century to Kazuo Ishiguro's *The Buried Giant* in the twenty-first. One of the most entertaining, but unfortunately little read, Arthurian romances is the fifteenth-century Middle English poem *The Wedding of Sir Gawain and Dame Ragnelle*, which recounts a story familiar to those who know Geoffrey Chaucer's *Wife of Bath's Tale*, one of the most famous selections of his larger *Canterbury Tales*. The plot of each is almost the same. A knight finds himself in a bind from which he will only escape if he can answer the binary, essentialist, and implicitly sexist, question *What do women want?* The answer, according to both tales, is "sovereignty," or authority over their husbands and their property. Yet the way that each arrives at this answer is remarkably different, because the anonymous writer of the *Wedding* composed the version as an adaptation of the folktale that Chaucer's widely known tale made famous.[71]

For example, one of the most fascinating changes that the *Wedding* poet makes is the insertion of an ethnographic research project conducted by knights. One of Arthur's most loyal vassals, Sir Gawain, recommends that he and Arthur answer the question *What do women want?* by surveying the countryside like a couple of chivalric anthropologists. He says:

> Ye, Sir, make good chere;
> Lett make your hors redy
> To ryde into straunge contrey;
> And evere wheras ye mete owther man or woman, in faye,
> Ask of them whate they therto saye.
> And I shalle also ryde anoder waye
> And enquere of every man and woman, and get whatt I may
> Of every man and woman answere,
> And in a boke I shalle them wryte. (lines 182–90)[72]

Arthur immediately accepts this writing assignment and leaves Gawain to interrogate every "man, woman, and other" (197). After discovering that some women want clothes, while others desire the pursuit of lusty men, he reconvenes with Gawain to conduct a kind of medieval writing workshop.

> Syr Gawen had goten answerys so many
> That had made a boke greatt, wytterly;
> To the courte he cam agayn.

> By that was the kyng comyn withe hys boke,
> And eyther on others pamplett dyd loke. (207–11)

Their individual writing projects become a collaborative endeavor, in which they collate their pieces of writing to determine the best answer to the question. Given the tendency in Arthurian romance to emphasize deeds over words, this instance is striking in its depiction of knights who attempt to write their way out of a problem.

This scene forces us to consider Arthur and Gawain as not just knights, but knights who write. We must then ask: From which perspective did they compose their "books"? Did they write in the third person, the conventional mode of Arthurian literature? Or more intriguingly, did they write in first person, a perspective rarely employed in Arthurian narration? These questions are left unanswered in the poem itself, but the prospect of an Arthurian text written in the voice of an Arthurian character suggests a kind of affective invitation to write that is absent in most legends of its kind. Many works of literature have been produced as a response to previous texts, and Arthurian literature is no exception. The Arthurian canon was produced, and is continually being produced, as a revision or elaboration of a basic plot that revolves around the exploits of England's legendary king and his knights of the Round Table. Still, the mere fact of accretive reception does not make Arthurian literature one of the earliest and most long-standing examples of what we today call fan fiction. As Anna Wilson aptly cautions us, "To define fan fiction only by its transformative relationship to other texts runs the risk of missing the fan in fan fiction—the loving reader to whom fan fiction seeks to give pleasure."[73] To identify "fans" within the premodern era, we can point to figures such as Petrarch, who writes adoring letters to Cicero, or even Margery Kempe, who imagines herself at the scene of Christ's death, offering comfort to the Virgin Mary.[74] Within most Arthurian romances, such intimate connections are unmentioned or unavailable, but in the case of the *Wedding*, we are invited to imagine texts produced by Arthur and Gawain, texts that would give us insight into their writerly voices. While this poem may not be properly called fan fiction, it invites an affective and performative response.

What then is the value of assuming such a role-playing habitus, particularly within the context of writing studies? I would argue that we do not want to promote an uncritical fandom of writing, which suggests that texts should be objects of worship and praise. For me, the goal, in fact, is almost the opposite. I want readers to be critical (though not necessarily suspicious) of all texts, whether they are canonical or not. Fan fiction encourages this by asking readers to inhabit texts and write their way through conflicts that include (among others), racism and white supremacy, sexuality and desire, gender identity, and authorship and authority. Additionally, the use of social platforms to disseminate this work may create what digital-culture theorist James Gee calls an "affinity space," which allows for a variety of levels of interactions via posting and commenting through the anonymity of avatars.[75] Ultimately, the digital presence that fan fiction now demands encourages readers and writers to think within the text and write and rewrite the very texts they inhabit.

Enchantment and critique do not have to be polarized, but our disputational habits often suggest that they do. It certainly is true that deep forms of immersion may lead to undesirable states in which "nothing else seems to matter" and that ardent forms of critique may lead to paranoid reading. While many are more than willing to discourage enchantment, few would jettison critique. However, should we be promoting forms of critique that do not allow for any level of enchantment? Cristina Bruns suggests, in fact, that critical reading (what she calls "reflective" reading) is "meaningless" without "immersive" reading.[76] Affective avenues into the text often nurture connections that are impossible to establish within supposedly indifferent critical modes. Without these immersive relationships, readers cannot truly claim they know these texts and cannot ascertain a stable position on which they can offer meaningful critiques. While enchantment comes naturally for many readers, anonymous online role-playing creates a ludic environment that offers the indifferent writer a safe space for immersion and critique. I would propose, in fact, that such modes of critical enchantment are the most ethical of all. They demand that readers attend to all details of the textual world, indulging in its pleasures as well as identifying its problems. This combination of enchantment and critique is perhaps best expressed by another of Ovid's letter writers, Phaedra, who offers these words to Hippolytus, the object of her affection: "Read to the end, whatever is here contained—what shall reading of a letter harm? In this one, too, there may be something to pleasure you; in these characters of mine, secrets are borne over land and sea" (IV.3–5).[77]

Anonymity and Transparency

While a disputational habitus exhibits productive potential for inhabiting and critiquing texts, role-play is often anonymous, introducing the danger of trolls who flame writing with impunity. Over the last decade, the protections of anonymous peer review have begun to be challenged, both within the classroom and within academic publishing. In their "Becoming Media" issue, the journal *Postmedieval: A Journal of Medieval Cultural Studies* decided to replace the traditional double-anonymous peer review with an open, transparent, and online review process. Editors Jen Boyle and Martin Foys embrace the term "crowd review" to characterize this process: "The concept of the crowd to some might seem particularly inimical to academic institutions or professionalism. Crowds imply mobs. Crowds imply amateur opinion, cajoling, and yelling. But crowds also now connect with activities like 'crowd sourcing,' an open call for collaboration among a large group of informed participants interested in exploring, creating, or solving. And crowds also change things. The crowd potentially embodies an exciting challenge to the isolation and insularity of traditional academic organizations, as an opportunity to experiment with the re-structuring of professional and disciplinary affiliation."[78] Rather than submit to the pejorative connotation of a "mob mentality," the editors challenge the supremacy of "Reviewer Two," inviting everyone to read and comment upon essays that have been posted to a blog. The only requirement is that every commenter must divulge their identities to keep the process transparent; this undermines anonymity, an aspect of peer review that many hold sacrosanct.

Anonymous review often mitigates personal biases and licenses the reviewer to evaluate the work on its merits alone. Yet transparency, particularly online, has benefits that may at times outweigh the advantages of anonymity. This is not always the case. After all, as I have suggested above, digital avatars, or anonymous online identities, provide writers safe and empowering perspectives to express their opinions boldly. Fan fiction writers often assume the points of view of characters in course texts, consistently compose lively prose, engage in heated debates, and even push the limits of the genres they inhabit. Even more importantly, the inability to identify fellow commenters democratizes the rhetorical situation: the expertise or knowledge of the writer can only be determined within the dynamic experience of online dialectic. That is, the anonymous contributor, who may be anyone under the sun, challenges traditional notions of epistemological authority, which rely upon an a priori location of authority in a credentialed specialist. Just like blogs and editable websites, especially Wikipedia, crowdsourced anonymous review platforms value a posteriori expertise— only through collaborative production, verification, and approval does information become authoritative. Wikipedians do not care if you are a distinguished professor or a high school dropout. As I suggest in chapter 3, authority is produced and sanctioned through popular and extensive compilation and collaboration, not through academic pedigree.

Despite the democratizing benefits of online anonymity, a transparency problem can arise, particularly when the stakes are raised. For instance, if someone manipulates information online in favor of a particular political program without divulging their allegiances or their identity, it is difficult for subsequent responders to evaluate the core assumptions behind the material. This in turn leads to what can be a mindless consumption of digitally produced media. Henry Jenkins suggests that twenty-first-century students have become increasingly adept at manipulating information online but surprisingly inept at evaluating it.[79] Sherry Turkle, one of our most influential media theorists, attributes this pervasive ineptitude to a lack of transparency, which she claims encourages "people to get used to manipulating a system whose core assumptions they do not see and which may or may not be 'true.'"[80] When identities, convictions, and sources are made transparent online, information can be evaluated responsibly and used more effectively. Within the academic structures of peer review, this means that critiques that need clarification or justification can be negotiated between writer and reviewer. Moreover, divulging the identity of the reviewer will also, in most cases, reveal the research programs, particular agendas, and sometimes even certain schools of thought that inform the critiques. This information allows the writer to situate the reviewer's responses within a specific context that may be otherwise unavailable through anonymous review.

Open Peer Review

Advocates for open-access publishing have been working tirelessly to make scholarly work freely available online without most copyright and licensing restrictions, offering a vigorous response to the price barriers that limit the availability of scholarship to readers.[81] The scientific community, for some time now, has been publishing research findings through open-access platforms such as the Public Library of Science (PLoS) to share their work in a timely manner.[82] Humanities scholars have been slow to embrace such platforms, but humanities-focused open access now appears in a variety of venues from library consortia, such as the Open Library of Humanities, to scholarly journals, such as *Kairos* and *Digital Humanities Quarterly*, to independent presses, such as Open Humanities Press and punctum books.[83] All of these open-access formats reflect a simple, yet seemingly radical, ideal: *scholarly writing wants readers*. This ideal, however, has an uncomfortable by-product: *if scholarly work becomes more accessible to readers, the work becomes more vulnerable and its reception becomes more transparent.* Among the multiple implications for this vulnerability and transparency within the context of open access, I want to conclude this chapter by offering one way we might transform our entrenched disputational habits: open peer review on social annotation platforms.

Reading has almost always been a social act, but one of the central claims of this book is that reading hasn't been this social since the Middle Ages. But an important distinction must be made. Whereas the social nature of reading now is enhanced through ubiquity and accessibility, reading was social then because of scarcity and inaccessibility. Digital texts thrive on speed, scale, and access, offering multiple opportunities for encounters with readers. Medieval manuscripts and their readers were relatively scarce, raising the value and utility of the single book, which might be used by generations of commentators for anything from interpretations of Aesop's fables in the classroom to legal glosses on canon law. From these two very different contexts emerge an emphasis on commentary and annotation, which establish a text's value and use.

Unfortunately, the potential of this social culture of commentary is often squandered, especially within traditional methods of double-anonymous peer review. Kathleen Fitzpatrick and Martin Paul Eve, among others, have argued that open peer review (even in partially open formats) offers more benefits than double-anonymous peer review.[84] Their work and this history of disputational writing suggest that we should consider adopting open review for the following reasons:

Open review makes commentary more transparent. Open peer review is the equivalent of a Microsoft Word document that tracks changes, showing markup. Many medieval manuscripts and early printed books were produced in anticipation of this marked-up state, with complex textual apparatus, including space for interlineal glosses and marginalia. Within open review formats, the comments of writers and reviewers are made available to all, encouraging vigorous dialogue. For example, the Modern Language Association (MLA) Commons hosted an open review of the volume *Digital Pedagogy in the Humanities*, which uses a commentary platform that allows for discussion between reviewers and writers.[85] Such an open format allows writers to evaluate the feedback, as attested by open review experiments, such as the one hosted by *Postmedieval* mentioned above. Writers can assess feedback by asking themselves questions, such as, is this just one reviewer's perspective or is this critique shared by others? Perhaps most importantly, the transparency of open review reveals bias. If a reviewer's remarks are clearly prejudicial, the community of reviewers can help to identify it and correct it.

Open review enhances the utility and relevance of the commentary. Within open review platforms, reviewers are often self-selected, based on their investment and expertise, as opposed to responding to a request from an editor to review a manuscript (which may not reflect the reviewer's interests or expertise).

Open review allows for a larger number of reviewers. Rather than limit the task of review to a handful of reviewers, work shared in open review is crowdsourced and potentially subject to a large volume of commentary. The work of reviewing could then be distributed, making it less of a burden upon individual reviewers and enriching and enlarging the community invested in the work.

Open review treats writing as it always is: work-in-progress. We recognize that finished work is a myth, despite our emphasis on "products." Another experimental project, *The Open Access Companion to the Canterbury Tales*, refers to its first incarnation as a kind of Netflix-like "first season," recognizing that its value will be maintained or enhanced through accumulation and evolution.[86]

Open review maximizes the value, relevance, and impact of the work. We often change our minds, especially after encountering persuasive critiques of our work. Open review formats could therefore continue "post-print," making book reviews more significant and useful. The book review process would become more dynamic—authors (and other reviewers) could respond to and correct outrageous or uninformed claims in reviews.

All of this suggests that we should be moving toward open review practices and publicly accessible review platforms, but given the precarious positions of many writers and publishers, we should proceed with caution. Anonymous forms of review, after all, have often allowed work to stand on its own and protected scholars from bias and career-damaging critiques. Keeping in mind Kathleen Fitzpatrick and Avi Santo's important call for "structured flexibility" in developing protocols and tools for open review,[87] I offer the following recommendations:

Make comments publicly available, even within double-anonymous formats. Whereas anonymity often protects the identities of reviewers who might be given little consideration because of their status, there is little benefit from keeping commentary hidden, especially on open-access platforms. While the redaction of comments keeps some critiques out of the hands of tenure review committees, such transparency would allow the larger scholarly community to redress critiques that are useless, unfair, or biased. Even within such an open platform, however, editors would need to moderate commentary, especially to prevent trolling, spamming, and harassment. If editors want to limit the feedback the authors receive, they could open the comments only to selected reviewers, which could provide a forum for reconciling confusing or contradictory feedback, before the responses are sent to the authors.

Adopt single-anonymous formats, in which the author remains anonymous and the names of reviewers are divulged. This kind of limited open review maintains transparency during the review process, while at the same time mitigating the possible embarrassment or damage to the promotion of a scholar whose work results in public rejection. Many publishers already use a limited form of single-anonymous review, revealing the name of the author to two or three reviewers only known by the editor. This format protects the reviewers, which can be beneficial for junior or less established scholars who want their reviews to be taken seriously, but it also licenses reviewers to pursue critiques they may not be willing to stand behind. By contrast, an open review platform that reveals the names of reviewers to the public would encourage responsible critiques and provide valuable contexts, such as a reviewer's scholarly perspectives or preferences, for feedback that would otherwise be unavailable to authors.

Establish multistage processes that combine anonymous and open review formats. Even within double-anonymous review, established authors are often identifiable because of their reputations for particular kinds of scholarship or areas of expertise. For such known quantities, even the most transparent forms of open review may be appropriate. New scholars to a field, however, may benefit from multistage processes, in which their work is subject first to anonymous review before being deemed "publishable" and then vetted through open review. The open-access journal *Kairos* pays special attention to what its editors Douglas Eyman and Cheryl Ball call the "social infrastructure of digital scholarship," which refers to the "multitiered" and "partially open" peer review procedures, which include both closed editoral review and open collaborative peer review.[88] These hybridized formats would be especially appropriate for well-established journals and presses who already have active and vigorous scholarly communities who are seeking to make their work more available to the public at large.

Create spaces for "post-publication" open review. Many medieval manuscripts survive marked and mediated by the hands of multiple marginal commentators, creating a readerly trail that medievalists follow to track the way the work has been received over time. Today, our book reviews are too often limited to the views of individual scholars, who may not be invested in the work they are reviewing. Post-publication book or article review spaces would open up and crowdsource the reception of the work, providing opportunities for authors to respond to feedback from multiple interested reviewers and make important revisions to their publications.

It is important to stress that open-access publishing, even in its most liberal forms, does not require open review—double-anonymous processes can continue unabated. Open-access publishers who continue to use anonymous review will not undermine their efforts to make scholarly work *accessible*. However, those publishers will not fully succeed in making this work *open* or suitable for challenging the limits of our disputational habitus. The democratic potential and ethic of openness is not fully realized without open review, which would provide opportunities for scholarly dialogue and critique throughout the writing process and beyond. The quality, range, and significance of work could be greatly enhanced, offering a distributed network of invested writers and reviewers, rather than small cohorts of experts and exclusive publishing priesthoods.

We might assume that we have long since shed the binary habitus of medieval disputation, but everything from our debate pedagogy to our political parties to our reviewing practices remain firmly lodged within this dialogic structure. Even early Enlightenment thinkers like John Locke glorified their notions of the autonomous rational individual by condemning this disputational habit as form of "artificial ignorance, and learned gibberish [that] prevailed mightily in these last ages, by the interest and artifice of those who found no easier way to that pitch of authority and dominion they have attained, than by amusing the men of business, and ignorant, with hard words, or employing the ingenious and idle in intricate disputes about unintelligible terms, and holding them perpetually entangled in that endless labyrinth."[89] Locke instead attributes governmental security and freedom to individual statesmen who broke away from the oppression of these scholastic practices. As Novikoff points out, however, "Locke seriously underestimated his own indebtedness to scholastic learning. . . . He assumed that the form and content of scholastic learning did not, and could not, affect the world beyond the academic arena. Over time, the notion of breaking free from the constraints of idle medieval debates has only been reinforced by modern scholars who insist on rupture with the scholastic past when continuity, change, and reform might equally be stressed."[90] In the succeeding centuries, we have witnessed little divergence from this disputational disposition, which has left its mark on all aspects of public life, especially political conversation, from the "both-sides" rhetoric of reproductive rights to the ubiquity of counterprotests.[91] Attempts to democratize dialogue even further and to expand conversations to multiple contributors have also faced resistance, particularly from academic circles reluctant to jettison their principles of exclusion. In his address before the Concord Lyceum in April 1838, Henry Thoreau complained that "the mass never comes up to the standard of its best member, but on the contrary degrades itself to a level with the lowest."[92] Most would agree that mobs, particularly the kinds that incite violent riots, indeed degrade their participants, warranting Thoreau's pessimism. Within the aftermath of the 2020 US presidential election, which was disrupted and contested by insurgent collectives, it is difficult not to agree with Thoreau. Networks can develop a political sovereignty that can systematically oppress the most vulnerable, even in the name of "democratic" protocols that claim to value the contributions of all, no matter their race, sex, or class.

On the other hand, serious forms of disputational play, such as fable writing and Arthurian fiction, reveal that the creative additions to existing dialogues offer opportunities for crowds of readers to exceed "the standard of [their] best member[s]." What makes many of these knowledge-producing networks so powerful and pervasive is that they do not insist on individual genius or even equal contribution. As Clay Shirky suggests in *Cognitive Surplus*, crowdsourcing on sites like Wikipedia succeeds because

> *Wikipedia* offers potential participants the ability to do as much writing or editing as they like, but also as little. If you fix a typo and never do anything on *Wikipedia* again, that still has more value than if you hadn't fixed it. *Wikipedia* makes it as easy as possible to effect these small changes, not even making users set up an account before they start editing. This low threshold of participation invites the accumulation of the smallest units of value—no one would create an account just to fix a single typo. By making the size of the smallest contribution very small, and by making the threshold for making that change small as well, *Wikipedia* maximizes contributions across an enormous range of participation.[93]

By making contributions as labor intensive as the contributor desires, collaborative work becomes less a matter of community obligation and more a matter of investment by an enthusiastic subject. This means that the "imbalance" of effort inherent to group work—that some participants will do more work than others—is not a problem for the work itself. This inequity becomes an obstacle, however, when we assess individual contribution, which is difficult, if not impossible, when contributions are completely anonymous. Transparency, on the other hand, adds an element of disputational responsibility to collaborative work, which is especially productive within high-stakes modes such as peer review. If contributions can be tracked to their contributors, reviewers must carefully consider the delicate nature of sharing and responding to scholarly work. More importantly, when review becomes the responsibility of a crowd of identifiable participants, the value of the collective response can greatly exceed the sum of its parts.

As this chapter suggests, the legacy of medieval disputation arises prominently within the structures of peer review, which depend upon the good faith and goodwill of scholarly and artistic communities. Such a system is set within the dialectical tension between anonymity and transparency that pervades all forms of digital delivery. While both playful and serious forms of anonymity may welcome an entirely new demographic of peer producers, they also perpetuate the infuriated networks that exploit the generosity of crowdsourcing and the reliability of information disseminated online. This exploitation relies upon one of the most persistent and insidious strains of medieval disputational rhetoric: the fantasy of two sides to any question or controversy. Such a rigid understanding of dialogue assumes the guise of objectivity, all the while obscuring the imbalances of power between the positions and the relationship of each side to a set of facts. This reduction of dialogue to two perspectives has grave political and moral consequences, as exhibited by Donald Trump's claim that there were "some very fine people on both sides" when referring to the deadly conflict between white supremacists and anti-racist protestors in Charlottesville, Virginia, on August 12, 2017.[94] As digital writing platforms continue to gain knowledge-making capital through increasingly swift and sweeping modes of circulation, this history of disputation challenges all of us to resist this rigid myth of disputational equality and to evaluate the responsible balance between anonymous creation and transparent reception.

5 | Amplification

Inhabiting and Annotating the Page

> And so, from a little water, much water arises.
> —**Geoffrey of Vinsauf,** *Documentum de modo et arte dictandi et versificandi* (Instruction in the method and art of composing in prose and in verse)

> Habit is a form of accumulation of memory and repetition in the body. Where memory represents and imagines the past, habit acts and repeats it.
> —**Elizabeth Grosz,** "Habit Today"

"Going viral" is a rhetorical phenomenon that seems impossible without the circulating capital of digital image- and video-sharing platforms such as YouTube, TikTok, and Instagram. Viral memes—ranging from Bernie Mittens to Obama Hope to Grumpy Cat—obtain their prominence and cultural capital through their capacity to be amplified by small additions, such as new captions and image edits. These rhetorical accretions impact their audiences because they build upon common templates that can easily be recognized as a common platform for accumulating meaning. Increasingly, scholars of rhetorical circulation have turned to the rapid and massive distributive and reproductive capital of digital platforms to demonstrate the ways in which tweets can become amplified and realities can become augmented. After all, digital media have played an enormous role in shaping the habitus of information sharing. When, for example, a 2017 study reveals a 62.7 percent increase in public commentary about issues that are covered by news outlets, we naturally focus on the quantitative power and influence of the news media itself.[1] As Whitney Phillips puts it, "What journalists report, people discuss; civic discourse gets its shape from the news."[2] Algorithms capture each click on a news story, accelerating the speed and expanding the scale of the coverage that could have never been achieved before the advent of digital media.

While the common tendency is to quantify the extent of the infoglut or the scale of its reach, often the ways in which the quality or character of the circulated objects are expanded or intensified are not adequately defined. A remix of a meme, such as Obama Hope, gains its power from the accumulation of its interpretative layers—it builds upon the pervasiveness and authority, or the medieval *auctoritas*, of Shepard Fairey's Obama Hope image, which in turn gained its power from its use of the framing and posture of Jim Fitzpatrick's Che Guevara poster.[3] The more recognizable the meme, the greater its amplificatory and viral authority, or its capacity to be augmented by future authors (*auctores*). While such viral circulation relies on the alacrity and efficiency of graphic design software, computer servers, and social media platforms, one important rhetorical foundation for this compositional framework can be found in the teaching of *amplificatio* (amplification) within twelfth- and thirteenth-century writing instruction throughout Europe. University teachers of writing from Geoffrey of Vinsauf to John of Garland composed textbooks that included extensive treatments of methods of amplification, ranging from comparison to digression to exclamation. And while these techniques were largely focused on strategies for expanding a composition, especially letters, they also reflected a larger textual culture of accumulation, which was both habitual and material, encouraging interpretative multiplicity within books that accommodated amplification through varying sizes of script and page layouts with wide margins for annotation.

Glossing a text has long been a habit to be encouraged because it activates engagement and fosters dialogue, but printed margins are often thin and inhospitable to multiple future annotators. Web templates often foster the illusion that the online spaces for expansion are limitless, but these platforms are run on physical servers that become saturated with data in the same ways that medieval manuscripts became overwhelmed with marginalia and commentary. This chapter confronts the problem of space for rhetorical circulation by detailing its history within preprinted contexts, which reveals the pressing imperative to reshape a disposition, what I call an *amplificatory habitus*, for developing writable spaces on the digital page. The spatial stakes for circulation are many, but I will limit my analysis to one: the need to design interfaces that accommodate opportunities for users to amplify writing on the digital page, which in turn will open up, rather than close down, interpretative possibilities of circulated content.

Medieval Amplification

The salience of premodern amplification could be easily revealed within the commentary traditions of a number of theological texts, such as the *Glossa Ordinaria*, or legal books, such as the *Decretum*, but some of the most powerful examples for our purposes are the medieval classroom manuscripts that contain beast fables.[4] As discussed in chapter 4, students and teachers would adapt fable narratives and append extensive commentaries to fables in their manuscripts; these commentaries regularly occupied more space on the page then the fables themselves. In her groundbreaking study of nonhuman animal rhetoric, Debra Hawhee summarizes their expansive adaptability this way: "Because fables provide a bare scenario, without reference to a specific time other than at one point in the past (the genre of fables is often marked by the term 'once'), they are more customizable . . . leaving the audience members to work it out for themselves."[5] Within medieval rhetorical manuals, such fabular adaptability offers opportunities for textual amplification, exemplified by the well-known "Crow and the Water Jar" fable, in which a crow drops pebbles in a jar to make the water rise and enable the crow to drink. In teaching amplificatio, the medieval rhetorician Geoffrey of Vinsauf (fl. 1200) encourages his students to pile up words and phrases like this crow: "And so, from a little water, much water arises."[6] While this aqueous model of knowledge accumulation actively encourages readerly additions, each classroom manuscript had a saturation point, in which the accommodation of commentary caused the page to become flooded with annotation.

To comprehend the importance of rhetorical amplification for university instruction from the later European Middle Ages until our modern age, we should begin with the works of Geoffery of Vinsauf, arguably the most influential rhetorician after Quintillian and before Petrarch. In addition to writing an elementary composition textbook and some short poems, Geoffrey composed two important rhetorical manuals, the *Documentum de modo et arte dictandi et versificandi* (Instruction in the method and art of composing in prose and in verse) and the *Poetria nova* (*The New Poetics*). Only five copies of the *Documentum* remain, but the *Poetria nova* survives in over two hundred manuscripts, a massive number for a medieval text.[7] Many rhetorical treatises included sections on amplification, but Geoffrey's *Poetria nova* is one of the most cited and imitated. He begins his section on amplification with the following sumptuary metaphor to describe the technique of repetition (*repetitio*): "If you choose an amplified form, proceed first of all with this step: although the meaning is one, let it not come content with one set of apparel. Let it vary its robes and assume different raiment. Let it take up again in other words what has already been said; let it reiterate, in a number of clauses, a single thought. Let one and the same thing be concealed under multiple forms—be varied and yet the same."[8] With its emphasis on one meaning represented by one body ornamented with an assortment of clothes (or habits), such a statement appears to limit the transformative or interpretative potential of amplification. Yet Geoffrey's understanding of "the same thing concealed under multiple forms" refers more to the sameness of the object being amplified, in his case a word, than to the singularity of meaning. To demonstrate the productive potential of amplification, he proceeds to describe seven other techniques for expansion: circumlocution, comparison, exclamation, personification, digression, description, and opposition (lines 226–689). It is also no accident that this section on amplification is itself amplified—Geoffrey models each technique as he describes it, even abbreviating the subsequent section on "Abbreviation" (690–736). Geoffrey is so committed to practicing what he preaches that he even composes his entire poetics manual in hexameter verse.

The *Poetria nova* is structured according to the five classical canons of rhetoric (invention, arrangement, style, memory, and delivery) and the discussion of amplification appears, perhaps surprisingly, within arrangement (what we might call "design"), which addresses methods of ordering a composition from beginning to middle to end. Amplification is offered as a method for elaborating the "middle" or "body" of a work, but its techniques are also directly applicable to the following section on the canon of style, especially techniques of ornamentation (lines 765–1,587). Yet, as Geoffrey's *Poetria nova* was studied over the following centuries, future writing manuals began to resituate amplification within the canon of invention, which addresses methods for the selection and creation of subject matter. For example, John of Garland—an Englishman who studied at Oxford shortly after the *Poetria nova* was likely written and copied—associates amplification directly with invention in his *Parisiana poetria* (*Parisian Poetics*), a writing manual he composed around 1231–35 for his students at the University of Paris. In the beginning of the section "De Arte Inueniendi Materiam" (A way of inventing subject matter), he writes,

> Here is a device that is useful in certain kinds of writing; students particularly who aim to amplify and vary their subject matter may observe it.... Thus, suppose one of them is treating of his book. He might praise it or criticize it through the efficient cause, that is, through the writer; through the material cause, that is, through the parchment or the ink; through the

formal cause, as through the layout of the book or the size of the letters; or through the final cause, by considering for what purpose the book was made, namely, that in it and through it the ignorant may be made more knowledgeable.[9]

The references to "causes" are part of the pedagogical language of what Alastair Minnis calls the conventional "Aristotelian prologue" for introducing academic texts to readers. Whereas these causes were usually explained to identify the author of the text (efficient cause), the author's source material (material cause), the generic structure of the text (formal cause), and the purpose for the text (final cause), John of Garland interprets these causes as opportunities for invention, suggesting that writers are encouraged to create new compositions by amplifying previous texts.[10] Furthermore, John of Garland expands his treatment of the causes to include design concerns: the "material cause," usually understood to be the source text, refers to actual material objects, parchment and ink, that will be used to write the new text; and the "formal cause," usually understand to be the literary form or rhetorical arrangement, refers to the layout of the text on the page, including the size of the script. This attention to the material affordances and constraints of amplification are reflected within the changing interfaces of the manuscript page, which set aside space in the margins and between lines for readers to amplify texts through written commentary. And while these considerations are largely visual in nature, the size of the letters on the page also point to the manuscript's oral delivery, another anticipated and primary form of the text's circulation.

Amplification on the Page

Within the habitus of our late print culture, viral amplification is somewhat limited because print relies upon the centralized distribution and circulation of discrete and replicated objects—book and newspaper editors decide which material to print, how it will be printed, and how many copies will be distributed. Scholars of visual rhetoric such as Kevin DeLuca, Joe Wilferth, and Bradford Vivian have argued that we should relinquish our print-based methods and attend to the distracted and emergent nature of images, which are difficult to limit to particular contexts such as printed pages.[11] Laurie Gries has further suggested that, within our current culture of viral circulation, "the rhetorical force, circulatory range, and dynamic transformation of images only intensify," and she calls for attention "to the ways things are composed, produced, distributed, and transformed as well as the ways they induce assemblage, spark collective action, and catalyze change that registers on affective and rhetorical dimensions."[12] The visual character of circulation has appropriately intensified interest in multimodality, encouraging writers, in the manner of John of Garland, to consider modes for composition beyond the alphabetic, attending especially to digital design and its accommodation of audiovisual elements.

As many scholars of rhetoric have pointed out, the printed page has always been multimodal, accommodating varying verbal and nonverbal elements from illustration to punctuation.[13] It is the mass reproduction and conventionalization of its layout, its accepted fonts, and its thin margins that have given writing its pride of place on the printed page. In Sigrid Norris's terms, writing carries a high "modal intensity" on the printed page—it serves as the primary mode of meaning-making, carries the majority of the semiotic weight, commands attention, and structures interaction with other modes.[14] We can recognize the varying levels of intensity of many other nonverbal modes across printed pages in books or student essays but the vast majority of printed pages we encounter are dominated by writing. In fact, the extreme degree of the modal intensity of alphabetic text has led to the mistaken characterization of print culture as "monomodal," as if nonalphabetic ways of making meaning on the page have disappeared from view.

To punctuate the egregiousness of this error, John Trimbur and Karen Press go so far as to argue that "print culture is as thoroughly multimodal in its practices of text production as the present digital age, though in different ways, with different effects, accomplished by different means."[15] While Trimbur and Press helpfully recognize the limits and fallacies of using the term *multimodal* to characterize conceptual differences of communication over time, their argument does not account for what Norris would call "modal complexity," or the level of intricacy of the relationships between multiple modes.[16] As Bruce Horner forcefully argues, the usefulness of multimodality as a frame for analysis is extremely limited if it is reduced to the counting of modes within a given communicative event.[17] By calling a page multimodal, then, I am not referring to the fact that on any given page we can count "more-than-one" mode. Instead, I follow Gunther Kress's sense of modes as those socially constructed and materially available resources for making meaning through space and time.[18] Modes are neither fully isolatable from one another nor fully reducible to one another. In analysis, then, I prefer not to count modes—as if that were possible—but instead to think about the waxing and waning complexity of the interrelations among ways of representing meaning. Here, I focus on those interrelations as they appear on the page—a culturally available space for representing meaning and shaping human textual attention and developing what I have been calling *habitual rhetoric*.

Within editable web templates, for example, this modal complexity is often extremely acute, offering multiple modes of interaction through sound files, video illustration, and even space for readerly annotation. And while some printed contexts exhibit such high levels of modal intensity, I want to suggest that the page has not been as multimodally complex since the Middle Ages, before the age of mass-produced, printed book.

Prior to the advent of the printing press, the page—the medieval manuscript page—was often complexly multimodal, containing elaborate scripts, rubrications, and illuminations; the medieval page was a multimedia experience for its community of readers, viewers, and listeners.[19] Both writing and the page are and always were visual: rendered in multicolored acrostics, historiated initials, and varying sizes of script.[20] The knowledge of this history compels us to orient our reading and writing practices newly to the page, particularly its design elements: not just images and text, but the entire mise-en-page, the layout, the arrangement, and the spaces for annotation and interaction. In our "postprinted" era, digital texts—particularly within development of Web 2.0 writing technologies—have reinvigorated our attention to the page as a site of multimodality.[21] In terms of modal complexity, the digital page is multimodal in ways the printed page cannot be: in its speed and scale of activity, coordination of audio, moving image, and responsive design. But what comparing these two historical moments shows even more clearly is that the page is now a place that enables forms of textual activity both new and old: clicking, scrolling, reading, embedding, interacting, commenting, annotating.

For Johanna Drucker, this recognition of digital page design as a visual and dynamic form of knowledge production means that "we face the challenge of reading interface as an object and of understanding it as a space that constitutes reading as an activity."[22] Just as medieval scribes, rubricators, and illuminators designed the page with future glossators and commentators in mind, digital composers must consider page designs as interfaces that both facilitate the elegant reading of their alphabetic text and invite the interactions of future readers. We must then consider carefully the visual, spatial, and aural dimensions of the page as a multimodal interface. This chapter outlines both the history and argument for the amplifiable page as both a visual image and a space for writerly activity.

Amplification on the Preprinted Page

As Alberto Manguel cleverly puts it, "Like a skeleton supporting the skin of the text, the page disappears in its very function, and in that unprepossessing nature lies its strength."[23] In the midst of flipping through the average printed book, magazine, or student essay, it is often easy to forget about the page, which has become such a default habitation for reading that we rarely stop to notice its features. It is only when we encounter an awkward or unconventional page layout that we awaken to what Manguel calls "the page's tyranny," or the visual limitations of textual display, which dictate every presentational feature from the size of the font to the spaces for margins.[24] By allowing for bottomless "pages," expandable text, and hypertext navigation, digital environments promise to free us from this oppression, but it only takes a few clicks to arrive at a website that is nearly unnavigable in its labyrinthine architecture. To resolve this problem of eye scatter, graphic-user-interface designers create text columns that are approximately thirty characters in width, thereby maximizing readability and minimizing scrolling.[25] The effect of this design habitus is not only a remediation of the printed newspaper, which has always used columns for efficiency and space, but also a return to the page before print, or more specifically, a return to the *pagina*.

The *pagina* was not a page, but rather an eight to twelve-centimeter-wide block of writing on a papyrus scroll, which was designed to be read aloud from top to bottom as it was unrolled. Once the codex book arrived on the scene in the first century CE, the *pagina* became a feature of the page, retaining its lanky shape, but often in duplicate form, as two columns side by side.[26] Because the codex freed the hand that had been previously occupied to hold the scroll, allowing it to turn the discrete leaves of the book, these folios eventually absorbed the *paginae* they hosted, becoming what we now definitively call "pages."[27] The emancipated hand also had the luxury to assume a new, and what would become a basic, amplificatory habit, "glossing" or inscribing annotations between lines or into the margins of the page, a phenomenon that in the twelfth century led to a further innovation of the placement and size of columns, which varied according to space reserved for readerly commentary.

Malcolm Parkes has suggested that this development introduced a design challenge that compelled medieval authors and commentators to create an organization of subject matter (*ordinatio*) on the page that would make the books easier to consult, read, and annotate. This was often accomplished through the precise placement of rubrics, red-lettered or underlined words or phrases that would offer guidance to the reader seeking chapter titles, source citations, or even particular parts of an argument.[28] For Ivan Illich, this development means that "the visual page is no longer the record of speech but the visual representation of a thought-through argument."[29] Through this transformation, the page becomes more than a script for oral performance—it becomes a visual object that absorbs the text as merely one aspect of its pictorial repertoire. For the medieval commentator Peter Lombard, this reorientation of text as image enhances the usability of his work, so that "for him who searches it will not be necessary to turn through numerous volumes because the brevity offers him, without toil, what he is after."[30] By attracting the eye to particular colors and other visual markers, Lombard crafts his page as a graphical user interface that both amplifies its multimodality and abbreviates the labor and time required to consult it and comprehend its arguments.

In addition to enhancing the visuality of writing, medieval manuscripts were often produced with the anticipation of readerly interventions and additions. This orientation to the future of the book resulted in page layouts that either included wide margins for the insertion of annotations or even large sections of the page left vacant for extensive commentary. These pages then became spaces for potential accretion, designed for the use of additional text creators, who could then make their mark on the page and recirculate the page to yet other readers, who could continue to add text until all available spaces were filled. This attention to the delivery of the page is what Jim Ridolfo and Dànielle Nicole DeVoss call "rhetorical velocity," defined as "the strategic theorizing for how a text might be recomposed (and *why* it might be recomposed) by third parties, and how this recomposing may be useful or not to the short- or long-term rhetorical objectives of the rhetorician."[31] While Ridolfo and DeVoss are primarily describing the digital forms of delivery that consider the future appropriation, remix, and redistribution of material online, this design habit pervaded pre-printed environments such as the manuscript page, which situated columns of text strategically to enhance readability and encourage future additions, such as diagrams, translations, and especially commentary.

Aesopic Amplification

To demonstrate the circulatory power of rhetorical amplifications within pre-digital environments, I turn to Aesop's fables as they appear within fourteenth- and fifteenth-century manuscripts and early printed books. The classroom of the Middle Ages was defined by a method of call and response in which students were in constant dialogue with the schoolmaster over matters of grammar, style, and interpretation. Because of the scarcity of books in the Middle Ages, students and teachers worked from common codices inscribed with marginalia that had been accumulating over time. The schoolbooks that survive from this era are so excessively overrun with glosses that it is often difficult to distinguish the texts from their commentaries. As noted earlier, the primary text for such scholastic exercises was the beast fable, which contained moral and allegorical lessons that pupils were charged to decipher, absorb, and rewrite in their own compositions. Much like their corollaries of texting, tweeting, and tagging, the marginalia, manicules, and glosses that accompany these fables in their extant manuscripts required the reader to assume a participatory role in the production, authorization, and collection of knowledge.

After the twelfth century, the fable series known as the elegiac *Romulus* (also attributed to one "Walter of England") became the canonical "Aesop," which students and their teachers paraphrased and amplified through extensive glosses that accumulated in manuscripts and early printed books. The elegiac *Romulus* was comprised of sixty verse fables that survive in at least 170 manuscripts and fifty printed editions published in five countries by the end of the fifteenth century.[32] Because of the popularity of these fables, the writing spaces that housed medieval Aesopica became editable platforms, in which written corpora would be compiled, rearranged, and reinterpreted, stretching the limits of what we now call "fair use" and challenging later ideologies of "intellectual property." This fabular appropriation is epitomized by a figure discussed in chapter 4, the fifteenth-century Scottish schoolmaster Robert Henryson who composed one of the earliest and most influential fable collections known as the *Morall Fabillis*. Henryson demonstrates that the production of the Aesopic corpus during the Middle Ages depends upon its status as an open resource with which writers and readers intimately interact, actively revising and expanding fable collections and blurring the boundaries between the text and its critics. Yet, when we think of Aesop's fables, we think of brief, conventionalized proverbs, not expanding, divergent commentaries. Perhaps no literary genre satisfies the literary appetite for brevity more fully than fables, which are accompanied by concise morals that readers can readily devour. The popularity of this literary diet has resulted in an immensely expandable market for tales of speaking animals, in which spider-adoring pigs and bus-driving pigeons are served up for the delight and education of all, especially young children. At the same time that the tales themselves have become reproduced in new guises, their interpretations have become increasingly standardized. How did this happen?

As a familiar example of the fabular moral, I turn to the gustatory tale, "The City Mouse and the Country Mouse." Here is one version of this popular fable:

> A city mouse once happened to pay a visit to the house of a country mouse where he was served a humble meal of acorns. The city mouse finished his business in the country and by means of insistent invitations he persuaded

the country mouse to come pay him a visit. The city mouse then brought the country mouse into a room that was overflowing with food. As they were feasting on various delicacies, a butler opened the door. The city mouse quickly concealed himself in a familiar mouse hole, but the poor country mouse was not acquainted with the house and frantically scurried around the floorboards, frightened out of his wits. When the butler had taken what he needed, he closed the door behind him. The city mouse then urged the country mouse to sit back down to dinner. The country mouse refused and said, "How could I possibly do that? Oh, how scared I am! Do you think that the man is going to come back?" This was all that the terrified mouse was able to say. The city mouse insisted, "My dear fellow, you could never find such delicious food as this anywhere else in the world." "Acorns are enough for me," the country mouse maintained, "so long as I am secure in my freedom!" *It is better to live in self-sufficient poverty than to be tormented by the worries of wealth.*[33]

We are provided a simple and seemingly straightforward message, an acorn of a lesson we can take away from the story and easily consume. In fact, it is often difficult to blame a hungry reader for devouring such an instantly satisfying interpretation that follows the efferent precepts of moralistic fable reading. We are familiar with the pervasive sentiment that there is something tangible to be obtained from reading and that it is often one thing, often practical and often simplistic. Fables fulfill, it seems, some readers' greatest fantasy: a brief, easily understandable interpretation.

If we examine the early history of Aesop's fables, however, we discover not only that there is no single set of interpretations for each fable, but also that there is no single set of fables themselves. No original Greek Aesop has ever been identified. Instead, his status as the "author" was fashioned in Latin by a number of ancient and medieval translators known as Phaedrus, Avianus, and Romulus, who individually invoked Aesop as a means to "authorize" their versions.[34] The students and teachers of the Middle Ages—who effectively canonized Aesop as the author of these beast fables—only knew them in their later Latin forms. Furthermore, the manuscripts that contain the fables demonstrate little preference for one set of fables over the other. For example, one fourteenth-century Austrian manuscript, Codex Vindobonensis Palatinus 303, is a veritable cornucopia of Aesopica, containing six different versions, and one set, known as the prose *Romulus*, even appears twice.[35] The first time the prose *Romulus* fables appear, they appear as promythia, or prefaces to the metrical elegiac *Romulus*.[36] Given their appearance later in the manuscript, it is likely that these promythia were written by students in an attempt to demonstrate their knowledge of the fable tradition, which would require that they know the variations of each fable. As Willene Clark notes, it was common pedagogical practice after the twelfth century for pupils to produce paraphrases and imitations of texts in order to learn grammatical rules, identify rhetorical tropes, and improve their writing fluency. In response to fables, students would often compose promythia, prose introductions, or epimythia, prose conclusions that served as *moralitates* or "morals."[37]

Of course, the fact that this was common practice does not assure us that the promythia in Codex Vindobonensis Palatinus 303 were written by a student, but a comparison of the two sets of prose *Romulus* fables further suggests that a novice—whose knowledge of the tradition was incomplete—produced the first series. For example, if we turn to the promythium for "De lupo et agno" (The wolf and the lamb), we find both a repetition and an omission indicative of a tentative understanding of the standard fable. The writer repeats the phrase "the wolf was drinking upstream" (fol. 13r) and then omits the final summative line "this fable is written about those who falsely accuse others" that appears at the end of the later prose Romulan fable (fol. 132r).[38] Furthermore, the error-ridden promythia are accompanied by numerous marginal glosses, which suggest moments of teacherly intervention. This is just one example, but this kind of redundancy becomes the rule, rather than the exception.

If we follow these fables into the early print era, we see that the earliest printed book of fables, compiled by Heinrich Steinhöwel and printed by Johann Zainer at Ulm in 1476 or 1477, contains not only the curricular versions of Romulus and Avianus, but also selections of the popular fables of Rinuccio d'Arezzo, Petrus Alphonsus, and Poggio Bracciolini.[39] In a later, probably 1481, printing by Heinrich Knoblochtzer in Strasbourg, the elegiac *Romulus* is also followed by prose summaries that are reminiscent of the epimythia of the medieval classroom.[40] By 1501, Steinhöwel's collection had been expanded to three hundred fables by the famous schoolmaster Sebastian Brant.[41] The encyclopedic compilation of fables had clearly become the norm by the late fifteenth century, but this emphasis on accretion, over condensation, would soon come to an end as printers became increasingly selective in their choice of texts.

The death knell may have been sounded even earlier with the first publication of Steinhöwel's collection, which included German translations of the Latin fables. This edition, which only survives in ten copies, proved to be the only bilingual one. After its publication, the collection was split into two separate editions, one German and one Latin.[42] The intervention of the vernacular seems to have begun the canonization of Steinhöwel's version, because many other national languages followed suit. Julien Macho's translation of Steinhöwel's collection into French, which appeared in print in 1480 in Lyon, in turn served as William Caxton's base text for his English *Aesop*, which was published in 1484.[43] By 1485, a Dutch translation was printed in Gouda, and by 1488 a Spanish translation was printed in Toulouse.[44] The fate of Aesop was now in the hands of printers, who vernacularized and popularized the predominantly Latin curricular fables such as the elegiac *Romulus*, which previously could be elaborated upon by students and teachers in the margins of classroom manuscripts, in a typeset form that could only be changed or expanded at the behest and cost of printing houses.

The transition to print in the fifteenth and sixteenth centuries reflects the ways that writers and printers developed new page formats and organizational features that dispelled much of the confusion caused by such an emphasis on rhetorical velocity. In the case of Aesop's fables, the widely various and dynamic commentary tradition became reduced to a single, standardized commentary, the *Aesopus moralizatus* (*Aesop Moralized*), which eventually transformed fable-reading into an exercise in abbreviation, not amplification. This text contains academic commentaries that provide both moral and allegorical interpretations between, and sometimes in the margin of, each fable (fig. 5.1). Its accommodation of interpretation within the text itself reflects the long-standing medieval practice of allocating adequate space in the margins of the manuscript page for glosses and commentary by teachers or students. The printed versions of the *Aesopus moralizatus*, however, reproduce one canonical commentary, which is in great contrast to the variety of commentaries that exist in the manuscripts of their medieval predecessors. A. E. Wright therefore characterizes the printed commentary tradition to be "brief, simple, and predictable," which he suggests was likely "a result of the not inconsiderable technological challenges to be overcome in the reproduction of complex manuscript layouts on the printed page."[45] The prospect of printing unruly and lengthy commentaries, which often appeared in the margins, between lines, and even between selections of text, was surely formidable, and it is no surprise that printers chose more manageable and standardized layouts for their editions. Edward Wheatley suggests that these printed Aesops "represent only the final, fossilized form of what had earlier been a dynamic interpretative tradition: further reader response of the type in which medieval scribes engaged, that is, marginalia, remains largely absent from the

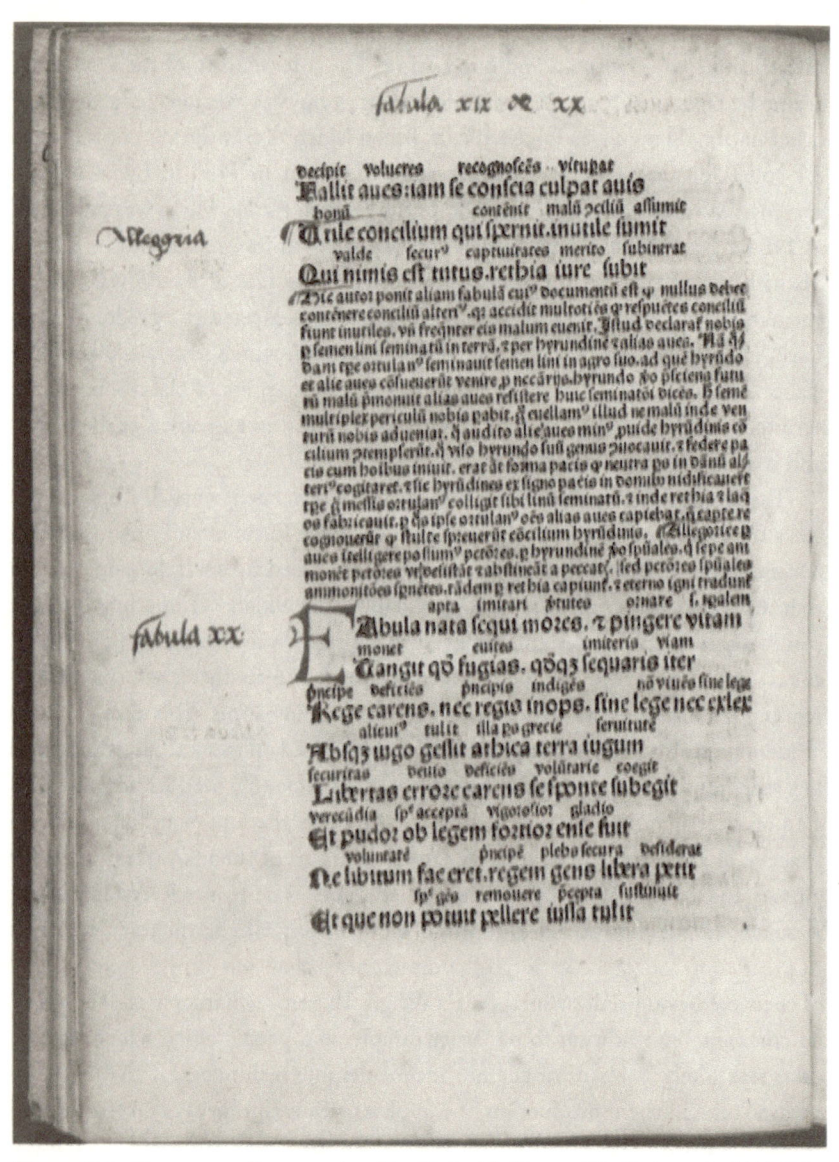

Figure 5.1. *Æsopus moralizatus*, printed by Heinrich Quentell in Cologne in 1489. RB 99974, Huntington Library, San Marino, California.

printed editions that contained their own commentaries."[46] Just as the accumulation and replication of fables had been more volatile, so too had been their interpretations.

In fact, the commentary of the earlier medieval classroom often displaced the fables themselves. For example, in one mid-fifteenth-century manuscript,

Figure 5.2. The prologue to the mid-fifteenth-century elegiac *Romulus*, in larger script, surrounded by overwhelming commentary, in smaller script. From Codex Claustroneoburgensis 1093, Stiftsbibliothek Klosterneuburg, fol. 350v–351r.

Codex Claustroneoburgensis 1093, the commentary that accompanies the elegiac *Romulus* is so lengthy that it overwhelms the fables inscribed in the middle of the pages (fig. 5.2). Even the prologue to the fables had to be divided into two parts to accommodate the effusive exegesis (fol. 350v–52r). In another fifteenth-century manuscript, Codex Vindobonensis Palatinus 3235, the glosses, marginalia, and even manicules are so pervasive that the commentary is occasionally indistinguishable from the fables (especially fol. 1r).[47] The most extreme example of commentary displacing fable, however, can be found in the fourteenth-century Codex S. Pauli in Carinthia 255/4, in which only the first two words, or lemma, of each fable are cited.[48] This was apparently sufficient identification of the fables, which were likely memorized in the classroom. The rest of the text is entirely devoted to commentary upon each fable. This excessive emphasis on commentary is so widespread in the existing manuscripts that Wheatley even goes so far as to suggest that the elegiac *Romulus* may have been composed specifically for the pedagogical production of classroom commentaries.[49] If this is the case, the text serves the commentary, overturning the standard assumption that interpretation is extraneous to its object. In the case of the medieval fable, the amplified commentary completes or authorizes the text.

Amplification

And if we turn to the content of these medieval commentaries, we discover that the complex and discursive habitus of the interpretations they contain are a far cry from the direct messages we have come to expect from Aesopica. As a representative example, let us return to the fable of "The Crow and the Water Jar":

> A thirsty crow noticed a huge jar and saw that at the very bottom there was a little bit of water. For a long time the crow tried to spill the water out so that it would run over the ground and allow her to satisfy her tremendous thirst. After exerting herself for some time in vain, the crow grew frustrated and applied all her cunning with unexpected ingenuity: as she tossed little stones into the jar, the water rose of its own accord until she was able to take a drink. *This fable shows us that thoughtfulness is superior to brute strength, since this is the way that the crow was able to carry her task to its conclusion.*[50]

Like "The City Mouse and the Country Mouse," this tale is accompanied by a pithy moral, one that suggests that reason, not might, makes right. If we examine medieval commentaries on this particular fable, we find a similar interpretation, but in an amplified form. For example, a fourteenth-century Copenhagen manuscript contains the following interpretation: "*Ingentem*. Here he teaches that cleverness is better than strength; and he teaches that through a quail, which, when it was thirsty, found an urn half-full of water in a field, and it could not tip the urn. But using its cleverness, it filled it with stones and drew out the water. The moral is this: The wise man is better than the strong" (fol. 139r).[51] Like the Carinthian manuscript discussed above, this Copenhagen codex only includes the lemma, or incipit, of each fable, which in this case is the word *ingentem*. As Wright observes, "the lemma is absolutely indispensable, not only serving the proper alignment of primary text and annotation, but also providing the internal articulation of the commentary accomplished in the other manuscripts by the regular alternation of prose with verse fables."[52] What Wright calls "proper alignment" I would call the displacement of the fable itself by its commentary, which is clearly deemed to be more important. A reader of this codex would have been expected to associate this commentary or read it along with other circulating manuscripts that contained these fables.

That said, is the interpretation of the fable in this commentary significantly different from our current understanding of the fable's meaning? A superficial comparison will tell us "no," since both suggest that wisdom is better than strength. Yet if we collate these with other medieval commentaries, we find amplifications of the fable's *moral* significance, which was associated with praxis in the Middle Ages. In fact, the standard hermeneutic framework was fourfold, following the exegetical formula "The literal presents the acts, the allegorical that which you ought to believe, the moral what you ought to do, the anagogical what you ought to hope."[53] Usually applied to biblical exegesis, these lines appear in a fourteenth-century fable collection in Biblioteca Marciana MS 4018, which suggests that fables themselves expressed multiple levels of theological meaning.[54] The moral, or "what you ought to do," is privileged over the other three modes in fable interpretation, and the commentators articulate the *moralitates* of each fable in diverse ways. In response to "The Crow and the Water Jar," one commentator in a fifteenth-century Wrocław manuscript claims that "in this fable we learn that there are many things which can be done more quickly by skill than by strength" (fol. 130r).[55] Here we have moved from the ontological realm of being wise or strong to the practical world of doing things with wisdom or strength. And in other commentaries we find even more urgent *moralitates* such as the following: "Here he urges us that we be more eager to acquire knowledge than power, because it is more useful" (fol. 9r).[56] While the previous commentator stresses the efficiency of skill, this commentator emphasizes knowledge, both its acquisition and utility.

The flexibility that medieval commentators exhibit through their interpretations reflects the dynamic nature of this scholastic enterprise. John Dagenais has suggested, "It is true that many medieval readers would have seen a potential for Christ or the devil behind a reference to 'lion.' But what were the rules that permitted medieval readers to determine, at a given moment of reading, that 'lion' meant 'Christ' and not 'the devil'? The key, then, lies not in a dictionary or code book . . . however complete, but in a grammar of medieval reading."[57] As Dagenais and other scholars have since argued, this "grammar of medieval reading" was far from prescriptive, leaving texts relatively open for what we might now call "unintended" uses. In his commentary on the Psalms, Honorius of Autun, one of our patron saints of Wikipedia (see chapter 3), even went so far as to claim, "The song of this book can be converted to any sense of intention whatsoever."[58] By referring to his text as *convertible*, Honorius endorses an interpretative sensibility that is shared by fable commentators: texts are readily adaptable for new purposes and uses.

Other commentaries become elaborations or compilations, incorporating both proverbial and homiletic material. In addition to the standard preference of wisdom over strength, the commentator of a Munich manuscript recites a relevant proverb: "Whence the saying: A man often conquers with knowledge

Amplification

those things that he could not do by force. This also urges us to rely more on wisdom and cleverness than on strength" (fol. 228v).[59] This inclusion of a similar maxim adds credence to the message of the fable and reflects the accretive nature of academic commentary. A more radical example of this accumulation of evidence can be found in a fifteenth-century codex in Budapest: "In this fable the author teaches us that we should seek knowledge, saying, 'You should know that knowledge is greater than strength and more valuable, because with wisdom a man can attain what he cannot with strength.' He continues saying that wisdom accomplishes the task begun by anyone. Thus Solomon in the Proverbs: 'Wisdom is stronger'" (fol. 15r).[60] The apparent redundancy of this interpretation should remind us of the repetitive habitus of the fables themselves. Yet the commentator cleverly turns the idea of strength (*viribus*) upon itself by suggesting not only that wisdom (*sapiencia*) is greater than strength, but also that it is stronger (*potencior*) than strength itself. By elaborating upon the basic principle "knowledge is greater than strength" (*prudencia est maior viribus*), the commentator interrogates the very nature of strength itself, a philosophical investigation that surely transcends simplistic interpretations so often associated with fables.

Some medieval commentators dare to go further than this, remixing the fables themselves within their commentaries to suit their particular contexts or audiences. Consider the following fifteenth-century commentary in a codex held in the University Library at Prague:

> *Ingentem sitiens*. Here the author demonstrates that wisdom is better and greater than strength. Thus, he urges us quite eagerly that we know that we should seek wisdom, which he shows by saying: A thirsty crow, flying across a field, came to a well, above which it saw a bucket hanging in which there was little water, which it could not pour out. Then, hoping to spill the vessel onto the ground, because the crow could not tip it, it nevertheless thought up a strategy in its cleverness; and gathering pebbles it dropped them into the bucket. When they had been put in, the water rose up, and thus the crow had an easy way to drink (fol. 22r).[61]

If we compare the plot details of this commentary with the fable itself, we find a number of innovations that not only appeal to the sensibilities of their academic audiences, but also prove to become standard elements in the future versions of the fable. As Wright puts it, "The conciseness of the verse fables . . . can verge on narrative reticence, and it can in fact come as no surprise that the late medieval annotators should have taken advantage of the freedom afforded them by the conventions of their own genre to introduce in the commentaries new motivations, causalities, or simple embellishments lacking in the verse fables."[62] In this case, the thirst of the bird and the method of quenching it are given explanations through implication and amplification: the bird has just flown over a field (*per campum*) and seeks refreshment from a bucket (*urnam*) that hangs above a well (*fontem*). It is clear that the word *urna*, which appears in the original fable and likely referred to a funerary urn, potentially caused confusion for the reader that this commentator sought to clarify by characterizing it as an urn, or bucket, that hung above the well. And as it turns out, this addition of the bucket and well persisted in the Aesopic tradition, as is evidenced by its appearance later in the same century in the woodcut that accompanies this fable in the many printed versions and translations of Steinhöwel's Aesop (fig. 5.3).[63]

Following the pioneering work of Paul Zumthor, medievalists have tended to characterize this textual malleability as *mouvance*, or variance, in an effort to distinguish the dynamic volatility of manuscript culture from the alleged fixity of print culture.[64] Even scholars working outside of medieval studies in the 1980s, such as Gerald Bruns, began to make stark distinctions between "the closed text of a print culture and the open text of a manuscript culture."[65] Bernard Cerquiglini used the strongest terms, claiming that "medieval writing does not produce variants; it is variance."[66] Such an emphasis on the radical elusiveness and multiplicity of texts within manuscript culture encouraged medievalists to revise their editorial procedures, sometimes eschewing emendation, in an effort to better represent the often untidy experience of reading a medieval text. This movement was marked in 1990 by a special issue in *Speculum* devoted to "The New Philology," in which contributors, led by Stephen Nichols, critiqued their predecessors' "preoccupation with scholarly exactitude based on edited and printed texts" and embraced "the representation of the past which went along with medieval manuscript culture: adaptation or *translatio*, the continual rewriting of past works in a variety of versions, a practice which made even the copying of medieval works an adventure in supplementation rather than faithful imitation."[67] This was a welcome paradigm shift for many medievalists, but it unfortunately led to simplifications and exaggerations about the supposed "static" or "exact" nature of print culture. It even led to some convenient McLuhanism, which allowed scholars, *pace* Bruns, to make essentialist claims about the nature of print rather than historicize particular developments within the multiple print eras, from movable type to mass production.[68] After all, it is clear that early printers continued to consider carefully the difficulty of representing multiple textual traditions, leaving space for reader involvement by allowing marginal space for commentary and appending errata lists for correction. And

bilia quidē forēt: sed nequaqȝ salubria aut lectura. Ħ Ðonet hec tabu
la dolosis cōsultoribꝰ nō esse habendā fidē. priusqȝ pspiciēs fore qȝ
fuerit q̄ cōsulit/ τ ppter qd̄. qȝ quid sit quod psuadet.

De cornice sitiente.

A gentem sitiens cornix aspexerat vrnam
Que tenuem fundo continuisset aquam:
Hanc enixa diu planis effundere campis:
Scilicet vt nimiam pelleret inde sitim.
Postqȝ nulla viam virtus dedit admouet omnes
Indignata noua calliditate dolos.
Nam breuibus mersis accrescens sponte lapillis
Potanti facilem prebuit vnda viam.
Viribus hec docuit quod sit prudentia maior:
Que ceptum volucris explicuisset opus.
Cornix sitibūda cū diutius vrnā putei intuita fuisset: illā
tñ se haurire nō posse intelligēs: calculos plures in vacuā
...

Figure 5.3. A crow dropping a pebble into a bucket in Heinrich Steinhöwel's *Aesop*. From Basel: Jakob Wolff von Pfortzheim, 1501.

as Daniel Wakelin has shown, scribes and readers of the later Middle Ages were often quite invested in emending manuscripts, making sure that variance did not undermine the authority of their projects.[69]

This kind of textual elaboration and its influence on subsequent fable writing, commentary, and even illustration suggest that the fable-commentary tradition's dynamic and expandable nature was an essential component of its academic use. An example from the commentary in an Erfurt manuscript demonstrates how even the fable of "The Crow and the Water Jar" itself can serve as a metaphor for the collaborative construction of knowledge. The commentator adds the following pedagogical summary to an interpretation of the fable: "Just as the crow could not spill the urn, so no student can attain any knowledge he desires; but he can acquire a certain portion of knowledge if he throws in a stone, that is to say if he applies effort and diligence" (fol. 35r).[70] Here the commentator warns readers that complete knowledge of anything is unachievable through individual pursuits. Instead, students can acquire knowledge by contributing stones, or offering their own efforts to the cumulative cause. A revision of this fable, which survives in at least two fifteenth-century manuscripts, even goes so far as to compare the act of writing itself to the accumulation of pebbles in a water-filled bucket: "In the same way as the author writes verses, so the crow drinks by skill."[71] Rhetorical amplification and revision are construed as the means to the attainment of knowledge. Wright aptly explains, "Here the act of writing is described as a process of patient accretion similar to the crow's gathering of pebbles."[72] I would take this a step further to suggest that this line characterizes the entire enterprise of writing fable commentary, which necessarily involves responding both to the individual fable and to the larger and ever-expanding corpus of fabular interpretation. Consider the words in the epigraph to this chapter of the medieval rhetorician Geoffrey of Vinsauf who, in teaching *amplificatio*, encourages his students to accumulate words and phrases in the manner of the crow: "And so, from a little water, much water arises." If each fable is a "little water" (*modica aqua*), the contributions of the commentators produce much water (*maxima aqua*) from which future fable readers will satisfy their thirst for knowledge.

One of those future fable readers was the late fifteenth-century Scottish schoolmaster Robert Henryson (discussed in chapter 4), who composed his own fables and commentaries that adopt the virtues of *amplificatio* to the extreme. If each commentary adds a pebble to the tradition, he tosses in a boulder. His commentaries, or what are commonly referred to as his *moralitates*, have been derided by modern critics such as J. A. Burrow, who suggests that they are "at best unpleasing and at worst desperately confusing."[73] At least some of the bewilderment must originate from Henryson's combination of his revision of well-known fables with an elaboration upon the fable commentary tradition.

Amplification

To make matters more complex, Henryson's commentaries often suggest possibilities rather than present answers, using tentative language to articulate his interpretations. He belies allegorical precision by using subjunctive terms such as "may" or figurative ones such as "liken": "This cok ... *may* till ane fule be peir" (141–42) (This cock ... *may* be compared to a fool); "this cok weill *may we call* / Nyse proude men" (590–91) (this cock well *may we call* foolish, proud men); "This volf I *likkin* to sensualitie" (1118) (This wolf I *liken* to sensuality); and "This selie scheip *may present the figure* / Of pure commounis" (1258–59) (This innocent sheep may represent the figure of the poor commoner).[74] By couching his interpretations in such qualified language, Henryson implies that his reading is simply one among many possibilities.[75] If, for example, we examine his commentary on "The City Mouse and the Country Mouse," the fable with which I began this section, we witness not only his distinctive narrative voice, but also his penchant for elaboration:

> Blissed be sempill lyfe withoutin dreid;
> Blissed be sober feist in quietie.
> Quha hes aneuch, of na mair hes he neid,
> Thoct it be littill into quantatie.
> Grit aboundance and blind prosperitie
> Oftytmes makis ane euill conclusioun.
> The sweitest lyfe, thairfoir, in this cuntrie,
> Is sickernes, with small possessioun.
>
> Of wantoun man that vsis for to feid
> Thy wambe, and makis it a god to be;
> Luke to thy self, I warne the weill on deid.
> The cat cummis and to the mous hes ee;
> Quhat is avale thy feist and royaltie,
> With dreidfull hart and tribulatioun?
> Thairfoir, best thing in eird, I say for me,
> Is merry hart with small possessioun.
>
> Thy awin fyre, freind, thocht it be bot ane gleid,
> It warmis weill, and is worth gold to the;
> And Solomon sayis, gif that thow will reid,
> "Vnder the heuin I can not better se
> Than ay be blyith and leif in honestie."
> Quhairfoir I may conclude be this ressoun:

>   Of eirthly ioy it beiris maist degre,
>   Blyithnes in hart, with small possessioun. (lines 373–96)[76]

Henryson begins with "Blissed be sempill lyfe withoutin dreid" (373), the common *moralitas* of this tale, but this is also his point of departure to a meditation on the blindness that accompanies prosperity and the security that follows from modesty. Moreover, his focus on "this cuntrie" (379) localizes his interpretation and speaks to the concerns of his audience, a rhetorical move that should remind us of the transformation of the funerary urn to the well and bucket in "The Crow and the Water Jar." And after this first stanza, he launches into an invective against human greed, ironically quoting one of the richest of Old Testament patriarchs, Solomon, whose proverb shifts the focus from possessions almost entirely. Henryson ultimately seems concerned with "Blyithnes in hart" (396), which accompanies modest living. And yet, when he includes phrases such as "I say for me" (387), "gif that thow will reid" (391), and "I may conclude" (394), he makes it abundantly clear that this is only his interpretation, subject to the volition, scrutiny, and amplification of future fable writers. These elements suggest that Henryson was fully aware of the flexible nature of fable interpretation and that *moralitates* were rarely codified or closed.

Henryson's expansion and revision of the standard *moralitas*, combined with his interpretative flexibility, offer a fitting climax to the historical volatility of the commentary tradition, which would slowly but surely become fixed and reduced into the abbreviated messages we have come to expect from Aesop's fables. Put another way, Henryson's fabular commentary represents a fleeting emergence of Roland Barthes's well-known "writerly text," for which "the goal of literary work . . . is to make the reader no longer a consumer, but a producer of the text."[77] Within this formulation, readers become writers, or in the case of the fables, readers become commentators who write the very text they read. While this kind of "writerly text" is possible within manuscript culture, in which readers write directly onto the texts they read, the emergence and widespread dissemination of the printed book made this kind communal reading and writing less common. Martin Foys suggests that it is important to consider "the large part that the cultural and economic dominance of the unvaried, mass-produced, and author-friendly print product plays in constructing the relationships of the written word as fixed, linear, and largely closed to alternative textualities."[78] While early printed texts are hardly "unvaried," printers in recent decades have undoubtedly played a large role in the facilitation of what Barthes calls "the pitiless divorce which the literary institution maintains between the producer of the text and its user, between its owner and its customer, between its author and its reader."[79] I believe this divorce is readily apparent when we consider the limits of fabular reading in the modern era.

While early printers worked valiantly to accommodate such Aesopic amplification, the demand to create editions that were mass-produced, readable, reproducible, and cost-effective led to the attenuation of their social function and annotative authority. The pages of printed books reduced the spaces previously open for future commentary, and the eventual inheritors of medieval manuscripts regularly cut off the margins of books altogether when they were rebound. This compromise resulted in a textually dominant and uniform design of the page that is almost completely determined by authors, editors, publishing companies, and software designers, which has in turn meant that the features of the page have become increasingly shaped by their value as commodified objects for individuals to consume, not produce.

By eliminating future readers as amplifiers of the page, printed text has come to pervade the page, so much so that such writing spaces are now considered monomodal. As John Trimbur and Karen Press suggest, such characterizations of print as monomodal are ideological claims that occlude the inherent multimodality of alphabetic text.[80] I recall this history of the printed page, however, to emphasize that the ideology of monomodality emerges from specific material conditions, which often make unavailable a rich array of composing modes previously available in the shared culture of medieval books, ranging from visual markers, such as manicules that refer future readers to key passages and invite commentary, to marginal apparatus, such as rubricated citations and key terms that facilitate hyperlinked connections within and across texts. And while multimodality represents its own neoliberal ideologies of innovation and countable objects of design,[81] the material conditions of digital pages make available social modes of readerly interaction, specifically the capacity to amplify and annotate web texts through audio, video, and illustration, which are high-speed and large-scale extensions of practices that predate the age of print. This historical context is crucial to consider, because digital pages are caught up in the same dilemma as printed pages: how can the page accommodate readerly additions and maintain readability? Put another way, how might we encourage designs of the page in which the elements of the page remain objects of critical inquiry and visual forms of knowledge production?

Digital Amplifications of the Page

In this chapter, I am arguing that the knowledge of the history of the page—difficult, partial, and in flux though it may be—compels us to orient our writing newly to textual design elements: not just individual modes, but to purposeful engagement with modal intensity and complexity. We must attend to the entire mise-en-page—the layout, arrangement, and spaces for readerly and writerly interaction that our texts might construct. Just as medieval scribes, rubricators, and illuminators designed the page with future glossators and commentators in mind, digital composers must consider designs that both facilitate the elegant reading of their alphabetic text and facilitate rhetorical velocity. In this section, I illustrate how digital annotation—one kind of engagement with the page, inflected through the material and social affordances of web templates—involves annotators in the history of and possible amplifications of the multimodal page.

The affordances of software that enable users to annotate web pages—that is, append writing, image, or video to existing digital texts, images, or videos—are so ubiquitous throughout the internet as to disappear "in their very function," to use Alberto Manguel's phrase. Almost every website invites user response through a variety of graphical features of the page, ranging from a "Contact Us" window, to a sidebar chat, to a commentary feed. While the data acquired from such annotations is often used to enhance user experience, it is also often used for product development or to create metrics for market analysis. This consumerist approach to web-page design leads to visually attractive and comfortable interfaces, but rarely do such pages accommodate divergent interests of their viewers, causing a slowing, if not a complete stoppage, of their rhetorical velocity, particularly if such recomposing is not oriented toward producing capital for the website's stakeholders. These pages are often designed to deliver content, not to enable dialogue or collaboratively produce new knowledge.

As we attend to the page as a unit of attention, then, we want also to consider the interpretative, cultural, economic, and political implications of graphic-user-interface design, particularly when incorporating space for viewer response or content creation. To accomplish this, it is important to engage critically with a wide variety of annotation platforms in an effort to identify the underlying assumptions that determine the place of readerly writing on the page.[82] Using different varieties of digital annotation and then reflecting on user experience, we can answer questions such as "How does the design of each page invite or disinvite certain types of annotation?" or "How do the annotations contribute to the visual representation or production of meaning on the page?" For the purposes of this chapter, I limit my discussion of these questions to one platform: the commercially successful site Genius.com.

Among the many annotation sites available, such as MIT's Annotation Studio, the University of Virginia's Prism, and Harvard University's Perusall, perhaps the most visually stimulating is Genius, which began as the hip-hop commentary platform Rap Genius in 2009 and has since expanded beyond rap and song lyrics to include a wide variety of annotatable objects, ranging from poetry to Netflix series' scripts to album cover art.[83] The site is particularly attractive because of its seemingly endless interactivity, including its manicules for upvoting or downvoting suggested annotations; its competitive and multifaceted system of gaining annotative and editorial authority through the accumulation of "IQ"; and its audio/visual options, including music videos, sound files of poems, and color-coded text highlighting. Meera Nair has developed one pedagogical approach to the site, called "Annotation Exercises for Fiction Boot Camp," which helps students create high quality annotations focused on tracking literary elements, particularly characterization and theme.[84] Consider, for example, the page devoted to Sylvia Plath's regularly anthologized poem "Metaphors," which contains the text of the poem in a column on the left side of page, as well as a slightly thinner column on the right dedicated to annotations for each line. Underneath the text of the poem is a row of social media icons, which allow the annotators to readily share the page to Twitter and Facebook, as well as to embed the page in their own websites. Annotations only appear when highlighted lines are clicked, which transforms the commentary into a digital palimpsest that can be peeled back to reveal annotations relevant to particular lines. Once a highlighted line is clicked, an annotation appears in the righthand column, followed below by a list of "improvements" to the annotation, which are suggestions for revision to the existing annotation.

While Genius's interface is provocative and motivating, its resistance to interpretative speculation challenges its usability and amplificatory capacity. At first glance, creating annotations is simple: commentators highlight a word or passage and then type a comment in a text box. However, annotations that are unverified by designated "editors" (users who have a high Genius IQ) are flagged in red, appear visually suspect, and may be eventually eliminated altogether. And in the case of short texts, such as "Metaphors," and those that have been extensively annotated, it is impossible to add a new annotation. Instead, users can merely suggest improvements to existing annotations, which then require additional approval by other users before they can be incorporated into the annotation itself. Riskier interpretations often get coded as a "Stretch" and rarely become added to existing annotations because the authorized comments are mostly descriptive or contextual in nature. The multivalence of a particular phrase such as Plath's "red fruit" is not valued because the purpose of Genius annotation is not to accommodate multiple interpretations of particular lines, but rather to create an authoritative commentary, much in the style of the *Aesopus moralizatus*, in which one moral per fable will suffice.

This annotative authority is also visually represented in the placement of the suggested improvements below the approved annotation. If we examine the comments on "red fruit," we find that the authoritative comment is focused on solving the riddle of the poem, which points to the "red fruit" as the flesh of the fetus being carried by the pregnant poetic persona. Joshua Colby's eight-year-old suggestion, which is now old enough to suggest it will never be incorporated into the annotation, offers an alternative reading to "red fruit." Colby sees it as referring to the forbidden fruit of Adam and Eve, an interpretation that addresses both the frustrated tone of the speaker of the poem and the resentful description of pregnancy itself (fig. 5.4). Without these subtleties, Plath's poem becomes merely a riddle to be decoded. While this kind of crowdsourced consensus clearly suits Wikipedia's verifiable and factually based compilation of knowledge about the world, Genius's creation of annotative authority through such a model reproduces the myth of the "right" reading of any text, a myth that is enabled through the strategic placement or effacement of readerly commentary. The result is a digital palimpsest that increasingly obscures the interpretative tensions beneath its surface, producing codified commentaries that declare interpretative authority through their visibility.

To consider how the design of such pages influences the reception and interpretation of the writing they contain, it is important to compare Genius to other social annotation sites, such as Annotation Studio and Prism. Students readily observe how easy it is to add comments to lines and passages in Annotation Studio, but they also find the annotation frame to be too crowded, making it difficult to distinguish between and respond to the comments of other annotators. While a variety of interpretations is valued on this site, the price of this textual accumulation is occasional unreadability, which undermines the purpose of social annotation altogether. On the other hand, a site like Prism offers color-coded forms of visual annotation, which limit the range of responses to a given text, but also provide visualizations of interpretation, indicating through highlighted text and pie charts the percentage of readers who, for example, view particular words/lines in Geoffrey Chaucer's *Wife of Bath's Prologue* as "feminist" or "sexist." Asking annotators to create their own "prisms" on this site engages them with the ways in which the placement and restriction of particular habits of responding to the text within the page have significant interpretative implications. As Johanna Drucker suggests, "to imagine new intellectual forms of interpretation is also to design the spaces and supports that structure interpretative

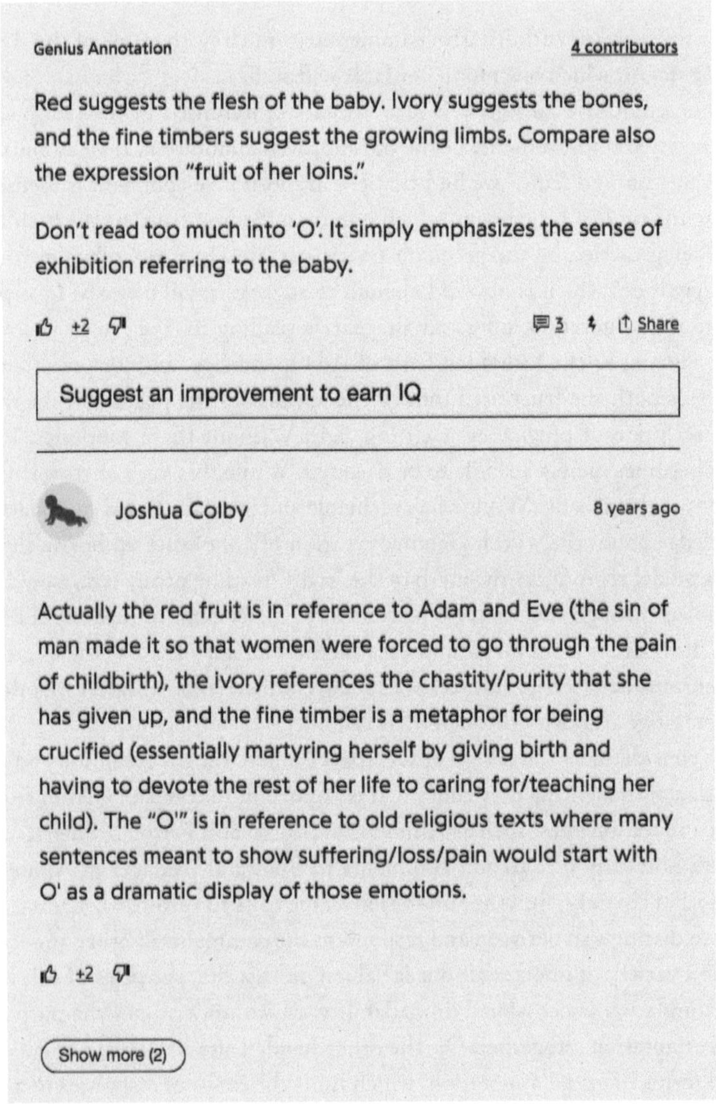

> **Genius Annotation**   **4 contributors**
>
> Red suggests the flesh of the baby. Ivory suggests the bones, and the fine timbers suggest the growing limbs. Compare also the expression "fruit of her loins."
>
> Don't read too much into 'O'. It simply emphasizes the sense of exhibition referring to the baby.
>
> 👍 +2 👎   💬 3   ⚡   ⬆ Share
>
> [Suggest an improvement to earn IQ]
>
> ---
>
> 👤 **Joshua Colby**   8 years ago
>
> Actually the red fruit is in reference to Adam and Eve (the sin of man made it so that women were forced to go through the pain of childbirth), the ivory references the chastity/purity that she has given up, and the fine timber is a metaphor for being crucified (essentially martyring herself by giving birth and having to devote the rest of her life to caring for/teaching her child). The "O'" is in reference to old religious texts where many sentences meant to show suffering/loss/pain would start with O' as a dramatic display of those emotions.
>
> 👍 +2 👎
>
> [Show more (2)]

Figure 5.4. A screen capture, August 22, 2022, of the Genius page devoted to Sylvia Plath's "Metaphors."

acts."[85] By asking users to design their own annotatable page layouts, Prism also makes users grapple with the ways in which graphical elements may both represent and produce interpretations, a prismatic dynamic dependent upon the careful placement of writing within a matrix of modes of meaning-making.

Attention to the history of the page and its contested status within digital environments should compel us to evaluate the quality of page design not only on its capacity to accommodate multiple modes or to deliver content, but also on its degree of modal intensity and complexity, which may invite or discourage readerly and writerly interactivity and amplification. Printed pages saturated with text, like many of our textbooks and student papers (and most of this chapter and book), afford writing a high degree of modal intensity and represent meaning effectively, but often do little to encourage multimodal activity or amplification. By contrast, the careful and limited intensity of fable text on the Aesopic manuscript page led to the accumulation of multiple interpretations of fables. This in turn led to the revision and recirculation of the fables themselves, even as it also challenged the limits of the printed page. Even innovative and interactive web template designs, multimodally intense and complex though they are, also risk the reproduction of certain print teleologies that value the visual, linear representation of knowledge over its production. For websites like Genius, which are highly dependent upon readerly contributions, it is imperative to consider the subtle ways in which stimulating page designs use visual modes to privilege certain kinds of interpretations and limit future amplifications of the page. Central to this consideration is the nuanced place of writing on the page, its modal intensity, and its increasingly vexed status as a visual object of attention. Until we recognize the page as a space that can both visually represent and produce meaning, alphabetic writing will neither shed its monomodal reputation nor achieve its powerful potential within the multimodally complex world of digital composition.

Amplification as Cohabitation

As a crowdsourced annotation platform, Genius attempts to strike a balance between a democratic spirit of participation and the strengthening of its authority as a reliable resource. By using their gamified Genius IQ as a metric for distinguishing between different levels of expertise, however, the site privileges the annotations of a particularly entrepreneurial set of editors, who gain fame through the upvoting star system, ascending the higher ranks through individual initiative and frequent annotative updates. To some extent, this glossarial disposition suits ancient understandings of *auctoritas*, in which, as Giorgio Agamben notes, "the auctor [author] is . . . the person who augments, increases, or perfects the act . . . of someone else."[86] Genius annotations are authorized through individual acts of augmentation: annotators "perfect" the annotations of others through suggested improvements, resulting in revised annotations that increase in authority by the upvotes of editors with high IQ. On the other hand, this is a crowdsourced model of participation in which, unlike Wikipedia, editors are rewarded individually for their contributions, granting them additional editorial access and capital as their Genius IQ increases. This emphasis on "genius" suggests a kind of discrete and intellectual novelty of the entrepreneurial annotator that belies any kind of democratic or collective process of augmentation or amplification that defines many forms of premodern *auctoritas*.

One way to understand the "augmented reality" of endlessly editable web templates like Genius is to consider the site a manifestation of our current "update culture." In a recent study of what he calls "template rhetoric," John Gallagher meticulously tracks the "afterlife" of digital writing, focusing on the ways in which individual writers persistently update their writing on user-friendly web templates, such as blogs and Amazon reviews, to address the constantly shifting responses, needs, and desires of their audiences. And while he draws upon premodern participatory cultures of reading and writing as precedents for such dynamic textual dialogue, Gallagher concludes that "digital writers on the internet can be described as entrepreneurs, perhaps even vertically integrated companies, who contend with the speed, scale, and frequency of social media and rapid content creation."[87] Such market-driven language envisions the aim of digital writing as the creation of web "content" achieved by individual initiative and persistence, essentially establishing what he calls the "economic value" of the labor of the digital entrepreneur.[88] By tracking individual contributions and their updates, Gallagher limits the work and authority of digital writing to discrete digital authors who occupy nodes on a social network actively enmeshed in capitalistic enterprise. Update culture then becomes inseparable from a neoliberal rhetoric of innovation, in which entrepreneurial writers must constantly update their work to compete within the online marketplace.

While Gallagher's vision of what we might call "always be updating" accurately reflects the competitive logic of commercial sites like Amazon, his focus on the fungible labor of the individual writer celebrates authorial genius over premodern notions of authority via amplification. As my analysis of amplification suggests, the potency of such individual agency is limited within these digital spaces. Web templates, like those of Genius analyzed above, are programmed to invite user interaction, but are designed by code that polices (and therefore prevents) particular kinds of user actions and contributions to designs of the page. As Wendy Hui Kyong Chun points out about such "everyone can edit" sites, "Celebrations of an all-powerful user/agent—YOU as the network, YOU as 'produser'—counteract concerns over code as law as police by positing YOU as the sovereign subject, YOU as the decider."[89] By celebrating the capital of the individual writer, the limits of encoded page design fade from view, and the fantasy of authorial sovereignty is maintained by each update a writer makes. In contrast to Gallagher's entrepreneurial view, Chun sees our current update culture as a persistent disruption of our habits, which she suggests are "creative anticipations based on past repetitions" in which "individual actions coalesce bodies into a monstrously connected chimera."[90] Updates therefore force changes in habits, forcing writers to remain unsettled and always connecting with others, even as they try to establish the distinctiveness of their voices. Chun puts it succinctly: "The constant update, that is, deprives habit of its ability to habituate."[91] For Chun, new media thrive on moments of crisis because crisis demands continual updates and changes to habits. Digital writers' habits are consequently tracked within networks and connected to big data sets that establish correlations between "user experience" and predictions about future consumer behavior.

I want to conclude by suggesting that this history of amplification demands that we reconsider such exploitation of writerly habits within premodern, and specifically rhetorical, conceptions of habitus. Katharine Breen, in her study of cultures of reading in medieval England, helpfully distinguishes between modern understandings of habit, which is often cast as "a pattern of mindless or unconscious repetition," and medieval understandings of habitus, which was largely considered to be a supplementation of "natural capacities through deliberate and diligent practice."[92] What Breen describes as "deliberate" supplementations, we might adapt Chun's proposition to call "creative [amplifications]" based on "past repetitions." The most frequently cited definition of *habitus* comes from none other than the rhetorical *auctor* himself, Marcus Tullius Cicero, who in his *De inventione* (*On Invention*) calls it "a stable and absolute constitution of mind or body in some particular, as, for example, the acquisition of some capacity or of an art, or again some special knowledge, or some bodily dexterity not given by nature but won by careful training and practice."[93] Cicero's habitus is neither fundamentally natural nor mindlessly behavioral, but rather an acquired condition, often attained through corporeal and artistic means.

Premodern rhetorical understandings of habitus are accordingly corporeal in nature. In addition to its dispositional character, *habitus* specifically refers to a distinctive dress or ornamental clothing, often associated with a religious order (e.g., a nun's "habit"). For example, if we return to the influential treatment of amplification in the *Poetria nova*, we see that Geoffrey of Vinsauf begins by addressing *repetitio* as a kind of "raiment" one puts on to present matter as "varied and yet the same" (225).[94] Amplification is therefore habitual rhetoric par excellence, creating the possibility of variety through repetition and establishing a writing practice that forms an embodied disposition, which others may take up and assume differently for particular rhetorical circumstances. When digital amplification is understood to be a habitus—as opposed to an updating habit that one is compelled to repeat in order to remain relevant, persistent, traceable, and marketable—the page becomes a space arranged to be inhabited by a variety of writerly bodies whose labor is encouraged, recognized, and made transparent to future inhabitants of the page. This is in contrast to the updating obsessions of habitual new media, what Chun calls "N(YOU) Media," oriented to the individualized work of Gallagher's entrepreneur, who becomes a node within capitalized networks designed to capture markets and predict consumer behavior. As a response to the destruction of a notion of any kind of digital democratic plurality, Chun proffers an understanding of "habit as a way to inhabit the inhabitable," pursuing "the possibilities of YOU as singular-plural," which would enable a vocative call for a "refusal of designs that undermine habituation by turning habits into forms of addiction, a refusal of undead information that renders us into zombies. It means inhabiting and discovering how our habits collect, rather than divide, us."[95] By reconceiving habit as habitus, rhetorical amplification becomes a disposition *and* practice that creates writing spaces designed for cohabitation. This is, after all, fundamental to the medieval monastic ideal, which attempts to reconcile a common state of being with a common rule for living. Agamben suggests, "To inhabit together thus meant for the monks to share, not simply a place or a style of dress, but first of all a *habitus*. The monk is in this sense a man who lives in the mode of 'inhabiting,' according to a rule and a form of life. It is certain, nevertheless, that cenoby represents the attempt to make habit and form of life coincide in an absolute and total *habitus*, in which it would not be possible to distinguish between dress and way of life."[96] If we understand amplification as a digital habitus, we are embracing both a rhetorical practice and disposition that anticipates and makes space for future amplifiers. Amplification then becomes cohabitation, both a deliberate action and a rhetorical way of life that attempts to accommodate the past, present, and future labor of the bodies that compose and circulate media objects.

6

Appropriation

Stealing Bodies and Properties

It's possible the work I've done some clerics might claim for their own—I wish no one to make that claim! ... Aesop men call this book, for he translated it originally from Greek into the Latin tongue. ... I in French verse have done the same, rightly, or such was my intent.
—**Marie de France**, "Epilogue" to *The Fables*

Plagiarism is to be avoided because it makes oneself appear ridiculous and shameful in public, like a clown in ill-fitting clothing, whose garments are not familiar to him.
—**Mary Carruthers**, *The Book of Memory*

In a famous literary dispute in 1841, Henry Wadsworth Longfellow accused Edgar Allan Poe of plagiarism. Attempting to reverse the charge, Poe offered his own account of the sequence and similarity of work:

I first published the H. P. ["The Haunted Palace"] in Brooks' "Museum" [*The Baltimore Museum*], a monthly journal of Baltimore, now dead. Afterwards, I embodied it in a tale called "The House of Usher" in Burton's Magazine. Here it was, I suppose, that Prof. Longfellow saw it; for, about 6 weeks afterwards, there appeared in the South. Lit. Mess [*Southern Literary Messenger*]: a poem by him called "The Beleaguered City," which may now be found in his volume. The identity in tide is striking; for by the Haunted Palace I mean to imply a mind haunted by phantoms—a disordered brain—and by the Beleaguered City Prof. L. means just the same. But the whole tournure of the poem is based upon mine, as you will see at once. Its allegorical conduct, the style of its versification & expression—all are mine.[1]

The corporeal features of Poe's "Haunted Palace" are unmistakable. After its publication in the "now dead" *Museum*, he claims to have "embodied" it in another text, "The House of Usher," which was then subsequently taken and redressed for "The Beleaguered City." This account effectively allegorizes the poem as a body that captivates another creator, who gives the body a makeover, complete with a new "tournure," or what we might call a "habit."

At its core, Poe's defense reveals plagiarism's most powerful threat: its challenge to the allegory of the author's body. When we refer to a writer's *corpus*, we are recognizing a body of writing that is uniquely attributed to that author. If Longfellow can fashion Poe's corpus to his liking, what happens to the proper "allegorical conduct" that is expected between an author and their text? In highlighting "allegorical conduct," Poe refers to the allegory in his poem that Longfellow has allegedly coopted, but this sly reference also casts the act of plagiarism itself as hostile to the allegorical relationship between his poem and its author. By claiming that "all are mine," Poe attempts to reclaim a poetic work that copyright attorneys would argue he establishes as his property.

Yet to say that style and versification are property is to mitigate the allegorical power of creative appropriation. If all creative work must pay homage to both a referent *and* an owner, the relationship is one of bondage and obligation, not one of reference and elaboration. Plagiarism, after all, is a form of allegory, albeit an often uncomplicated one. The spectrum of plagiarism even follows the spectrum of allegory, from the heavy-handed and transparent to the shrewdly nuanced and multivalent. When the allegorical referent or plagiarized text is too easily discerned, a crisis of authority emerges, the velocity of interpretation loses steam, and artistic production breaks down. When Poe sees his corpus dressed in Longfellow's tournure, he accuses his fellow poet of intellectual theft, but this desperate charge is based on an appropriation of "conduct," a kind of disposition or *habitus*, not on any transparent form of copying and pasting. Crucially, it is the tournure—not the body—of the work itself that Poe recognizes as his, a rhetorical sleight of hand that makes the stolen object a possession, a garment that can be removed and placed on another body. In effect, it is not a corpus that has been stolen—it is the outer covering or habit, which reflects Poe's fashion or what he calls "style." Through this clever bait and switch, Poe invokes the corporeal features of his work, while also employing the language of the ownership of objects.

I retell this story to highlight the slippery shift from *corporeal* to *proprietary* conceptions of creative production and appropriation that have been the basis for most subsequent legal claims to intellectual property. In response to defenses of "idea" ownership, Siva Vaidhyanathan urges, "We must revise our notion of intellectual 'theft.' You cannot 'steal' an idea, a style, a 'look and feel.' These things are the raw material of the next move in literature, art, politics, or music. And using someone's idea does not diminish its power."[2] For Vaidhyanathan, this proposed revision is a move away from the language of intellectual "property" toward responsible intellectual policy. Insofar as flight from the language of property may be necessary to release restrictions on creative work that relies on appropriation and reuse, I want to suggest that such a paradigm shift would also be a recognition of premodern forms of artistic production, or what I want to call an *appropriative habitus*, in which the creative nature of authorship and allegory is corporeal and accumulative.

In this chapter, I continue my examination of the medieval Aesop into the early age of print to reveal the creative tensions that arise between *corporeal* and *proprietary* understandings of artistic production. Building upon the highly accumulative, various, and expandable Aesopic tradition that thrived in the Middle Ages within scholastic manuscripts, the fifteenth-century fables of Robert Henryson and William Caxton confront movements to consolidate and transform Aesop's sprawling literary corpus into a singular printable property. At the same time that a single series of Aesop's fables, now known as the elegiac *Romulus*, became increasingly standardized within printed books, woodcut illustrations and textual descriptions increasingly normalized the physical features of Aesop's previously grotesque body, restructuring his corporeal habitus from that of an enslaved and nonverbal wordsmith to an eloquent and aristocratic poet. The simultaneous metamorphosis of Aesop's poetic and visual corpus reveals the premodern underpinnings of current efforts by publishing industries to immunize digital work from habitual acts of appropriation, mash-up, and remix—practices which had previously defined Aesopic textuality. As a response to this textual vulnerability, the collapse of Aesopic work into a singular entity reimagines the allegorical relationship between the author or publisher and the work as proprietary, not corporeal. Rather than an extension of a generative, deeply somatic, and grotesque process of multiple fabular authors and commentators, the modernized Aesop obtains value as a "property," paving the way for the notion that creative corpuses can be "owned," effectively stealing away corporeal features from intellectual production.

Within the context of twenty-first-century copyright law, the medieval Aesopic combination of critical commentary and literary "theft" challenges current understandings of "fair use." As Robin Wharton has demonstrated about the Court of Appeals for the Eleventh Circuit's decision in Suntrust Bank v. Houghton Mifflin (2001), interpretations of copyright have begun to separate literary "critique" from "creative" work.[3] To distinguish parody from satire as a literary genre that falls within fair use, the court in Suntrust determined that "[a] parody is a work that seeks to comment upon or criticize another work by appropriating elements of the original. 'Parody needs to mimic an original to make its point, and so has some claim to use the creation of its victim's (or collective victims') imagination.'"[4] Revisions of medieval fables also incorporate commentaries within their elaborations on the Aesopic imagination, but the result was hardly parodic and the previous fables were rarely victims of critique. Rather, new fables became new members attached to the Aesopic corpus, a ceaselessly expandable body of fabular work composed by innumerable Aesopic authors and commentators. Throughout the Middle Ages, the name *Aesop* obtained its own authorial habitus, an early example of what Michel Foucault famously calls the "author-function," a product of discourses that became "objects of appropriation" and "a form of ownership," which eventually reduce the authority of texts to "their membership in a systematic ensemble, and not the reference to the individual who produced them."[5] As the Aesopic traditions begin to appear in print, we see acts of "hacking" emerge in the form of mash-ups and remixes of fables—an especially poignant phenomenon in the printed life of Henryson's *Morall Fabillis*. Within these early printed contexts, we see striking evidence of critical appropriation, in which printers and readers remix fables for new audiences, all the while recognizing the authority of their original objects. I ultimately want to suggest that a premodern orientation toward intellectual bodies, instead of properties, may produce an appropriative habitus that encourages responsible uses, critiques, and reuses of artistic work and offers formidable challenges to self-interested uses of copyright law, as well as idealistic fantasies of a "creative commons."

From Body to Property

As I demonstrated in the previous chapter, the ossification of the Aesopic corpus is a relatively recent development that stands in stark contrast to its life in the medieval classroom, where individual fables were offered up for practice in written amplification and collaborative constructions of knowledge. In addition to a focus on amplification, appropriation became the signature pedagogy for many schoolmasters, including Robert Henryson. On the one hand, Henryson demonstrates that the production of the Aesopic corpus during the Middle

Ages depends upon its status as an open resource, in which writers and readers intimately interact, actively revising and expanding fable collections, blurring the boundaries between the text and its critics. On the other, his *Morall Fabillis* reflects the culminating tension between an older manuscript tradition, dependent upon multiple Aesopic writers and accumulative commentary, and a newer printed tradition, increasingly restricted by singular modes of authorship and standardized textual apparatus. This conflict is evident through two fascinating transformations in the early printed Aesopic corpus: (1) the emergence of "mash-ups" of fabular texts and images, and (2) the gradual normalization and standardization of depictions of Aesop's body. While these two phenomena represent two creative impulses—appropriation and codification—seemingly at odds with each other, I want to suggest that they are both attempts to reconcile challenges to the allegorical relationship between author and corpus posed by an expanding Aesopic writing community and nascent notions of "intellectual property."

According to John Willinsky, intellectual property has its origins in medieval monastic culture, which followed the Benedictine rule that required monks to live communally, renouncing all claims to private possessions, even the writing utensils they used to produce learned books.[6] Within a legal context, however, proprietary language for creative production did not emerge until 1624, when the English Parliament approved an act to prevent commercial monopolies and enhance the Crown's power over the issuing of patents.[7] And it was not until 1666 that booksellers embraced the language of authorial "property" in their defense against royalist claims that the Stationer encouraged piracy against the Crown. The booksellers and printers collectively argued that "the Author of every manuscript or copy hath (in all reason) as good right thereunto, as any Man hath to the Estate wherein he has the most absolute property."[8] Rather than allow the Crown to destroy the Stationer and its control over the registry of printings, this statement empowered authors to sell the rights of their works over to booksellers. Adrian Johns contends, "This may be the earliest explicit articulation of the idea of literary property—of an absolute right generated by authorship, which could serve as the cornerstone of an entire moral and economic system of print. Certainly the idea had no clear precedent behind it."[9] For contemporaries unfamiliar with the Crown's attempted literary land-grab, such a statement must have been stunning in its hyperbolic claims to writing as property. This statement is also striking in its advocacy for authors, not printers or booksellers. As Rebecca Curtin has pointed out, early printers were occasionally willing to engage in "alternative transactions," granting privileges to writers in order to encourage them to enter the book market, a situation that she claims has been replicated within open source software sharing movements in recent decades.[10] In retrospect, it is difficult not see to see a lost opportunity here, in which the rights of authors could be cast in corporeal, rather than proprietary, terms.

Johns is surely correct that no explicit precedent exists for the printers and booksellers' statement of 1666, but the transformation from the understanding of the book as a body to the book as a property, particularly for the medieval Aesop, in the preceding centuries suggests that the groundwork was already being prepared for such a claim. Quite literally, of course, the medieval book was a body with leaves of sheepskin, bound with animal glue, and enclosed with calfskin leather.[11] Figuratively, the body played a central role in the medieval imagination, a role that Guillemette Bolens divides into two types: contained bodies and articulated bodies. Within the articulation model, bodies are designed for motion with limbs connected by joints—suggesting the potentiality of movement that can only be severed through destruction or mutilation, such as Beowulf's wresting of Grendel's arm from its socket.[12] This dynamic view of corporeality was an alternative to the containment model, in which the body's outer layer would both define the body and prevent penetration from outside forces, such as weapons, poisons, or corruptions. This corporeal envelope was often understood to include protective or concealing clothing (skin, armor, or monastic habit), much in the manner of Poe's *tournure*.[13] The culture of books, in turn, provides its own rigorous structure of containment, words alphabetized and contained within the limited space of leaves of paper or parchment, selected folios bound together in discrete codices, held within bookcases within libraries. This containment model is continuous from manuscript to printed books and beyond, but as Paul Zumthor and Jan-Dirk Müller have argued, books begin to shed their corporeal habits after the arrival of the printing press.[14] As Johns points out, the threat of piracy compelled early printers to protect their industry by enclosing it within the moral comfort of domestic spaces: "A printing house was to be a printing *house*. At one point the law actually stipulated expressly that presswork could only be done at home. The idea was that activities carried out in a patriarchal household partook of the moral order implicit in that place."[15] Once books became associated more often with physical locations than physical bodies, they were ripe for the proprietary appropriations that would crescendo after the seventeenth century.

When we refer to the medieval Aesop, we are referring to both the ramifying sets of beast fables used in classroom instruction and the various conceptions of the author himself. In both cases, Aesop is undoubtedly a corpus, and (to use Bolens's term) a radically articulated corpus at that. In addition to the proliferating sets of fables and their commentaries, Aesop himself was sprawling and monstrous figure, whom William Caxton in his 1484 *Life of Aesop* describes as having "a grete hede / large visage / longe Iowes / sharp eyen / a short necke / corbe backed / grete bely / grete legges / and large feet" (27).[16] Moreover, this grotesquely articulated body is obsessed with linguistic modes of articulation, so much so that he serves cooked animal tongues to dinner guests (43–44). By giving his animal protagonists human tongues, he reverses their fates, engaging in an allegorical fantasy of monstrous speech. And, according to one young medieval reader, even this uncontained corpus—and by proxy his schoolmaster—was subject to the figural violence of its students. An annotation to the explicit in Lambeth Palace MS 431 ends with a call to arms: "Having finished this book, let us break the bones of the master" (fol. 136v).[17] Again and again, the medieval Aesop is described in corporeal terms, but as Aesop begins to appear in print, his body and fabular tradition are increasingly disarticulated and contained, inspiring "piratical" acts designed to appropriate, mash-up, and remix Aesopic work for new audiences.

Allegorical Body-Snatching

To understand the bond between Aesop's poetic corpus and his authorial body, it is useful to consider the following fable, whose unorthodox message and textual afterlife epitomize the corporeal habitus of medieval Aesopica. Late one evening, while guarding the bodies of criminals hanging from crosses, a soldier overhears the cries of a woman distraught by the death of her husband. Spying her from a distance, he observes that she is holding vigil over the tomb, clawing at her breast, and lamenting loudly. Despite the king's warning that the theft of the corpses would result in the death of the guard on watch, the soldier, unable to resist his attraction to the widow, relinquishes his post to comfort and feed her. Seduced by this compassionate gesture, she embraces the soldier and they copulate over her husband's tomb. When he resumes his watch, he discovers to his dismay that one of the bodies has been stolen. The widow is so moved by his earlier kindness to her that she tells him, "I would prefer to hang a dead man than kill a living one," offering to substitute the body of her dead husband for the missing criminal.[18] At her urging, they remove the husband's corpse from his tomb and hang it on the cross in the criminal's place (fig. 6.1).

This tale of grave robbing is a fitting allegory for the way this fable itself was exhumed, rewritten, and incorporated into other literary traditions. We may

Figure 6.1. The woodcut that accompanies "De Viro et Uxore" in Heinrich Steinhöwel's *Aesop*. From Basel: Jakob Wolff von Pfortzheim, 1501.

recognize this story as the "Matron of Ephesus" from the *Satyricon*, Petronius's first-century CE satire of Roman excess, but the tale was more frequently known throughout the Middle Ages as a standard fable in the elegiac *Romulus*.[19] This may seem surprising, since we can identify next to nothing Aesopic in this one, which contains nary a talking nonhuman animal and includes lascivious content that cannot be easily moralized. While the elegiac *Romulus* emerged as the predominant pedagogical series of fables and the basis for one popular printed version, known as the *Aesopus moralizatus*, the number of variations of each fable and their commentaries suggests that the medieval fable corpus had been extensively revised and remoralized.[20]

For example, the *moralitas* or standard "moral" that concludes the graveyard seduction fable, known as "De Viro et Uxore" (The man and the wife) in the elegiac *Romulus*, spawned a number of revisions and variations of its caustic antagonism toward women. The final lines offer the following message of the fable: "Only a woman oppresses the living with fear and the entombed with punishment; the work of women does not end well."[21] We can imagine that commentators accustomed to offering moralistic interpretations of fables such as "The City Mouse and the Country Mouse" were befuddled by this scurrilous tale of illicit sex and tomb raiding. One reader of this fable was also unsettled by the possibility that the widow's husband would have been discovered to be a different corpse from that of the stolen criminal. To correct this non sequitur, this commentator revised the tale (the revision appears prominently in British Library MS Additional 11897), adding a new scene in which the guard recalls that the criminal did not have any teeth, motivating the compliant widow to grab a stone nearby and unscrupulously smash out the teeth from her dead husband's mouth.[22] This revision is one example that suggests that these fables were considered to be flexible works in progress, ripe for correction and appropriation, rather than finished products to be consumed "as is."

Some commentators even exerted herculean efforts to allegorize this tale and justify its status as material for classroom instruction. The interpretation that eventually became the canonical reading in the *Aesopus moralizatus* was the following:

> Allegorically, by the woman the soul of a rational person can be understood, and by the man the chaste body itself or the world. At last comes death, that is the delight of the world, and captures (them), that is leads the man to sins and pulls the flesh to vanities. But the woman, that is the soul remaining around the grave, laments and weeps in the night, that is in

hidden conscience. Then the guard of the thief, that is a good angel, visits that place, directing his attention to that contrite one, and then he leads that soul into marriage, that is into eternal blessedness.[23]

Testing the limits of allegoresis, this selective reading weighs heavily upon the virtuous nature of the widow's grief and the compassion of the adoring soldier, all the while ignoring the mutilation of the corpse and the soldier's dereliction of duty. The Christian allegory even goes so far as to recast the illicit union of the soldier and widow as the marriage of the soul with divine bliss. This might seem like a surprising, and possibly sacrilegious, *moralitas* for this fable, but this awkward exegesis is representative of the tension represented in contemporary commentary traditions, such as the *Ovidius moralizatus*, which employs allegory to Christianize the classical tales devoid of any obvious moral content, such as scenes of incest.[24]

This fable also offers an allegory for common types of online theft, usually associated with certain types of academic thievery, such as copying and pasting, full-scale textual appropriation, and silent citation, that have become increasingly visible in this early digital age. Failing to produce an "original" text, the intellectual thief exhumes an obsolescent corpus for undead consumption. While we might reasonably object to this harrowing form of textuality—the reanimation of dead bodies of work—it must be admitted that this practice has always defined creative labor. On the one hand, acknowledging this poorly kept secret—that our so-called new work relies upon the old labor of someone else—threatens to weaken our claims to "credit" for a particular discovery. On the other, we have developed rigorous criteria for citing our sources, such as footnotes and endnotes, that simultaneously recognize and marginalize the material we rely on, all the while retaining our rights to authorship of the compiled corpus we have assembled. Whether we want to admit it or not, we often "prefer to hang a dead man than kill a living one."

Premodern Remixing

The medieval Aesopic tradition is attractive to book historians, but this corpus is not exclusively defined by the exigencies of its material environments. Nor do I think it is useful to distinguish types of Aesopic authorship according to the stark Bonaventuran categories of scribe, compiler, commentator, and author.[25] As Matthew Fisher has pointed out, Bonaventure offers this fourfold schema within a sacred tradition of theological commentary, not as a taxonomy for understanding medieval textuality more broadly, which is how it has too often been applied.[26] Within literary and historical manuscripts, the identities of scribe, compiler, commentator, and author often become blurred and irreducible to these categories.

I want to suggest, instead, that Aesopic practices of fable revision and exegetical allegorization are premodern examples of the pervasive digital habit of remixing. While remixing typically refers to music sampling and alternative mixes of previously recorded material, the rhetoric of remixing draws on the allegorical habitus of medieval school texts, of which Aesopica serves as an exemplar, or the musical "master" recording, so to speak. While there are various kinds of sampling, such as the extended remix (i.e., an elaborated version of an original track), Aesopic writing is most accurately characterized by what Eduardo Navas calls "reflexive" remixing, which "allegorizes and extends the aesthetic of sampling, where the remixed version challenges the 'spectacular aura' of the original and claims autonomy even when it carries the name of the original."[27] To establish a distinction between what he calls the "original" and its remix, Navas invokes Walter Benjamin's conception of the "aura" or cult authority of an art object, which is increasingly eliminated through new forms of mechanical reproduction.[28] Unlike Benjamin, who views the liquidation of the aura (or the destruction of art's "ritual" value) as the creation of art's political potentiality,[29] Navas suggests that the reflexive remix recognizes *and* challenges the authority of the aura through allegory.[30]

Such acts of appropriation and sampling have been characterized by Alan Liu as "destructive creativity," a kind of neo-avant-garde aesthetics that responds to the neoliberal push for constant innovation through acts of "creative destruction."[31] This is a provocative way of understanding the subversive value of remixing, but as Patricia Ingham points out, "When even 'sampling' figures as a tool of 'creative destruction'—rather than, say, an innovative act of ambivalent *homage*, we have bought entirely the notion that innovation lays waste to what has come before."[32] After all, acts of sampling and remixing gain power through their ability to preserve the material they are reconstructing and their facility to expose their sources at the same time that they are appropriating and revising them. If a source is destroyed, it becomes unrecognizable, thereby evacuating its potency as an "act of ambivalent *homage.*" *Ambivalent homage* aptly characterizes the medieval development of the beast fable corpus, which clings to the aura of Aesop, all the while expanding the collection through elaborations, additions, and variations under other names such as Phaedrus, Avianus, and Walter of England.[33]

The reflexive remixes familiar to most of us, such as alternative versions of popular books, songs, or movies, have been produced for decades behind the closed doors of publishing houses, music studios, and film editing rooms, but the emergence of writable platforms such as web templates render such textual and visual mash-ups much more visible. As Martin Irvine has astutely pointed out, their ubiquity tempts us to call everything a remix, which empties the term of its utility. At the same time, Irvine suggests, it "has become a convenient metaphor for a mode of production assumed (incorrectly) to be specific to our post-postmodern era and media technologies (though with some earlier 'precursors'), and usually limited to describing features of cultural artifacts as 'outputs' of software processes (especially in music, video, and photography."[34] Rather than limit remixing to materials and genres, Irvine proposes a semiotic model, drawing on the work of C. S. Peirce, to demonstrate the generative, dialogic, and recursive nature of all meaning-making. If we accept remixing as inherent to all types of expression, "then the *material form* of an expression appears as a *moment of orchestrated combinatoriality* in the ongoing interpretative, collective, meaning-making processes that necessarily precede and follow it."[35] Aesopic fables and commentary, as they appear within individual manuscripts and printed books, operate as *orchestrated* compilations that both recognize and challenge their predecessors, inviting future readers to do the same. While digital materials present new and accelerated forms of remixing, Raffaele Simone predicts that the future of these and related practices will lead to the disintegration of textual corpora, in which "the protective membrane of the texts will decompose and they will once more become open texts as in the Middle Ages with all the standard concomitant presuppositions."[36] According to Simone, this textual decomposition will return us to medieval writing, in which writing could be "convertible" to any particular use. Medieval texts were not as open as Simone or Honorius seem to imply, but the digital practices of creating new texts out of old ones complicate the claims to "copyright protection" or "membrane"—so cherished by publishing houses and intellectual property attorneys—in ways that anonymous medieval fable writers, commentators, and glossators would have considered necessary for their own writing or classroom pedagogy. Irvine suggests that his semiotic model for remix "can counter misrecognitions about original authorship and proprietary artifacts that sustain copyright law and confuse the popular understanding of Remix as something outside the normative and necessary structures of meaning-making in ordinary, daily expression."[37] For Irvine, our obsessions with copyright and ownership are based on erroneous conceptions about artistic originality and intellectual property, which could recuperate remixing as a creative act. As Kathleen Fitzpatrick has suggested, the characterization of creative or scholarly work as remixing might shift us "away from a sole focus on the production of unique, original new arguments and texts to consider instead curation as a valid form of scholarly activity, in which the work of authorship lies in the imaginative bringing together of multiple threads of discourse that originate elsewhere, a potentially energizing form of argument via juxtaposition."[38] Refashioning the publication of research as a form of remixing, as Fitzpatrick advocates, would acknowledge the creative appropriations that scholars already tacitly embrace, effectively making transparent their conversion of old texts into new ones.

Mixing Flowers and Fruits in Fables

The medieval expansion and canonization of Aesopic fables, for example, would have been impossible without the capacity to remix previous textual corpora. And in at least one sense, "mixing" and "appropriation" have always been central values of fable writing and reading. Take for example the opening lines of the standard prologue to the elegiac *Romulus*, which employs horticultural language to express the ways in which fables are composed and then used by their readers: "This present work ventures to be pleasurable and useful; serious things are more alluring when they are embellished with sport. This garden brings forth fruit with flowers. The flower and the fruit win favor, the one by its flavor and the other by its beauty. If the fruit pleases you more than the flower, select the fruit; if the flower more than the fruit, select the flower; if both, take both" (lines 1–6).[39] This rhetorical enterprise mixes the serious with the playful, and more precisely the serious "embellished" by the playful. The word used here is *picta*, which refers to something "painted," implying that the sport inherent in fable telling serves as a veneer or habit for what lies underneath. Yet the fruit (the serious message) is not privileged over the flower (the aesthetic attributes of the fables). Instead, the fabulist uses the verbs *lege* (select) and *carpe* (take) to explain what readers might do to the fable text, taking either the fruit or the flower, or both. While we might expect that readers would select particular aspects of a text to take away, the writer perceives the material as an open source, in which "both" or "all" may be taken. This acknowledgment of the entirety and variety of produce that might be harvested from the text suggests that appropriation is a rhetorical habit expected of the fable reader.

One poet who embraced this habitual thievery was Robert Henryson. In his own version of the Romulan prologue, Henryson offers the following line, translated almost directly from his source: "And clerkis sayis, it is richt profitabill / Amangis ernist to ming ane merie sport" (lines 20–21) (And clerks say that it is very profitable to mix merry sport amongst serious things).[40] By claiming that he learned this mantra from "clerkis," he characterizes the elegiac *Romulus* as a collection compiled by a number of unnamed authorities. Perhaps more interestingly, he alters slightly the relationship between "sport" and "ernist" ("serious things"), moving away from the Latin "seria picta iocis," or "sport painted upon serious matter," towards a more balanced "mix," the result of Henryson's "to ming." He appears to endorse appropriation and remixing as characteristics of fable writing, but his next use of "ming" a few lines later is accompanied by a direct citation of a singular authority.

> With sad materis sum merines to ming
> Accordis weill; thus Esope said, I wis,
> *Dulcius arrident seria picta iocis.*[41] (26–28)

By naming Aesop, Henryson recognizes the aura of his fabular object and reflexively remixes his source material, distilling the vast number of compilers and commentators who contributed to the elegiac *Romulus* into the authority of a single author.

On the one hand, it was conventional to cite Aesop as the origin for fables, but on the other, Henryson attributes the sentiment of mixing "merry sport amongst serious things" to anonymous "clerkis." Aesop was a particularly elusive author to pin down, since he was considered to be the singular progenitor of beast fables, while simultaneously performing Foucault's "author-function" for a host of fabular authors and commentators. Even though the phenomenon of hanging a corpus on the name of an *auctor*, such as Cato, was fairly common among medieval school authors, even Cato's *Distichs* was not attributable to other identifiable authors in the ways that beast fables were associated with multiple Aesopic authors such as Phaedrus and Avianus.[42] In an act of excessive homage, Henryson recites three different versions of the same Romulan phrase within the space of ten lines.[43] In the first instance, he offers a fairly faithful rendering of the aphorism, making just one significant substitution: rather than translate *dulcius* as "sweeter" or "more alluring," he selects "richt profitabill" (very profitable), which privileges the moral profit of the fables over their aesthetic delights. The second version, however, offers a more qualified perspective than the first: rather than suggest that any kind of frivolity may be mixed with serious things, he tweaks it slightly, saying "With sad materis sum merines to ming" (to mix some merriments with solemn matters). As if he is dissatisfied with either translation, his third version is the original Latin line itself: *Dulcius arrident seria picta iocis.* While this kind of translation and citation might seem egregiously repetitive, this redundancy reflects the redundant nature of many fable collections, which offer multiple versions of the same fable in the same manuscript.[44] Henryson may have been influenced by his immersion in this pedagogical tradition, but it is also important to note that his three renderings of the line cleverly mimic the three levels of appropriation encouraged by the Romulan prologue: selecting one, or selecting another, or taking the whole thing. Understood this way, Henryson first takes the fruit, next takes the flower, and then, having decided he wants them both, he takes both, offering his own remix of the Aesopic mantra.[45]

Aesopic Mash-Ups in the Early Age of Print

In addition to serving as a source of inspiration for Henryson, the medieval fable offers practice in literary amplification and collaborative constructions of knowledge that set the stage for the fifteenth- and sixteenth-century printers of Aesop who attempted to codify their editions through compilation, or what could be likened to the digital mash-up. Within remix culture, the mash-up is an aesthetic mode that combines two or more discrete and recognizable artistic objects (e.g., images, sounds, words) to extend or elaborate upon their meaning or significance. One of the best examples in the world of music is Danger Mouse's *Grey Album*, which is a mash-up of Jay-Z's *Black Album* and the Beatles' *White Album*.[46]

In the case of early printers, they combined disparate series of fables, commentaries, and images into single editions, expecting readers to play an active role in their reception and interpretation. Henryson's adoption of remixing as an appropriative habit also encourages his early readers and illustrators to appropriate his text in kind. One manuscript in particular, British Library MS Harley 3865, is an intriguing case in point. The handcrafted illumination that accompanies the fable, "The Preaching of the Swallow," presents a scene that serves as a mash-up of previous elements from a variety of Aesopic images (fig. 6.2). To begin to comprehend the peculiar nature of this illustration, a brief summary of the fable is in order: The narrator, happening upon a flock of birds gathering around a swallow perched in a hawthorn tree, hides behind a hedge to listen to their conversation. The swallow, warning fellow birds to dig up the hempen seed that a fowler has just sown, predicts that these seeds will eventually become the rope that the fowler will use to fashion a net, which he will then use to catch and kill the birds that feed on the crops. Mocking the swallow's prudence, the birds ignore her advice and allow the seeds to germinate in the soil. A year passes, and the narrator returns to the scene to find the seeds have now sprouted short stalks, which the swallow again implores the birds to pull up. Spurning her counsel once again, the birds allow the stalks to grow to full bloom, until the fowler harvests them to construct a net. He places the net on

Appropriation

Figure 6.2. The illustration that accompanies Robert Henryson's "The Preaching of the Swallow." © British Library Board, Harley MS 3865, 43v.

the ground and casts fresh seed for the birds to eat. For the third time the swallow warns the birds, but they greedily devour the new seed as the fowler catches them up in his net and kills them. Henryson offers an allegory for this fable, in which the swallow represents a preacher who warns her flock (the birds) against the entrapments of the devil (the fowler).

Given the presence of the human preacher at the pulpit and the audience of birds in the tree, it is clear that the Harley illustrator tried to accommodate both literal and allegorical elements of the fable. This conflation might seem appropriate for a genre heavily inflected by allegory, but this combination of two interpretative modes is a radical departure from the standard image that would accompany this fable, which depicts the fowler casting seed in view of the swallow and the birds (fig. 6.3). The unique nature of the Harley illustration suggests an "original" creation, but upon further inspection, it would be more appropriately called a "reflexive mash-up" of other previously published Aesopic figures. Navas defines the reflexive mash-up as a "form [that] uses samples from two or more elements to access specific information more efficiently, thereby taking them beyond their initial possibilities."[47] To understand how this illustration operates as a reflexive mash-up, the printing history of these Aesopic images must be considered.

The Harley manuscript dates to the latter part of the sixteenth century, approximately a century after Henryson likely composed it (ca. 1485), which would make it a handwritten copy of a text that had been in print for a significant length of time.[48] Based on this chronology, I want to suggest that three of the elements of the Harley illustration—the bird in the hand, the preacher at a pulpit, and the disembodied head on the hill (lower left corner)—were lifted from the standard frontispiece to the earliest printed book of fables, first compiled by Heinrich Steinhöwel in 1476, which contained not only the standard Latin fables of the medieval curriculum, but also their German translations (fig. 6.4).[49] The frontispiece that serves as the primary source for the Harley illustrator, however, was not Steinhöwel's edition, but rather that of Thomas Bassandyne, the resemblances of which are clear through visual comparison (fig. 6.5). In the lower right-hand corner is a clear depiction of the bird in the hand, and in the lower left-hand corner a preacher in a pulpit-pedestal is located adjacent to the lower left edge of Aesop's toga. A head on a hill is not readily apparent in this frontispiece, but the image of a man falling down an embankment lies to the left of the pulpit-pedestal.

Let us consider first the preacher in the pulpit-pedestal, the most striking and complicated image in the Harley illustration. While the preaching figure matches exactly the preacher in Bassandyne's frontispiece, Bassandyne's preacher differs significantly from Steinhöwel's statuesque man atop the pedestal that occupies the same position on the page. We know this figure to be Aesop be-

altaria:nec sacrificijs pepercisti:quid vis ergo quod orem? Audiat hec qui commisso malo:audet in malis suis loca sancta circuire maculatus:sed faciem eius & manus lauare debet:vt facta eius mala prius deleantur. Audiat & ille qui omnibus semper contrarius/ multos lesit: & malis sibi instātibᵒ querit auxiliū. Nam in psperitate/ queuis qui offenderit/in aduersis sibi amicū reperit neminē.

De hyrundine et ceteris auibus.

Et linum pariat lini de semine:linum
Nutrit humus,sed aues tangit hyrundo metu.
Hec ait,hoc semen nobis mala damna minatur:
Vellite pro nostris semina sparsa malis.
Turba fugit sanos monitus/vanosq̃ timores
Arguit,exit humum semen/et herba viret:
Rursus hyrundo monet instare pericula,ridet
Rursus aues,hominem placat hyrundo sibi.

Figure 6.3. The woodcut that accompanies "De hyrundine et ceteris auibus" in Steinhöwel's *Aesop*. From Basel: Jakob Wolff von Pfortzheim, 1501.

Figure 6.4. Frontispiece to Steinhöwel's *Aesop*. From Basel: Jakob Wolff von Pfortzheim, 1501.

Figure 6.5. Frontispiece to Bassandyne's edition of Henryson's *Morall Fabillis*. Edinburgh, 1571.

cause many of the images represented in Steinhöwel's frontispiece refer directly to scenes in the *Vita Aesopi* (Life of Aesop) that commonly prefaced fable collections after the thirteenth century and served as the source for Caxton's *Ae-*

sop.⁵⁰ The episode in question, in which the Babylonian king constructs a statue in Aesop's honor, is also illustrated in one of Steinhöwel's other woodcuts (fig. 6.6), as is the case for most all of the images that appear in the frontispiece. In this sense, this titular collage of Aesopic images serves as a visual index for the illustrations to come. We can easily imagine, for example, a linkable version of the frontispiece, in which the viewer would click the images to gain access to episodes in the life of Aesop. But Henryson's fables do not include the *Vita Aesopi*, making the Bassandyne frontispiece a partial homage (an orphaned link) to Steinhöwel's woodcuts. The preacher in the pulpit-pedestal, which appears to originate in the Bassandyne edition, complicates this reflexive relationship to the Steinhöwel frontispiece and recasts Aesop on the pedestal as a preacher, who will appear in a remediated form in the "Preaching of the Swallow" fable that appears in Henryson's collection.

The Harley illustrator, by contrast, viewed the titular collage less as a set of premodern hyperlinks to prior or subsequent Aesopic texts than as raw material for a new meme. In the case of Henryson's fable, the actual appearance of Aesop at a pulpit-pedestal would have seemed entirely appropriate, particularly because of his direct invocation at the outset of the *moralitas*, in which he is described as a "nobill clerk ... ane poet worthie to be lawreate" (lines 1888–89) (noble clerk ... a poet worthy to be a laureate) who composed this fable for "gude morall edificatioun" (line 1893) (good moral edification). The tension identified earlier in Henryson's prologue—between fables produced by many anonymous clerks and a singular Aesop—emerges again, this time in a vexed attempt to cast laurels on the fable. This shift in written authority from the multiple clerical collaborators to classroom *auctor* is dramatized in the Harley illustration, which includes an accretive figure that is a swallow, a preacher, and finally Aesop himself.

The third remixed element of the Harley illustration, the disembodied head, is perhaps the most peculiar contribution to this increasing tension between multiple and singular models of authorship. Given the fact that the head is bereft of any discernible body and lacking the color of other figures in the illustration, it is easy to overlook. It is quite possible, in fact, that the illustrator remained undecided about what to do with this head, leaving it unfinished. The only reasonable explanation for its existence is its juxtaposition with what appears to be the "hedge" (line 1729) that the narrator hides behind to eavesdrop on this parliament of fowls. Inserting a witness into a fable is a departure from the conventions of the genre and a complication of point of view that Henryson champions throughout his collection. Despite his deferral to Aesop's authority throughout his fables, Henryson consistently asserts himself as an interpreta-

menses,trabes triginta sunt ipsoȝ mensiū dies,femine dūe / dies et
nox esse dicunt̃:que se alternatim cōtinuo discurretes sequunt̃.Tūc
Nectanabo suis inqt magnatibus: tributa regi lycurgo me mittere
ius est. Unus ex illis ait: Etiā aliud pblema interrogemus:scȝ qd
sit illud:qd nunqȝ vidimus:neqȝ audiuimus? Tūc rex ait Esopo:
Dic queso Esope:qd illud est:qd nos nunqȝ vidim° neqȝ audium°
Esopus ait:Die crastino vobis respōdebo. Itaqȝ pfect° domū syn
graphū astu finxit:quo Nectanabo rex ofitebať:se mutuo babuisse
a rege lycurgo mille talēta: que Nectanabo reddere,pmittit ad ter-
minū quedā:q eo tpe pfinitus erat. Ac syngraphū regi mane apud
regiā reddidit.recitato syngrapho:Rex admirās inqt,pcerib° suis
Audistis ne autvidist̃ me a lycurgo pecuniā mutuo babuisse vnqȝ:
tūc ait esop°:si id qd dicit̃ verū ē:qstio soluta ē.Tūc nectanabo inqt Beať es lycurge q tali viro potiri̧:atqȝ esopū cū tributo remisit.

Esopus babyloniā regressus: que i egypto egerat lycur
gum edocuit:ac tributū reddidit. Quas ob res lycurg°
vt statua aurea esopo publice statueref:mādauit. Isbau
cos post dies Esopus visendi greciā cupidus/veniȝ a

Figure 6.6. Illustration of the Babylonian king's creation of a statue of Aesop in Steinhöwel's *Aesop*. From Basel: Jakob Wolff von Pfortzheim, 1501.

tive interloper in one way or another. The Harley illustrator seemed to sense
the authorial conflict represented by a narrative figure who could threaten the
credibility and coherence of Aesop, the well-established author of the fable. As

176   Habitual Rhetoric

a possible compromise, the illustrator returns to the frontispiece, but this time to a low point in Aesop's life, his violent demise—or what we might view as an allegorical moment of authorial death that makes his corpus available for reanimation by future fabulists like Henryson. This image of a man falling down a hill is actually an illustration of Aesop being tossed over a cliff, an episode from the *Vita Aesopi* absent from Henryson's fables and the Bassandyne print (fig. 6.7).

The correspondence between the two images in their entirety, a floating head and a prostrate body, are unconvincing replicas of one another. But if we examine the position of Aesop's body in relationship to his statue, we see that his head is placed in a similar position as the disembodied head, both situated below the pulpit-pedestal. If we are expected to associate these two images, a crisis of written authority arises, because the head behind the hedge would presumably be the narrator or Henryson himself. Furthermore, his disembodiment, and arguably his botched erasure from the scene, reflects an attempt by the illustrator to privilege the figure of the preacher Aesop, a figure who would increasingly become the exclusive *auctor* of all beast fables.

Aesop's Grotesque Body in an Age of Print Reproduction

During the latter part of the fifteenth century, when Henryson was composing his fables, the Aesopic corpus experienced a transformation that coincided with the arrival of the printing press. This newly mechanized system of textual production witnessed a division and dismemberment of fable collections into discrete traditions, now available in a variety of vernaculars, including English, French, German, and Italian. Printers were then faced with the daunting prospect of distilling a highly dynamic and encyclopedic genre, which contained multiple sets and variations of fables and their commentaries, into a reproducible form that could be easily absorbed by a new reading public. Despite Aesop's new public facade, readers were increasingly faced with what Walter Benjamin called "graduated and hierarchized mediation," still a far cry from his description of the state of the press in the late-nineteenth century, in which "an increasing number of readers became writers."[51] Rather, I would suggest, this unstable moment of transition in the fifteenth century between script and print led to increasing efforts to contain the authorial aura of Aesop, which can be witnessed in the changing nature of descriptions and illustrations of his physical body. And even more fascinatingly, this corporeal transformation is accompanied by attempts to consolidate the widely varied and dynamic fable corpora into a singular and reproducible Aesopic property.

aliam narrauit fabulam:sic inquiens:Uir quidam amore filie captus
rus misit vxorem:7 apud se retinuit filiam:quam cum viciaret:patri
filia inquit:pater psana facis.velim equidē potius a viris centum/
quā abs re vno/huiusmodi pati scelus.Et ego delphij,psani ac sce
lesti:eligerē potius totā circuire Siciliā:ac Scyllā charybdinq̃ se
pius transire:q̃ a vobis sic per cōtumeliā interfici.

Execro vos vestram patriam. Ac deos deasq̃ omnes ob
testor:vt me iniuste pereuntem exaudiāt:ac digna devo
bis supplicia sumant.   Uerum illi obaudientes/ ipsũ̧
ex rupe ardua precipitem dederunt.Et sic misere esopus
vitam siniuit.Mortuo Esopo:pestis 7 fames:ac vehemens quidā
mentis furor delphios cōprehendit. Qua super re cousulti a polli
nem,oraculum habuerunt: vt manes Esopi placarent. Igitur con
scientia compuncti: quod Esopum iniuste occiderant/ templum sibi
construxerūt. Preterea principes grecie ac prouincie presides/au
dita morte Esopi/ delphos pfecti : habita diligentius inquisitiōe/
dignis supplicijs vlti sunt eos/qui mortis Esopi auctores fuerūt.

Figure 6.7. Illustration of Aesop's death in Steinhöwel's *Aesop*. From Basel: Jakob Wolff von Pfortzheim, 1501.

One text mentioned above that was often retained from earlier manuscripts, but absent in the Bassandyne Henryson, was the biographical *Vita Aesopi*, the standard preface to the curricular fables, which provides a surprisingly monstrous illustration of Aesop's physical body. As reported above, Caxton describes Aesop as an enslaved man who was "dyfformed and euylle shapen / For he had a grete hede / large visage / longe Iowes / sharp eyen / a short necke / corbe backed / grete bely / grete legges / and large feet" (27). It is no accident, of course, that Caxton's striking description matches the figure of Aesop in Steinhöwel's frontispiece, crafted only eight years earlier. Perhaps more than any other depiction of Aesop, this humpbacked barefoot giant could be described as grotesque, incompatible with the traditional image of the classical author represented in Romanesque sculpture. Furthermore, his status as a venerated medieval classroom authority is belied by what is described in the text as his initial stuttering of a language comprehensible only to himself, a disability that highlights the corporeality of poetic production and threatens the very possibility of an Aesopic literary corpus. As Peter Travis suggests, "the figure of Aesop—a disruptive anti-hero—is scarcely a model of the humanistic male ideal the liberal arts curriculum was designed to fashion. Rather, he is a curiously transgressive hybrid—a bricoleur, wordsmith and trickster—whose counter-establishment words and gestures evoke a kind of subaltern admiration in his young readers."[52] Yet this "bricoleur" is neither the Aesop nor the model of authorship that has persisted in our fabular imaginations.

As printed Aesops were reproduced over time, the grotesque corporeal features of Aesop became increasingly difficult to detect. For example, if we turn to the 1571 frontispiece of the Bassandyne print of Robert Henryson's fables, we find a more normalized authorial figure (see fig. 6.5). This more symmetrically shaped Aesop is still, however, an odd match for Henryson's own physical description of the fabulist that appears in his "Lion and the Mouse" fable. The narrator even goes so far as to present Aesop as the most beautiful man he had ever seen (line 1348):

> His gowne wes off ane claith als quhyte as milk,
> His chymmeris wes off chambelate purpour broun,
> His hude off scarlet, bordowrit weill with silk
> On hekillit wyis untill his girdill doun,
> His bonat round, and off the auld fassoun,
> His beird wes quhyte, his ene wes grit and gray,
> With lokker hair quhilk over his schulderis lay.[53] (1349–55)

While we can easily identify the "spectacular aura" of the corporeal metamorphosis between the Aesops that appear in the frontispieces of the Steinhöwel (1476) and the Bassyndyne (1571) printed editions, Henryson's bearded and gray-eyed Aesop bears no likeness to the bumbling "disruptive anti-hero" of Caxton's *Aesop*.

Like the insertion of disparate graphical features of Aesop into the remixed Harley illustration of "The Preaching of the Swallow," Henryson's introduction of a curly-haired fabulist is a symptom of a growing conflict between competing and highly racialized notions of written authority in the fifteenth and sixteenth centuries. On the one hand, written and visual fabular corpora had largely been open sources, ripe for conversion for new uses and audiences. On the other, the encyclopedic accumulation and expansion of fable collections required printers to develop editorial apparatus to create an appearance of textual control. Stuck in the middle of these competing forces is the racialized body of Aesop, who is described by Caxton and announced in the Bassandyne Henryson as being from Phrygia, modern-day Turkey. Yet in Henryson's "The Lion and the Mouse," Aesop not only dons a white habit and sports a white beard, but also claims that he was born in Rome (line 1371). Henryson's Aesop has adopted a westernized habitus that seeks to enhance his authorial force for a new, and predominantly white, print reading audience, a premodern phenomenon analogous to what Cedric Burrows calls "whitescaping" in American civil rights film, which "visually shows how groups should present an acceptable form of their identity, thereby creating a racialized reality for how African Americans should behave when interacting with whites."[54] Within Henryson, this "racialized reality" is palpable, simultaneously acknowledging appropriation as a core value of fabular production while offering a singular model of authorship through a whitescaped Aesop. It is therefore hardly a coincidence that the physical body of Aesop experiences a dramatic makeover at the same time that the Aesopic corpus becomes increasingly codified and closed.

Corporate Writing and an Aesopic Commons

Through a remixing of manuscript and print technologies, the Harley illustrator demonstrates that it would be enormously reductive and technologically deterministic to conclude that the printing press ushered in this move toward singular authorship and literary property. After all, the Aesopic corpus experienced a number of educational and political transformations throughout the late sixteenth and seventeenth centuries, as witnessed in the printed editions of John Brinsley (1617 and 1624), John Ogilby (1651 and 1668), Sir Roger L'Estrange (1692), and Jean de la Fontaine (1668–94).[55] Within late seventeenth-century pedagogical discourse, however, we begin to see less of an emphasis on fable interpretation and more of a focus on the fable itself, particularly as it would relate to childhood development.[56] Throughout the subsequent centuries, Aesopica would play a central role within the development of the speaking animal tale of children's literature, a progenitor for Lewis Carroll's *Alice's Adventures in Wonderland* (1865) and Kenneth Grahame's *The Wind in the Willows* (1908). By the mid-twentieth century, the effacement of the fabular interpretative tradition had become so acute that the classicist Lloyd W. Daly could publish a collection entitled *Aesop without Morals*, an English translation of the fables with their morals relegated to an appendix, much in the manner of answers in the back of a schoolbook. Condemning the simple one-line morals as an "encumbrance" and "little more than an insult to our intelligence," Daly offers the fables in isolation as "mirror[s] of self-reflection."[57] While he acknowledges the variability of the Aesopic tradition, he refers to the fables as both a "literary product" and a "floating, common property," suggesting that the fables are designed to promote individual intellectual development.[58] By unmooring the fables from their morals, Daly's fables "float" as unified objects of reflection, affording them a romantic completeness that suggests that their artistic evolution had come to an end. Aesop's fables could now become common products designed for select, private, and individual consumption.

While we might be tempted to view Daly's "amoral" approach as idiosyncratic, even more recent editions, such as Olivia and Robert Temple's *Aesop: The Complete Fables* (1998), reflect this modern tendency to reduce Aesop to a containable property. In a Penguin paperback designed for the mass market, the translators bypass the unruly medieval Latin tradition entirely and rely exclusively on Émile Chambry's 1927 edition of the Greek prose fables. They justify their choice in a "Note on the Text" this way: "We have taken Chambry's text to represent the 'complete' fables for the purposes of this volume, although every scholar would probably alter the text by taking away some and adding others according to his or her own personal choices. . . . The 'complete fables of Aesop' is whatever the editor of its Greek text chooses to say it is."[59] In the Temples' claim that the editor determines the "completeness" of the corpus—the qualifying scare-quotes of which are eliminated in the title and back cover description of the edition—Aesop becomes a commodified property with boundary lines that are defined by "personal choices" and particular "purposes," euphemisms for market demands that ride on hyperbolic claims such as "the first translation *ever* to make available the complete corpus."[60] This contention relies upon both the denigration of Aesopic authors such as Babrius and Phaedrus, whom Robert Temple calls "second- or third-rate adapters," and the devaluation of the dynamic commentary tradition, represented by some "appalling, even idiotic"

Appropriation

morals that the Temples separate from the fables.⁶¹ Such an attempt to purify the Aesopic corpus from its grotesque literary history and messy commentary tradition effectively makes Aesop a property defined by mass-market objectives and idiosyncratic editorial limitations.

This transformation of Aesop from written body to written property, I want to suggest, represents the way open-source material, particularly creative work produced before (or outside of the restrictions of) copyright, can become consolidated and redefined as intellectual "property," often at the expense of its corporeal identity, as well as its free and "open" use. Consider the example of incunabules, the first texts printed during the latter half of the fifteenth century. While these printed volumes are often available to the public within rare book archives, most of us only know English incunabules through their availability via the online database Early English Books Online (EEBO). Produced centuries before the introduction of copyright, these books were regarded as open sources that scholars could easily reproduce and use without restriction . . . until 2011. The updated terms of service developed by ProQuest, the publishing company that owns EEBO, at the time stated, "The electronic versions of any public domain works that may be included in EEBO are the copyright of ProQuest LLC. For all works in the collection, the printing or saving of texts is permitted only for private or educational use. Further reproduction is prohibited."⁶² This attempt by ProQuest to control an entire corpus of microfilmed early editions demonstrates how far we have strayed from the corporeal nature of textual production, in which hands and bodies produce, embody, and perform writing. As Jen Boyle and Martin Foys have suggested, this policy implies that "the digital translation of an older media form into a newer one renders it *able to be owned anew.*"⁶³

To some extent, even the early association of books with libraries perpetuated this shift. Michael Camille suggests, "The whole history, development, and, to some extent, the institutional aims of the modern library have been to exclude the body from the site of reading, to make a silent desomatized optics of the *biblioteca* the simulacrum of purely mental experience, a process that will only accelerate in the future with the increasing incorporeality of the electronic word."⁶⁴ Within the recent emergence of digital libraries, texts have migrated even further from the body to become consolidated into databases, hidden behind the most indulgent proprietary fantasy of all: the paywall. To protect the online value of these intellectual properties, publishers have erected password-protected screens that require readers to pay a premium for full access to content. Blaming the decline of print subscription and advertisement, scholarly journals and the news media justify the blocking of free access as their only means of revenue generation. The paywall is also a proprietary metaphor that reveals the foundation of many institutions that produce knowledge, from the university to the newsroom: an artificial barrier that creates scarcity, enhances value, and accumulates capital. Moreover, the forms of access the paywall regulates are unevenly distributed across universities, and even across fields in ways that map onto the unequal structures of funding that have come to define the modern university. In this sense, the paywall not only offers a means toward understanding how the contemporary university has become an engine of inequality, but also contributes to it directly.[65] Given the high institutional cost of subscribing to EEBO, ProQuest perverts the Romulan "take both" mantra in order to recast this incunabular body as an intellectual property whose doors are closed to many users. It is locked, fixed, monetized, and controlled by a singular entity, a move presaged by Aesopic printers and modern editors, who increasingly consolidated Aesop's expandable corpus into one classical figure.

Many have now joined the "open access revolution," which seeks to resist the increasing author-facing charges and subscription fees imposed by academic publishers. Yet even for digital initiatives such as the Text Creation Partnership (TCP), which creates freely available XML/SGML encoded editions of early printed books, including those on EEBO, the access to the books is limited to their textual transcriptions. And while the EEBO-TCP is enormously valuable for cross-corpus searching, lexicographical study, and textual analysis, these printed codices are effectively reduced to data, alphabetic texts that have shed their codicological features. These "books" are now encoded text files of digital scans available on EEBO, which are themselves desomatized images of individual pages from early printed books. As Rebecca Welzenbach notes, users "who want to quickly get at the content of the texts, not work with the data itself, XML files are not useful unless they are indexed by a search engine and presented in a web interface."[66] By reducing them to data, the physical features of the books that are represented visually on EEBO—namely, the marginalia, the illustrations, the textual layouts, the fonts, and even handwritten corrections—are eliminated, effectively stripped of the corporeal traces of author, printer, or reader. The texts are now available to be transmitted to new locations and uploaded to new interfaces: EEBO-TCP users are even encouraged "not to worry about where they discover the data, but where it comes from."[67] While the TCP clearly provides a valuable resource for many digital humanists and early book scholars, it also perpetuates the increasingly proprietary character of the digital book, which has become defined more by "where" we find it, than "who" created it or "what" it is. For example, Henryson is not even listed as the author of the

Morall Fabillis on EEBO-TCP's "Author" browse feature. Instead, the credit is given to Aesop, yet another example of the consolidation of this corpus into one authorial figure.[68] More importantly, these text files are in danger of becoming metonyms for the books themselves, just one member of the corpus standing in for all.

Such proprietary attempts to claim copyright effectively kill the vitality of these texts, cutting them off from what we now, thanks to Lawrence Lessig, call the creative commons.[69] From the perspective of Aesopic poets and early humanists like Henryson, this privileging of one member of a corpus (i.e., one author, one text) at the expense of the others (i.e., illustrators, commentators, etc.) would have seemed inimical to the common good, especially to many in the fifteenth century who had been thoroughly schooled in Ciceronian notions of the body politic. In his *De Officiis*, Cicero uses a corporeal metaphor to describe the danger of self-interested proprietary claims: "Suppose, by way of comparison, that each one of our bodily members should conceive this idea and imagine that it could be strong and well if it should draw off to itself the health and strength of its neighboring member, the whole body would necessarily be enfeebled and die; so if each one of us should seize upon the property of his neighbors and take from each whatever he could appropriate to his own use, the bonds of human society must inevitably be annihilated."[70] For Cicero, if the act of appropriation itself can be appropriated and limited to one member, the communal body cannot thrive.

His insistence on the body as a symbol of a republic is, in turn, replicated in the fable "The Belly and the Members" that became a central feature in many Aesopic collections, including the elegiac *Romulus* and Caxton's *Aesop*, as well as a contentious political metaphor in England for the relationship between monarchs and their subjects throughout the seventeenth century.[71] Henry Turner calls this hierarchical conflict "the problem of the 'more-than-one,'" or the tension between the part and the whole, as well as "the laws and power necessary to regulate relationships among people and the values that justify this regulation."[72] Just as this conflict arises for artists caught between the protections of copyright law and the free culture of the creative commons, this struggle is palpable for Henryson and his contemporaries, who were trapped in the cradle of their incunabular moment, vying with printers for their share of the marketplace. According to Turner, this contention gave rise to the sixteenth-century "corporation," which attempted to actualize the corporeal identity of political and knowledge communities: "At once an 'artificial person' and a fictive community, the corporation is both 'one' and 'many,' enjoying rights and freedoms that are simultaneously rights of persons and rights of collectivities."[73] As both a singular figure and a textual community of authors and commentators, the medieval Aesop serves as a prototype of the early modern corporation and a representative of an intellectual gift economy, in which scholarly or artistic work is transparently shared and used. But just as medieval practices of appropriation have become exploited for privatized and monetized within digital databases, the corporation has become too often an entity that immunizes stakeholders against risks at the exclusion of others.

Moreover, the corporeal quality of the premodern Aesopic interpretative tradition should encourage us to reconsider twenty-first-century mash-ups and remixes not simply as piratical products, but as unfinished, radically articulated bodies. As Mikhail Bakhtin influentially suggested in his study of grotesque realism, the grotesque body—exemplified by Aesop's corpus (both corporeal and textual)—is perpetually "in the act of becoming. It is never finished, never completed; it is continually built, created, and builds and creates another body."[74] The work of grotesque textualities will never be finished because it will spawn new modes of production, forms of commentary, and hybridized languages. Drawing on Bakhtinian dialogism, Martin Irvine extends his argument about remix to contend that "any work produced and received in a culture, when decrypted from the copyright ontology force field of assignable property, is, necessarily, a materialized symbolic structure encoding an interpretative dialogic pattern of combinatorial units, meanings, values, and ideas that came from somewhere and are on their way to somewhere else."[75] As the canonization of a normalized Aesop demonstrates, these carnivalesque bodies will always eventually meet institutional resistance, which will force their insurgent energies toward new directions and resources.

This historically inflected understanding of remix culture and technological transition should also encourage us to reconsider our own perceptions of scholarly originality, ownership, and even the very nature of critical commentary. As Carolyn Guertin has recently argued about our current era of "digital prohibition," the attempts by transnational corporations to create greater restrictions on uses of media are accompanied by "acts of remixing media and ideas that produce new insights and deep critique" as well as "political expression of resistance to the spectacle of consumer culture via the innovative reuse of existing materials."[76] On the practical level, we might support the efforts of scholars attempting to taxonomize digital remix culture or develop responsible reforms to copyright law.[77] Yet any resistance to copyright restrictions must be accompanied by changes in intellectual dispositions, moving away from myths of in-

Appropriation

dividuality, genius, and property rights, and toward an appropriative habitus that recognizes all of the bodies involved, from the laboring scholar or graphic designer to the bodies of work they compile and produce. As Michele Kennerly suggests in her recognition of the "corpus care" that pervades ancient poetics and rhetoric, her concept of "'editorial bodies' gestures not only to the corporeal vocabulary of writing, editing, and book-rolls but also to the bodies of writers who took pains to edit and to the critical bodies that received and evaluated their work."[78] New-media theorists such as Navas point to Benjamin's enthusiastic analysis of newspaper publishing for origins for the "rise of the collaborator" and digital read-write platforms, but this limited historical understanding fails to account for our persistent emphasis on premodern principles of compilation, amplification, and allegoresis that produce written bodies of work.[79]

Allegorical Communities and Immunities

In closing this chapter, I want to consider the challenge that such an appropriative habitus offers to standard assumptions about appropriation. Even if we attempt to reclaim the corporeal nature of intellectual work, as I believe the literary history of Aesop's fables challenges us to do, how do we move beyond the proprietary language that grips our conception of a creative commons? On the one hand, if we understand a creative commons as shared property, appropriation cannot exist. We cannot appropriate what is already "proper" to us. If, on the other hand, we agree with Roberto Esposito that our understanding of the commons is "the totality of persons united not by a 'property' but precisely by an obligation or a debt," then any assertion of subjectivity or interpretation cannot exist either.[80] Any contribution to the community is defined by a duty (based on the Latin root *munus*) to be performed, not the participation of a desiring subject. The opposite of community, for Esposito, is immunity, which negates any participation or indebted fulfillment of office.[81] This cynical impulse is embodied by restrictive claims to intellectual "ownership" championed by copyright attorneys and publishing corporations like ProQuest. Immunity opens the space for subjectivity, but it is exclusively hostile to any notion of a creative community or appropriative habitus.

And while some communities, namely those that oppress others, should be subject to critique and sanction, creative communities cannot survive on cycles of destruction and immunization. If we want such an appropriative habitus to thrive, we must reject, following Esposito and Vaidhyanathan, any understanding of community based in common property, since such a proprietary conception of knowledge production only leads to restrictive claims to intellectual property and copyright, which are often at odds with creative and interpretative habits, particularly within the contexts of Aesopic writing and digital remix. In this sense, some might go so far as to challenge the very use of the term *appropriation*, or taking for one's own what is proper to another, since this fundamentally suggests the use of someone else's property. Yet as postcolonial analyses have shown, even cultural appropriation may not be simply reduced to "theft" and often becomes, as Kathleen M. Ashley and Véronique Plesch suggest, a "two-way process, one in which exchange and creative response may take place."[82] Such dialogic artistic habits may indeed operate as acts of "ambivalent homage," obscuring the language of property within the act of appropriation. At the same time, we must also reject communities based on obligation, since any contribution is limited by the perceived duties and allegiances of its members, the kind of dutiful obeisance that Poe and Longfellow expected of each other. Any attempt to tailor or interpret previous material results in the ostracism of the remixed material and its curator.

Aesop's fables and EEBO's incunabules are now available in more libraries and databases than ever before, but the cost of their massive distribution has been the gradual diminution of their corporeal habitus. Whereas Aesopica had been produced by multiple fabulists and commentators and early printed books had been mashed up by their readers and illustrators, these corpora have increasingly become a "floating, common property" and a textual landscape to be "mined." Within the *longue durée* of remixing and the increased assertion of intellectual property rights, it is difficult to imagine a neo-Aesopic corporation through which appropriation and interpretation are no longer immunized, or without office. There may be, however, a *munificent* way to conceive of creative communities that synthesizes Esposito's biopolitics with Turner's theorization of the early modern "group person."[83] As Esposito notes, the Latin root *munus* of community can mean both an obligation and a gift. And while Esposito goes to great lengths to reject the "voluntary" connotation of *munus* by demonstrating the gift's requirement of gratitude, we only need to turn to the Aesopic invitation to "take both" to find a communal body based in generosity, goodwill, and the production of new fabulists, such as Avianus, Marie de France, and Robert Henryson.[84]

This addition of *auctores* to Aesopica is a model of what we might call an articulated corporation, a singular artistic corpus that invites and accumulates new members. Within such a grotesque vision of artistic production, intellectual work is no longer a property to be owned, but a multimembered body to be fed, nurtured, and continually reshaped and redressed for new occasions and new creators. The sharing of creative work that licenses its appropriation and interpretation by others is inspired, I believe, by what Cicero calls friendship or that which is bound by "mutual goodwill and affection."[85] While healthy communities are not always defined by friends, I would suggest that they are defined by what Cicero calls *benevolentia*, or goodwill. Unfortunately for Aesop, the drive to immunize his corpus has been too strong, consolidating multiple authors and commentators into a singular author and impoverishing the fable genre to reductive allegories. Within the current era of digital remix and mash-up, I suggest we try to reimagine a neo-Aesopic habitus through which appropriation and interpretation are no longer immunized, or without office—indeed they may have a space to thrive.

7 | Salutation

The Public Intimacy of Social Networks

> If the pictures of our absent friends are pleasing to us, which refresh the memory and lighten our longing by a solace that is unreal and unsubstantial, how much more pleasant are letters, which bring us real traces, real evidences, of an absent friend.
> —**Seneca,** *Ad Lucilium Epistolae Morales*

> On Facebook, friendship means more than anything else a willingness to listen (and to like): it is a site where you tell your story to your friends and listen to theirs in return. And the story you tell is an accumulation of fragments that trickle into your friends' newsfeed over days, weeks, years.
> —**Jay David Bolter,** *Digital Plenitude*

The moment we login to Facebook, we are faced with an up-to-the-second archive of vacation photographs, cat videos, political screeds, and daily frustrations of our close friends and distant acquaintances. While we rarely think of it this way, such a collection of memories is both highly intimate and fundamentally rhetorical. Instagram brings to us images of what our friends had for breakfast and where they went on vacation, drawing us into the personal remembrances of their daily lives. At the same time, the curation of material on these sites creates a kind of rhetorical archive, a persona composed of collected memories. These digital feeds of friendly correspondence operate from a conception of memory that is more than a private storage chest of familiar things—it is an integral part of the process of recollecting, composing, and representing relationships.

In characterizing memory as one of the canons of the medieval arts of rhetoric, Mary Carruthers suggests that "memory craft is a stage in composing a work; presupposed is the axiom that recollection is an act of investigation and recreation in the service of conscious artifice. . . . Recollection is a kind of composition, and by its very nature is selective and formal."[1] Twitter feeds may be sequenced by algorithms, but these formulas for curating a particular user's experience are based in "likes," affective and robotic responses that filter and structure relationships with other users. Carruthers further notes, "Successful memory schemes all acknowledge the importance of tagging material emotionally as well as schematically, making each memory as much as possible into a personal occasion by imprinting emotional associations. . . . Successful recollection requires that one recognize that every kind of mental representation, including those in memory, is in its composition sensory and emotional."[2] Within social networks like Facebook, "tagging material" through liking and sharing becomes a way to express affection rhetorically that seems remarkably distinct from most modern habits of epistolary intimacy, in which letters are written for specific and private audiences. While nothing has ever matched the massive scope and speed of online social networking, I want to suggest that correspondence in the digital world is as archival and public as it was within medieval letter-writing cultures.

Social media databases are merely the most recent repositories of friendship, which have ranged from the mental storehouses developed through ancient mnemonic techniques to the monastic archives of the medieval world. The library has historically been a destination for those collecting and seeking materials—notably books, deeds, and wills—that document relationships and shared property between family and friends, both real and imagined. Yet libraries, like social archives such as Twitter, have been questioned as sites of intimacy because of their accessible and public nature, which would seem to undermine their personal or private value. In her critique of social media, Christine Rosen writes, "Because friendship depends on mutual revelations that are concealed from the rest of the world, it can flourish only within the boundaries of privacy; the idea of public friendship is an oxymoron."[3] Such a limited definition of friendship depends on a private archive of correspondence, a romanticized and nostalgic vision of handwritten letters kept in shoeboxes hidden away from public view underneath beds and in the corners of closets.

By contrast, danah boyd's study of teen perception of the public and private nature of social media provides a more complicated view of their potential for intimacy: "At first blush, the desire to be in public and have privacy seems like a contradiction. But understanding how teens conceptualize privacy and navigate social media is key to understanding what privacy means in a networked world, a world in which negotiating fuzzy boundaries is par for the course."[4] Teens actively seek intimacy with each other on Instagram, TikTok, and other public online spaces because these open digital venues are the default locations where teens come together, the equivalent of the public park or the shopping mall. Recognizing the archival and rhetorical nature of these sites, teens actively curate their pages to present themselves and their past in ways that suit multiple audiences of peers or even parents.[5] This conception of intimacy, in which personal correspondence is assumed to be public and available to a wide variety of readerships, may be a far cry from the private letter or diary but, as I will demonstrate, it is based in the principles, or *habitus*, of the *ars dictaminis*, otherwise known as the medieval art of letter writing.

In this chapter, I track the ways that premodern conceptions of friendship are reemerging within the networked environments that have come to define twenty-first-century internet culture across the globe, addressing specifically the history of social networking, notably the Twitter and Facebook post, whose instantaneous and abbreviated character has transformed written correspondence. In an effort to trace the precedents of this digital communication, I examine the medieval art of writing letters, known as *ars dictaminis* or *dictamen*, which established the rhetorical habits (i.e., salutation, securing of goodwill, narration, petition, conclusion) for most Western epistolary genres, from the memorandum to the email to the text message. For many scholars of letter writing, this medieval art was essentially an impersonal formula for producing a high volume of letters, written primarily for bureaucratic purposes. According to Ronald Witt, "*Dictamen*'s tyranny of stylistic prescriptions . . . discouraged the spontaneity and direct expression of thought and feeling that, at other times in history, have given the personal letter its distinctive character. With the diffusion of the prescription of *ars dictaminis* the personal letter as such disappeared."[6] Following the pioneering work of Paul Kristeller, scholars generally agree that such prescriptive teaching was gradually superseded in the fourteenth and fifteenth centuries by the work of early humanists, who preferred the less hierarchical expressions of friendship represented by the treatise *De Amicitia* and actual letters of the Roman politician Marcus Tullius Cicero.[7] Such a fundamental shift suggests that later medieval writers such as Geoffrey Chaucer abandoned the restrictive habits of *dictamen* in favor of the social networks that could be maintained through humanistic imitation of classical models.

Medieval letters of the twelfth through the fourteenth centuries have also been characterized by scholars as highly formulaic and impersonal, because written correspondence was assumed to be the documentary in nature, causing some to underestimate or discount the context of their oral delivery. According to Ben McCorkle, "the development of largely writing-based rhetorics such as the *artes poetica, dictaminis,* and *praedicandi* [arts of poetry, letter writing, and preaching] supported a philosophical view of language that regarded words as a material manifestation of mental activity rather than an embodied, performative practice."[8] McCorkle's argument about the decline of delivery within late medieval rhetoric is largely focused on the rise of print, but this claim does not account for the extensive focus within writing and preaching manuals on oral performance, which ranged from attention to tone of voice to treatises on rhythmic punctuation, the audible cues to readers about the ending of sentences. As Witt observes about medieval epistolary pedagogy, "the private letter . . . was not formally distinguished from the public letter and like public communication was assumed to be something very like a speech and amenable to oratorical teachings."[9] Letters were often recited aloud to listening audiences, who expected the deliverer to be a public orator who would adhere to Ciceronian rhetorical principles. Private audiences for letters were the exception, not the norm, within many premodern epistolary cultures.

When personal correspondence from the Middle Ages has been recovered, as is the case for the twelfth-century love affair of Abelard and Héloïse, the letters still assume a potentially public reception. In the opening lines of her letter to Abelard, Héloïse admits, "Not long ago, my beloved, by chance someone brought me the letter of consolation you had sent a friend. I saw at once from the superscription that it was yours, and was all the more eager to read it since the writer is so dear to my heart."[10] No apology is offered for what a modern reader might expect for such a breach of confidentiality. In fact, the "someone" (*quidam*) who brought her the letter is distinguished from the "friend" (*amicum*), the original addressee, indicating that Abelard's missive had been in public circulation. Abelard's famous letter, known as the *Historia calamitatum* (*The Story of My Misfortunes*), provides intimate details about his life, including his affair with Héloïse and his punishment of castration.[11] This kind of premodern "status update" that provides, perhaps "too much," personal information betrays the notion that medieval epistolary culture was dominated by impersonal formulas and bureaucratic salutations.

Even with such a poignant example as the love letters of Abelard and Héloïse, scholars continue to distinguish so-called Renaissance humanism of the fourteenth and fifteenth centuries from the medieval *ars dictaminis* by claiming that the recovery of the classical "familiar" letter inaugurated a new "personal" style of writing. Kathy Eden even goes so far as to mark Petrarch's 1345 discovery of Cicero's personal letters to Atticus in a cathedral archive in Verona as "the primal scene for the Renaissance rediscovery of intimacy."[12] For Petrarch, his discovery of Cicero's letters was the discovery of a long-lost pen pal. This transhistorical moment of epistolary intimacy is also situated as a kind of violation of Ciceronian privacy, assuming that Cicero must have distinguished his private letters from his public oratory. Petrarch is then given credit for establishing a humanist style of letter writing that provides the means for intimate amicable (or even amatory) engagement, which had been nearly absent for hundreds of years.

While this narrative of a "Renaissance rediscovery" of the personal in letter writing is attractive and pervasive, it does not accurately capture important distinctions between private and public forms of intimacy. As Daniel Hobbins has suggested about Jean Gerson (1363–1429), widely considered to be a humanist of the Petrarchan stripe, the French theologian and poet "approached writing not as a private, monastic retreat from the world" but rather "as an entry into a medieval public sphere that brought him into contact with a variety of textual consumers."[13] Gerson may have adopted a classicizing style in some of his early works, but all of his writing, like that of many schoolmen of his era, reflects a careful attention to the dictaminal training he received in the university classroom. The *ars dictaminis*, as taught in the fourteenth and fifteenth centuries at Bologna, Oxford, and Paris, works from the assumption that all writing is potentially public, interwoven within a hierarchical network of writers, and crafted for oral delivery. This performative character of correspondence naturally attends to the affective connections each correspondent is challenged to maintain within a social letter-writing network.

Such epistolary intimacy could be demonstrated in the works of Gerson or Petrarch, but I turn in this chapter to the fourteenth- and fifteenth-century vernacular writing of the British Isles, often considered to be a "late-adopter" of humanistic habits. Geoffrey Chaucer and the so-called Scottish humanists, Gavin Douglas and Archibald Whitelaw, offer a trenchant challenge to the notion that rhetoric, particularly the teachings of the *ars dictaminis*, is merely a set of learned techniques that one assumes to persuade an audience. *Dictamen* is instead a habitus, or public disposition, that actively creates, sustains, and archives networks of distributed friendships. The center of gravity of such correspondence is the salutation, the part of the letter that received the most attention in the dictaminal manuals. As the gateway to correspondence, the salutation governs the spectrum of intimacy available in a given letter and provides the most direct appeal to the personal, naming and characterizing the relationship between the writer and the reader.

A History of the Salutation

While often highly personal in nature, the salutation is generally understood to be one of the most conventional elements of an epistolary exchange. It is the part of the letter or email that establishes the relationship between the writer and the reader and sets the tone for the writing to come. "Dear" has become such a standard opening of the letter or email that we often forget about how intimate the word *dear* is. When used to describe persons, "dear," according to the *Oxford English Dictionary*, means "regarded with personal feelings of high estimation and affection," a definition that fails to match the sentiment of most written correspondence, especially the bureaucratic memorandum or even the legal subpoena. In his only reference to letter-writing in his *English Composition* lectures that were published in 1891, Barrett Wendell emphasizes the increasing conventionality of the salutation: "When we write letters, we begin them with the adjective *dear*. Now, the occasions when we mean by this word to express even the smallest degree of personal affection are so rare that at such moments we often feel called upon to change the word to *dearest*, or *very dear*, or *darling*."[14] Within writing manuals produced in the late nineteenth and early twentieth centuries, letters began to play a diminishing role because of their association with such emotionless prescriptions.[15] As J. B. Fletcher and George Carpenter put it in their late-nineteenth-century composition textbook, "letters are, roughly speaking, of two kinds, impersonal and personal. In the impersonal or business letter the writer restrains himself from all extraneous adornment of style, or even any particular display of individuality."[16] By the middle of the twentieth century, letter-writing instruction had all but vanished from composition pedagogy.[17] Now, as we proceed into early twenty-first-century writing, one of the most ubiquitous complaints about the rise of digital communication, especially through social networking sites and text messaging, is the dwindling degrees of intimacy that accompany such distributed forms of personal correspondence. Even as early as 2004, when texting was just beginning to its rise to ubiquity, linguists were already lamenting the demise of the traditional greeting, leading Carmen Frehner to conclude that "the most significant characteristic of salutations is their absence."[18] Within the swift exchanges of Facebook messaging and Snapchat, there is seemingly no time to address a recipient formally. And there is simply no need to identify the sender, whose identity has already been revealed through the automated population of contact lists and usernames.

Yet the formal address to the recipient is only one part of the medieval dictaminal greeting. The Latin salutation was originally composed of three parts: the *intitulatio* (the name of the sender), the *inscriptio* (the name of the recipient), and the *salutatio* (the initial expression of good will).[19] While the first two parts often adhere to a prescribed formula, dictated by the status of the sender and recipient and the nature of their relationship, the latter part, what we will call, *pace* Carol Dana Lanham, the *salutatio* (to distinguish it from the full salutation), offers more flexibility and opportunity to express varying degrees of intimacy. According to the twelfth-century Bolognese letter-writing manual *Rationes dictandi* (*The Principles of Letter-Writing*), a *salutatio* for the Pope might express "steadfastness of due obedience" while a *salutatio* for a friend might express "the sweetness of imperishable love."[20] The *artes dictandi* (letter-writing manuals) of the succeeding centuries continue to focus on the ornamentation of the salutation, offering long lists of examples for every kind of rhetorical occasion, which might be an academic warning from teacher to pupil or a plea for help from a child to a parent. While these manuals also attend to other parts of the letter such as the *petitio* (the request), most focus almost exclusively on the language of the salutation, particularly the different approaches to the *captatio benevolentiae* (securing of goodwill), a part of the letter that is increasingly treated within the *artes dictandi* in tandem with the salutatio. Its importance is articulated best by Brunetto Latini in his thirteenth-century *Rettorica*: "I say that the salutation is the doorway of the epistle, that which illuminates, in an orderly fashion, the names and the merits of the person addressed, and the affection of the sender."[21] As the threshold to the letter, the salutation balances the formulaic convention of addressing the status of the sender with the variable degrees of intimacy expressed.

As we move into digital correspondence, we see that the first two parts of the salutation, the *intitulatio* (sender) and *inscriptio* (recipient) have become almost completely automated, embedded within email headings and Twitter handles and tags. The most malleable part of the digital salutation is the salutatio, or the expression of affection for the recipient. While emails typically rely upon rhetorical formulations, such as "sending best wishes" or "many thanks for your kind response," texting and other forms of instant messaging employ a vast array of emojis, visual icons that express a range of emotions from sympathy to happiness to gratitude. Facebook has recognized the salutatio as one of the most powerful engines of engagement, engineering its algorithms to catalog the patterns of "likes" and strong reactions and to create networks that become intimate, often highly exclusionary, bubbles of like-minded "friends." But despite the important concerns of media scholars such as Siva Vaidhyanathan, who argues that Facebook is fundamentally antisocial and destructive, these social networks thrive because online epistolary cultures have embraced premodern dictaminal habits, in which personal correspondence is fundamentally public and performative.[22] To understand this development, I turn to representations of medieval *dictamen*, specifically Geoffrey Chaucer's *The Legend of Good Women*, which stages an interrogation of what I call "rhetorical intimacy," the capacity of the letter to develop the salutational habitus of the sender and apostrophize friendship—that is, distribute affection to unaddressed future recipients.

Rhetorical Intimacy

While Chaucer was most certainly aware of the bureaucratic and formulaic nature of the *ars dictaminis*, if not thoroughly trained in it, his epistolarity is also steeped in the Ovidian tradition of the *Heroides*, a series of intimate letters written from the points of view of mythical lovers, such as Paris and Helen, Hero and Leander, and Acontius and Cydippe. Many of these poetic epistles, notably those of Phaedra, Dido, and Medea, are essentially "dead letters," since they are addressed to an inaccessible or unresponsive audience, such as Hippolytus, Aeneas, and Jason. Whereas academic commentators provided their own *moralitates* to these suicide notes and vernacular translators situated these cautionary letters within Trojan historiography, Chaucer replies to Ovid with what I want to call "rhetorical intimacy" in *The Legend of Good Women*. Rather than merely translate or moralize Ovid's epistles, he recognizes their inherently rhetorical character, in which their authenticity matters less than their potential capacity to express love, friendship, and affection. As a challenge to the assumption that epistolary intimacy relies more on an exchange of genuine feeling between interlocutors and less upon "stylistic prescriptions," Chaucer replies to Ovid's dead letters with a kind of vernacular *dictamen* that showcases the power of rhetoric to express amatory desire, even in the absence of an identifiable audience.

As discussed in chapter 4, the works of Ovid play a central role in many premodern educational cultures in the West, and his *Heroides* received extensive attention by commentators because of their unique receptivity to habitual practice in both the rhetorical arts and allegorical interpretation. To some extent, however, they emerged more often as cautionary tales of bad behavior than eloquent expressions of virtuous desires. In his early sixteenth-century letter-writing treatise, *De conscribendis epistolis* ("On the Writing of Letters"), Erasmus suggests that while these love epistles offer examples of heroism, they also demonstrate that "the common good must take precedence over private grief."[23]

This dismissive view of the mourning of Dido, Ariadne, Phaedra, and Ovid's other abandoned women is fairly typical of premodern commentators. An alternative to this indifference is offered by one of the great Scottish "makars," Gavin Douglas, in his earliest surviving work, *The Palyce of Honour*. Rather than condemn their behavior, his narrator praises their literary achievements:

> I had gret wondir of thair layis sere
> Quhilkis in that arte mycht have na way compere
> Of castis quent, rethorik colouris fyne
> So poete-lyk in subtyle fair manere
> And eloquent, fyrme cadens regulere.[24] (817–21)

Referring to their "poet-like" habitus, he applauds both their use of rhetorical color and their eloquent rhythms, as if they, not Ovid, had composed these epistolary verses. Douglas imagines these women as writers who exhibit the skills typically acquired in the classroom, notably "cadence," a vernacular term that may refer directly to the Latin *cursus*, one of the central teachings of *dictamen*, particularly in Britain.[25] In addition to teaching the rhetorical parts of the letter (i.e., the salutation, the securing of goodwill, the narration, the petition, and the conclusion), medieval schoolmasters who taught letter writing (*dictatores*) trained their students in *cursus*, a method of rhythmical punctuation, which employs regular spondaic and dactylic stress patterns to mark the ending of clauses and sentences.[26] What is perhaps most striking, then, is that Douglas's narrator attributes this colorful cadence to the Ovidian women, who offer models of rhetorical and prosodic proficiency, rather than models of virtue or vice.

This momentary removal of Ovid from the scene of writing, however, does not prevent Douglas from demonizing Dido and other women of the *Heroides*.[27] Instead, I want to suggest, Douglas's recognition of the "poet-like" habits of the Ovidian women points to Chaucer's rhetorical replies to Ovid's epistles in *The Legend of Good Women*. This silent Chaucerian citation in the 1501 *Palyce* paves the way for Douglas's later ostracism of Chaucer in the prologue to the 1513 *Eneados*, in which Douglas famously derides Chaucer for offending Virgil, claiming that Chaucer is "all womanis frend."[28] While critics such as Marilynn Desmond have rightly focused on the gender politics of this claim,[29] the use of the word *friend* directly invokes Ciceronian notions of *amicitia*, which had been embraced by Italian letter writers, such as Petrarch, as the desirable epistolary mode of correspondence among intimates. At the advent of the printing press in the fifteenth century, enthusiasm for Ciceronian epistolary style was at its apex, even motivating the Venetian printer Giovanni da Spira in 1469 to select Cicero's

Epistolae ad familiares (*Letters to His Friends*) as the first book he would publish. And while readers of Italian books—both printed and handwritten—continued to make clear connections between the medieval rhetorical modes of the letter and Ciceronian eloquence and friendship,[30] the teaching of the *ars dictaminis* appeared to decline, evidenced by the infrequency with which dictaminal manuals were printed in the later fifteenth century.[31]

Whereas Douglas's epistolary training may have distinguished bureaucratic *dictamen* from Ciceronian intimacy, Chaucer's dream visions would have caused him to question this distinction altogether. For Chaucer, friendship is highly rhetorical, which means that it could be used as a destructive tool for verbal manipulation. In *The House of Fame*, Chaucer's narrator Geffrey laments the fate of Dido, who like many women is falsely wooed under the pretense of "frendshippe" (1.307).[32] After condemning Aeneas's infidelity, Geffrey concludes:

> Therefore be no wyght so nyce,
> To take a love oonly for chere,
> Or speche, or for frendly manere,
> For this shal every woman fynde,
> That som man, of his pure kynde,
> Wol shewen outward the fayreste,
> Tyl he have caught that what him leste. (1.276–82)

Speech, in this case, is associated with a "friendly manner," but speech is not explicitly linked to friendship. Jill Mann notes, however, that this treatment of Dido is notably Ovidian because it "encourage[s] us to identify with Dido's perspective on the desertion, instead of seeing it, as we do in the *Aeneid*, framed and qualified within the dictates of Aeneas's historic destiny."[33] Within *The House of Fame*, friendship is a rhetorical habitus that reflects little to no authentic feeling of intimacy or love, and therefore should be viewed only as a means of "securing goodwill" in the service of persuasion, one of the central tenets of dictaminal teaching.

By the time Chaucer writes *The Legend of Good Women*, however, friendship acquires a new valence, one that bridges the divide between the persuasion of rhetoric and the sincerity of emotion. This time, the amicable disposition or habitus is attributed to Dido, rather than Aeneas. In response to Aeneas's woes since his flight from Troy, Dido offers comfort:

> She seyde, certes, that she sory was
> That he hath had swych peryl and swich cas;

> And, in hire frendly speche, in this manere
> She to hym spak, and seyde as ye may here. (1082–85)

In a revision of *The House of Fame*'s account, Dido displaces Aeneas as the friendly rhetor, who offers a compassionate response to Aeneas's complaint. To emphasize this change, Chaucer transforms *The House of Fame*'s "Or speche, or for frendly manere" to the *Legend*'s "And, in hire frendly speche, in this manere," attributing friendliness to speech instead of manner. This could either be a change of significance, that is, a transfer of *amicitia* from manner to speech, or it could indicate the interchangeability of manner and speech, emphasizing the performative nature of habitus. Given the largely sympathetic portrayal of Dido and her obvious sincerity in this scene, I read the attribution of "friendly" qualities to her speech as Chaucer's attempt to recuperate friendship from its more sophistic connotations, suggesting instead that *amicitia* can operate as rhetoric that expresses genuine intimacy. And when we consider Douglas's characterization of Chaucer as a "woman's friend" and the Ovidian women as writers trained in dictaminal *cursus*, we can begin to see how Chaucer's Dido in the *Legend* offers a challenge to prevailing assumptions about the gendered habitus of rhetoric and friendship. In other words, Dido is less a "good" woman or casualty of Roman history than imitable *rhetorica* and *amica*.

To understand fully the way the *Legend*'s Dido explores the affective possibilities of rhetoric, we should recognize that Chaucer's emphasis on "friendly speech and manner" emerges from a prior, specifically Italian, epistolary tradition that had been increasingly challenging the distinctions between the bureaucratic *dictamen* and Ciceronian *amicitia* throughout the fourteenth century. For example, Giovanni di Bonandrea, the foremost teacher of writing at the University of Bologna at the beginning of the fourteenth century (discussed in chapter 1), did not distinguish dictaminal education from Ciceronian rhetoric. His *Brevis introductio ad dictamen* (*Brief Introduction to Writing*), the most popular writing textbook of its time, champions the communal nature of writing and orients instruction for civic and practical use, adapting Ciceronian rhetorical categories for writing that could be used to develop social networks among professional communities outside the university.[34] The impact of his writing manual is exhibited not only by future teachers' marginalia, but also by its attachment to Cicero's *De Amicitia* (*On Friendship*), the pseudo-Ciceronian *Rhetorica ad Herennium* (*Rhetoric for Herennius*), and Ciceronian quotations in surviving Bolognese codices.[35] As James Banker has demonstrated, Giovanni distinguishes his approach from his predecessors by suggesting that letter writing is not the exclusive province of ecclesiastical and aristocratic circles.[36] In addition to providing formulas for greeting superiors, Giovanni provides a new rhetorical category for letters that could be addressed to those "habitu precellentium" or "distinguished by habitus" (77r).[37] On the one hand, *habitus* could refer to "quality," or those who have proven their merit in ways that transcend ecclesiastical or aristocratic titles. Giovanni attempts to clarify his understanding of habitus by explaining that it is "some proportion of the body not given by nature but collected by study and industry" (77r).[38]

Given the Ciceronian context of Giovanni's rhetoric, habitus offers a new category for written correspondence, one that embraces the collection of knowledge through learning and work, as well as the capacity for amicable, non-hierarchical exchange. Therefore, when Chaucer describes Dido's "friendly manner" and Douglas describes the Ovidian women's "fair manere," they may be directly invoking this rhetorical category of habitus. As Giorgio Agamben points out in his analysis of medieval "manner" in *The Coming Community*, "perhaps the only way to understand this free *use of the self*, a way that does not, however, treat existence as a property, is to think of it as a *habitus*, an *ethos*. Being engendered from one's own manner of being is, in effect, the very definition of habit.... And this being engendered from one's own manner is the only happiness really possible for humans."[39] For Chaucer's Dido in the *Legend*, her "free use of the self," or friendly habitus, is her means of access to happiness.

To speak of happiness for a woman who proceeds to fall on her own sword out of the anguish of abandonment strikes a flat note, but it is important to understand that Chaucer's Dido emerges as a respondent to earlier incarnations of Ovidian women. Whereas one medieval commentator understands the *intentio auctoris* (intention of the author) of the *Heroides* as "how one may be solicited through letters,"[40] Chaucer's Dido demonstrates how one may express affection through rhetorical habits. Ovid's Dido is easily appropriated in the service of medieval education because she writes a letter that is "dead" in at least two senses. First, her epistle is a letter after Jacques Derrida's heart, one that never reaches its destination, purloined by a medieval "Dead Letter Office" for unintended pedagogical use.[41] Second, it is written as a prelude to Dido's death, which effectively renders it a suicide note that preserves the memory of her desire and pain. By contrast, Dido's letter in Chaucer's *Legend* is published posthumously. The vernacularized text of her letter, while described as written "byforen or she deyde" (line 1353), appears only in abbreviated form after she has fallen on Aeneas' sword (1351–65). Desmond aptly notes, "The composition of the love letter at the point of death provides the textual mechanism by which [Dido]'s desire survives her death and continues to exert a claim on her lover."[42] The legend becomes more a rhetorical lesson of Dido's desiring manner than a homily of her exemplary devotion.

Chaucer therefore achieves a kind of friendly habitus in two ways. Firstly, he purloins Ovid's letter and offers a preemptive reply. By devoting most all of his legend to Dido's intimate exchanges with Aeneas—what I would call examples of Ciceronian *amicitia*—Chaucer provides a context for the suffering that Ovid's epistle describes. Before he urges readers to "Rede Ovyde" (1367) at the end of the legend, Chaucer establishes Dido's ethos, which makes her one of Giovanni's epistolary agents distinguished by quality, manner, or habitus. Secondly, Chaucer's legend provides an historical background for Dido's rhetoric of intimacy, which encourages readers to conceive of her letter (and all letters by Ovidian women) as plausible letters written by plausible women, not simply produced from Ovid's imagination. This is perhaps why Douglas perceives Chaucer to be "all womanis frend" and praises the epistolary acumen of the Ovidian women.

Tweeting Dido

If Chaucer is attempting to reproduce Dido's expression of intimacy, why then does he abbreviate her letter? Ralph Hexter suggests that, as "dead letters" addressed to inaccessible or unresponsive audiences, the poetic epistles of the *Heroides* "model the writer reaching out across a void to an absent other."[43] Among these Ovidian women, Dido was especially attractive to academic commentators, who often amplified her letter with *moralitates*. By contrast, Chaucer's *Legend of Good Women* dramatically abbreviates Dido's letter, urging readers to recover the full letter in the Ovidian archive. Chaucer's Dido, a rhetor of "frendly speche [and] manere" (1084) follows her loving desire for Aeneas to her death, only letting loose "a word or letter" (1362) in her swan-like complaint. The abbreviated lines of Dido's epistle function as a premodern tweet to a readership who can purloin the letter for a new life, one that bears the distributed traces of Dido's acts of rhetorical intimacy.

This interpretation of Dido's epistolarity takes as its point of departure Desmond's argument that *The Legend of Good Women* is Chaucer's attempt "to dramatize a sort of interpretative mastery," a kind of textual power-grab that "relies on a binary set of heterosexist possibilities for the performance of gender."[44] Within this hermeneutic opposition, the *Legend* represents, as Carolyn Dinshaw describes it, a "text as a woman read and interpreted by men."[45] Christopher Baswell attributes more agency to Dido through her "queenliness," but he also insists that her attempts to gain sovereignty are "finally blasted, transfixed by the sword of Aeneas" that she uses to kill herself shortly after composing her letter.[46] All of these interpretations focus on Dido's written authority, the Ovidian fiction of female epistolary agency that is rewritten and reimagined by Chaucer.

While I agree with these previous readings of Dido, I want to shift the focus from the writing subject, Dido the letter-writer, to the writing object, the letter itself, to recognize both the vitality and ephemerality of its material presence. In this way, I am adopting a similar posture to that of Jacques Lacan in his "Seminar on 'The Purloined Letter,'" in which he argues that the stolen letter in Edgar Allan Poe's detective tale operates as a "pure signifier," necessarily disconnected from its meaning, or the controversial content that made it an attractive object for theft. For Lacan, the materiality of the letter is of utmost importance to its singularity as a letter, which does not "allow of partition. Cut a letter into small pieces and it remains the letter that it is."[47] Within Poe's narrative, the letter's meaning is irrelevant. Rather, the letter's materiality possesses symbolic capital, a potentiality that drives the plot of the tale to its resolution. Without the recognition of the material presence of the letter, the narrative loses its force.

For the *Legend*'s Dido, her letter possesses a symbolic power that Chaucer connects directly to its location in an Ovidian archive. Rather than relate the full extent of the letter's contents, Chaucer's narrator excerpts the letter and ends the tale with the couplet, "But who wol al this letter have in mynde, / Rede Ovyde, and in hym he shal it fynde" (1366–67). Through this rhetorical abbreviation, Chaucer refers readers who desire "al this letter" to the Ovidian corpus, where the full letter may be found. Chaucer employs this technique earlier in the *Legend* to shorten Virgil's account of Venus's conversation with Aeneas, adding the comment, "I coude folwe, word for word, Virgile, / But it wolde lasten al to longe while" (1002–3). While the rationale for this abbreviation is narrative efficiency, the direct citation of these sources offers the opportunity for expansion, if the reader so desires. Such textual references are far from uncommon, but in the *Legend* they are specifically linked to books as objects of memory. Among all of Chaucer's work, Carolyn Collette identifies the *Legend* and *Troilus and Criseyde* as texts "where Chaucer most frequently references books, citing 'olde bokes' as the sources of our knowledge . . . creat[ing] a world of book ownership, of readership, of ready access to books which become guides to thinking and understanding, as well as historical knowledge."[48] Within the *Legend*, the word *book* appears often and variously, referring once to "oure bok" (1721) and another time to the sad state of loving "withoute bok" (1608). When Chaucer urges his audience to "Rede Ovyde, and in hym he shal it fynde," he equates Ovid with a book, in which Dido's letter may be found.

The logic of this abbreviation and potential for expansion by a future unidentified audience is the very logic that shapes the digital habitus of tweeting. When we send out a tweet into the Twitterverse, our 280 (or fewer) characters become a voice crying out in the wilderness, an abbreviated object reaching out for an expanded life. Once recipients recognize the tweet, it is favorited, retweeted, or (best of all) replied to—rhetorical habits that create various afterlives for this digital epistle. And even when its series of lives fade into the background, superseded by newly trending tweets, this networked object is archived, available for recovery or revival by a future digital friend (or enemy). This epistolary habitus explains a surprising affinity between premodern and digital writing: they are both object-oriented, that is, focused on the coded relationships between material objects, represented by the networks of glossed books or RSS feeds.

Dorothy Kim has suggested, "If the medieval manuscript is a recording medium that allows scholar[s] now to see the conversations and connected marginal glosses of individual readers, then Twitter is the digital medium that replicates this practice the most but with comments all the time and in real time for individual thinkers."[49] Marginalia and tweets both operate as nodes of connection between textual objects, expanding drastically the temporal field of interpretation for texts and their material environments. In her book *Medieval Twitter*, Alicia Spencer-Hall observes, "The tweet is also a time-capsule, one that can be dug up by anyone with its location—even years after the fact. The Twitter algorithm offers up a roadmap, with 'in case you missed it' notifications inserting 'old,' but noteworthy, content into a user's feed. Reading that tweet after sundown, after *that* sun has gone down, allows the past to puncture our present, for the linear order of things to be disrupted, if only for an instant. This temporal unruliness is amplified by tweets which, in the present tense, recount the past, explicitly acknowledged as such."[50] When Chaucer follows Dido's abbreviated letter with the command to "Rede Ovyde," he inserts a common marginal gloss within his narrative, essentially hyperlinking his text to Ovid's, where the full letter has been transhistorically archived.

As ephemeral as a tweet may seem, Twitter is a networked repository of information that may be retrieved from physical servers, often with just a minimal exertion of labor. The fact that online archives require little effort to access creates the illusion that the virtual world is immaterial or that digital objects do not possess physical qualities or habitations. Matthew Kirschenbaum corrects this misperception through his own "forensic" investigations of computational materials—such as drives and disks—that support the operation of digital code. He argues that "every contact leaves a trace," demonstrating that digital writing relies on inscription and storage technologies that constitute two types of computational materiality: forensic, which refers to manufactured structures such as hardware; and formal, which refers to layout or design.[51] Through these definitions, Kirschenbaum establishes a vital distinction between two materialist methodologies: the formal analysis of a text's script, organization, or relationship to extratextual elements such as images and margins; and the forensic analysis of the text's physical environment, its state of corruption, and its storage capacity. Assuming it is a social good to preserve and publish knowledge, archive-loving academics tend to neglect thoroughgoing forensic investigations—despite (or perhaps because of) the US Department of Defense's abiding concern with what Kirschenbaum calls the "remarkably, stubbornly, perniciously stable and persistent" state of electronic data.[52] Unlike political regimes who safeguard state secrets, the academy does not seem to view the indestructibility of data as a problem.

Likewise, when Chaucer tells his audience to read Ovid, he assumes that a book of Ovid will be available to them. Even the couplet "But who wol al this letter have in mynde, / Rede Ovyde, and in hym he shal it fynde" echoes his previous (and well-known) meditation on books as containers of memory in the prologue to the *Legend*:

> Than mote we to bokes that we fynde,
> Thurgh whiche that olde thinges ben in mynde, ...
> And yf that olde bokes were aweye,
> Yloren were of remembraunce the keye. ...
> And as for me, though that I konne but lyte,
> On bokes for to rede I me delyte,
> And to hem yive I feyth and ful credence,
> And in myn herte have hem in reverence
> So hertely, that ther is game noon
> That fro my bokes maketh me to goon. (F.17–18, 25–26, 29–34)

In contrast to the indestructibility of digital data, Chaucer dwells on the fear that "olde thinges" would be "[y]loren" (lost) if books were unavailable. This forensic nightmare displays little confidence in the human capacity to memorize, suggesting instead that the destruction of or distance from books would cause memory loss. Most importantly, these lines emphasize the vital status of the book as a storage device, which contains "olde thinges" such as Dido's letter to Aeneas. Dido's abbreviated epistle and reference to Ovid therefore recognizes the forensic materiality of the medieval book as a kind of open-access hard drive.

Yet this recognition of the book's storage capacity does not exhaust the material range or rhetorical velocity of Dido's excerpted letter. At the same time that a tweet leaves a trace in the digital archive, it also disseminates data over a range of potential networks, which in turn rely upon substructures such as wiring and circuits. Johanna Drucker refers to this partitioning of the digital object as "distributed materiality," in which a "digital 'entity' is dependent on servers, networks, software, hosting environments and the relations among them just as surely as a biological entity depends upon atmospheric and climatic conditions."[53] These multiple points of contact leave traces throughout digital networks, which disseminate the object's materiality into disparate spaces and locations.

If we consider Dido's abbreviated letter in this context, parts of her epistle have material presences in various books: in the multiple copies of Ovid's *Heroides* in medieval libraries and schools, in the multiple vernacular versions of Ovid's works, and even in the multiple copies of Chaucer's *Legend*, a text which famously survives in two (often irreconcilable) versions. What is striking about Chaucer's example is its self-conscious assertion that the letter has an expanded life elsewhere, a recognition that this premodern tweet will lead readers to other distribution centers of Dido's lament. In contrast to Lacan's insistence on the singular "materiality of the signifier," Dido's letter is purloined and partitioned, disseminated in pieces throughout the medieval network of Ovidian books. As Drucker suggests, "distributed-ness disturbs assumptions of singularity or stability. A quality, materiality, whose identity depends on contingencies cannot be mistaken for a self-evident object."[54] In the case of the *Legend*, a crucial contingency is the relationship between Chaucer's text and the larger Ovidian network, a relationship that transcends a mere citation of a weightier textual authority. It is a dynamic distribution of epistolary parts across an interrelated network of medieval books.

By making this argument, I am not suggesting that every textual citation or allusion is a recognition of the distributed materiality of books. It is this Chaucerian scene, in particular—in which Dido's grief is given both a sympathetic context (one that is openly critical of Aeneas's abandonment of Dido) and an archival record (a kind of digital object identifier)—that provides a compelling glimpse into the forensic world of medieval books. The fact that her lament is not just spoken, but recorded in writing, enhances the emphasis on written matter. In the epigraph to this chapter drawn from Seneca's letters to Lucilius, an epistolary collection of enormous importance to medieval letter writers, Seneca writes, "I never receive a letter from you without immediately being in your

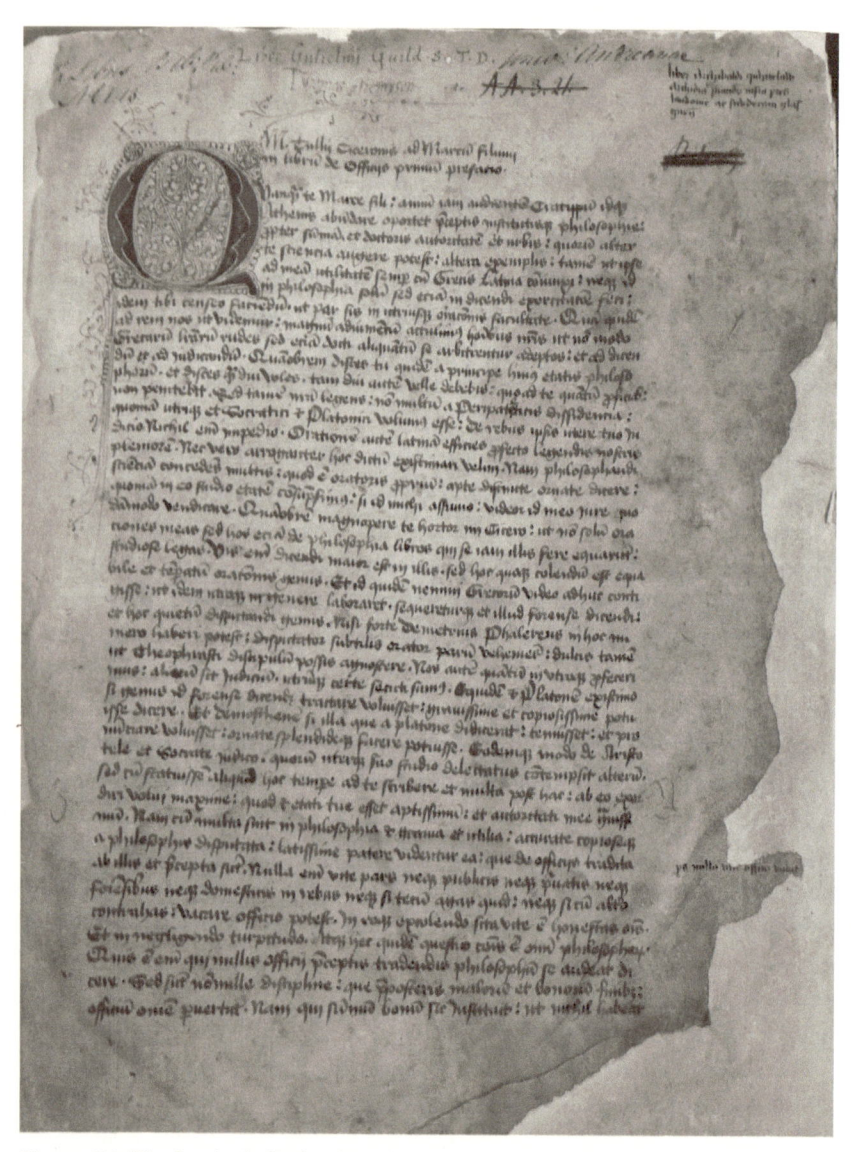

Figure 7.1. The first leaf of Whitelaw's handwritten copy of Cicero's *Opera Philosophica* (ca. 1480). Courtesy of the University of St. Andrews Libraries and Museums, Cicero, 'Opera Philosophica,' msPA6295.A2A00.

company. If the pictures of our absent friends are pleasing to us, which refresh the memory and lighten our longing by a solace that is unreal and unsubstantial, how much more pleasant are letters, which bring us real traces, real evidences, of an absent friend. For that which is sweetest when we meet face to face is afforded by the impress of a friend's hand upon his letter,—recognition" (40.1).⁵⁵ When Dido inscribes her letter, she leaves both a record of her grief and the Senecan "impress" of her hand, a material marker that signifies her presence. But her letter is "dead," never reaching Aeneas, relinquishing its potential to conjure her absent presence for her addressee. Dido even anticipates this loss, noting "my name is lost thourgh yow ... I may wel lese on yow a word or letter" (1361–62). Yet the lost connection between Dido and Aeneas is the event that releases and distributes the traces of her intimacy into the Ovidian archive, real evidence that can be recovered by Chaucerian readers. Shifting the focus from reading Dido to tweeting Dido, we can supplement our formal analysis of individual manuscripts with investigations of the forensic and distributed materiality of medieval books.

Friending Cicero

After Chaucer's legacy began to fade during the later fifteenth century in Britain, dictaminal rhetoric gradually began to lose its grip on both Latin and the vernacular, perhaps because of its prescriptive and hierarchical nature, which was perceived to be a hindrance to the development of more intimate social networks based upon Ciceronian ideals of *amicitia*. The obsolescence of *dictamen* in Britain was therefore accompanied by the importation of Cicero's works printed on the continent. An important figure in this development was Scotland's Archibald Whitelaw, royal secretary and tutor to James III, who studied and taught at St. Andrews University, all the while amassing an archive of classical works.⁵⁶ Considered to be one of the earliest Scottish humanists, Whitelaw possessed a library of printed books, including four from Venice, which specialize in all things Ciceronian.⁵⁷ Cicero was so beloved among Venetians that their first printer, Giovanni da Spira, selected Cicero's *Epistolae ad familiares* (*Letters to His Friends*) as the first (and second) book he would print in Venice.⁵⁸ Whitelaw appears to have been grappling with continental Ciceronianism when he encountered the 1471 Roman edition of Cicero's *Opera Philosophica*.⁵⁹ St. Andrews University's library holds a manuscript copy (ca. 1480) of this printed book (fig. 7.1), written in a script that imitates a humanist hand.⁶⁰ While this paleographic feature is worthy of investigation in itself, even more revealing is Whitelaw's marginalia, which is signed and distinguishable throughout the manuscript (fig. 7.2). As the length and number of his comments indicate, Whitelaw was clearly engaged with Cicero's *De Amicitia* (*On Friendship*), but his greatest dedication was to Cicero's *De Officiis* (*On Duties*), a vastly influential work of moral and political philosophy.

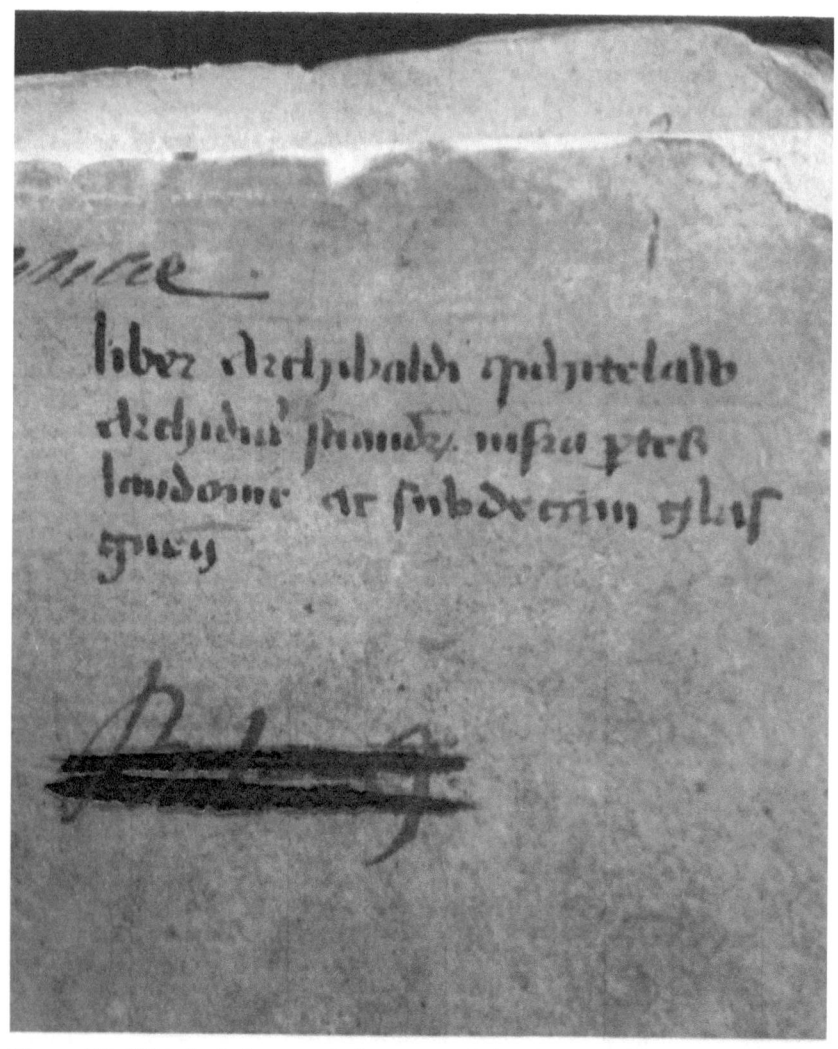

Figure 7.2. Whitelaw's signature in the upper righthand corner of fol. 1r. Courtesy of the University of St. Andrews Libraries and Museums, Cicero, 'Opera Philosophica,' msPA6295.A2A00.

    Whitelaw's investment in *De Officiis* is relevant for two reasons. First, Petrarch and later humanists considered it to be an intimate letter of advice from father to son.[61] Whitelaw's interest may reflect his engagement with this "new" epistolary style, a kind of political rhetoric of friendship. Second, *De Amicitia* and *De Officiis* share a common concern with the role of utility (or advantage) in human affairs. In *De Amicitia*, the relationship is one of the chicken and the egg:

208　　　　　　　　　　　　　　　　　　　　　　　　　Habitual Rhetoric

"It is not the case, therefore, that friendship attends upon advantage, but, on the contrary, that advantage attends upon friendship."[62] Whitelaw appears to have this dictum in mind when he approaches Book Three of *De Officiis*, the most heavily glossed book in the manuscript. To highlight a similar point that Cicero makes about using others for personal advantage, Whitelaw adds the summative gloss, "Nature does not permit that we increase our power with the spoils of others."[63] This comment highlights his unassuming dedication to friends, especially when we consider Norman Macdougall's claim that Whitelaw was "the survivor of more political crises than any other royal servant," a man who endured the tumult of the reign and eventual overthrow of his tutee James III.[64] Without Whitelaw's marginalia, we would have limited access to his thoughts on friendship, which could only be inferred from the surviving contents of his library, historical records, and his address to King Richard III.[65] His glosses comprise a network of commentary on friendship that would be archived and later extended by the book's future owners, swapping words with imagined friends, much in the style of Cicero and Petrarch.

Social networks such as Twitter, Facebook, and TikTok may happen in "real time," but they are shaped by this premodern habitus of archival friendship, with the number of comments and "likes" indicating the level of collaborative investment of one's "friends." Within these interactive platforms, social networks are established and tracked through digital correspondences that we call "following" and "friending." While such forms of friendship are sometimes empty gestures devoid of any sincere feeling of affection, these rhetorical habits often express a real desire for intimacy, even in the absence of a sympathetic recipient. Most importantly, these epistolary friendships have a distributed material life within these spaces, wherein digital objects of intimacy can be recorded, disseminated, archived, searched, and even recovered.

Rhetorical Friendship within Social Networks

"Oh, my friend, there is no friend."[66] This famous proverb by Michel de Montaigne, which he attributes to Aristotle, expresses skepticism about the possibility of perfect friendship, one in which intimacy is equally shared between two people. Within the constraints of mutual affection, Facebook is most certainly not our friend. To suggest otherwise would be ignore the capital-driven mission of such a social network, which profits from the intimacies it facilitates. Yet it is important to acknowledge that the technocrats who develop these platforms recognize the potential of public, performative, and distributed forms of friendship, all of which thrive on the human desire to connect with others. In the absence of an identified recipient, Twitter has developed an infuriated hive of "followers" who swarm around retweets, a massive amplification of the forwarded email, reaching readers who could be friends, enemies, or even robots. Critics have justifiably condemned these social-media corporations for their monetization of user data, selling it to advertisers and, in some cases, violating users' privacy rights. All of these efforts to capture this market would have been futile, however, without the willingness or desire of social-media users to share their personal information over these networks. Even though it is now commonplace to consider the rise of exhibitionist correspondence as a post-Enlightenment digital phenomenon, public and archival forms of friendship have a rich history that has important implications for current and future research in rhetorical memory and delivery. Ultimately, a recognition of this inherited habitus fundamentally challenges our assumptions about the existence of a friendly reading audience itself.

Since the classical canons of memory and delivery were developed primarily with orators, not writers, in mind, they have often been neglected within modern scholarship on rhetoric. In one particularly compelling response, Collin Brooke reevaluates the salience of these canons, arguing that digital platforms force us to reconsider the importance of persistence and performance within new media.[67] Social networks like Facebook rely upon an archive of memories that is constantly updated, automatically indexed, easily accessed, and instantly shared. Each posted photo and accompanying caption becomes a multimodal epistle to the online world and an annotated remembrance for the accumulating archive. Moreover, each time we "like," comment, or share a friend's post, these affective habits are tracked and filtered for the production of future content on our feeds. For Brooke, such a practice of tagging material—embodied as well by metadata, RSS, or tag clouds—transforms our traditional understanding of memory as storage into a persistent practice of pattern-making. This digital form of memory is what he calls "persistence of cognition," which he defines as "the ability to build and maintain patterns, although those patterns may be tentative and ultimately fade into the background."[68] Brooke importantly demonstrates that algorithmic new-media platforms challenge the presence/absence binary, which has accordingly limited discussions of the role of memory within rhetorical theory.

While the Twitter aggregators that track "trending" topics and other kinds of software-encoded operations that do this work in the "background" certainly comprise a new, decidedly posthuman, memory practice, the method of constructing and sustaining structures for memory retrieval was a central medieval mnemonic technique for the production of speech and writing. Historians of rhetoric have long recognized the importance of the pseudo-Ciceronian *Rhetorica ad Herennium* (*Rhetoric for Herennius*), an authoritative Latin treatise on rhetoric from the first century BCE that addresses both memory and delivery at length; but the significance of its medieval reception and application of these oratorical precepts to manuscript culture have been underestimated. One of the most well-known teachers of *dictamen* in the early thirteenth century, John of Garland, treats the importance of memory for letter writing in his *Parisiana poetria* (*Parisian Poetics*), which sets out a three-column system for remembering material within the composition process. Even though John of Garland claims to be following the intercolumnar principles of the *Rhetorica*, Mary Carruthers calls the treatise a "garbled adaptation" that demonstrates a greater indebtedness to the twelfth-century mnemonic theory of Hugh of St. Victor, who developed a grid system organized by place, time, and number that could be associated easily with the layout of a page in a book.[69]

John of Garland claims that material from the memory could be selected, his alternative for classical invention, from a set of sections in the mind that are each devoted to particular compositional content. He even claims that one part of the column

> should be imagined as containing, in separate compartments, examples and sayings and facts from the authors, and the teachers from whom we heard them, and the books in which we have read them. If memory should fail us on some point, we must then call to mind the time, be it vivid or hazy, when we learned it, the place in which, the teacher from whom, his dress, his gestures, the books in which we studied it, the page—was it white or dark?—the position on the page and the colors of the letters; because all these will lead to the things that we want to remember and select.[70]

This cognitive map for structuring and archiving things that must be remembered (*memoranda*) is the basis for future visual representations of memory, including printed multicolumn layouts of encyclopedias and textbooks, especially sectioned webpages and social-networking sites, which run feeds of text, image, and video in columns within interactive interfaces. As Carruthers notes, "the development of tabular lay-outs and the advice to use them mnemonically went hand in hand, since there is a clear, persistent theme in all medieval mnemonic advice: to take advantage of the presentation of the physical page as a fixative for memory."[71] This technological innovation within the codex is an important element in the design of social media sites, especially Facebook, which relies upon such mnemonic visualization in the development of an interface that juxtaposes vibrant images and favorite quotations within easily organizable tabular spaces.

While digital forms of epistolary writing such as tweeting and updating rely heavily upon such oral and manuscript memory systems, their reliance upon forms of medieval rhetorical delivery are equally significant. Brooke makes an important distinction between what he calls "transitive" and "intransitive" understandings of delivery, or what he prefers to distinguish between delivery as "medium" (an object to be delivered) and delivery as "circulation" (a continual act of performance).[72] Brooke uses Wikipedia as his central example of a platform that is in a constant state of delivery through edits and updates, but we could also cite a number of social-media sites, especially Twitter, which rely on retweets to circulate messages to the larger online world. Because print publications are often understood to be discrete entities (i.e., everyone gets their own copy), only the text they host and distribute is considered to be a shared object. The supposed innovation of the electronic word is the capacity of a text to be shared within a common interface, such as a website or blog, available to be annotated or, in the case of Wikipedia, edited by interested readers. Each edit of a page, each comment on a blog, each revision of website is a new performance, a new delivery of the text—hence its intransitive nature. Yet this same social sensibility of textual interaction pervades premodern writing, from the continually amplified interfaces of the manuscript book to the copying and circulation of manuscript letters, which often include the annotations and abbreviated replies of multiple recipients anticipated by Chaucer's Dido and Whitelaw's Cicero.

This emphasis on intransitive forms of digital delivery clearly has its own premodern roots, but it is also imperative that we recognize what Kathleen Welch identifies as the significance of the "medium," which could be a television screen or a tabular online interface that facilitates delivery.[73] Brooke offers a critique of Welch's argument about the role of the medium by citing the limits of established genres such as blogs, limits which constrain their performative value. For Brooke, blog-writing develops its own set of static rules that, if considered a medium for delivery, limit the dynamic potential of blogs.[74] If, however, we do not equate genres, such as blog-writing, with the media that host or circulate them, such as blog platforms, and instead refer to media as material interfaces, such as manuscript letters or social media templates, then we can rehabilitate the rhetorical capacity of the medium to the canon of delivery.

Drawing on Welch's arguments, James Porter has persuasively argued for a more capacious definition of delivery, identifying five categories: body/identity, distribution/circulation, access/accessibility, interaction, and economics. Rather than draw the line between Brooke's transitive and intransitive forms, Porter demonstrates the ways in which delivery can operate across digital objects and modes of new-media performance, analyzing faculty profile pages, circulation of printed texts, interfaces usable by people with various disabilities, platforms that facilitate a range of participation, and the capital-driven forces that shape file-sharing databases. Yet even Porter falls prey to the same "renaissance rediscovery" and "digital innovation" narrative that occludes the principles of the medieval arts of writing that undergird all of his stated categories. Beginning his rhetorical history of delivery with Aristotle and Quintillian, Porter asks us to "fast forward to the early Renaissance," otherwise known as the later Middle Ages, to consider Christine de Pisan's *Treasure of the City of Ladies* (1405), which provides what he claims is "an integrated view of rhetoric and the body that we do not often see represented in the Western rhetorical canon."[75] As the chapter 6 has demonstrated, medieval writing *often and regularly* relies upon the rhetorical body of the author, the text as a corpus, designed to be expanded and translated for future readers and writers. Chaucer's aforementioned Dido explicitly connects the fate of her body with the fate of her epistle, a dead letter to an absent audience, which can only be revived through the manuscript books of Ovid that preserve and distribute her memory. This turn away from an identifiable or familiar recipient to a future or unknown respondent is therefore not just the "true revolution of the Internet," in which an editable website such as a blog "actively invites the audience to become a co-producer of content."[76] Instead, it is the elevation of the persistent value of the amplificatory, appropriative, compilational, circulatory, performative, and translational habits and media of premodern writing cultures that make digital forms of delivery so salient.

Rather than distinguish between transitive and intransitive delivery models or posit the revolutionary character of digital writing, I want to conclude by suggesting that the medieval salutation establishes fundamental assumptions for the public intimacy that pervades our social-networking rhetorics. Montaigne's maxim "O, my friends, there is no friend" is a type of salutation called an apostrophe, an ancient rhetorical device for addressing an absent or inanimate audience. As one kind of "strophe" or "turn," an apostrophe is a "turning away" from a narrative or subject at hand to offer a lyrical speech to a recipient outside of the text. As an important method for expressing emotion, such as exclamation or lament, the apostrophe plays a central role within medieval writing manuals, including Geoffrey of Vinsauf's *Poetria nova* (*The New Poetics*), which devotes nearly two hundred lines to the apostrophe as one of several methods of poetic amplification.[77] Its ubiquity within medieval writing indicates its popularity as a lyric expression of desire for a captive, albeit abstracted, audience that was bifurcated into two recipients: the unavailable addressee and the actual reader/listener. Given the dictaminal assumption of public reception, such an apostrophic salutation invokes an indirect addressee, one who could potentially reply and establish an intimate connection in the style of Héloïse, who replies to Abelard's letter addressed to another friend. This kind of indirect, almost voyeuristic, friendship circulates widely within social media, which rely upon the one-to-many distribution of online correspondence. A tweet, which often hosts a complaint or lament, epitomizes this premodern apostrophic expression, which is neither completely transitive nor completely intransitive. While a tweet may express intransitive forms of delivery, refashioned by likes, replies, or retweets, it also has a transitive habitus as a digital object that is delivered, inscribed on a server, and embedded within feeds of followers.

Digital salutations are therefore fundamentally apostrophic in nature, public expressions of friendship that reach into the void, like Dido, for the "absent other," without expectation of reciprocity or reply. In so doing, they assemble archives of intimacy, based in dynamic medieval systems of memory and delivery that undergird our basic principles of digital correspondence. This epistolary habitus demonstrates what writers ranging from Giovanni di Bonandrea to Chaucer to Montaigne clearly recognized: friendship is highly rhetorical, and always has been.

Conclusion

Breaking Bad *Habitus*

It has reached a point where today, knowledge is increasingly defined as knowledge for the market.... Since markets themselves are increasingly turning into algorithmic structures and technologies, the only useful knowledge today is supposed to be algorithmic. Instead of actual human beings with a body, history, and flesh, big data and statistical inferences are all that count, and both are mostly derived from computation.
—**Achille Mbembe,** *Necropolitics*

When we look at the elaborated commentaries that decorate the pages of manuscripts in the Middle Ages, when conventions of navigation, reading, and writing were being established as customs for use, we see the origins of our habits alongside the opportunities that had to be let go within the constraints of printed forms.
—**Johanna Drucker,** *Graphesis*

Anything described as "data-driven" has an undeniable rhetorical force. This phrase is nearly ubiquitous in advertisements about any new mobile technology, any new pharmaceutical, or any new educational policy. As Achille Mbembe suggests in the passage quoted in the epigraph, *data* is part of a vocabulary of computation that privileges binary logic over embodied experience, often in service of the technology markets. By relying on large datasets, digital networks perpetuate the fantasy of representing truth in a democratic fashion, promising a kind of transparent access to knowledge that had previously been obscured by print-based publishing structures. Within this data-driven dream,

Johanna Drucker observes, "data pass themselves off as mere descriptions of *a priori* conditions" that then accordingly justify the creation of visualizations of data in maps and charts that "pass as unquestioned representations of 'what is.'"[1] Big data, or massive sets of quantitative information, possess an even greater persuasive capital because they signify a large-scale and high-speed acquisition of evidence about the world that is pervasive and relevant for any object of research. In response, Drucker forcefully argues that "*data are capta*, taken not given, constructed as an interpretation of the phenomenal world, not inherent in it."[2] In other words, all data are captured information, based on particular assumptions and collected for particular purposes. For critical theorists such as Mbembe and media scholars such as Wendy Hui Kyong Chun, this "capta"-driven culture primarily benefits international technology markets, which thrive on web-scraping and data-mining to capture, analyze, and monetize patterns of human habits. Our individual contributions to such algorithmic knowledge are so habitual, suggests Chun, that "through habits users become their machines: they stream, update, capture, upload, share, grind, link, verify, map, save, trash, and troll. Repetition breeds expertise, even as it breeds boredom."[3] With each somnolescent click, we *give* information that will be used to *capture* our behavior, which technology companies from Google to Apple present as "data" that they argue will change the world, and even our habits.

As I have attempted to demonstrate in this book, many of our rhetorical habits—from translating to compiling to disputing to amplifying to appropriating to salutating—have deep histories within premodern manuscript cultures, yet they are often assumed to be "given" to us by the speed and scale of digital technologies. The prevalence of this techno-determinism has, on the one hand, inspired important studies of posthuman rhetoric, ranging from Thomas Rickert's analyses of nonhuman ambient agency to Casey Boyle's examination of embodied material practices, which recognize how writing is not, and has never been, an autonomous human act.[4] On the other hand, the illusion that big data and artificial intelligence provide a future free from human bias has led to an uncritical embrace of the notion of computer code as a great equalizer and engine of social justice. In her analysis of what she calls the "New Jim Code," Ruha Benjamin points out, "Posthumanist visions assume we have all had a chance to be human," emphasizing how regularly Black communities are dehumanized by the algorithms created by white software engineers.[5] From the racialized bias programmed within Google searches to the surveillance of names coded and tracked as Black, we have too often overlooked the roles that humans actively play within the digital architectures that reinforce racism.[6] In *Habitual*

Rhetoric, I have attempted to demonstrate the limits of such posthuman technodeterminism, arguing that human rhetorical actors and their nonhuman material environments have always been inseparable bodies, always interacting to shape particular writing habits and particular writing interfaces over time. As Drucker points out in the passage quoted in epigraph, examining the traces of human inscription and illustration on medieval manuscripts allows us to see the "origins of our habits alongside the opportunities that had to be let go within the constraints of printed forms."[7] Such manuscript evidence captures snapshots of rhetorical principles that we can track into the present, suggesting that these habits reflect ongoing social and embodied dispositions that transform and are transformed by the ambient features of their material environments. We are therefore assuming the habits of varying rhetorical *habitus* that have been structured as much by the affordances and constraints of writing technologies as by repetitive writing practices that transcend both space and time.

I want to conclude by offering two recommendations that follow from the two main claims of this book. If we accept the first argument—that digital writing habits were established before digital technology—we should then work to define the digital habitus, both singular and plural, that we currently inhabit. This requires an acknowledgment of the history of these habits, which have significant ethical consequences as much for those they have included and privileged as for those they have excluded and oppressed. As James Baldwin famously put it, "the great force of history comes from the fact that we carry it within us, are unconsciously controlled by it in many ways, and history is literally *present* in all that we do."[8] This history manifests itself within our habitus, our way of being in the world that has been structured over time by our varying identities, often defined by categories ranging from race to nationality to class to gender to sexuality. If we, like medieval rhetoricians Geoffrey of Vinsauf, Hermannus Alemannus, or Giovanni di Bonandrea, consider our rhetoric itself to be a habitus, a disposition that conditions and produces all discourse, we must also identify the writing habits that we "carry . . . within us" and "are unconsciously controlled by." When we edit Wikipedia, or annotate a PDF, or paste text from one Google doc to another, we are repeating ancient rhetorical acts, adapting and maximizing their capabilities within new habitations. Recognizing the persistence of these habits within our writing practices allows us to identify how our habitus have stabilized creative forces from the past and limited our means of production for the future.

Once we have defined the history and nature of our rhetorical dispositions, we are prepared to consider my second recommendation, which follows from the second argument of this book. If social media have accelerated the speed and expanded the scale of our translating, compiling, disputing, amplifying, appropriating, and salutating habits—reducing these corporeal collaborations to consumable commodities, obscuring the human labor and material conditions that afford and constrain them—then we must take steps to break our bad habitus, transform them, and make them stable agents of change. For those familiar with Pierre Bourdieu's definition of *habitus* as "the durably installed generative principle of regulated improvisations," such a potential transformation of a largely unconscious and deeply enculturated dispositional force is much easier said than done.[9] Yet the premodern writers examined in this book consistently demonstrate that rhetorical habitus is fundamentally both something *said* and something *done*, both an articulated set of techniques and an ongoing repetitive practice. Whereas Bourdieu's habitus determines action but doesn't necessarily determine discourse—explaining why, for example, those who announce their commitment to antiracism continue to perpetuate racism through their behavior—medieval authors often perceive a dynamic interplay between word and deed, suggesting that, contra the maxim, the habit makes the monk. This book therefore proposes a habitual rhetoric that requires both a recognition of our habituated dispositions and activates our capacity to change deeply ingrained habits through the repetition of techniques. Since I see, like Casey Boyle, "writing as a continuous cultivation of habits,"[10] I offer, as a conclusion, a set of example practices and questions that seek to maintain a dynamic balance between words and deeds, repetition and difference, stability and metamorphosis. Once we get in the habit of defining our habitus, I believe we will become better attuned to break the habits that constrain us and to develop the habits that may set us free.

Recommendation No. 1: Define our Digital Habitus

As I complete this book in the midst of the ongoing COVID-19 pandemic, it has become difficult for me *not* to see how our varying habitus have empowered or limited our rhetorical capacities. Those of us with high-speed internet, high-quality health care, and safe working environments have continued our lives relatively unabated, with the ability and energy to post our complaints about mask-wearing on Twitter or engage in highly partisan political dialogue about vaccination mandates on Facebook. Those of us without one or more of these privileges have endured an entirely different rhetorical situation, one whose power was blocked by limited bandwidth, frequent hospital visits, or life-threatening workplace conditions. Yet these socioeconomic factors are just the tip of the iceberg. Rather than a world of two habitus on "both sides" of a digital divide, we can discern a varying prevalence of writing habits even within communities composed of particular racial groups or social classes and practiced within particular material environments. As Annette Harris Powell points out in her study of underserved middle-school Black girls in a technology camp, student computer literacies are not exclusively determined by race or class: "The rules of the game are clearly different . . . despite their seemingly similar socio-economic status."[11] For Powell, the differing learning habits of these students compel us to challenge the narrative that the so-called digital divide will be closed by making sure underserved students merely "have" a computer. Rather than focusing on this false binary, Powell urges us to consider the students' habitus as defined by a "practice of access" which transcends particular material environments, allowing for "the habitation of *space*."[12] This kind of habitation is cultivated through a pedagogy of reflective *and* repetitive practice that understands writing habits to be potentially both stable and in flux, as well as structured by changing physical surroundings, varying educational preparations, and shifting identities.

While our rhetorical habitus is defined by numerous factors, I limit my purview in this conclusion to the six writing habits examined in this book.

The first, *translation*—directly related to Powell's "practice of access"—often provides content to new and expanded audiences. Yet as I argue, translation too often transfers power to elites. Within impoverished understandings of access, merely providing Chromebooks to students who need them is a successful translation of technological power from the haves to the have-nots. The question we should ask ourselves is this: *do we recognize and resist or do we ignore and perpetuate the inequalities inherent within linguistic and cultural translations of digital authority and knowledge?* Once we attempt to define our translational habits, we can begin to see, for example, whether we believe easy access to online degree programs is more beneficial or more harmful to the students it aims to serve.

The second habit, *compilation*, promises democratic modes of participation, all the while privileging those who possess the most authority, knowledge, and capital to contribute. If a compilational habitus is structured by the contingent and multilayered nature of representing knowledge, do we use writable sites like Wikipedia primarily for the consumption or production of information about the world? Relatedly, *do our compilational practices of editing, combining, and updating contribute to a multiverse of knowledge production or a monoculture of information consumption?* Our response to this question will help us identify our disposition toward knowledge that has been compiled by anonymous contributors.

The third habit, *disputation*, produces a kind of dialogue that both assumes an equal level of participation and promises a kind of balanced treatment of any given subject, yet often obscures the multiple perspectives and imbalances of power and access to achieve its rhetorical force. Our disputational habitus have developed and accelerated a culture of dialogue across social platforms like Twitter, but our debates have become bifurcated and polarized to create the fiction that there are only two sides to any issue. We must then ask, *do our disputational practices of online role-playing and peer reviewing encourage multiplicity and transparency, or do they limit the terms of debate and perpetuate a cynical culture of "both sides"?* Our answers will help us determine which impulses (e.g., opposition, correction, promotion, circulation) motivate our participation in online disputes.

The fourth habit, *amplification*, offers means of elaboration and circulation that enhance the depth, exposure, and expandability of our writing, but which also introduce interface design challenges and information saturation. If our amplificatory habitus allow us to add new knowledge to old within annotatable spaces from common books to editable web templates, how then do we respond to social media platforms increasingly reducing user contributions to data points and editorial upvotes? We must ask, *do our amplifications primarily expand opportunities for communal participation, or do they obstruct the contributions of others?* Our responses will help us identify the principles that shape our digital annotation and circulation practices on sites ranging from Genius to Twitter.

The fifth habit, *appropriation*, constitutes a continual reuse of writing and a continual challenge to claims of "intellectual property," yet it threatens to destabilize authorial autonomy and sanction acts of plagiarism. Our appropriative habitus generate remixes that build and often improve upon prior work, but these creative acts are increasingly obstructed by copyright restrictions and subscription paywalls. We should then ask, *do our appropriations recognize the corporeal labor that produces the work we use, reuse, and critique, or do they transfer public bodies of knowledge into private properties of the market?* Our answers will flesh out our appropriative dispositions, which structure rhetorical practices ranging from copying and pasting to creating mash-ups and memes.

The sixth habit, *salutation*, encompasses a wide range of epistolary acts seeking to establish public forms of intimacy that can establish lasting friendships across time and space but also violate privacy through surveillance and harassment. Even though our salutatory habitus are based in principles of affection and goodwill, social media platforms such as Facebook and Twitter have perpetuated political enmity and exposed underprivileged populations, especially people of color, to hate and oppression. We must ask, *do our salutations contribute* more to public friendships and solidarity with others or to the private interests and profits of social media corporations? Our responses will help us identify the principles that shape our social media habits, ranging from updating to tweeting to liking to sharing.

Collectively, our working definitions of these habitus can be combined to provide a kind of social profile of our digital writing habits, helping us identify those habits we want to nurture and those we may want to break.

Recommendation No. 2: Break Our Bad Habitus

Defining our digital habitus relies upon the effectiveness of reflection, the metacognitive act of "thinking about thinking" that has been central to rhetoric and composition studies. As an alternative to our common, and highly humanist, emphasis on reflective practice, Boyle proposes a turn towards a posthumanist "practice as a serial exercise of a body's tendencies to activate greater capacities."[13] Understanding rhetorical habits as repetitions of bodily activities, Boyle's focus on seriality resonates with premodern conceptions of rhetorical *habitus* discussed in this book, which are fundamentally corporeal, repetitive, and accumulative in nature. And like Boyle, their prehumanist vision of the rhetorical body is capacious, including the skins of cows and feathers of birds that were used to create parchment books and the material environments that actively shaped the writing that inhabited their pages. Yet Boyle's claim that "rhetorical processes depend on ongoing material relationships more so than an individual's conscious awareness of available means" positions writers in somewhat subjected and less agential roles than the rhetorical habitus of premodern writing manuals, such as Giovanni di Bonandrea's *Brevis introductio ad dictamen* (*A Brief Introduction to Writing*), would accommodate.[14] From the seventh-century encyclopedist Isidore of Seville, who urges writers to wrench the club from Hercules, to the fifteenth-century schoolmaster Robert Henryson, who encourages readers to pluck both fruits and flowers from fables, humans possess great capacities to change their habits and their relationships with their environments.

Whereas Boyle and many posthumanists would attribute more rhetorical power to nonhuman material forces and most humanist discourses would attribute more rhetorical power to human actors, premodernist writers often understood composition to be a corporeal act irreducible to discrete members, what might be considered the "limbs" of a rhetorical body. Rather, rhetoricians like John of Garland would often apprehend the "invention" of any text by its "causes," which include its writer (the efficient cause), its parchment and ink (the material cause), its layout and letterforms (the formal cause), and its purpose (the final cause).[15] Each of these "causes" are both human and nonhuman affordances and constraints of a book that would be encountered by future readers who would inhabit its pages, potentially altering its habitus by adding new members and establishing new relations through serialized acts of reflection, such as annotation, reproduction, appropriation, or even translation. These repetitive habits are both reflective and accretive, turning back *and* pressing forward, recognizing previous forms of authority and creation while accumulating new meanings and reaching new audiences.

Reflection is therefore a central feature of habitual rhetoric. Even for Bourdieu, who emphasizes the durability of acquired social habits, our "collectively orchestrated" habitus can be identified, and sometimes altered, through reflective practice. According to Boyle, this is only possible because Bourdieu "sees practice as social relations that develop between humans and collections of humans against a backdrop of materiality."[16] Yet as I discuss in the introduction, it is important to recognize that Bourdieu first begins to articulate his theory of practice in his "Postface" to his French translation of Erwin Panofsky's *Gothic Architecture and Scholasticism*, a book that argues for a reflexive relationship between the oppositional dialectics of disputation and the symmetrical designs of cathedrals.[17] Bourdieu is particularly influenced by what he calls

> the logic of a certain system of schemes of thought, perception, and action that Panofsky reveals when he observes that the pointed arches of Caen and Durham started to speak before they acted, whereas the flying buttresses started to act before they spoke, other elements of the edifice having never ceased to speak and act at once. These human works that the rib vault, the break of Gothic handwriting, or the flying buttress represent have, to use the language of scholasticism, an *intention* that is ambiguous in that they can be apprehended and appreciated either for their mere technical function or for their "optical value," which supposes a "special interest in form." This objective intention, which can never be reduced to the creator's intention, depends on the schemes of thought, perception, and action the creator owes to his belonging to a society, an epoch, and a class.[18]

Panofsky's observation that varying features of Gothic architecture speak and act synchronously and asynchronously provides Bourdieu with a habitus that both refuses clear distinctions between words and deeds and imbues nonhuman edifices with a rhetorical force acquired through Scholastic habit, a premodern dialectical disposition learned within medieval schooling. Materiality is more than a "backdrop" that provides the scene for writing or rhetorical action. Scribal practice reflects both the efficient usability of Gothic letterforms and symmetrical beauty of Gothic architecture. After all, medieval university rhetorical manuals made little distinction between the "technical function" of writing (e.g., its notarial or legal purpose) and its "optical value," emphasizing writing as an "art" (an *ars dictaminis* or *ars poetriae*) that could both act and speak. These "schemes of thought" structure the tastes of learned classes, from the scribal to the notarial to the legal, that are cultivated both through professional habit and through Scholastic instruction, suggesting that habitus can be learned, defined, and transformed by reflective *and* repetitive writing practices.

If an instructional method, such as quodlibetal disputation, can shape the physical structures of medieval cathedrals, then we can surely cultivate compositional strategies that can improve the designs of our digital interfaces. I want to conclude this book by offering a description of some digital writing practices that may be able to break the bad habitus of online spaces that too often perpetuate inequality, monopolize information-gathering, polarize debate, silence resistant voices, conceal corporeal labor, and privatize public domains. To do so, I propose principles for writing habits that have the potential to transform the dispositions of writers, the infrastructure of writing spaces, the design of interfaces, and the purpose of the writing. Therefore, I have organized these inventional practices into their Aristotelian "causes," as defined by John of Garland: *causae efficiens* (writers), *causae materialis* (infrastructures), *causae formalis* (designs), and *causae finalis* (purposes).[19]

Causae efficiens (writers): As I have been suggesting throughout this book, the figure of a singular and autonomous authority for writing was merely a fantasy within medieval manuscript culture. The "author" of a text was not always its "writer," who was often a scribe or a compiler, who recorded an author's dictation or copied selections from manuscripts at hand. Furthermore, future readers of books often became its writers through extensive commentary and marginal annotation. As I discuss in chapters 5 and 6, Aesopic annotators transformed the habitus of books through amplification, sometimes even revising or expanding the fables themselves. Within digital environments, writable websites, ranging from Wikipedia to WordPress offer opportunities for eager editors to contribute, but such spaces are highly templated and curated, which too often prevent minority voices from being represented. It is therefore crucial that we seek to support and enable writers, especially writers of color, to offer their "counterstories," what Aja Y. Martinez characterizes as "a methodology that functions through methods that empower the minoritized through the formation of stories that disrupt the erasures embedded in standardized majoritarian methodologies."[20] One example of the habitual and disruptive practice of counterstory is #BlackTwitter, a collaborative thread that continuously annotates and narrates the various experiences of Black social and political life. Keith Gilyard and Adam J. Banks observe, "#BlackTwitter as a rhetorical and communal space takes on functions of the church, the public arena, the soapbox, the studio, the corner, the hip-hop cipher, the gathering place for small collectives, and more."[21] Twitter can therefore provide a habitation for writers to host their counterstories, offering a challenge to narratives that have become standardized within other, often majoritarian, communities. These inventional interventions suggest the following writerly disposition, which is also exhibited by Aesopic annotators: *writers should seek to fill, support, and amplify writing environments that provide opportunities for including, extending, and revising the work of other writers.*

Causae materialis (infrastructures): Twitter provides space for such *causae efficiens*, but the ease with which disinformation and harassment spreads through retweets highlights the need to reconfigure the material habitus of such platforms. As Diana Ascher demonstrates in her study of "yellow journalism," human social-media managers disseminate inaccurate and racist news headlines less often than automated software, which in turn accelerate the retweeted Twitter narratives.[22] When combined with Google search results that reproduce stereotypes of women and people of color, we are left with what Safiya Umoja Noble calls "algorithmic oppression" and what Ruha Benjamin calls "the New Jim Code": "the employment of new technologies that reflect and reproduce existing inequities but that are promoted and perceived as more objective or progressive than the discriminatory systems of a previous era."[23] Just as Gothic cathedrals replicate the normative disputational structures of the medieval university, so too do the seemingly innocuous and supposedly "neutral" digital platforms codify the implicit racism and sexism of their programmers. As I suggest in chapter 4, we will remain locked within such systems of oppression as long as we cling to pretenses to the objectivity of "both-sides" rhetoric, as represented by scholarly habits such as double-anonymous peer review, leaving insidious systemic bias hidden from view. In addition to heeding the "coding literacy" and "rhetorical code studies" proposals by Annette Vee and Kevin Brock, we should consider what Boyle formulates for understanding infrastructure as a rhetorical body: "This function should not be understood as an interface between two (or more) known things but instead as an amplification process whose activation of connections of prior embeddedness through multiple registers and within a wider milieu makes it difficult to make distinctions on which an interface (or transmitter or medium) traditionally relies."[24] For example, open forms of peer review activate and expand connections across a scholarly corpus, offering access to prior debates and providing the reviewing contexts necessary to situate the scholarship. We should therefore establish our writing environments upon the following principle: *the foundational relationships between the material elements and human actors that collectively create the infrastructures for our writing spaces and practices should be made available for all to see, question, and rebuild.*

Causae formalis (designs): The *causae materialis* of our compositional environments will naturally determine their design capacities, or what we might call the affordances and constraints of their quotidian uses. As I discuss in chapter 5, the layouts of the interface, from the columned scroll to the skimmable codex to the hyperlinked screen, encourage and limit certain kinds of writing activity. Some are easily searchable and some are easily annotatable, but most every format experiences standardization, which may increase usability but often decreases changeability. In the case of the Aesopic corpus, the normalization of the interface and reduction of its margins for annotation eventually eliminated the multiplicity of fable interpretations, reducing these animal tales to oversimplified morals. How then should we create nimble designs that avoid such a fossilized result? Drucker proposes the following:

> We have to imagine the design of a situation of a sustained activity, a series of events . . . so the creation of digital environments for interpretative writing will refer back to earlier precedents and extend their possibilities. . . . The critical design of interpretative interface will push beyond the goals of "efficient" and "transparent" designs for the organization of behaviors and actions, and mobilize a critical network that exposes, calls to attention, its madeness—and by extension, the constructedness of knowledge, its interpretative dimensions. This will orchestrate, at least a bit, the shift from conceptions of interface as things and entities to that of an event-space of interpretative activity.[25]

Within this design vision, the formal habitus of online spaces would be both serial and reflective, anticipating the interventions of future writers and highlighting its past constructions, providing formats that attempt to offer universality and particularity. For Tara McPherson, this means questioning the computational "logic of modularity," which threatens to obscure the possibility to create designs that celebrate race and gender differences.[26] We should then strive to adhere to the following principle for design: *writing spaces should seek to be both prospective and retrospective, designed to anticipate future users and to recognize past* contributions, creating hospitable habitations for writing that accommodate difference.

Causae finalis (purposes): Social media corporations promise to realize two fundamental objectives: create collaborative networks and amplify individual voices. While this book suggests that they often achieve the first, they frequently struggle with the second. Rather than emphasize the first person *I* or *we*, Wendy Hui Kyong Chun argues, social media platforms like YouTube "relentlessly emphasize you," a shift in individual focus that "is central to the changing value of the Internet, to the transformation of the Internet into a series of poorly gated communities that generate YOUs value."[27] Instagram and Facebook encourage their users to turn their phone cameras on themselves, reflecting themselves to themselves, persistently documenting individual experience, often without much connection to the others who have adopted the same self-interested social media habits. And even if connections become established as meaningful forms of public intimacy, like the salutations of the *artes dictandi* of chapter 7, rarely do they develop habitus—through writing practices, infrastructural forces, or formal designs—that seek relationships with communities of different genders, races, classes, or sexual identities because of their (often algorithmic) tendencies to value sameness over difference and to prefer retweets to resistance. Achille Mbembe takes this a step further, suggesting these computational habits allow us to "finally become our own spectacle, our own scene, our own theater and audience, even our own public. In this age of endless self-curation and exhibition, we can finally draw our own portrait."[28] The drive of this algorithmic narcissism for "likes" and retweets is so strong that we separate our words from our actions, merely performing altruistic dispositions towards oppression, all while maintaining our private enmities toward the oppressed. To transform these self-promotional habitus, we should therefore pursue the following principle for our purposes for writing: *writing should strive to establish forms of public intimacy, not through the avoidance of conflict or counterstory, but through negotiation of difference, desire for social justice, and abundance of care.*

Breaking our bad habitus will not be easy, and we will not transform our habits without the passing of time, the destruction of oppressive systems, and a collective desire for change. An app will not suffice. As Vannevar Bush predicted, the accumulation of data required for such software is well beyond our interpretive control. Yet when the Latin West faced a similar crisis in the dramatic expansion of written records in the eleventh and twelfth centuries, the institution of the "university" was developed, at least in part, to train lawyers, Chancery clerks, and notaries to produce documents, ranging from writs to deeds to letters. To do so, university teachers such as Giovanni di Bonandrea and John of Garland composed the rhetorical manuals, the *artes dictandi*, that provided techniques and examples of written amplification and epistolary salutation. In the afterword of her study of what she calls "graphesis" or "visual forms of knowledge production," Drucker asks,

> Where are the manuals of rhetoric for the electronic age? What grammars will take their place beside those that stood for years, such as those of the great fourth century BCE Sanskrit scholar, Panini, and the Latinist, Priscian, from the beginning of the sixth CE? What treatises of rhetoric will expand the principles of ethos, pathos, and logos from Aristotle or build on Quintillian's concepts of invention, arrangement, style, presentation, memory, and action in ways appropriate to the media of our times? Such guides would have to engage with the tenets of graphical knowledge production, with order and sequence, hierarchy and proximity, temporal dimensions and spatial axes, with concepts of derivation and replication, of continuity and juxtaposition, as ordering elements of communicative systems.[29]

This challenge has already been taken up by numerous writing-studies scholars, especially those working on multimodal composition, so I want to end this book by suggesting the premodern prototype for future digital-rhetorical manuals. For me, the treatise that best embodies the basic tenets of a habitual rhetoric, one that seeks to foster habits that combine speech and action, is none other than the *Poetria nova* of Geoffrey of Vinsauf. As discussed at numerous points throughout this book, Geoffrey composed this poetics manual in verse, offering examples of each rhetorical habit, much in the manner of Scott McCloud's *Understanding Comics*, which teaches graphical terminology through the visual representations of the terms themselves.[30] One of the students of the *Poetria nova* offered the following annotation about Geoffrey's embodied tactic: "It is one thing to speak about rhetoric, another to speak rhetorically. A rhetorician speaks about rhetoric, an orator rhetorically. This author does both; he speaks about rhetoric and does so rhetorically. Similarly, it is one thing to write about verse, another to write in verse. . . . This author does both."[31] This commentator observes a central feature of the habitus of Geoffrey's treatise: it speaks and acts at once, reflecting the principles of writing through writing. As we reflect upon our own digital habits, we should strive to match our words with our deeds, composing writing that "does both": speak and act.

This means that reflective practices by themselves are insufficient. After all, machines have already learned to create digital habitus for us, grouping our online habits into homogenous, flattened, and robotic dispositions that are ready-made for an accelerated and large-scale form of capitalist consumption. These commodified profiles may be useful to the analyst who seeks a flat network, but, as Alberto Romele and Dario Rodighiero suggest, this "notion of *habitus* ends up reducing the supposedly most authentic actions and intentions of a social actor to those of all other members of her dominating or dominated social group."[32] If algorithms capture our online behavior and categorize us according to our connections with "dominating" or "dominated" people, we will only reproduce and perpetuate the inequalities and exclusion that already exists. For Wendy Hui Kyong Chun, this polarization is not an accident of online, crowdsourced media. It is the dystopian goal, which has been achieved through homophily, the fundamental tendency of people to associate with those similar to themselves. As she puts it, "Homophily is used to create agitated clusters of individuals whose angry similarity and overwhelming attraction to their common object of hatred both repel them from one another and glue them together."[33] Over time, these similar groupings have become echo chambers, resulting in varying levels of discrimination, from filter bubbles to segregated neighborhoods.

Any progress in breaking such bad habitus will require the uncomfortable recognition and complex negotiation of difference. If we individualize our habits and perceive any potential change to come from our own entrepreneurial initiative, we fail to see how our speaking and acting in the world is inseparable from the surroundings or habitations that make speech and action possible. Elizabeth Grosz suggests, "Habits are the ways in which living beings accommodate more of their environments than the constitution of instincts generally permits: habits are how environments impact and transform the forms of life they accommodate and are themselves impacted and transformed by these forms of life."[34] In order for our digital habitus to become transformative dispositions, we must collectively accommodate—or consistently seek habitations for—difference, which entails both a willingness to be persuaded and change and a desire to adopt new habits and create spaces for disagreement. We cannot achieve our *causae finalis*, our rhetorical purposes, without the recognition of difference within our *causae materialis* and *causae formalis*, the design of our material infrastructures. When we acknowledge the habitual nature and history of our rhetorical practices, we can activate the creative forces of the habits from the past to negotiate sameness and difference within our social dispositions and environments. Only then will this socially embodied and difference-oriented digital habitus be capable of producing complete forms of discourse, design, and life that challenge the data-driven, disembodied, discriminating, and dystopian objectives of digital media.

Notes

Introduction | Digital Writing before Digital Technology

1. Haas, "Wampum as Hypertext"; Banks, *Digital Griots*.

2. *The Digital Humanities Manifesto 2.0*, http://www.humanitiesblast.com/manifesto/Manifesto_V2.pdf, 2. According to Todd Presner, this document was the product of approximately a hundred contributors, including himself, Jeffrey Schnapp, and Peter Lunenfeld. See "Digital Humanities Manifesto 2.0 Launched," last modified June 22, 2009, http://www.toddpresner.com/?p=7.

3. Bolter and Grusin, *Remediation*.

4. *Digital Humanities Manifesto 2.0*, 1.

5. Brantley, "Medieval Remediations," 210. For similar approaches that combine media and medieval studies, see Brylowe and Yeager, *Old Media and the Medieval Concept*; Davis, Mahoney-Steel, and Turnator, *Meeting the Medieval in a Digital World*.

6. Hayles and Pressman, "Introduction," ix. They acknowledge the previous work that has interrogated the complexity of media across time, such as Bolter's *Writing Space* and Cayley's "The Code Is Not the Text (Unless It Is the Text)."

7. Mak, *How the Page Matters*, 4.

8. McLuhan, *Understanding New Media*; Eisenstein, *Printing Press*; Brantley, "Medieval Remediations," 203.

9. Ridolfo and Hart-Davidson, *Rhetoric and the Digital Humanities*. The work of dig-

ital rhetoricians appears within many of the books of the *Debates* series: Bianco, "This Digital Humanities"; Bogost, "Turtlenecked Hairshirt"; Losh, "Hacktivism and the Humanities"; Sayers, "Dropping the Digital"; Sayers, *Making Things and Drawing Boundaries*.

10. OpenAI, "ChatGPT," accessed December 13, 2022, https://openai.com/blog/chatgpt/.

11. For some of the influential work on rhetorical circulation, see Ridolfo and DeVoss, "Composing"; Porter, "Recovering Delivery"; Gries, *Still Life*.

12. Eyman, *Digital Rhetoric*, 15.

13. Their publications in this area are too numerous to count, but some explicit challenges to the lack of attention to medieval rhetoric within rhetorical histories can be found in Camargo and Woods, "Writing Instruction"; Copeland, *Emotion and the History of Rhetoric*; Carruthers, *Book of Memory*; Enders, *Medieval Theater of Cruelty*; Glenn, *Rhetoric Retold*; Camargo, "Between Grammar and Rhetoric."

14. See Eyman, *Digital Rhetoric*; Banks, *Digital Griots*; Losh, *Virtualpolitik*; Brooke, *Lingua Fracta*; Welch, *Electric Rhetoric*.

15. Losh, *Virtualpolitik*, 47.

16. Hawhee and Olson, "Pan-Historiography," 90–91.

17. Hawhee and Olson, 90.

18. Hawhee and Olson, 91.

19. Hawhee and Olson, 92.

20. Nagel and Wood, *Anachronic Renaissance*, 29.

21. Nagel and Wood, 45. See their discussion of the anachronic example of Jorge Luis Borges's Pierre Menard, who copies Cervantes's *Don Quixote* word for word.

22. Griffiths, "Comparative Method," 498.

23. Dimock, "Historicism, Presentism, Futurism," 257–58.

24. Dimock, 258.

25. "Animi aut corporis constantem et absolutam aliqua in re perfectionem, aut virtutis, aut artis alicius preceptionem, aut quamvis scientiam et item corporis aliquam commoditatem non natura datam, sed studio et industria partam." See Cicero, *On Invention*, 1.25.36; 72–73.

26. Banker, "Giovanni di Bonandrea," 3–20.

27. Panofsky, *Gothic Architecture and Scholasticism*, 59, 64.

28. Bourdieu, "Postface," 233.

29. Bourdieu, *In Other Words*, 63.

30. See Latour, *Reassembling the Social*; Mol, *Body Multiple*; Thrift, *Spatial Formations*; Chun, *Updating to Remain the Same*; Rickert, *Ambient Rhetoric*.

31. Chuh, *Difference Aesthetics Makes*; la paperson, *Third University Is Possible*.

32. Burrows, *Rhetorical Crossover*.

33. Asad, *Genealogies of Religion*, especially 189–93.

34. Copeland, *Rhetoric*, 3.

35. Wikipedia, s.v. "compiler," accessed August 6, 2021, https://en.wikipedia.org/wiki/Compiler.

36. Chaucer, *Treatise on the Astrolabe*, 1.61, in *Riverside Chaucer*, 662.

37. Bahr, *Fragments and Assemblages*, 3. Bahr builds upon and challenges previous definitions of compilation, including Rouse and Rouse, "*Ordinatio* and *Compilatio* Revisited"; Minnis, "*Nolens Auctor Sed Compilator Reputari*"; Parkes, "Influence of the Concepts."

38. "Wikipedia: Introduction," Wikipedia, http://en.wikipedia.org/wiki/Wikipedia:Introduction.

39. Glott, Ghosh, and Schmidt, "Wikipedia Survey"; Hill and Shaw, "Wikipedia Gender Gap Revisited."

40. O'Neil, "Sociology of Critique," 3.

41. Karras, *From Boys to Men*, 83–95.

42. For recent analyses of information overload, see Andrejevic, *Infoglut*; and Baron, *Words Onscreen*, especially 56–58. For an explanation of a similar phenomenon in the early age of print, see Blair, *Too Much to Know*.

43. See Jenkins, *Textual Poachers*; Jenkins, *Fans, Bloggers, and Gamers*.

44. Baron, *Words Onscreen*, 235.

45. Shirky, *Here Comes Everybody*, 81–108; *Cognitive Surplus*.

46. Blair, *Too Much to Know*, 6.

47. See Lessig, *Remix*; Vaidhyanathan, *Copyrights and Copywrongs*.

48. Liu, *Laws of Cool*, 9.

49. Schumpeter, *Capitalism, Socialism, and Democracy*, 83–4, 83. Italics appear in the original.

50. See Mueller, *Translating Troy*, especially 3–4.

51. Critical Art Ensemble, *Electronic Civil Disobedience*. See Liu's discussion of their approach in his chapter on "Destructive Creativity" in *Laws of Cool*, 317–71, at 367.

52. Ingham, *Medieval New*, 14.

53. Kennedy, *Medieval Hackers*, 4.

54. Jenkins, "Confronting the Challenges of Participatory Culture," 14.

55. Miller, *On the End of Privacy*, 18.

56. Turkle, *Alone Together*, 1.

57. See Lambert, *Intimacy and Friendship*, especially 19–28.

58. dj readies, *Bureaucratic Intimacies*, 10.

59. For one example, see Greenblatt, *Swerve*.

60. See Struever, "Rhetoric of Familiarity"; LeClercq, "L'amitié"; Folena, "Pluristilismo," 263.

61. Eden, *Renaissance Rediscovery of Intimacy*, 50.

62. Constable, *Letters and Letter-Collections*, 11.

63. Camargo, "Special Delivery."

64. Nowviskie, "Alternate Futures/Usable Pasts." Italics appear in the original.

1 | Habitual Rhetoric

Epigraphs: Hermannus Alemannus, in his translation of Averroes's Middle Commentary on Aristotle's *Poetics*, in Copeland and Sluiter, *Medieval Grammar and Rhetoric*, 744; Pierre Bourdieu, "Postface" to his translation of Erwin Panofsky's *Gothic Architecture and Scholasticism*, in Holsinger, *Premodern Condition*, 230.

1. Bourdieu, *In Other Words*, 170.

2. Bourdieu, *Outline*, 214. Italics appear in the original.

3. Bourdieu, 86.

4. Bourdieu, *In Other Words*, 63.

5. Aristotle, *Nicomachean Ethics*, I.x.1100b2.

6. Aristotle, II.i.1103b22–24.

7. Nederman, "Nature, Ethics, and the Doctrine of Habitus," 96.

8. Colish, "'Habitus' Revisited."

9. "Animi aut corporis constantem et absolutam aliqua in re perfectionem, aut virtutis, aut artis alicius preceptionem, aut quamvis scientiam et item corporis aliquam commoditatem non natura datam, sed studio et industria partam." See Cicero, *On Invention*, 1.25.36; 72–3.

10. For a full discussion of the relationship between *habitus*, *studium*, and *affectio*, see Copeland, *Emotion*, 22–57.

11. Banker, "Giovanni di Bonandrea," 13.

12. Vecchi, *Il magistero*, 20–21.

13. "Corporis aliquam commoditatem non natura datam sed studio et industria comparatam." See Giovanni di Bonandrea, *Brevis introductio ad dictamen*, Biblioteca Universitaria di Bologna, Lat. MS 2461 (1303–4). Quotations of Giovanni's treatise are from this manuscript. For the influence of Giovanni's *Brevis introductio*, see Banker, "Ars dictaminis and Rhetorical Textbooks."

14. "De adiectivatione personarum habitu precellentium." *Brevis introductio*, fol. 77r.

15. For a short discussion of Hermannus Alemannus's rhetorical influence, see Copeland and Sluiter, *Medieval Grammar and Rhetoric*, 735–40.

16. Copeland and Sluiter, 744.

17. For English translations of the Arabic commentaries of al-Fārābī, Avicenna, and Averroes on Aristotle's *Rhetoric*, see Ezzaher, *Three Arabic Treatises*.

18. Boggess, "Hermannus Alemannus' Rhetorical Translations," 247–49.

19. Camargo, *Tria sunt*, 3.53.

20. Agamben, *Highest Poverty*, 16.

21. "principium importans ordinem ad actum." See Aquinas, *Sancti Thomae Aquinatis Opera omnia*, I–II, q. 49 art. 3c.

22. Panofsky, *Gothic Architecture and Scholasticism*, 59, 64.

23. For a discussion of objections to Panofsky's argument, see O'Donnell, "Erwin Panofsky's Neo-Kantian Humanism," 176–89.

24. Panofsky, 21.

25. Bourdieu, "Postface," 233. For the French translation, see Panofsky, *Architecture gothique et pensée scolastique*. All English translations of Bourdieu's postface refer to Laurence Petit's translation in Appendix II of Holsinger's *Premodern Condition*, 221–42.

26. Bourdieu, "Postface," 235; Marichal, "L'Écriture latine."

27. See especially Bourdieu, *Distinction*.

28. Breen, *Imagining an English Reading Public*, 7–8.

29. See Bourdieu's discussion of Marichal's analysis of medieval manuscripts in "Postface," 233–35.

30. Bourdieu, "Postface," 232.

31. Latour, *Reassembling the Social*, 209.

32. Latour, 16.

33. Latour, 196.

34. Murphy, *Rhetoric in the Middle Ages*, 258–63.

35. Mol, *Body Multiple*, 13. Italics appear in the original.

36. Mol, 21.

37. Thrift, *Spatial Formations*, 43.

38. Shotter, *Cultural Politics of Everyday Life*, 14; quoted in Thrift, *Spatial Formations*, 38–39.

39. Venturini and Latour, "Social Fabric."

40. Romele and Rodighiero, "Digital Habitus," 104–5.

41. Romele and Rodighiero, 98–99.

42. Gallagher and Holmes, "Empty Templates," 272.

43. Holmes, *Rhetoric of Videogames*. See also Bogost, *Persuasive Games*.

44. Gallagher, *Update Culture*, 157.

45. Bourdieu, *Outline*, 78.

46. Chun, *Updating to Remain the Same*, 3. See also Anderson, *Imagined Communities*.

47. Chun, *Updating to Remain the Same*, 85.

48. Rickert, *Ambient Rhetoric*, 3.

49. Bourdieu and Wacquant, *Invitation to Reflexive Sociology*, 127.

50. For some examples, see Rickert, *Ambient Rhetoric*, 1–37; and Haas, "Wampum as Hypertext."

51. Bourdieu, "Postface," 230.

52. Smith, "Africa Writes Back."

53. Smith.

54. Chuh, *Difference Aesthetics Makes*, 2.

55. Chuh, 4.

56. See the chapter "A Third University Exists within the First" in paperson, *Third University Is Possible*.

57. McPherson, *Feminist in a Software Lab*.

58. Drucker, *Graphesis*.

2 | Translation

Some material in this chapter was previously published as "A Prehistory of Resistance to Writing across the Curriculum," *Studies in Medieval and Renaissance Teaching* 19, no. 2 (2012): 117–42. The original Latin in the epigraph by Horace is "Publica materies privati iuris erit, si / non circa vilem patulumque moraberis orbem, / nec verbo verbum curabis reddere fidus / interpres." See Horace, *Satires, Epistles, and Ars poetica*, 131–34. The translation is from Copeland, *Rhetoric, Hermeneutics, and Translation in the Middle Ages*, 29.

1. "Quasi captiuos sensus in suam linguam uictoris iure transposuit." See Jerome's *Epistula 57, Ad Pammachium*, 511.

2. See Geary, *Furta Sacra*.

3. Newman, "Online Ed Key."

4. Konrad, "Access Fatigue," 181.

5. Wikipedia, s.v. "List of Wikipedias," accessed March 18, 2022, https://meta.wikimedia.org/wiki/List_of_Wikipedias.

6. All textual citations of the *Dialogue* and its accompanying *Epistle* refer to the following edition produced by Stephen Shepherd: Wogan-Browne et al., *Idea of the Vernacular*, 130–38.

7. Newfield, "When Are Access and Inclusion Also Racist?"

8. Bady, "MOOC Moment," III.

9. Bady, IV.

10. Newfield, "Aftermath of the MOOC Wars," 13.

11. Losh, *War on Learning*, 133.

12. Bourdieu, *Practical Reason*, 80.

13. Parr, "Not Staying the Course."

14. Adams, "Meet the English Professor."

15. Ginder, Kelly-Reid, and Mann, "Graduation Rates."

16. Adams, "Meet the English Professor."

17. Neem, *What's the Point of College?*, 90.

18. Horace, *Satires, Epistles, and Ars poetica*, 131–34.

19. WGU receives federal funds, despite the US inspector general's claim in 2017 that they did not offer the minimum level of faculty-student interaction required for distance learning. If not for the intervention of the US Department of Education in early 2019, WGU would have had to repay $712 million in federal aid. See "US Department of Education Issues Final Audit Determination for WGU," US Department of Education, January 11, 2019, https://www2.ed.gov/documents/press-releases/20190111-wgu-audit.pdf.

20. Adams, "Meet the English Professor."

21. Higden, *Polychronicon*, 158–61. For the history of this development, see Orme, *English Schools*, 59–86, at 73.

22. Cannon, "From Literacy to Literature," 351; see also Meech, "Early Treatise," 84. Latin grammars written in English did not emerge until after the first quarter of the fifteenth century. See Thomson's introduction to *An Edition of the Middle English Grammatical Texts*, xii and xxxi–xxxii.

23. Emily Steiner further suggests that the Lord's perspective suits the universal character of Higden's narrative: "According to the Lord, the totality represented defines the universality of translation; translation realizes linguistically the *Polychronicon*'s generic claims." "Radical Historiography," 184.

24. Russell, *Writing in the Academic Disciplines*, 37; Kimball, *Orators and Philosophers*.

25. The result of this homogeneity was a curricular resistance to the specialized discourses that began proliferating in the vernacular languages after the eighteenth century. See Ong, *Orality and Literacy*, 112–15.

26. Russell, *Writing in the Academic Disciplines*, 37–38.

27. MSS London, British Library Additional 24194, Cambridge, St. John's College 204, Aberdeen University Library 21, Liverpool Public Library f909 HIG, Princeton Univ. Library, Garrett 151.

28. Waldron, "John Trevisa," 178.

29. Hanna, "Sir Thomas Berkeley," 891–92.

30. "Ce nos ont nostre livre apris, / Que Grece ot de chevalerie / Le premier los et de clergie. / Puis vint chevalerie a Rome / Et de la clergie la some, / Qui or est an France venue. / Deus doint qu'ele i soit retenue / Et que li leus li abelise / Tant que ja mes de France

n'isse. / L'enor qui s'i est arestee, / Deus l'avoit as autres prestee: / Car de Grejois ne de Romains / Ne dit an mes ne plus ne mains; / D'aus est la parole remese / Et estainte la vive brese." See Chrétien de Troyes, *Les Romans*, 25–42. The English translation is taken from Chrétien de Troyes, *Arthurian Romances*, 123.

31. This is especially apparent in the early debate about the two different temporalities of Christ. See his argument in Trevisa, *Trevisa's Dialogus*, 6.

32. Steiner, *John Trevisa's Information Age*, 106–42.

33. Steiner, 126.

34. Brereton, *Origins of Composition Studies*, 3.

35. Brereton, 28. See especially LeBaron Russell Briggs, "The Harvard Admission Examination in English," in Brereton, 57–73.

36. Villanueva, "Politics of Literacy."

37. Burrows, *Rhetorical Crossover*, 46.

38. Canagarajah, "Rhetoric."

39. Bazerman and Russell, "Writing across the Curriculum."

40. The practice of submitting written speeches in English had been prevalent at Harvard since the mid-eighteenth century. See Halloran, "From Rhetoric to Composition," 159.

41. Perrin, "Teaching of Rhetoric," 137.

42. Hill, "Answer to the Cry"; Carpenter, "English Composition in Colleges."

43. See Briggs, "Harvard Admission Examination in English," in Brereton, *Origins of Composition Studies*, 57–73, at 62.

44. Brereton, 61.

45. Connors, "Mechanical Correctness," 65.

46. Brereton, *Origins of Composition Studies*, 58.

47. Crowley, *Composition in the University*, 46–78.

48. "National Council of Teachers."

49. Wilcox, *Comprehensive Survey*, x, 82; Smith, "Composition Requirement Today," 138; Connors, "Abolition Debate," 57.

50. Halloran, "From Rhetoric to Composition," 167.

51. Connors, "Rhetoric in the Modern University"; Bazerman et al., *Reference Guide*, 15.

52. Spring, *American School*, 194.

53. Berlin, *Rhetoric and Reality*, 59.

54. Thurber, "English in the Secondary Schools," 476.

55. Browne, "Successful Combination"; Searson, "Determining a Language Program," 274–79; Taylor, *National Survey*.

56. The communications movement led by I. A. Richards also played a significant

role. Richards argued that rhetoric is properly the "study [of] all types of discourse as functions of linguistics behavior," a claim that associated language skill with critical thinking and emphasized the foundational practices of reading, writing, speaking, and listening in all disciplines. See Richards, *Philosophy of Rhetoric*, 3; Progressive Education Association, *Language in General Education*, 32; Bazerman et al., *Reference Guide*, 19. According to David Russell, this capacious view of language instruction established "the groundwork for a revival of interest in rhetoric in the 1960s, which in turn led to the WAC movement in the 1970s." See *Writing in the Academic Disciplines*, 256–57.

57. Berlin, *Rhetoric and Reality*, 111.

58. Lounsbury, "Compulsory Composition in Colleges," 878 (my emphasis). For a full discussion of his influence, see Russell, "Romantics on Writing."

59. Lounsbury, "Compulsory Composition in Colleges," 881.

60. Campbell, "Failure of Freshman English," 185. See also, Russell, "Romantics on Writing," 138–39.

61. Smith, "Composition Requirement Today," 139.

62. Russell, *Writing in the Academic Disciplines*, 274.

63. Daniels, *Famous Last Words*, 138.

64. Witte et al., *National Survey*, 14.

65. Crowley, *Composition in the University*, 1.

66. Connors, "Mechanical Correctness."

67. Knoblauch and Brannon, "Writing as Learning," 465–66.

68. McLeod and Maimon, "Clearing the Air," 574–75.

69. Mike Rose calls such a belief a "myth of transience" in "The Language of Exclusion."

70. Fulwiler and Young, "Afterword," 290.

71. Russell, "Writing across the Curriculum and the Communications Movement," 191.

72. Cremin, *Transformation of the School*, 8.

73. Waldron, "John Trevisa," 171–202; Bennett, "Court of Richard II," 7.

74. Fowler, "John Trevisa and the English Bible." William Caxton claimed that Trevisa produced an English Bible, but if it ever existed, it does not survive. Therefore, critics now generally agree that Trevisa only "participated" in the early workings of the Wycliffite Bible. Waldron suggests that Trevisa "may have been influential" in the project. See Waldron, "John Trevisa," 173.

75. Hanna, "Sir Thomas Berkeley," 892.

76. For this larger phenomenon of correction, see Wakelin, *Scribal Correction*.

77. See John Lydgate, *Troy Book*, in Wogan-Browne et al., *Idea of the Vernacular*, 48.209–12.

78. See Guy de Chauliac, *Cyrurgie*, in Wogan-Browne et al., *Idea of the Vernacular*, 63.37–39.

79. Gonzales, *Sites of Translation*, 57.

80. Hanna, "Sir Thomas Berkeley," 895.

81. Manly and Rickert, *Text of the Canterbury Tales*; Manly and Rickert, *Writing of English*.

82. Brereton, *Origins of Composition Studies*, 429.

83. Knapp, "Chaucer Criticism," 335–36.

84. Manly and Rickert, *Writing of English*, iii.

85. Manly and Rickert, 286.

86. Manly and Powell, *Better Business English*.

87. Peter Elbow is famous for his pioneering work *Writing without Teachers*, but he also published *Oppositions in Chaucer* early in his academic career. Cheryl Glenn wrote the widely used *Harbrace Guide to Writing*, but she is also known for her work on Margery Kempe and Julian of Norwich in *Rhetoric Retold: Regendering the Tradition from Antiquity through the Renaissance*. David Russell is best known for his *Writing in the Academic Disciplines*, but he also published a paper entitled "A Technique for Teaching Exposition: Medieval and Modern" that he presented at the Meeting of the Oklahoma Council of Teachers of English in Stillwater, Oklahoma, on April 16–17, 1982.

88. Elbow, "Vernacular Englishes," 127.

89. Fradenburg, *Staying Alive*, 41.

3 | Compilation

Some material in this chapter was previously published as "Wikipedia as *Imago Mundi*," *Studies in Medieval and Renaissance Teaching* 17, no. 2 (Fall 2010): 11–25. The original Latin in the epigraph by Isidore of Seville is "Hoc scelere quondam accusabatur Mantuanus ille vates, cum quosdam versus Homeri transferens suis permicuisset et conpilator veterum ab aemulis diceretur. Ille respondit: 'Magnarum esse virium clavam Herculi extorquere de manu'" (10.44). The Latin text, here and in subsequent citations, is from Isidore of Seville, *Etymologies*. The English translations of the *Etymologies* are all from Irvine, *Making of Textual Culture*.

1. Leuf and Cunningham, *Wiki Way*, 14.

2. Reagle, *Good Faith Collaboration*.

3. Singel, "Veni, Vidi, Wiki."

4. Parkes, "Influence of the Concepts," 52–58.

5. Bahr, *Fragments and Assemblages*, 11.

6. WikiLeaks, accessed May 17, 2021, https://wikileaks.org.

7. Tkacz, *Wikipedia*, 3.

8. All citations of Chaucerian texts refer to *The Riverside Chaucer*.

9. Ricoeur, *Freud and Philosophy*, 356.

10. WikiLeaks, "Latest Releases," accessed June 16, 2014, https://wikileaks.org. This list of information was available on the site at the date of access—the content has been updated since.

11. Dinshaw, *How Soon Is Now?*, 30–31.

12. McCorkle, *Rhetorical Delivery*, 77. McCorkle builds upon the work of Ong, Ramus, and Bolter, *Writing Space*.

13. Baron, *Better Pencil*, 49.

14. Roszak, "Shakespeare."

15. Baron, *Better Pencil*, 52.

16. OpenAI, "ChatGPT," accessed December 13, 2022, https://openai.com/blog/chatgpt/.

17. Plato, *Phaedrus*, 550–54. See also Ong's discussion of this debate in *Orality and Literacy*, 78–80.

18. Ong, *Orality and Literacy*, 95.

19. "Cito post inquietauit rex quosdam ex magnatibus terre per iusticiarios suos scire volens quo Waranto tenerent terras et si non haberent bonum varentum saysiuit statim terras illorum; vocatusque est inter ceteros Comes de Warenna coram justiciarios regis et interrogatus quo Warento teneret produxit in medium gladium antiquum et eruginatum et ait 'Ecce domini mei ecce Warentum meum. Antecessores enim mei cum Willelmo bastardo uenientes conquesti sunt terras suas gladio et easdem gladio defendam a quocunque eas occupare volente.'" See *The Chronicle of Walter of Guisborough*, 216. For a discussion of this story and its status as a popular legend see Clanchy, *From Memory*, 36–43.

20. Harrington, Shermis, and Rollins, "Influence of Word Processing," 207.

21. Haswell, "Error and Change," 494–96.

22. See Vee, *Coding Literacy*.

23. Head and Eisenberg, "How Today's College Students."

24. See Darnton, *Business of Enlightenment*.

25. On Isidore's being named the patron saint of the internet, see Brandon Hawk's blog post: "Isidore of Seville & Old Media," *Brandon W. Hawk* (blog), April 4, 2016, https://brandonwhawk.net/2016/04/04/isidore-of-seville-old-media/. Bolter, *Writing Space*, 82–83. For the loss of texts in the Byzantine East and Latin West from the sixth through the eighth centuries, see Reynolds and Wilson, *Scribes and Scholars*, 47–48, 75–76.

26. Bolter, *Writing Space*, 84. For similar innovations by Hugh of St. Victor and Vincent of Beauvais, see also Châtillon, "Le *Didascalicon*"; and Lemoine, "Le oeuvre."

27. Collison, *Encyclopaedias*, 51–53. For more on the life and writing of Honorius, see Endres, *Honorius Augustodunensis*; and Sanford, "Honorius."

28. Collison, *Encyclopaedias*, 60, 63.

29. Caxton, *Caxton's Mirrour of the World*, v. All citations of Caxton's *Mirrour of the World* refer to this edition.

30. Bolter, *Writing Space*, 90.

31. Bush, "As We May Think." For an application of Bush's ideas to technological innovations such as Wikipedia, see Stettler, "Reframing Semiotic Telematic Knowledge Spaces."

32. Bush, "As We May Think."

33. Bush.

34. Hayles, *How We Think*, 12.

35. Brooks, *Design of Design*.

36. Bolter, *Writing Space*, 27, 66; Camille, "Sensations of the Page," 44.

37. Nunberg, "Place of Books," 22. See also Camille, "Sensations of the Page," 45.

38. Camille, "Sensations," 45.

39. Carruthers, *Book of Memory*, 237. For a discussion of the reemergence of this readerly authority in digital culture, see Wahlstrom and Scruton, "Constructing Texts/Understanding Texts," 314.

40. "Multa ille igitur de beluis deque auibus ac piscibus, quot leo pilos in uertice, quot plumas accipiter in cauda, quot polipus spiris naufragum liget, ut auersi coeunt elephantes biennioque uterum tument, ut docile uiuaxque animal et humano proximum ingenio et ad secundi tertijque finem seculi uiuendo perueniens; ut phenix aromatico igne consumitur ustusque renascitur; ut echinus quouis actam impetu proram frenat, cum fluctibus erutus nil possit; ut uenator speculo tigrem ludit, Arimaspus griphen ferro impetit, cete tergo nautam fallunt; ut informis urse partus, mule rarus, uipere unicus isque infelix, ut ceci talpe, surde apes, ut postremo superiorem mandibulam omnium solus animantium cocodrillus mouet." Petrarch, *De sui ipsius*, 24.50–66. The translation is Ernest Cassirer's, from Petrarch, *On His Own Ignorance*, at 56–57. For another discussion of this passage, see Mazzota, "Humanism," 114.

41. Mazzota, 115.

42. Brehaut, *Encyclopedist of the Dark Ages*, 42–43.

43. Wikipedia, s.v. "Five Pillars," accessed August 10, 2021, http://en.wikipedia.org/wiki/Five_pillars_of_Wikipedia.

44. O'Neil, *Cyberchiefs*, 150.

45. Irvine, *Making of Textual Culture*, 210. For the reception of the *Etymologies*, see Beeson, *Isidor-Studien*; Bischoff, "Die europäische Verbreitung"; Reydellet, "La Diffusion des *Origines*."

46. Wikipedia, s.v. "Wikipedia: Size Comparisons," accessed May 17, 2021, https://en.wikipedia.org/wiki/Wikipedia:Size_comparisons.

47. Head and Eisenberg, "How Today's College Students."

48. Bahr, *Fragments and Assemblages*, 3.

49. Irvine, *Making of Textual Culture*, 241–42. The italics appear in the original. See also Hathaway, "Compilatio."

50. Head and Eisenberg, "How Today's College Students." See also Lim, "How and Why."

51. Isidore, *Etymologies*, 242. The Latin reads as follows: "Conpilator, qui aliena dicta suis praemiscet, sicut solent pigmentarii in pila diversa mixta contundere. Hoc scelere quondam accusabatur Mantuanus ille vates, cum quosdam versus Homeri transferens suis permiscuisset et conpilator veterum ab aemulis diceretur. Ille respondit: 'Magnarum esse virium clavam Herculi extorquere de manu'" (10.44).

52. Irvine, *Making of Textual Culture*, 242.

53. Dunger, *Die Sage*.

54. "nulla quidem esset apibus gloria, nisi in aliud et in melius inventa converterent. Tibi quoque, siqua legend meditandique studio reppereris, in favum stilo redigenda suadeo." Petrarch, *Prose*, 1.8.23–24.

55. Carruthers, *Book of Memory*, 273.

56. "Apes, ut aiunt, debemus imitari, quae vagantur et, flores ad mel faciendum idoneos carpunt" (84.3). All Latin quotations of these letters refer to Seneca, *Epistulae morales*. The English translations are slightly adapted from Carruthers, *Book of Memory*, 237, 435n8.

57. "ut quicquid lectione collectum est, stilus redigat in corpus" (84.2).

58. Anderson and Sayers, "Metaphor and Materiality of Layers," 80.

59. *The Colbert Report*, episode 128, "Wikiality," aired on July 31, 2006 on Comedy Central.

60. Liu, *Wikipedia Revolution*, 201–2.

61. Wikipedia, s.v. "Geoffrey Chaucer," March 24, 2005, 5:20 p.m., http://en.wikipedia.org/w/index.php?title=Geoffrey_Chaucer&oldid=11476382.

62. Wikipedia, s.v. "Geoffrey Chaucer," March 24, 2005, 7:00 p.m., http://en.wikipedia.org/w/index.php?title=Geoffrey_Chaucer&oldid=11679015.

63. Wikipedia, s.v. "Geoffrey Chaucer," November 28, 2006, 12:59 p.m., https://en.wikipedia.org/w/index.php?title=Geoffrey_Chaucer&oldid=90650525.

64. Wikipedia, s.v. "Wikipedia: No Original Research," accessed August 10, 2021, http://en.wikipedia.org/wiki/Wikipedia:No_original_research.

65. Brooke, *Lingua Fracta*, 191.

66. Brehaut, *Encyclopedist of the Dark Ages*, 15–34.

67. "Etymologia est origo vocabulorum, cum vis verbi vel nominis per interpretationem colligitur. Hanc Aristoteles σύμβολον, Cicero adnotationem nominavit, quia nomina et verba rerum nota facit exemplo posito; utputa 'flumen,' quia fluendo crevit, a fluendo dictum. . . . Omnis enim rei inspectio etymologia cognita planior est" (1.29).

68. This call was titled "Appeal to the English-Speaking and English-Reading Public to Read Books and Make Extracts for the Philological Society's New Dictionary." For a discussion of this publication, see Lerer, *Inventing English*, 236–37.

69. "Wikipedia: Introduction," Wikipedia, accessed August 6, 2021, http://en.wikipedia.org/wiki/Wikipedia:Introduction.

70. Cohen, "Don't Like Palin's Wikipedia Story?"

71. Common Core State Standards Initiative, "Common Core State Standards for English Language Arts & Literacy in History/Social Studies, Science, and Technical Subjects," 31, 57, accessed December 14, 2022, https://ccsso.org/sites/default/files/2017-12/ADA%20Compliant%20ELA%20Standards.pdf.

72. Common Core State Standards Initiative, "Common Core State Standards for English Language Arts & Literacy in History/Social Studies, Science, and Technical Subjects," 58, accessed December 14, 2022, https://ccsso.org/sites/default/files/2017-12/ADA%20Compliant%20ELA%20Standards.pdf.

73. National Assessment Governing Board, US Department of Education, "Reading Framework for the 2009 National Assessment of Educational Progress" (Washington DC: US Government Printing Office, 2008), 7, http://www.nagb.org/content/nagb/assets/documents/publications/frameworks/reading09.pdf.

74. Common Core State Standards Initiative, "Common Core State Standards for English Language Arts & Literacy in History/Social Studies, Science, and Technical Subjects," 5, accessed December 14, 2022, https://ccsso.org/sites/default/files/2017-12/ADA%20Compliant%20ELA%20Standards.pdf.

75. Rosenblatt, *Literature as Exploration*; Rosenblatt, *Reader, the Text, the Poem*.

76. Blau, *Literature Workshop*, 145.

77. Common Core State Standards Initiative, "Common Core State Standards for English Language Arts & Literacy in History/Social Studies, Science, and Technical Subjects," 8, accessed December 14, 2022, https://ccsso.org/sites/default/files/2017-12/ADA%20Compliant%20ELA%20Standards.pdf.

78. Tyre, "Writing Revolution." For another discussion of Coleman and the Common Core, see Goldstein, "Schoolmaster."

79. Lynch, *You Could Look It Up*, 389.

4 | Disputation

The Latin in the epigraph by Abelard is "Et quoniam dialecticarum rationum armaturam omnibus philosophie documentis pretuli, his armis alia commutaui et trophies bellorum conflictus pretuli disputationum." Abelard, *Historia calamitatum*, 23–26. The translation is J. T. Muckle's in *The Story of Abelard's Adversities*, 12. For the implications of this passage for the drama of disputation, see Enders, *Rhetoric and the Origins of Medieval Drama*, 93.

1. Welch, *Electric Rhetoric*, 188–89.

2. See especially Welch's chapter "Technologies of Electric Rhetoric," in *Electric Rhetoric*, 137–89. See also McCorkle, *Rhetorical Delivery as Technological Discourse*; and Morey, *Rhetorical Delivery and Digital Technologies*.

3. Welch, *Electric Rhetoric*, 156; Carruthers, *Book of Memory*; Enders, "Memory"; Enders, "Music."

4. Welch, *Electric Rhetoric*, 172; Ong, *Orality and Literacy*, 43–44.

5. Marenbon, *Later Medieval Philosophy*, 20–23; Maierù, *University Training*, 65–69, 127–37; Courtenay, *Schools and Scholars*, 45; Weisheipl, "Curriculum of the Faculty of Arts," 147, 153–56, 176–85.

6. Fowler, *Life and Times of John Trevisa*, 69.

7. Chaucer, General Prologue, *The Canterbury Tales*, in *The Riverside Chaucer*, 23–37. Future citations of *The Canterbury Tales* refer to this edition.

8. Novikoff, *Medieval Culture of Disputation*, 135.

9. "Non curamus . . . rationem humanam, aut sensum nostrum in talibus, sed auctoritatis verba solummodo" (Abelard, *Operum Pars Prima*, 147). The Latin text here and future citations are from *Operum Pars Prima*. Translations and citations of this passage are from Betty Radice's translation in *The Letters of Abelard and Heloise*.

10. "Et erat praesto liber quem secum ipse detulerat. Revolvi ad locum, quem noveram, quem ipse minime compererat, aut qui nonnisi mihi nocitura quaerebat. Et voluntas Dei fuit, ut cito occurreret migi quod volebam. Erat autem sentential intitulata: Augustinus De Trinitate lib. I (*cap*. 1): 'Qui putat ejus potentiae Deum, ut seipsum ipse genuerit, eo plus errat quod non solum Deus ita non est; sed nec spiritalis creatura, nec corporalis. Nulla enim omnino res est, quae seipsam gignat.' Quod cum discipuli ejus, qui aderant, audissent, obstupefacti erubescebant. Ipse autem, ut se quoquomodo protegeret: 'Bene, inquit, est intelligendum.' Ego autem subjeci [*al*. subjunxi], 'hoc non esse novellum, sed ad praesens nihil attinere, cum ipse verba tantum, non sensum requisisset'" (147–48).

11. Novikoff, *Medieval Culture of Disputation*, 133–71.

12. Gruwell, "Wikipedia's Politics of Exclusion," 118.

13. For the original survey, see Glott, Ghosh, and Schmidt, "Wikipedia Survey." For the updated survey, see Hill and Shaw, "Wikipedia Gender Gap Revisited."

14. Losh et al., "Putting the Human Back."

15. Ong, *Fighting for Life*, 118–48; Courtenay, *Schools and Scholars*, 29–30; Enders, "Theater of Scholastic Erudition," 341–63; Karras, *From Boys to Men*, 90–95.

16. Ong, *Rhetoric, Romance, and Technology*, 17.

17. Karras, *From Boys to Men*, 93.

18. O'Neil, "Sociology of Critique in Wikipedia," 3.

19. Marino, "Why We Must Read the Code."

20. Brock, *Rhetorical Code Studies*. Brock builds upon Ian Bogost's definition of "procedural rhetoric" as "the practice of using processes persuasively" in *Persuasive Games* (28).

21. For a discussion of the birching of boys, see Orme, *Medieval Schools*, 144–45. See especially figure 40, which depicts a fourteenth-century teacher birching a student (164). For a helpful overview of modern pedagogical ideals, particularly for writing instruction, see Knoblauch and Brannon, *Rhetorical Traditions*. For a critique of Knoblauch and Brannon's claim that students ought to be "nurtured, rather than 'taught'" (4), see Woods, "Among Men—Not Boys," 18.

22. Orme, *Medieval Schools*, 345.

23. Sayers, *Lost Tools of Learning*.

24. Knoblauch and Brannon, *Rhetorical Traditions*, 51–52; see also Knoblauch, "Modern Composition Theory"; Corbett, "John Locke's Contributions"; Stewart, "Some Facts Worth Knowing"; Connors, "Rise and Fall."

25. For a response to Knoblauch and Brannon, see Lloyd-Jones, "Using the History of Rhetoric," 18–19. Knoblauch and Brannon offer their own reflection on the critiques in *Critical Teaching*, 143–44.

26. Woods, "Teaching of Writing," 77. She includes the following histories of rhetoric within the corpus of scholarship that neglects the medieval period: Corbett, *Classical Rhetoric for the Modern Student*; Kennedy, *Classical Rhetoric and Its Christian and Secular Tradition from Ancient to Modern Times*; Vickers, *In Defense of Rhetoric*; Covino, *Art of Wondering*.

27. Freire, *Pedagogy of the Oppressed*, 71–86.

28. Orme, *Medieval Schools*, 57. See also Orme's figure 18, the title page of *Hornbyes Hornbook*, which depicts this posture.

29. "Et quia in toto praeexercitamine erudiendorum nihil utilius est quam ei quod fieri ex arte oportet assuescere, prosas et poemata cotidie scriptitabant, et se mutuis exercebant collationibus, quo quidem exercitio nihil utilius ad eloquentiam, nihil expeditius ad scientiam, et plurimum confert ad uitam, si tamen hanc sedulitatem regat caritas, si in profectu litteratorio servetur humilitas." John of Salisbury, *Ioannis Saresberiensis Metalogicon*, 1.24.109–15. For another translation, see John of Salisbury, *Metalogicon of*

John of Salisbury, 70. For another discussion of John's thoughts on Bernard's teaching, see Woods, "Some Techniques," 98–99.

30. Geoffrey of Vinsauf, *Poetria nova*; for the Latin, see Faral's edition in *Les arts poétiques du XIIe et du XIIIe siècle*, 194–262.

31. "[L]oquitur de arte ita quod ex arte, versificatur dans precepta de uersibus. Et ita ipse agit quod docet, quod est boni doctoris de consuetudine." Woods, *Early Commentary on the Poetria nova of Geoffrey of Vinsauf*, 6.53–54.

32. Orme, *Medieval Schools*, 181. For more on William Wheatley, see Emden, *Biographical Register*, 2030–31. For more on John Seward, see Galbraith, "John Seward," 85–104.

33. Lelamour's herbal is contained in Sloane MS 5, ff. 13r–57r in the British Library. See Orme, "Cathedral School," 574. For more on Barclay, see Orme, *Education and Society*, 259–65.

34. Henryson, *Poems of Robert Henryson*, xiii–xxv.

35. The reference to Henryson appears in line 82 of Dunbar's poem "I that in heill wes," in *Poems of William Dunbar*, 1.97.

36. See Mapstone, "Robert Henryson," 243–55.

37. Henryson, *Testament of Cresseid*.

38. *Munimenta Alme Universitatis Glasguensis*, 2.69.

39. Mapstone, "Robert Henryson," 243.

40. Jill Mann tracks this Aesop/Reynard mashup in *From Aesop to Reynard*, 262–305.

41. Citations of Henryson's fables refer to line numbers in Denton Fox's edition, *The Poems of Robert Henryson*.

42. Jenkins, "Confronting the Challenges," 4 and 28–31.

43. Bogost and Losh, "Rhetoric and Digital Media," 763.

44. Jenkins, "Confronting the Challenges," 22–25.

45. "Mes n'i ad fable de folie / U il n'en ait philosophie." See Marie de France, *Fables*, 28.23–24. The English translation is from Dorothy Gilbert's edition, *Marie de France*, 176.23–24.

46. Pearsall, *The Nun's Priest's Tale*, 12.

47. Mann, *From Aesop to Reynard*, 250–61.

48. Donaldson, *Speaking of Chaucer*, 150.

49. Mann, *From Aesop to Reynard*, 25–61.

50. Barker, *1381: The Year of the Peasant's Revolt*, 265–66.

51. See David Wallace's chapter "In Flaundres" in *Premodern Places*, 91–138, at 117.

52. Quoted in Murray, *Reason and Society in the Middle Ages*, 236.

53. See *The Trials and Joys of Marriage*.

54. "Un coq se redresse contre un autre, et se hérisse." See Lecoy de la Marche, *La Chaire française au moyen âge*, 452.

55. Koh, "Political Power of Play."

56. Enders, *Rhetoric*, 160; Lebègue, *Etudes*, 15.

57. "Ecquid, ut adspecta est studiosae littera dextrae, / Protinus est oculis congnita nostra tuis—/ an, nisi legisses auctoris nomina Sapphus, / hoc breve nescires unde movetur opus?" Citations and translations are from Ovid, *Heroides, Amores*.

58. See Goold's "In Appreciation of the *Heroides*" in Ovid, *Heroides, Amores*, 8.

59. Ricoeur, *Freud and Philosophy*, 356.

60. Felski, "Suspicious Minds," 216.

61. Latour, "Why Has Critique Run Out of Steam?" 225–48.

62. Felski, *Uses of Literature*, 54.

63. See Bacon-Smith, *Enterprising Women*.

64. FanFiction, accessed August 12, 2021, http://www.fanfiction.net.

65. See Black, *Adolescents*.

66. Black, "Online Fan Fiction," 409–10.

67. Black, 410.

68. Woods, *Weeping for Dido*, 10–11.

69. "Est metrice describere . . . qualiter latuit in chiro insula in aula lycomedis in habitu muliebri." Venice, Biblioteca Nazionale Marciana Zanetti Lat. 541, fol. 1r. For the translation and discussion, see Woods, *Weeping for Dido*, 66–67.

70. "Thetis ad motus et mores femineos rudem instruxit puerum." Wolfenbüttel, Herzog August Bibliothek, Codex Guelf. 52 Gudian Lat. 2°, fol. 124r. See Woods, *Weeping for Dido*, 71.

71. According to James Wilhelm, the poem likely dates to 1450. See his introduction to the tale in *The Romance of Arthur*, 467. Chaucer's *Tales* were written, and never completed, at the end of his life, between 1387 and 1400, but it is likely that he completed *Wife of Bath's Tale* between 1392 and 1395. See Larry Benson's editorial introduction to *The Riverside Chaucer*, xxix. For more on the sources of the *Wedding*, see Thomas Hahn's edition of the text in *Sir Gawain*, 41–44.

72. Line references to the *Wedding* are from *The Wedding of Sir Gawain and Dame Ragnelle* in Wilhelm, *Romance of Arthur*, 467–88.

73. Wilson, "Role of Affect," 1.2.

74. See Wilson, "Immature Pleasures."

75. Gee, *Situated Language and Learning*, 77–90.

76. Bruns, *Why Literature?*, 78.

77. "Perlege, quodcumque est—quid epistula lecta nocebit? / te quoque in hac aliquid quod iuvet esse potest; / his arcana notis terra perlagoque feruntur."

78. Boyle and Foys, "Editor's Vision Statement."

79. Jenkins, "Confronting the Challenges," 14.

80. Turkle, *Life on the Screen*, 70.

81. An earlier version of this section of the chapter was originally published as "The Case for Open Review" in *Inside Higher Ed*, May 16, 2016, https://www.insidehighered.com/views/2016/05/16/open-peer-review-journal-articles-offers-significant-benefits-essay.

82. Public Library of Science, accessed August 12, 2021, https://www.plos.org.

83. Open Library of Humanities, accessed August 12, 2021, https://www.openlibhums.org; *Kairos: Rhetoric, Technology, and Pedagogy*, accessed August 12, 2021, http://kairos.technorhetoric.net; *Digital Humanities Quarterly*, accessed August 12, 2021, http://www.digitalhumanities.org/dhq/; Open Humanities Press, accessed August 12, 2021, http://openhumanitiespress.org; punctum books, accessed August 12, 2021, https://punctumbooks.com.

84. See Fitzpatrick, *Planned Obsolescence*; Eve, *Open Access and the Humanities*.

85. Digital Pedagogy in the Humanities (New York: MLA, 2016), https://digitalpedagogy.mla.hcommons.org.

86. Candace Barrington, Brantley L. Bryant, Richard H. Godden, Daniel T. Kline, and Myra Seaman, "Call for Contributors and Collaboration: The Open Access Companion to the Canterbury Tales," *In the Middle*, January 6, 2016, http://www.inthemedievalmiddle.com/2016/01/call-for-contributors-and-collaboration.html. For the companion itself, see Barrington et al., *Open Access Companion to the Canterbury Tales*.

87. Fitzpatrick and Santo, "Open Review," 4.

88. Eyman and Ball, "Digital Humanities Scholarship," 73.

89. Locke, *Essay Concerning Human Understanding*, 3.10.9.

90. Novikoff, *Medieval Culture of Disputation*, 224.

91. For more on these examples, see Kleinman and Ezzell, "Opposing 'Both Sides'"; Trice, "Gamergate."

92. Thoreau, *Journal*, 36.

93. Shirky, *Cognitive Surplus*, 200.

94. Gray, "Trump Defends White-Nationalist Protesters."

5 | Amplification

The Latin by Geoffrey of Vinsauf is "Et sic ex modica maxima crescit aqua." Geoffrey of Vinsauf, *Documentum de modo et arte dictandi et versificandi* in *Les arts poétiques du xiie et du xiie siècle*, 283. Subsequent Latin citations of the works of Geoffrey of Vinsauf are from this edition. The English translation is mine. See also Wright, *"Hie lert uns der meister,"* 41.

1. King, Schneer, and White, "How the News Media."
2. Phillips, "Oxygen of Amplification," 2.32.
3. See Laurie Gries's study of the circulation of this meme in *Still Life with Rhetoric*.
4. See Saloman, *Introduction to the Glossa Ordinaria*; Winroth, *Making of Gratian's Decretum*.
5. Hawhee, *Rhetoric in Tooth and Claw*, 77.
6. Geoffrey of Vinsauf, *Documentum*, 283.
7. For a brief discussion of Geoffrey and his works, see Martin Camargo's "Introduction to the Revised Edition" in Geoffrey of Vinsauf, *Poetria nova*, 4–16.
8. "Si facis amplum, / Hoc primo procede gradu: sententia cum sit / Unica, non uno veniat contenta paratu, / Sed variet vestes et mutatoria sumat; / Sub verbis aliis praesumpta resume; repone / Pluribus in clausis unum; multiplice forma / Dissimuletur iden; varius sis et tamen idem" (lines 219–25). All English translations of the *Poetria nova* are from Nims's edition, Geoffrey of Vinsauf, *Poetria nova*.
9. "Hoc artificio vtendum est in aliis orationibus, quod pueri uolentes ampliare et uariare materiam obseruent.... Ut, si tractet de libro suo, commendet eum uel uituperet per causam efficientem, idest per scriptorem; per causam materialem, idest per pargamenum et incaustum; per causam formalem, ut per libri disposicionem et litterarum protractionem; per causam finale, considerando ad quid factus est liber, ad hoc uidelicent ut in eo et per eum nescientes scientes reddantur." John of Garland, *Parisiana Poetria*, 1.26, 52–55.
10. Minnis, *Medieval Theory of Authorship*, 28–29.
11. Deluca and Wilferth, "Foreword"; Vivian, "In the Regard of the Image."
12. Gries, *Still Life with Rhetoric*, 17, 20.
13. The following sections of this chapter are adapted from part of an essay coauthored with Matthew Davis. See Davis and Mueller, "Places of Writing."
14. Norris, *Analyzing Multimodal Interaction*, 83.
15. Trimbur and Press, "When Was Multimodality?" 22.
16. Norris, *Analyzing Multimodal Interaction*, 79.
17. Horner, "Modality as Social Practice."
18. Kress, *Multimodality*, 79–81.
19. See Carruthers, *Book of Memory*; Mak, *How the Page Matters*.
20. See Mitchell, *Picture Theory*; Drucker, *Graphesis*.
21. See Shipka, *Toward a Composition Made Whole*; Wysocki, "awaywithwords"; Yancey, "Made Not Only in Words."
22. Drucker, "Reading Interface," 213.
23. Manguel, *Reader on Reading*, 120.
24. Manguel, 123.

25. Vandendorpe, *From Papyrus to Hypertext*, 136–42.

26. Mak, *How the Page Matters*, 4.

27. Vandendorpe, *From Papyrus to Hypertext*, 135–36.

28. Parkes, *Scribes, Scripts, and Readers*, 36–58.

29. Illich, *In the Vineyard of the Text*, 99.

30. "ut non sit necesse quarenti, librorum numerositatem evolvere, cui brevitas, quod queritur, offert sine labore." Lombard, *Sentences*, I.4. The translation from Latin is mine.

31. Ridolfo and DeVoss, "Composing for Recomposition."

32. Hervieux, *Les Fabulistes Latins*, 1:472; Dicke and Grubmüller, *Die Fabeln*, lxvi–lxviii.

33. Aesop, *Aesop's Fables*, 190–91.

34. For a brief reception history of Aesop's fables through the Middle Ages, see Laura Gibbs's useful website, Aesopica: Aesop's Fables in English, Latin, and Greek, http://www.mythfolklore.net/aesopica/. In this section of the chapter, I rely on A. E. Wright's manuscript readings and translations in *"Hie lert uns der meister,"* especially those found in chapter 1, *"Moraliter, Allegorice, Scholastice,"* 1–73.

35. Vienna, Österreichische Nationalbibliothek, Codex Vindobonensis Palatinus 303.

36. See Wheatley, "Aesopic Corpus Divided."

37. Clark, *Medieval Book of Beasts*, 103. This teaching technique is described by Quintillian in *The Orator's Education*, 1.9.2–1.9.3, 208–11. See also Reynolds, *Medieval Reading*, 8–11.

38. "Sursum bibebat lupus . . . Haec in illos dicta est fabula qui hominibus calumniantur."

39. Wheatley, *Mastering Aesop*, 19.

40. San Marino (California), Huntington Library, 102140.

41. The first edition was printed in Basel by Jakob Wolff von Pforzarim (Huntington Library 110966). For a discussion of this new Brant-Steinhöwel compilation, see Carnes, "Heinrich Steinhöwel," 5.

42. Carnes, 4.

43. Hervieux, *Les Fabulistes Latins*, 602–19; Caxton, *Caxton's Aesop*, 4.

44. Holbek, *Æsops levned og fabler*, 117; Beardsley, *Hispano-Classical Translations*, 20–21; Keller and Kincade, *Iconography in Medieval Spanish Literature*, 93.

45. Wright, *"Hie lert uns der meister,"* xxiii.

46. Wheatley, *Mastering Aesop*, 62.

47. Vienna, Österreichische Nationalbibliothek, Codex Vindobonensis Palatinus 3235.

48. Carinthia, Stiftsbibliothek, Codex S. Pauli in Carinthia 255/4.

49. Wheatley, "'Fabulae' of Walter of England," 71–153.

50. Aesop, *Aesop's Fables*, 208.

51. *"Ingentem.* Hic docet quod ingenium preualet uiribus, et hoc per coturnicem que dum sitiret in quodam campo urnam semiplenam aqua inuenit, quam uiribus inclinare non potuit. Sed eam ingenio lapillis inpleuit et istam aquam extraxit. Fructus talis est: Melior est sapiens forti uiro." Copenhagen, Kongelige Bibliotek, GKS 1905 4°. See Wright's reading of this manuscript in *"Hie lert uns der meister,"* 23. It's also apparent that this commentator, or a previous scribe, misread *cornicem*, which means "crow," as *coturnicem*, which means "quail."

52. Wright, *"Hie lert uns der meister,"* 24.

53. "Lictera gesta refert, quod credas aligoria / Moralis quod agas, quod speres anagogia."

54. Hervieux refers to this "Liber Catonianus" manuscript by its former shelf mark, MS LXXXVIII, Class. XI. See *Les Fabulistes Latins*, 1:595. For a discussion of this distich, see Wheatley, *Mastering Aesop*, 67–69.

55. "In hoc appologo docemur quod multa sunt que citius fiunt per artem quam per vires." Wrocław, Biblioteka Uniwersytecka, MS Codex IV.Q.126.

56. "Hic monet nos ut studiosius acquiramus scientiam quam vires, quia magis proficit." Berlin, Staatsbibliothek, Preußischer Kulturbestiz, cod. Q 536. Similar admonitions can be found in Munich, Bayerische Staatsbibliothek, clm 391, fol. 29v; and Vienna, Österreichische Nationalbibliothek, Codex Vindobonensis Palatinus 15071, fol. 68v.

57. Dagenais, *Ethics of Reading*, 57.

58. "Carmen huius libri . . . est convertibile ad omnem sensum cuisulibet intentionis." Honorius of Autun, *Selectorum Psalmorum Expositio*, 172:274.

59. "Vnde: Homo sepe vincit illa per sapientiam que per vires non faceret. Eciam monet nos ut studiosius sapientia et ingenio insistamus magis quam viribus." Munich, Bayerische Staatsbibliothek, cgm 3974.

60. "In hoc appollogo auctor docet nos quod queramus prudenciam, dicens 'Tu debes scire quod prudencia est maior viribus et prevalet eam, quia per sapienciam vincet homo qui viribus vincere non posset.' Ideo subiungit dicens quod sapiencia complet opus cuiuslibet hominis inceptum. Vnde Salomon Prouerbiorum: 'Potencior est sapiencia.'" Budapest, Magyar nemzeti múzeum, ms. lat. med. aev. 123 (referring to Prov. 24:5: "vir sapiens et fortis est et vir doctus robustus et validus.")

61. "Ingentem sitiens. Hic actor ostendit quod prudencia est melior et maior viribus. Ergo studiosius admonet ut sciamus et prudenciam acquiramus, quod probat dicens: Quedam sitiens cornix volans per campum venit ad vnum fontem, quem circa vidit pendere vnam vrnam in qua modicum aque fuit, quam haurire non valebat. Post hec cupiens effundere vrnam planis campis, quia cornix nusquam potuit inclinare, tandem

invenit sua arte calliditatem, et congregans lapillos in vrnam misit. Quibus immissis aqua sursum ascendit et sic habuit facilem viam potandi." Prague, Universitní Knihovna, ms. 546.

62. Wright, "*Hie lert uns der meister,*" 29.
63. Wright, 29.
64. Zumthor, *Essai de poétique médiévale.*
65. Bruns, *Inventions,* 44.
66. "L'écriture médiévale ne produit pas de variants, elle est variance." Cerquiglini, *Eloge de la variante,* 111.
67. Nichols, "Introduction," 2–3.
68. For one critique of this approach, see Price, "Introduction," 14.
69. Wakelin, *Scribal Correction.*
70. "Licet sicud cornix non potuit effundere vrnam, sic nullus scholaris studens potest quamlibet scientiam acquirere; set potest acquirere aliquam partem scientie si proiciat lapidem, id est si adhibit laborem et dilegenciam." Erfurt, Stadtbücherei, Amplon.Q.21.
71. "Versus cev scribit, taliter arte bibit." "Novus Avianus," Munich, Bayerische Staatsbibliothek, clm 14703; and Vienna, Österreichische Nationalbibliothek, Codex Vindobonensis Palatinus 303; edited in Hervieux, *Les fabulistes latins,* 3:443, line 10.
72. Wright, "*Hie lert uns der meister,*" 41.
73. Burrow, "Henryson," 35. For a similar critique, see Kinsley, *Scottish Poetry,* 18. On the opposite extreme is Henderson's "Having Fun with the Moralities." For a more measured response, see Mann, *From Aesop to Reynard,* 262–305.
74. Quotations are taken from Fox's edition, *The Poems of Robert Henryson.* The translations of Henryson are mine.
75. Henderson, "Having Fun with the Moralities," 72–73; Gray, *Robert Henryson,* 129; Powell, *Fabula docet,* 181; Bright, "Henryson's Figurative Technique," 20. Mann alternatively suggests that "these phrases bring the moralizing narrator, and particularly his intellectual ingenuity, to the forefront of our attention." See *From Aesop to Reynard,* 295.
76. "Blessed be a simple life without fear; blessed be a temperate feast in peace. Whoever has enough, though it is little in quantity, has no need of more. Great abundance and blind prosperity often produce a bad conclusion. Therefore, in this country the sweetest life is security with modest possessions. O greedy man, accustomed to feed your stomach and make it a god, look to yourself, I warn you in all earnest. That cat comes, and has an eye on the mouse. What is the use of your feasting and splendor, with a fearful heart and tribulation? Therefore, the best thing on earth, I say for my part, is a merry heart with modest possessions. Your own fire, friend, though it is only a coal, warms well, and is worth gold to you. And Solomon says, if you care to read him, 'Under the heaven I can see

nothing better than to be always happy and live virtuously.' Wherefore, I may conclude with this saying: 'The highest degree of earthly joy comes from blitheness of heart, with modest possessions.'"

77. Barthes, *S/Z*, 4.

78. Foys, *Virtually Anglo-Saxon*, 40.

79. Barthes, *S/Z*, 4.

80. Trimbur and Press, "When Was Multimodality?" 21.

81. Horner, "Modality as Social Practice."

82. I am grateful here to Paul Schacht and Meera Nair, whose work on using annotation platforms, including Genius, informs my own thinking. I hope to draw from the best of their insights—about the democratic potential of annotation and its usefulness in teaching certain genres of writing, respectively—and add to them specific attention to the role that multimodality plays in achieving those ends. See Nair, "Annotate the Plot"; Schacht, "Annotation."

83. Annotation Studio, http://www.annotationstudio.org; Prism: A Tool for Collaborative Interpretation of Texts, http://prism.scholarslab.org/; Perusall, https://perusall.com; Genius, https://genius.com.

84. Schacht, "Annotation."

85. Drucker, *Graphesis*, 180.

86. Agamben, *State of Exception*, 76.

87. Gallagher, *Update Culture*, 11–14 and 156.

88. Gallagher, 160.

89. Chun, *Updating to Remain the Same*, 84.

90. Chun, 3.

91. Chun, 85.

92. Breen, *Imagining*, 43.

93. "Animi aut corporis constantem et absolutam aliqua in re perfectionem, aut virtutis, aut artis alicius preceptionem, aut quamvis scientiam et item corporis aliquam commoditatem non natura datam, sed studio et industria partam." See Cicero, *On Invention*, 1.25.36; 72–73.

94. "varius sis et tamen idem."

95. Chun, *Updating to Remain the Same*, 171, 172.

96. Agamben, *Highest Poverty*, 16.

6 | Appropriation

Some material in this chapter was previously published as "Stealing a Corpus: Appropriating Aesop's Body in the Early Age of Print," *Digital Humanities Quarterly* 12, no. 2 (Fall 2018). http://www.digitalhumanities.org/dhq/vol/12/2/000382/000382.html.

The French in the epigraph by Marie de France is "Put cel ester que clerc plusur / Prendreient sur eus mun labur. / Ne voil que nul sur le le die! / . . Esope apel'um cest livre, / Qu'il translate e fist escrire, / Del griu en latin le turna. / . . E jeo l'ai rime en franceis, / Si cum jeo poi plus proprement" (5–7, 13–15, 18–19). See Marie de France, *Fables*, 256, 258. The English translation is from Dorothy Gilbert's edition, *Marie de France*, 200.

1. Edgar Allan Poe to Rufus Griswold, May 29, 1841, Griswold MS 835, Boston Public Library.

2. Vaidhyanathan, *Copyrights and Copywrongs*, 15.

3. Wharton, "Digital Humanities," 32–38.

4. Suntrust Bank v. Houghton Mifflin, 286 F.3d 1257 (2001).

5. Foucault, "What Is an Author?" 211–13.

6. Willinsky, *Intellectual Properties of Learning*, 21–48, at 41.

7. Johns, *Piracy*, 28.

8. *The case of the booksellers and printers stated with answers to the objections of the patentee* (1666). British Library, Wing / C1017.

9. Johns, *Piracy*, 38.

10. Curtin, "Hackers and Humanists," 136.

11. For a treatment of animals as parchment, see Holsinger, "Of Pigs and Parchment," 616–23.

12. See Bolens, "*Beowulf*."

13. See Young, *Bodylore*; Rubin, "Person in the Form," 100–22; Daileader, *Eroticism*; Cohen, *Medieval Identity Machines*.

14. Zumthor, *La lettre*; Müller, "Body of the Book."

15. Johns, *Piracy*, 27.

16. Caxton, *Caxton's Aesop*. Future citations refer to this edition.

17. "Finito libro, frangamus ossa magistro." Cited in Wheatley, *Mastering Aesop*, 94. Unless otherwise indicated, the translations from Latin to English in this chapter are mine.

18. "Malo mortuum impendere quam vivum occidere." Petronius, *Petronii Arbitri Satyricon reliquiae*, 112.7–8.

19. Wheatley, *Mastering Aesop*, 82–84. See also Wheatley, "Aesopic Corpus."

20. Wright, "Hie lert uns der meister," xxiii; Wright, "Readers and Wolves"; Cramer, "Æsopi wolff."

21. "Sola premit uiuosque metu penaque sepultos / Femina: femineum non bene finit opus." Hervieux, *Les Fabulistes Latins*, 2:341.

22. Hervieux, 2:341n1.

23. "Allegorice per mulierem potest intelligi anima rationalis et per virum ipsum corpus castum sive mundum. Tandem venit mors, id est delectatio mundi, et capit, id est du-

Notes to Pages 156–164

cit hominem ad peccata et trahit carnem ad vanitates. Sed mulier, id est anima, residens circa tumulum, plorat et flet in nocte, id est in conscientia occulta. Tandem custos furis, id est bonus angelus, visitat illum locum attendens illam contritionem et tandem ipsam animam trahit in coniugem, id est in eternam beatitudinem." Cited and translated by Wheatley in *Mastering Aesop*, 83.

24. Hexter, *Ovid and Medieval Schooling*.
25. See Minnis, *Medieval Theory of Authorship*, 94–95.
26. Fisher, *Scribal Authorship*, 71–72.
27. Navas, *Remix Theory*, 60.
28. Benjamin, "Work of Art," 221.
29. Benjamin, 224.
30. Navas, *Remix Theory*, 67.
31. Liu, *Laws of Cool*, 317–71.
32. Ingham, *Medieval New*, 14.
33. For an extensive list of Aesopic authors and texts, see Laura Gibbs's website Aesopica: Aesop's Fables in English, Latin, and Greek, http://www.mythfolklore.net/aesopica/.
34. Irvine, "Remix," 15.
35. Irvine, 33. Italics are mine.
36. Simone, "Body of the Text," 249.
37. Irvine, "Remix," 33.
38. Fitzpatrick, *Planned Obsolescence*, 79.
39. "Ut iuvet et prosit conatur pagina presens: / dulcius arrident seria picta iocis. / Ortulus iste parit fructum cum flore, favorem / flos et fructus emunt: hic sapit, ille nitet. / Si fructus plus flore placet, fructum lege, si flos / plus fructu, florem, si duo, carpe duo." Line numbers in the elegiac *Romulus* refer to Busdraghi, *L'Esopus*.
40. Quotations are taken from Denton Fox's edition, *The Poems of Robert Henryson*. Translations of Henryson are mine.
41. "It is fitting to mix some merriments with solemn matters; indeed Aesop said so. Serious things are more alluring when embellished with sport."
42. Compare, for example, the discussion of Cato as author of the *Distichs* to the discussion of Avianus as an Aesopic author in Huygens, *Accessus ad auctores*, 21–22; for an English translation, see Minnis and Scott, *Medieval Literary Theory*, 15–16.
43. Repetition is one of the central habits of what Carolyn Guertin calls—via Giorgio Agamben's analysis of Guy DeBord's films—the "aesthetics of appropriation" that define digital remixing projects. See Guertin, *Digital Prohibition*, 51; Agamben, "Difference and Repetition," 328–33.
44. For example, one fourteenth-century Austrian manuscript, Codex Vindobonen-

sis Palatinus 303 (Vienna, Österreichische Nationalbibliothek), is an amplified Aesopic compilation that contains six different fable versions, with even two copies of the prose *Romulus*.

45. If we move beyond Henryson's prologue, we find that he applies this practice of remixing to texts beyond the fable tradition. Jill Mann suggests that Henryson is not content simply to rewrite Aesopic mainstays; rather, he merges the fable genre with the *Roman de Renart*, another animal corpus that centers on the exploits of one Reynard the fox. See Mann, *From Aesop to Reynard*, 262–305.

46. See Navas, *Remix Theory*, 96.

47. Navas, 93.

48. For more on the dating of the manuscript and its relationship to printed editions, see Denton Fox's discussion in *Poems of Robert Henryson*, lii–liv.

49. Carnes, "Heinrich Steinhöwel and the Sixteenth-Century Fable Tradition," 4.

50. Travis, "Aesop's Symposium," 37.

51. Benjamin, "Work of Art," 235, 232.

52. Travis, "Aesop's Symposium," 46.

53. "His gown was of a cloth as white as milk, his shirt was of a deep purple fabric, his hood was scarlet, bordered skillfully with silk, fringed unto his girdle below, his bonnet was round like the old fashion, his beard was white, his eyes were large and grey, with curly hair which lay over his shoulders."

54. Burrows, *Rhetorical Crossover*, 71.

55. Patterson, *Fables of Power*; Blake and Santos, *Arthur Golding's "A Moral Fabletalk*,*"* 13–28.

56. Lerer, *Children's Literature*, 104–28.

57. Daly, *Aesop without Morals*, 267–307, at 12 and 11.

58. Daly, 12 and 15.

59. Temple and Temple, *Aesop*, xxiv.

60. Temple and Temple, back cover.

61. Temple and Temple, xviii and xv.

62. This language used to be in "Terms of Service," *Early English Books Online*, http://eebo.chadwyck.com/about/terms.htm (accessed October 24, 2012). This link no longer leads to a page that includes these terms.

63. Boyle and Foys, "Becoming Media," 2.

64. Camille, "Book as Flesh," 40.

65. I am indebted to my colleague Emilio Sauri for these observations about the social function of the paywall and its effects on access within higher education.

66. Welzenbach, "Making the Most," 5.

67. Welzenbach, 12.

68. "Aesop. *The morall fabillis of Esope the Phrygian*," Early English Books Online—Text Creation Partnership (Ann Arbor and Oxford: Text Creation Partnership, 2003), http://name.umdl.umich.edu/A08136.0001.001.

69. For more information about these open-source licenses, see Creative Commons, http://creativecommons.org.

70. "Ut, si unum quodque membrum sensum hunc haberet, ut posse putaret se valere, si proximi membri valetudinem ad se traduxisset, debilitari et interire totum corpus necesse esset, sic, si unus quisque nostrum ad se rapiat commoda aliorum detrahatque quod cuique possit, emolumenti sui gratia, societas hominum et communitas evertatur necesse est." Cicero, *De Officiis*, 3.5.22. One of Henryson's Scottish contemporaries, Archibald Whitelaw (discussed in chapter 7), royal secretary and tutor to James III, owned a manuscript of the 1471 Roman print of Cicero's *Opera Philosophica* (St Andrews University Library MS PA6295.A2A00). As the length and number of his marginal comments indicate, Whitelaw was clearly engaged with Cicero's *De Amicitia* ("On Friendship"), but his greatest dedication was to Book 3 of *De Officiis*, which is accompanied by the greatest concentration of glosses throughout the manuscript.

71. Patterson, *Fables of Power*, 111–37.

72. Turner, "Problem of the More-than-One," 416–17.

73. Turner, 427n46.

74. Bakhtin, *Rabelais and His World*, 317.

75. Irvine, "Remix," 33.

76. Guertin, *Digital Prohibition*, 39–40.

77. Lessig, *Remix*.

78. Kennerly, *Editorial Bodies*, 15.

79. Navas, *Remix Theory*, 120.

80. Esposito, *Communitas*, 6.

81. Esposito, 6.

82. Ashley and Plesch, "Cultural Processes," 6.

83. Turner, *Corporate Commonwealth*.

84. Esposito, *Communitas*, 4–5.

85. "Benevolentia et caritate consensio." Cicero, *De Senectute*, 6.20, 130–31.

7 | Salutation

The Latin by Seneca, quoted in the epigraph, is, "Numquam epistulam tuam accipio ut non protinus una simus. Si imagines nobis amicorum absentium iucundae sunt, quae memoriam renovant et desiderium [absentiae] falso atque inani solacio levant, quanto iucundiores sunt litterae, quae vera amici absentis vestigia, veras notas afferunt?" The

Latin and English are from G. P. Goold's edition, Seneca, *Seneca IV*. Future citations are from this edition.

1. Carruthers, *Book of Memory*, x.
2. Carruthers, 75.
3. Rosen, "More, But Not Merrier."
4. boyd, *It's Complicated*, 57.
5. boyd, 54–76.
6. Witt, *Two Latin Cultures*, 254.
7. Kristeller, "Humanism and Scholasticism."
8. McCorkle, *Rhetorical Delivery*, 87.
9. Witt, "Medieval 'Ars Dictaminis,'" 8.
10. "Missam ad amicum pro consolatione epistolam, dilectissime, vestram ad me forte quidam nuper attulit. Quam ex ipsa statim tituli fronte vestram esse considerans tanto ardentius eam coepi legere, quanto scriptorem ipsum charius amplector . . ." Héloïse, *Epistola II*, in Abelard, *Operum Pars Prima*, 181. The translation is from *The Letters of Abelard and Heloise*, 47.
11. Abelard, *Historia calamitatum*; Abelard, *Story of Abelard's Adversities*.
12. Eden, *Renaissance Rediscovery of Intimacy*, 50.
13. Hobbins, *Authorship and Publicity*, 10.
14. Wendell, *English Composition*, 25.
15. Gage, "Vestiges of Letter Writing."
16. Fletcher and Carpenter, *Introduction to Theme-Writing*, 7.
17. Gage, "Vestiges of Letter Writing," 229.
18. Frehner, *Email-SMS-MMS*, 91.
19. Lanham, *Salutatio Formulas*, 7.
20. "Debite subiectionis perseuerantiam," "indissolubilis amoris dulcedinem." The Latin is from Rockinger, *Briefsteller*, 13, 15. The translation is from Anonymous of Bologna, *Principles of Letter-Writing*, 10, 13.
21. "Et io dico che la salutazione è porta della pistol, la quale ordinatamente chiarisce le nomora e'meriti delle persone e l'affezione del mandante." Latini, *La Rettorica*, 76.27. The English translation is by Justin Steinberg in Copeland and Sluiter, *Medieval Grammar and Rhetoric*, 778–79.
22. Vaidhyanathan, *Anti-Social Media*.
23. "Publicum commodum priuato dolori anteponendum." Erasmus, *De Conscribendis Epistolis*, 232.13. The translation is from Erasmus, "On the Writing of Letters," in *Collected Works of Erasmus*, 25:24. For a helpful discussion of his epistolary theory, see Henderson, "Humanism and the Humanities."

24. Douglas, *Palyce of Honour*. "I experienced great wonder of their diverse lays, which in that art they might have no peer at all of ingenious expressions, fine rhetorical colors so poet-like in subtle, fair manner and eloquent, steady, regular cadence." The modern English translation is mine.

25. See Martin Camargo's introduction to *Medieval Rhetorics of Prose Composition*, 1–34.

26. Cornelius, "Rhetoric of Advancement," 314.

27. For a helpful analysis of Douglas's misogyny, see Desmond, *Reading Dido*, 179–83.

28. Douglas, *Virgil's Aeneid Translated into Scottish Verse*, 1.449.

29. Desmond, *Reading Dido*, 163–67.

30. Fifteenth-century books that contain Cicero's *Episotlae ad familiares* and rhetorical glosses include Biblioteca Universitaria di Bologna (BUB) Lat. MS 1 VIII; BUB Lat. MS 467; BUB Lat. MS 2283; Cambridge University Library (CUL), classmark Inc.3.B.3.152 [1857]; CUL, classmark Inc.2.B.3.85 [1659]; CUL, classmark Inc.2.D.2.25 [2713]; CUL, classmark Inc.2.B.7.2 [4336]; Cambridge, St. John's College Library, classmark Ii.2.10. Fifteenth-century books that contain the *Rhetorica ad Herennium* and glosses referring to Ciceronian *amicitia* include BUB Lat. MS 1282. Fifteenth-century books that contain Cicero's *De Amicitia* and rhetorical glosses include BUB Lat. MS 2051; CUL, classmark Inc.3.B.3.104 [1736]. For more on the Cambridge incunables, see Wakelin, *Humanism*, 140–47.

31. Murphy claims that "no dictaminal treatises" were printed during this period in "Trends in Rhetorical Incunabula," 390.

32. All citations of Chaucerian texts refer to Chaucer, *The Riverside Chaucer*.

33. Mann, *Feminizing Chaucer*, 9.

34. Banker, "Giovanni di Bonandrea."

35. BUB Lat. MS 313 (contains *De Amicitia*); BUB Lat. MS 2461 (contains *Ad Herennium*); BUB Lat. MS 1754 (contains model letters as well as a compilation of Ciceronian quotations on friendship).

36. Banker, "Giovanni di Bonandrea," 11.

37. Giovanni di Bonandrea, *Brevis introductio ad dictamen*, BUB, Lat. MS 2461 (1303–4). Quotations of Giovanni's treatise are from this manuscript. Unless otherwise indicated, translations from Latin to English are mine.

38. "Corporis aliquam commoditatem non natura datam sed studio et industria comparatam."

39. Agamben, *Coming Community*, 27–28.

40. "Quo modo aliquis per epistolas sollicitaretur." Huygens, *Accessus ad auctores*, 32. For a discussion of this *accessus*, see Copeland, *Rhetoric, Hermeneutics, and Translation*, 187–88.

41. Derrida, *Post Card*, 124–25.

42. Desmond, "*Translatio* of Memory and Desire," 199.

43. Hexter, "Ovid in the Middle Ages," 418.

44. Desmond, *Reading Dido*, 160, 162.

45. Dinshaw, *Chaucer's Sexual Politics*, 12.

46. Baswell, *Virgil in Medieval England*, 268.

47. See Lacan, *Écrits*, 23, 16.

48. Collette, *Rethinking Chaucer's Legend of Good Women*, 24–25.

49. Kim, "#medievaltwitter."

50. This quotation, which I include here with permission, is from Alicia Spencer-Hall's forthcoming book, *Medieval Twitter* (York: ARC Humanities).

51. Kirschenbaum, *Mechanisms*, 25–74.

52. Kirschenbaum, 27.

53. Drucker, "Performative Materiality," 21.

54. Drucker, 21.

55. "Numquam epistulam tuam accipio ut non protinus una simus. Si imagines nobis amicorum absentium iucundae sunt, quae memoriam renovant et desiderium [absentiae] falso atque inani solacio levant, quanto iucundiores sunt litterae, quae vera amici absentis vestigia, veras notas afferunt? Nam quod in conspectu dulcissimum est, id amici manus epistulae impressa praestat, agnoscere."

56. Macdougall, "Whitelaw, Archibald."

57. Durkan and Ross, *Early Scottish Libraries*, 159.

58. Incunabula Short Title Catalogue (ISTC) ic00504000 and ic00505000.

59. ISTC ic00505000.

60. Lyall, "Books and Book Owners," 249.

61. Eden, *Renaissance Rediscovery of Intimacy*, 59.

62. "Non igitur utilitatem amicitia, sed utilitas amicitiam secuta est." Cicero, *De Senectute, De Amicitia, De Divitatione*, 14.51.

63. "Natura non patitur ut aliorum spoliis nostra copias augeamus." Cicero, *De Officiis*, 3.5.

64. Macdougall, "Whitelaw, Archibald."

65. Whitelaw [Whytelaw], "Oratio Scotorum," 19a, 41–48; Whitelaw, "Address to King Richard III," 193–99.

66. "O mes amis, il n'y nul amy." Montaigne, "De l'amitié," 226. The translation is mine.

67. Brooke, *Lingua Fracta*, 143–93.

68. Brooke, 157–66, at 157.

69. Carruthers, *Book of Memory*, 156.

70. "Debent intelligi distingui exempla et dicta et facta autentica, et magistri a quibus audiuimus, et libri quos legimus. Si aliquid deciderit nobis a memoria, debemus recolere tempus clarum uel obscurum in quo didicimus, locum in quo, magistrum a quo, in quo habitu, in quo gestu, libros in quibus studuimus, paginam candidam uel nigram, disposiciones et colores litterarum; quia hec omnia introductiua erunt rerum memorandarum et nobis eligendarum." The Latin and English translation are from John of Garland, *Parisiana poetria*, 2.8, 64–66.

71. Carruthers, *Book of Memory*, 163.

72. Brooke, *Lingua Fracta*, 169–93.

73. Welch, *Electric Rhetoric*, 137–89.

74. Brooke, *Lingua Fracta*, 175.

75. Porter, "Recovering Delivery," 209.

76. Porter, 218.

77. See Geoffrey of Vinsauf, *Poetria nova*, in *Les arts poétiques*, lines 264–460.

Conclusion | Breaking Bad *Habitus*

1. Drucker, *Graphesis*, 125.

2. Drucker, 128.

3. Chun, *Updating to Remain the Same*, 1.

4. Rickert, *Ambient Rhetoric*; Boyle, *Rhetoric as a Posthuman Practice*.

5. Benjamin, *Race after Technology*, 32.

6. See Noble, *Algorithms of Oppression*.

7. Drucker, *Graphesis*, 168.

8. Baldwin, *Collected Essays*, 723.

9. Bourdieu, *Outline*, 78.

10. Boyle, *Rhetoric as a Posthuman Practice*, 55.

11. Powell, "Access(ing) Habits," 28.

12. Powell, 33.

13. Boyle, *Rhetoric as a Posthuman Practice*, 22.

14. Boyle, 22; Giovanni di Bonandrea, *Brevis introductio ad dictamen*, Biblioteca Universitaria di Bologna, Lat. MS 2461.

15. John of Garland, *Parisiana Poetria*, 1.26, 52–55.

16. Bourdieu, *Outline*, 72; Boyle, *Rhetoric as a Posthuman Practice*, 48.

17. Bourdieu, postface, in Panofsky, *Architecture gothique*, 135–67.

18. This translation is by Laurence Petit, Appendix II in Holsinger's *Premodern Condition*, 238–39.

19. For a brief explanation of their Aristotelian character, see Minnis, *Medieval Theory of Authorship*, 28–29.

20. Martinez, *Counterstory*, 3.

21. Gilyard and Banks, *On African-American Rhetoric*, 88.

22. Ascher, "New Yellow Journalism."

23. Noble, *Algorithms of Oppression*, 4; Benjamin, *Race after Technology*, 5–6.

24. Vee, *Coding Literacy*; Brock, *Rhetorical Code Studies*; Boyle, *Rhetoric as Posthuman Practice*, 70.

25. Drucker, *Graphesis*, 176–78.

26. McPherson, *Feminist in a Software Lab*, 106.

27. Chun, *Updating to Remain the Same*, 3–4.

28. Mbembe, *Necropolitics*, 114.

29. Drucker, *Graphesis*, 194–95.

30. McCloud, *Understanding Comics*.

31. "Aliud est enim agree de rethorica et aliud rethorice. Rhetor enim agit de rethorica, orator autem rethorice. Iste auctor utrumque facit; agit de rethorica et hoc rethorice. Item aliud est agree de uersibus et aliud uersifice . . . Iste auctor utrumque facit." Woods, *Early Commentary*, 44–47 and 49.

32. Romele and Rodighiero, "Digital Habitus," 120.

33. Chun, *Discriminating Data*, 82.

34. Grosz, "Habit Today," 219.

Bibliography

Abelard, Peter. *Historia calamitatum.* Edited by Alexander Andrée. Toronto: Pontifical Institute of Mediaeval Studies, 2015.

Abelard, Peter. *Operum Pars Prima.—Epistole.* In *Patrologiae Cursus Completus.* Series Latina, vol. 178. Edited by J. P. Migne. Paris: Garnier, 1885.

Abelard, Peter. *The Story of Abelard's Adversities.* Translated by J. T. Muckle. Toronto: Pontifical Institute of Mediaeval Studies, 1954.

Adams, Susan. "Meet the English Professor Creating the Billion-Dollar College of the Future." *Forbes,* March 28, 2019. https://www.forbes.com/sites/susanadams/2019/03/28/meet-the-english-professor-creating-the-billion-dollar-college-of-the-future/#29b8c12f426b.

Aesop. *Aesop's Fables.* Translated by Laura Gibbs. Oxford: Oxford University Press, 2008.

Agamben, Giorgio. *The Coming Community.* Translated by Michael Hardt. Minneapolis: University of Minnesota Press, 1993.

Agamben, Giorgio. "Difference and Repetition: On Guy DeBord's Films." In *Art and the Moving Image: A Critical Reader,* edited by Tanya Leighton, 328–33. London: Tate, 2008.

Agamben, Giorgio. *The Highest Poverty: Monastic Rules and Form-of-Life.* Stanford, CA: Stanford University Press, 2013.

Agamben, Giorgio. *State of Exception*. Translated by Kevin Attell. Chicago: University of Chicago Press, 2005.

Anderson, Benedict. *Imagined Communities: Reflection on the Origin and Spread of Nationalism*. London: Verso, 1991.

Anderson, Daniel, and Jentery Sayers. "The Metaphor and Materiality of Layers." In Ridolfo and Hart-Davidson, *Rhetoric and the Digital Humanities*, 80–95.

Andrejevic, Mark. *Infoglut: How Too Much Information Is Changing the Way We Think and Know*. New York: Routledge, 2013.

Anonymous of Bologna. *The Principles of Letter-Writing*. In *Three Medieval Rhetorical Arts*, edited by James J. Murphy, 1–25. Berkeley: University of California Press, 1971.

Aquinas, Thomas. *Sancti Thomae Aquinatis Opera omnia: iussu impensaque, Leonis XIII. P.M. edita*. Rome: Typographia Polyglotta, 1882.

Aristotle. *Nicomachean Ethics*. Edited and translated by H. Rackham. Cambridge, MA: Harvard University Press, 1934.

Asad, Talal. *Genealogies of Religion: Discipline and Reasons of Power in Christianity and Islam*. Baltimore, MD: Johns Hopkins University Press, 1993.

Ascher, Diana. "The New Yellow Journalism." PhD diss., University of California, Los Angeles, 2017.

Ashley, Kathleen M., and Véronique Plesch. "The Cultural Processes of 'Appropriation.'" *Journal of Medieval and Early Modern Studies* 32, no. 1 (2002): 1–15.

Bacon-Smith, Camille. *Enterprising Women: Television Fandom and the Creation of Popular Myth*. Philadelphia: University of Pennsylvania Press, 1992.

Bady, Aaron. "The MOOC Moment and the End of Reform." *The New Inquiry*, May 15, 2013. https://thenewinquiry.com/blog/the-mooc-moment-and-the-end-of-reform/.

Bahr, Arthur. *Fragments and Assemblages: Forming Compilations of Medieval London*. Chicago: University of Chicago Press, 2013.

Bakhtin, Mikhail. *Rabelais and His World*. Translated by Helene Iswolsky. Cambridge, MA: MIT Press, 1968.

Baldwin, James. *Collected Essays*. New York: Library of America, 1998.

Banker, James R. "The *Ars dictaminis* and Rhetorical Textbooks at the Bolognese University in the Fourteenth Century." *Medievalia et Humanistica*, no. 5 (1974): 153–68.

Banker, James R. "Giovanni di Bonandrea and Civic Values in the Context of the Italian Rhetorical Tradition." *Manuscripta*, no. 18 (1974): 3–20.

Banks, Adam J. *Digital Griots: African American Rhetoric in a Multimedia Age.* Carbondale: Southern Illinois University Press, 2011.

Barker, Juliet. *1381: The Year of the Peasants' Revolt.* Cambridge, MA: Harvard University Press, 2014.

Baron, Dennis E. *A Better Pencil: Readers, Writers, and the Digital Revolution.* Oxford: Oxford University Press, 2009.

Baron, Naomi S. *Words Onscreen: The Fate of Reading in a Digital World.* Oxford: Oxford University Press, 2015.

Barrington, Candace, Brantley L. Bryant, Richard H. Godden, Daniel T. Kline, and Myra Seaman, eds. *The Open Access Companion to the Canterbury Tales* (2015–17). https://opencanterburytales.dsl.lsu.edu.

Barthes, Roland. *S/Z.* Translated by Richard Miller. New York: Hill and Wang, 1974.

Baswell, Christopher. *Virgil in Medieval England: Figuring the Aeneid from the Twelfth Century to Chaucer.* Cambridge: Cambridge University Press, 1995.

Bazerman, Charles, Joseph Little, Lisa Bethel, Teri Chavkin, Danielle Fouquette, and Janet Garufis. *Reference Guide to Writing across the Curriculum.* West Lafayette, IN: Parlor Press, 2005.

Bazerman, Charles, and David R. Russell. "Writing across the Curriculum as a Challenge to Rhetoric and Composition." In *Landmark Essays on Writing across the Curriculum*, edited by Charles Bazerman and David R. Russell, xi–xvi. Davis, CA: Hermagoras Press, 1994.

Beardsley, Theodore S., Jr. *Hispano-Classical Translations Printed between 1482 and 1699.* Pittsburgh, PA: Duquesne University Press, 1970.

Beeson, C.H. *Isidor-Studien.* Munich: C. H. Beck, 1913.

Benjamin, Ruha. *Race after Technology.* Cambridge: Polity, 2019.

Benjamin, Walter. "The Work of Art in the Age of Mechanical Reproduction." In *Illuminations*, translated by Harry Zohn and edited by Hannah Arendt, 217–51. New York: Schocken, 1968.

Bennett, Michael. "The Court of Richard II and the Promotion of Literature." In *Chaucer's England: Literature in Historical Context*, edited by Barbara Hanawalt, 3–20. Minneapolis: University of Minnesota Press, 1992.

Berlin, James A. *Rhetoric and Reality, Writing Instruction in American Colleges, 1900–1985.* Carbondale: Southern Illinois University Press, 1987.

Bianco, Jamie "Skye." "This Digital Humanities Which Is Not One." In Gold, *Debates in the Digital Humanities*, 96–112.

Bischoff, Bernard. "Die europäische Verbreitung der Werke Isidors von Sevilla."

In *Mittelalterliche Studien: Ausgewählte Aufsätze zur Schriftkunde und Literaturgeschichte*, 1:171–94. Stuttgart: Hiersemann, 1966.

Black, Rebecca W. *Adolescents and Online Fan Fiction*. New York: Peter Lang, 2008.

Black, Rebecca W. "Online Fan Fiction, Global Identities, and Imagination." *Research in the Teaching of English* 43, no. 4 (2009): 397–425.

Blair, Ann. *Too Much to Know: Managing Scholarly Information before the Modern Age*. New Haven, CT: Yale University Press, 2010.

Blake, Liza, and Kathryn Vomero Santos, eds. *Arthur Golding's "A Moral Fabletalk" and Other Renaissance Fable Translations*. Cambridge: Modern Humanities Research Association, 2017.

Blau, Sheridan. *The Literature Workshop: Teaching Texts and Their Readers*. Portsmouth, NH: Heinemann, 2003.

Boggess, W. "Hermannus Alemannus' Rhetorical Translations." *Viator*, no. 2 (1971): 227–50.

Bogost, Ian. *Persuasive Games: The Expressive Power of Videogames*. Cambridge, MA: MIT Press, 2007.

Bogost, Ian. "The Turtlenecked Hairshirt." In Gold, *Debates in the Digital Humanities*, 241–42.

Bogost, Ian, and Elizabeth Losh. "Rhetoric and Digital Media." In *The Oxford Handbook of Rhetorical Studies*, edited by Michael J. MacDonald, 759–71. Oxford: Oxford University Press, 2017.

Bolens, Guillemette. "Beowulf et les anneaux du squelette." In *La Logique du Corps Articulaire: Les articulations du corps humain dans la littérature occidentale*, 145–81. Rennes: Presses Universitaires de Rennes, 2000.

Bolter, Jay David. *Digital Plenitude: The Decline of Elite Culture and the Rise of Digital Media*. Cambridge, MA: MIT Press, 2019.

Bolter, Jay David. *Writing Space: Computers, Hypertext, and the Remediation of Print*. 2nd ed. New York: Routledge, 2001.

Bolter, Jay David, and Richard Grusin. *Remediation: Understanding New Media*. Cambridge, MA: MIT Press, 2000.

Bourdieu, Pierre. *Distinction: A Social Critique of the Judgement of Taste*. Translated by Richard Nice. Cambridge, MA: Harvard University Press, 1984.

Bourdieu, Pierre. *In Other Words: Essays towards a Reflexive Sociology*. Translated by M. Adamson. Cambridge: Polity, 1994. Originally published as *Choses dites* (Paris: Les Éditions de Minuit, 1987).

Bourdieu, Pierre. *Outline of a Theory of Practice*. Translated by Richard Nice. Cambridge: Cambridge University Press, 1977. Originally published as *Es-

quisse d'une théorie de la pratique: Précédé de trois études d'ethnologie kabyle (Geneva: Droz, 1972).

Bourdieu, Pierre. "Postface to Erwin Panofsky, *Gothic Architecture and Scholasticism.*" Translated by Laurence Petit. In Bruce Holsinger, *The Premodern Condition: Medievalism and the Making of Theory*, 221–42. Chicago: University of Chicago Press, 2005.

Bourdieu, Pierre. *Practical Reason: On the Theory of Action*. Cambridge: Polity, 1998.

Bourdieu, Pierre, and Löic J. D. Wacquant. *An Invitation to Reflexive Sociology*. Chicago: University of Chicago Press, 1992.

boyd, danah. *It's Complicated: The Social Lives of Networked Teens*. New Haven, CT: Yale University Press, 2014.

Boyle, Casey. *Rhetoric as a Posthuman Practice*. Columbus: Ohio State University Press, 2018.

Boyle, Jen, and Martin Foys. "Becoming Media." *Postmedieval: A Journal of Medieval Cultural Studies*, no. 3 (2012): 1–6.

Boyle, Jen, and Martin Foys. "Editor's Vision Statement." *Postmedieval—Crowd Review*. http://postmedievalcrowdreview.wordpress.com/editors-vision-statement/.

Brantley, Jessica. "Medieval Remediations." In *Comparative Textual Media: Transforming the Humanities in the Postprint Era*, edited by N. Katherine Hayles and Jessica Pressman, 201–20. Minneapolis: University of Minnesota Press, 2013.

Breen, Katharine. *Imagining an English Reading Public, 1150–1400*. Cambridge: Cambridge University Press, 2010.

Brehaut, Ernest. *An Encyclopedist of the Dark Ages: Isidore of Seville*. New York: Burt Franklin, 1912.

Brereton, John, ed. *The Origins of Composition Studies in the American College, 1875–1925: A Documentary History*. Pittsburgh, PA: University of Pittsburgh Press, 1995.

Bright, Philippa M. "Henryson's Figurative Technique in *The Cock and the Jasp.*" In *Words and Wordsmiths. A Volume for H.L. Rogers*, edited by Geraldine Barnes, John Gunn, Sonya Jensen, and Lee Jobling, 13–21. Sydney: University of Sydney Press, 1989.

Brock, Kevin. *Rhetorical Code Studies: Discovering Arguments in and around Code*. Ann Arbor: University of Michigan Press, 2019.

Brooke, Collin. *Lingua Fracta: Towards a Rhetoric of New Media*. Cresskill, NJ: Hampton Press, 2009.

Brooks, Frederick P., Jr. *The Design of Design: Essays from a Computer Scientist*. Boston: Pearson, 2010.

Browne, G. H. "Successful Combination against the Inert." *Leaflet*, no. 3 (1901): 1–4.

Bruns, Cristina Vischer. *Why Literature? The Value of Literary Reading and What It Means for Teaching*. New York: Continuum, 2011.

Bruns, Gerald. *Inventions: Writing, Textuality, and Understanding in Literary History*. New Haven, CT: Yale University Press, 1982.

Brylowe, Thora, and Stephen Yeager, eds. *Old Media and the Medieval Concept: Media Ecologies before Early Modernity*. Montreal: Concordia University Press, 2021.

Burrow, J. A. "Henryson: *The Preaching of the Swallow*." *Essays in Criticism*, no. 25 (1975): 25–37.

Burrows, Cedric D. *Rhetorical Crossover: The Black Presence in White Culture*. Pittsburgh, PA: University of Pittsburgh Press, 2020.

Busdraghi, Paola, ed. *L'Esopus attribuito a Gualtero Anglico*. Favolisti Latini Medievali 10. Genova: Università di Genova, 2005.

Bush, Vannevar. "As We May Think." *Atlantic Monthly*, July 1945. https://www.theatlantic.com/magazine/archive/1945/07/as-we-may-think/303881/.

Camargo, Martin. "Between Grammar and Rhetoric: Composition Teaching at Oxford and Bologna in the Late Middle Ages." In *Rhetoric and Pedagogy: Its History, Philosophy, and Practice: Essays in Honor of James J. Murphy*, edited by W. B. Horner and M. Leff, 83–94. Mahwah, NJ: Erlbaum, 1995.

Camargo, Martin. "Special Delivery: Were Medieval Letter Writers Trained in Performance?" In *Rhetoric beyond Words: Delight and Persuasion in the Arts of the Middle Ages*, edited by Mary Carruthers, 173–89. Cambridge: Cambridge University Press, 2010.

Camargo, Martin, ed. *Medieval Rhetorics of Prose Composition: Five English Artes Dictandi and Their Tradition*. Medieval and Renaissance Texts and Studies 115. Binghamton, NY: Center for Medieval and Early Renaissance Studies, 1995.

Camargo, Martin, ed. and trans. *Tria sunt: An Art of Poetry and Prose*. Cambridge, MA: Harvard University Press, 2019.

Camargo, Martin, and Marjorie Curry Woods. "Writing Instruction in Late Medieval Europe." In *A Short History of Writing Instruction: From Ancient Greece to the Modern United States*, 4th ed., edited by James J. Murphy and Christopher Thaiss, 129–64. New York: Routledge, 2020.

Camille, Michael. "The Book as Flesh and Fetish in Richard de Bury's *Philo-

biblon." In *The Book and the Body*, edited by Dolores Warwick Frese and Katherine O'Brien O'Keeffe, 34–77. Notre Dame, IN: University of Notre Dame Press, 1997.

Camille, Michael. "Sensations of the Page: Imaging Technologies and Medieval Illuminated Manuscripts." In *The Iconic Page in Manuscript, Print, and Digital Culture*, edited by George Bornstein and Theresa Tinkle, 33–53. Ann Arbor: University of Michigan Press, 1998.

Campbell, Oscar James. "The Failure of Freshman English." *English Journal*, coll. ed. 28 (1939): 177–85.

Canagarajah, A. Suresh. "A Rhetoric of Shuttling between Languages." In *Cross-Language Relations in Composition*, edited by Bruce Horner, Min-Zhan Lu, and Paul Kei Matsuda, 158–79. Carbondale: Southern Illinois University Press, 2010.

Cannon, Christopher. "From Literacy to Literature: Elementary Learning and the Middle English Poet." *PMLA* 129, no. 3 (2014): 349–64.

Carnes, Pack. "Heinrich Steinhöwel and the Sixteenth-Century Fable Tradition." *Humanistica Lovaniensia: A Journal of Neo-Latin Studies*, no. 35 (1986): 1–29.

Carpenter, George R. "English Composition in Colleges." *Educational Review*, no. 4 (1892): 338–46.

Carruthers, Mary. *The Book of Memory: A Study of Memory in Medieval Culture.* 2nd ed. Cambridge: Cambridge University Press, 2008.

Cayley, John. "The Code Is Not the Text (Unless It Is the Text)." *Electronic Book Review*. Last modified September 10, 2002. http://electronicbookreview.com/essay/the-code-is-not-the-text-unless-it-is-the-text/.

Caxton, William. *Caxton's Aesop.* Edited by R. T. Lenaghan. Cambridge, MA: Harvard University Press, 1967.

Caxton, William. *Caxton's Mirrour of the World.* Edited by Oliver H. Prior. Early English Text Society, Extra Series, 110. 1913. Reprint, London: Oxford University Press, 1966.

Cerquiglini, Bernard. *Eloge de la variante: Histoire critique de la philologie.* Paris: Éditions du Seuil, 1989.

Châtillon, J. "Le *Didascalicon* de Hughues de Saint-Victor." *Journal of World History*, no. 9 (1966): 539–52.

Chaucer, Geoffrey. *The Riverside Chaucer.* Edited by Larry Benson. Boston: Houghton Mifflin, 1987.

Chrétien de Troyes. *Arthurian Romances.* Translated by William W. Kibler. London: Penguin, 1991.

Chrétien de Troyes. *Les Romans de Chrétien de Troyes: Cligés*, vol. 2. Edited by Alexandre Micha.

The Chronicle of Walter of Guisborough. Edited by H. Rothwell. 3rd series, 89. London: Camden Society, 1957.

Chuh, Kandice. *The Difference Aesthetics Makes: On the Humanities "After Man."* Durham, NC: Duke University Press, 2019.

Chun, Wendy Hui Kyong. *Control and Freedom: Power and Paranoia in the Age of Fiber Optics*. Cambridge, MA: MIT Press, 2006.

Chun, Wendy Hui Kyong. *Discriminating Data: Correlation, Neighborhoods, and the New Politics of Recognition*. Cambridge, MA: MIT Press, 2021.

Chun, Wendy Hui Kyong. *Updating to Remain the Same: Habitual New Media*. Cambridge, MA: MIT Press, 2016.

Cicero, Marcus Tullius. *De Officiis*. Translated by Walter Miller. London: W. Heinemann, 1947.

Cicero, Marcus Tullius. *De Senectute, De Amicitia, De Divinatione*. Translated by William Armistead Falconer. London: W. Heinemann, 1923.

Cicero, Marcus Tullius. *On Invention. The Best Kind of Orator. Topics*. Translated by H. M. Hubbell. Loeb Classical Library 386. Cambridge, MA: Harvard University Press, 1949.

Clanchy, M. T. *From Memory to Written Record: England 1066–1307*. 2nd ed. Oxford: Blackwell, 1993.

Clark, Willene B. *A Medieval Book of Beasts: The Second-Family Bestiary: Commentary, Art, Text, and Translation*. Woodbridge: Boydell, 2006.

Cohen, Jeffrey Jerome. *Medieval Identity Machines*. Minneapolis: University of Minnesota Press, 2003.

Cohen, Noam. "Don't Like Palin's Wikipedia Story? Change It." *New York Times*, August 31, 2008. http://www.nytimes.com/2008/09/01/technology/01link.html.

Colish, Marcia L. "'Habitus' Revisited: A Reply to Cary Nederman." *Traditio*, no. 48 (1993): 77–92.

Collette, Carolyn P. *Rethinking Chaucer's Legend of Good Women*. Woodbridge: York Medieval Press, 2014.

Collison, Robert. *Encyclopaedias: Their History throughout the Ages*. 2nd ed. New York: Hafner, 1966.

Connors, Robert J. "The Abolition Debate in Composition: A Short History." In *Composition in the Twenty-First Century: Crisis and Change*, edited by Lynn Z. Bloom, Donald A. Daiker, and Ed M. White, 47–63. Carbondale: Southern Illinois University Press, 1996.

Connors, Robert J. "Mechanical Correctness as a Focus in Composition Instruction." *College Composition and Communication* 36, no. 1 (1985): 61–72.

Connors, Robert J. "Rhetoric in the Modern University: The Creation of an Underclass." In *The Politics of Writing Instruction: Postsecondary*, edited by R. Bullock and J. Trimbur, 55–84. Portsmouth, NH: Boynton/Cook, 1991.

Connors, Robert J. "The Rise and Fall of the Modes of Discourse." *College Composition and Communication*, no. 32 (1981): 444–55.

Constable, Giles. *Letters and Letter-Collections*. Turnout: Brepols, 1976.

Copeland, Rita. *Emotion and the History of Rhetoric in the Middle Ages*. Oxford: Oxford University Press, 2021.

Copeland, Rita. *Rhetoric, Hermeneutics, and Translation in the Middle Ages: Academic Traditions and Vernacular Texts*. Cambridge: Cambridge University Press, 1995.

Copeland, Rita, and Ineke Sluiter, eds. *Medieval Grammar and Rhetoric*. Oxford: Oxford University Press, 2009.

Corbett, Edward P. J. *Classical Rhetoric for the Modern Student*. 2nd ed. New York: Oxford University Press, 1971.

Corbett, Edward P. J. "John Locke's Contributions to Rhetoric." In *The Rhetorical Tradition and Modern Writing*, edited by James J. Murphy, 73–84. New York: Modern Language Association, 1982.

Cornelius, Ian. "The Rhetoric of Advancement: *Ars Dictaminis, Cursus*, and Clerical Careerism in Late Medieval England." *New Medieval Literatures*, no. 12 (2010): 287–328.

Courtenay, William J. *Schools and Scholars in Fourteenth-Century England*. Princeton, NJ: Princeton University Press, 1987.

Covino, William A. *The Art of Wondering: A Revisionist Return to the History of Rhetoric*. Portsmouth, NH: Boynton/Cook, 1988.

Cramer, Thomas. "Æsopi wolff." In *Festschrift Walter Haug und Burghart Wachinger*, edited by Johannes Janota, Paul Sappler, Frieder Schanze, Benedikt K. Vollmann, Gisela Vollmann-Profe, and Hans-Joachim Ziegeler, 955–66. Tübingen: Niemeyer, 1995.

Cremin, Lawrence A. *The Transformation of the School: Progressivism in American Education*. New York: Vantage, 1961.

Critical Art Ensemble. *Electronic Civil Disobedience and Other Unpopular Ideas*. Brooklyn: Autonomedia, 1996.

Crowley, Sharon. *Composition in the University: Historical and Polemical Essays*. Pittsburgh, PA: University of Pittsburgh Press, 1998.

Curtin, Rebecca Schoff. "Hackers and Humanists: Transactions and the Evolution of Copyright." *Legal Studies Research Paper Series* 54, no. 1 (2014): 105–57.

Dagenais, John. *The Ethics of Reading in Manuscript Culture: Glossing the "Libro de Buen Amor."* Princeton, NJ: Princeton University Press, 1994.

Daileader, Celia R. *Eroticism on the Renaissance Stage: Transcendence, Desire, and the Limits of the Visible.* Cambridge: Cambridge University Press, 1998.

Daniels, Harvey. *Famous Last Words: The American Language Crisis Reconsidered.* Carbondale: Southern Illinois University Press, 1983.

Darnton, Robert. *The Business of Enlightenment: A Publishing History of the Encyclopédie, 1775–1800.* Cambridge, MA: Harvard University Press, 1987.

Davis, Matthew, and Alex Mueller. "The Places of Writing on the Multimodal Page." In *Writing Changes: Alphabetic Text and Multimodal Composition*, edited by Pegeen Reichert Powell, 103–22. New York: Modern Language Association of America, 2020.

Davis, Matthew Evan, Tamsyn Mahoney-Steel, and Ece Turnator, eds. *Meeting the Medieval in the Digital World.* Amsterdam: Amsterdam University Press, 2018.

Daly, Lloyd W., trans. and ed. *Aesop without Morals: The Famous Fables, and a Life of Aesop.* New York: A.S. Barnes, 1961.

DeLuca, Kevin Michael, and Joe Wilferth. "Foreword." *Enculturation: A Journal of Rhetoric, Writing, and Culture* 6, no. 2 (2009). http://enculturation.net/6.2/foreword.

Derrida, Jacques. *The Post Card: From Socrates to Freud and Beyond.* Translated by Alan Bass. Chicago: University of Chicago Press, 1987.

Desmond, Marilynn R. *Reading Dido: Gender, Textuality, and the Medieval Aeneid.* Minneapolis: University of Minnesota Press, 1994.

Desmond, Marilynn R. "The *Translatio* of Memory and Desire in *The Legend of Good Women*: Chaucer and the Vernacular *Heroides.*" *Studies in the Age of Chaucer*, no. 35 (2013): 179–207.

Dicke, Gerd, and Klaus Grubmüller. *Die Fabeln des Mittelalters und der Frühen Neuzeit: Ein Katalog der deutschen Versionen und ihrer lateinischen Entsprechungen.* Munich: Wilhelm Fink, 1987.

Dimock, Wai Chee. "Historicism, Presentism, Futurism." *PMLA* 133, no. 2 (2018): 257–63.

Dinshaw, Carolyn. *Chaucer's Sexual Politics.* Madison: University of Wisconsin Press, 1989.

Dinshaw, Carolyn. *How Soon is Now?: Medieval Texts, Amateur Readers, and the Queerness of Time.* Durham, NC: Duke University Press, 2012.

dj readies [Craig J. Saper]. *Bureaucratic Intimacies: A Manifesto*. Brooklyn: punctum books, 2012.

Donaldson, Talbot. *Speaking of Chaucer*. Durham, NC: Labyrinth Press, 1983.

Douglas, Gavin. *The Palyce of Honour*. Edited by David J. Parkinson. 2nd ed. TEAMS Middle English Texts Series. Kalamazoo, MI: Medieval Institute Publications, 2018.

Douglas, Gavin. *Virgil's Aeneid Translated into Scottish Verse by Gavin Douglas*. Edited by David F.C. Coldwell. 4 vols. Edinburgh: Scottish Text Society, 1957–64.

Drucker, Johanna. *Graphesis: Visual Forms of Knowledge Production*. Cambridge, MA: Harvard University Press, 2014.

Drucker, Johanna. "Performative Materiality and Theoretical Approaches to Interface." *Digital Humanities Quarterly* 7, no. 1 (2013). http://www.digitalhumanities.org/dhq/vol/7/1/000143/000143.html.

Drucker, Johanna. "Reading Interface." *PMLA* 128, no. 1 (2013): 213–20.

Dunbar, William. *The Poems of William Dunbar*. Edited by Priscilla Bawcutt. 2 vols. Glasgow: Association for Scottish Literary Studies, 1998.

Dunger, Hermann. *Die Sage vom troyanischen Kriege in den Bearbeitungen des Mittelalters und ihre antiken Quellen*. Leipzig: F.C.W. Vogel, 1869.

Durkan, John, and Anthony Ross. *Early Scottish Libraries*. Glasgow: J.S. Burns, 1961.

Eden, Kathy. *The Renaissance Rediscovery of Intimacy*. Chicago: University of Chicago Press, 2012.

Eve, Martin Paul. *Open Access and the Humanities: Context, Controversies, and the Future*. Cambridge: Cambridge University Press, 2014.

Eisenstein, Elizabeth L. *The Printing Press as an Agent of Change: Communications and Cultural Transformations in Early Modern Europe*. 2 vols. Cambridge: Cambridge University Press, 1979.

Elbow, Peter. *Oppositions in Chaucer*. Middletown, CT: Wesleyan University Press, 1975.

Elbow, Peter. "Vernacular Englishes in the Writing Classroom: Probing the Culture of Literacy." In *ALT DIS: Alternative Discourses and the Academy*, edited by Christopher Schroeder, Patricia Bizzell, and Helen Fox, 126–38. Portsmouth, NH: Heinemann, 2002.

Elbow, Peter. *Writing without Teachers*. 2nd ed. New York: Oxford University Press, 1998.

Emden, A. B. *A Biographical Register of the University of Oxford to A.D. 1500*. 3 vols. Oxford: Oxford University Press, 1957–59.

Enders, Jody. *The Medieval Theater of Cruelty: Rhetoric, Memory, Violence.* Ithaca, NY: Cornell University Press, 1999.

Enders, Jody. "Memory and the Psychology of the Interior Monologue in Chrétien's *Cliges.*" *Rhetorica*, no. 10 (1992): 5–23.

Enders, Jody. "Music, Delivery, and the Rhetoric of Memory in Guillaume de Machaut's *Remède de Fortune.*" *PMLA* 107, no. 3 (1992): 450–64.

Enders, Jody. *Rhetoric and the Origins of Medieval Drama.* Ithaca, NY: Cornell University Press, 1992.

Enders, Jody. "The Theater of Scholastic Erudition." *Comparative Drama* 27, no. 3 (1993): 341–63.

Endres, Josef. *Honorius Augustodunensis: Beitrag zur Geschichte des geistigen Lebens im 12. Jahrhundert.* Munich: Jos. Koesel, 1906.

Erasmus, Desiderius. *De Conscribendis Epistolis.* In *Opera Omnia: Desiderii Erasmi Roterodami*, edited by Jean-Claude Margolin, series 1, vol. 2, 85–580. Amsterdam: North-Holland, 1971.

Erasmus, Desiderius. "On the Writing of Letters / *De conscribendis epistolis.*" In *Collected Works of Erasmus*, edited by J. K. Sowards, translated by Charles Fantazzi, 25–26. Toronto: University of Toronto Press, 1985.

Esposito, Roberto. *Communitas: The Origin and Destiny of Community.* Translated by Timothy Campbell. Stanford, CA: Stanford University Press, 2010.

Eyman, Douglas. *Digital Rhetoric: Theory, Method, Practice.* Ann Arbor: University of Michigan Press, 2015.

Eyman, Douglas, and Cheryl Ball. "Digital Humanities Scholarship and Electronic Publication." In Ridolfo and Hart-Davidson, *Rhetoric and the Digital Humanities*, 65–79.

Ezzaher, Lachen Elyazghi, trans. *Three Arabic Treatises on Aristotle's Rhetoric: The Commentaries of al-Fārābī, Avicenna, and Averroes.* Carbondale: Southern Illinois University Press, 2015.

Felski, Rita. "Suspicious Minds." *Poetics Today* 32, no. 2 (2011): 215–34.

Felski, Rita. *Uses of Literature.* Hoboken, NJ: Wiley, 2009.

Fisher, Matthew. *Scribal Authorship and the Writing of History in Medieval England.* Columbus: Ohio State University Press, 2012.

Fitzpatrick, Kathleen. *Planned Obsolescence: Publishing, Technology, and the Future of the Academy.* New York: New York University Press, 2009.

Fitzpatrick, Kathleen, and Avi Santo. "Open Review: A Study of Contexts and Practices." *Andrew K. Mellon Foundation*, December 2012. https://mellon.org/media/filer_public/20/ff/20ff03e0-17b0-465b-ae82-1ed7c8cef362/mediacommons-open-review-white-paper-final.pdf.

Fletcher, J. B., and G. R. Carpenter. *Introduction to Theme-Writing*. Boston: Allyn & Bacon, 1897.

Folena, Daniela Goldin. "Pluristilismo del *Familiarum rerum liber.*" In *Motivi e forme della "Familiari" di Francesco Petrarcha*, edited by Claudia Berra, 261–90. Milan: Cisalpino, 2003.

Foucault, Michel. "What Is an Author?" In *Aesthetics, Method, and Epistemology*, translated by Robert Hurley et al. and edited by James D. Faubion, 205–22. New York: New Press, 1998.

Fowler, David C. "John Trevisa and the English Bible." *Modern Philology*, no. 58 (1950): 81–98.

Fowler, David C. *The Life and Times of John Trevisa, Medieval Scholar*. Seattle: University of Washington Press, 1995.

Foys, Martin. *Virtually Anglo-Saxon: Old Media, New Media, and Early Medieval Studies in the Late Age of Print*. Gainesville: University Press of Florida, 2007.

Fradenburg, L. O. Aranye. *Staying Alive: A Survival Manual for the Liberal Arts*. Brooklyn, NY: punctum books, 2013.

Frehner, Carmen. *Email-SMS-MMS: The Linguistic Creativity of Asynchronous Discourse in the New Media Age*. Bern: Peter Lang, 2008.

Freire, Paulo. *Pedagogy of the Oppressed: 30th Anniversary Edition*. Translated by Myra Bergman Ramos. New York: Continuum, 2000.

Fulwiler, Toby, and Art Young. "Afterword: The Enemies of Writing across the Curriculum." In *Programs that Work: Models and Methods for Writing across the Curriculum*, edited by Toby Fulwiler and Art Young, 287–94. Portsmouth, NH: Boynton/Cook, 1990.

Gage, John T. "Vestiges of Letter Writing in Composition Textbooks, 1850–1914." In *Letter-Writing Manuals and Instruction from Antiquity to the Present: Historical and Bibliographic Studies*, edited by Carol Poster and Linda C. Mitchell, 200–229. Columbia: University of South Carolina Press, 2007.

Galbraith, V. H. "John Seward and His Circle." *Medieval and Renaissance Studies*, no. 1 (1941–43): 85–104.

Gallagher, John R. *Update Culture and the Afterlife of Digital Writing*. Logan: Utah State University Press, 2020.

Gallagher, John R., and Steve Holmes. "Empty Templates: The Ethical Habits of Empty State Pages." *Technical Communication Quarterly* 28, no. 3 (2019): 271–83.

Geary, Patrick J. *Furta Sacra: Thefts of Relics in the Central Middle Ages*. Princeton, NJ: Princeton University Press, 1990.

Gee, James Paul. *Situated Language and Learning: A Critique of Traditional Schooling.* New York: Routledge, 2004.

Geoffrey of Vinsauf. *Documentum de modo et arte dictandi et versificandi.* In *Les arts poétiques du XIIe et du XIIIe siècle: Recherches et documents sur la technique littéraire du moyen âge,* edited by Edmond Faral, 265–320. Paris: Champion, 1962.

Geoffrey of Vinsauf. *Poetria nova.* In *Les arts poétiques du XIIe et du XIIIe siècle: Recherches et documents sur la technique littéraire du moyen âge,* edited by Edmond Faral, 194–262. Paris: Champion, 1962.

Geoffrey of Vinsauf. *Poetria nova.* Translated by Margaret F. Nims. Revised ed. Toronto: Pontifical Institute of Mediaeval Studies, 2010.

Gilyard, Keith, and Adam J. Banks. *On African-American Rhetoric.* New York: Routledge, 2018.

Ginder, Scott A., Janice E. Kelly-Reid, and Farrah B. Mann. "Graduation Rates for Selected Cohorts, 2009–14." US Department of Education, December 2018. https://nces.ed.gov/pubs2018/2018151.pdf.

Glenn, Cheryl. *The Harbrace Guide to Writing.* Boston: Wadsworth Cengage Learning, 2009.

Glenn, Cheryl. *Rhetoric Retold: Regendering the Tradition from Antiquity through the Renaissance.* Carbondale: Southern Illinois University Press, 1997.

Glott, R., R. Ghosh, and P. Schmidt. "Wikipedia Survey." Technical report. UNU-MERIT, Maastricht, Netherlands, 2010. https://www.merit.unu.edu/wp-content/uploads/2019/03/Wikipedia_Overview_15March2010-FINAL.pdf.

Gold, Matthew K., ed. *Debates in the Digital Humanities.* Minneapolis: University of Minnesota Press, 2012.

Gold, Matthew K., and Lauren F. Klein, eds. *Debates in the Digital Humanities 2016.* Minneapolis: University of Minnesota Press, 2016.

Goldstein, Dana. "The Schoolmaster." *Atlantic,* October 2012. http://www.theatlantic.com/magazine/archive/2012/10/the-schoolmaster/309091/.

Gonzales, Laura. *Sites of Translation: What Multilinguals Can Teach Us about Digital Writing and Rhetoric.* Ann Arbor: University of Michigan Press, 2018.

Gray, Douglas. *Robert Henryson.* Leiden: Brill, 1979.

Gray, Rosie. "Trump Defends White-Nationalist Protesters: 'Some Very Fine People on Both Sides.'" *Atlantic,* August 15, 2017. https://www.theatlantic.com/politics/archive/2017/08/trump-defends-white-nationalist-protesters-some-very-fine-people-on-both-sides/537012/.

Greenblatt, Stephen. *The Swerve: How the World Became Modern.* New York: W.W. Norton, 2011.

Gries, Laurie. *Still Life with Rhetoric: A New Materialist Approach for Visual Rhetorics.* Logan: Utah State University Press, 2015.

Griffiths, Devin. "The Comparative Method and the History of the Modern Humanities." *History of Humanities* 2, no. 2 (2017): 473–505.

Grosz, Elizabeth. "Habit Today: Ravaisson, Bergson, and Deleuze and Us." *Body & Society* 19, nos. 2/3 (2013): 217–39.

Gruwell, Leigh. "Wikipedia's Politics of Exclusion: Gender, Epistemology, and Feminist Rhetorical (In)action." *Computers and Composition,* no. 37 (2015): 117–31.

Guertin, Carolyn. *Digital Prohibition: Piracy and Authorship in New Media Art.* London: Continuum, 2012.

Haas, Angela M. "Wampum as Hypertext: An American Indian Intellectual Tradition of Multimedia Theory and Practice." *Studies in American Indian Literatures* 19, no. 4 (2007): 77–100.

Halloran, S. Michael. "From Rhetoric to Composition: The Teaching of Writing in America to 1900." In *A Short History of Writing Instruction: From Ancient Greece to Twentieth-Century America,* edited by James Murphy, 151–82. Davis, CA: Hermagoras Press, 1990.

Hanna, Ralph. "Sir Thomas Berkeley and His Patronage." *Speculum* 64, no. 4 (1989): 878–916.

Harrington, Susanmarie, Mark D. Shermis, and Angela L. Rollins. "The Influence of Word Processing on English Placement Test Results." *Computers and Composition,* no. 17 (2000): 197–210.

Haswell, Richard H. "Error and Change in College Student Writing." *Written Communication* 5, no. 4 (1988): 479–99.

Hathaway, Neil. "Compilatio: From Plagiarizing to Compiling." *Viator,* no. 20 (1989): 19–44.

Hawhee, Debra. *Rhetoric in Tooth and Claw: Animals, Language, Sensation.* Chicago: University of Chicago Press, 2017.

Hawhee, Debra, and Christa J. Olson. "Pan-Historiography: The Challenges of Writing History across Time and Space." In *Theorizing Histories of Rhetoric,* edited by Michelle Ballif, 90–105. Carbondale: Southern Illinois University Press, 2013.

Hayles, N. Katherine. *How We Think: Digital Media and Contemporary Technogenesis.* Chicago: University of Chicago Press, 2012.

Hayles, N. Katherine, and Jessica Pressman. "Introduction: Making, Critique:

A Media Framework." In *Comparative Textual Media: Transforming the Humanities in the Postprint Era*, edited by N. Katherine Hayles and Jessica Pressman, vii–xxxiii. Minneapolis: University of Minnesota Press, 2013.

Head, Alison J., and Michael B. Eisenberg. "How Today's College Students Use *Wikipedia* for Course-Related Research." *First Monday* 15, no. 3 (2010). https://journals.uic.edu/ojs/index.php/fm/article/view/2830/2476.

Henderson, Arnold Clayton. "Having Fun with the Moralities: Henryson's *Fables* and Late-Medieval Fable Innovation." *Studies in Scottish Literature*, no. 32 (2001): 67–87.

Henderson, Judith Rice. "Humanism and the Humanities: Erasmus's *Opus de Conscribendis Epistolis* in Sixteenth-Century Schools." In *Letter-Writing Manuals and Instruction from Antiquity to the Present*, edited by Carol Poster and Linda C. Mitchell, 141–77. Columbia: University of South Carolina Press, 2007.

Henryson, Robert. *The Poems of Robert Henryson*. Edited by Denton Fox. Oxford: Clarendon, 1981.

Henryson, Robert. *The Testament of Cresseid & Seven Fables*. Translated by Seamus Heaney. New York: Farrar, Straus and Giroux, 2009.

Hervieux, Léopold, ed. *Les Fabulistes Latins depuis le siècle d'Auguste jusqu'a la fin du moyen Âge*. 5 vols. New York: Burt Franklin, 1960.

Hexter, Ralph J. *Ovid and Medieval Schooling: Studies in Medieval School Commentaries on Ovid's "Ars Amatoria," "Epistulae ex Ponto," and "Epistulae Heroidum."* Münchener Beiträge zur Medievalistik und Renaissance-Forschung 38. Munich: Arbeo-Gesellschaft, 1978.

Hexter, Ralph J. "Ovid in the Middle Ages: Exile, Mythographer, and Lover." In *Brill's Companion to Ovid*, edited by Barbara Welden Boyd, 413–42. Leiden: Brill, 2002.

Higden, Ranulph. *Polychronicon*. Edited by Churchill Babington. Vol. 2. Rolls Series. London: Longmans, Green, & Company, 1869.

Hill, Adams Sherman. "An Answer to the Cry for More English." *Good Company*, no. 4 (1879): 234–35.

Hill, B. M., and A. Shaw. "The Wikipedia Gender Gap Revisited: Characterizing Survey Response Bias with Propensity Score Estimation." *PLoS ONE* 8, no. 6 (2013): e65782. https://doi.org/10.1371/journal.pone.0065782.

Hobbins, Daniel. *Authorship and Publicity before Print: Jean Gerson and the Transformation of Late Medieval Learning*. Philadelphia: University of Pennsylvania Press, 2009.

Holbek, Bengt. *Æsops levned og fabler: Christiern Pedersens oversættelse af Stainhöwels Æsop*. Vol. 2. Copenhagen: J.H. Schultz, 1962.

Holmes, Steve. *The Rhetoric of Videogames as Embodied Practice: Procedural Habits*. New York: Routledge, 2018.

Holsinger, Bruce. "Of Pigs and Parchment: Medieval Studies and the Coming of the Animal." *PMLA* 124, no. 2 (2009): 616–23.

Holsinger, Bruce. *Premodern Condition: Medievalism and the Making of Theory*. Chicago: University of Chicago Press, 2005.

Honorius of Autun. *Selectorum Psalmorum Expositio*. In *Patrologia Cursus Completus*. Series Latina, vol. 172. Edited by J. P. Migne. Paris: Garnier, 1854.

Horace. *Satires, Epistles, and Ars poetica*. Edited and translated by H. Rushton Fairclough. Loeb Classical Library. Cambridge, MA: Harvard University Press, 1926.

Horner, Bruce. "Modality as Social Practice in Written Language." In *Writing Changes: Alphabetic Text and Multimodal Composition*, edited by Pegeen Reichert Powell, 21–40. New York: Modern Language Association of America, 2020.

Huygens, R. B. C., ed. *Accessus ad auctores: Bernard d'Utrecht; Conrad d'Hirsau, Dialogus super auctores*. Leiden: Brill, 1970.

Illich, Ivan. *In the Vineyard of the Text: A Commentary to Hugh's Didascalicon*. Chicago: University of Chicago Press, 1993.

Ingham, Patricia Clare. *The Medieval New: Ambivalence in an Age of Innovation*. Philadelphia: University of Pennsylvania Press, 2015.

Irvine, Martin. *The Making of Textual Culture: "Grammatica" and Literary Theory, 350–1100*. Cambridge: Cambridge University Press, 1994.

Irvine, Martin. "Remix and the Dialogic Engine of Culture: A Model for Generative Combinatoriality." In *The Routledge Companion to Remix Studies*, edited by Eduardo Navas, Owen Gallagher, and xtine burrough, 15–42. London: Routledge, 2014.

Isidore of Seville. *Etymologies*. Edited by W. M. Lindsay. Oxford: Clarendon, 1911.

Jenkins, Henry. "Confronting the Challenges of Participatory Culture: Media Education for the 21st Century." *Building the Field of Digital Media and Learning*. Chicago: MacArthur Foundation, 2006. https://www.macfound.org/media/article_pdfs/jenkins_white_paper.pdf.

Jenkins, Henry. *Fans, Bloggers, and Gamers: Exploring Participatory Culture*. New York: New York University Press, 2006.

Jenkins, Henry. *Textual Poachers: Television Fans and Participatory Culture*. Updated 20th anniversary ed. New York: Routledge, 2013.

Jerome. *Ad Pammachium de optimo genere interpretandi. Corpus scriptorium ecclesiasticorum latinorum* 54. S. Eusebii Hieronymi opera sec. I, pars. I, epistularum pars I, I–LXX. Ed. I. Hilberg. Vienna: Tempsky, 1910.

John of Garland. *Parisiana Poetria*. Edited and translated by Traugott Lawler. 1974. Cambridge, MA: Harvard University Press, 2020.

John of Salisbury. *Ioannis Saresberiensis Metalogicon*. Edited by J. B. Hall. Turnhout: Brepols, 1991.

John of Salisbury. *The Metalogicon of John of Salisbury: A Twelfth-Century Defense of the Verbal and Logical Arts of the Trivium*. Translated by Daniel D. McGarry. Berkeley: University of California Press, 1955.

Johns, Adrian. *Piracy: The Intellectual Property Wars from Gutenberg to Gates*. 2nd ed. Chicago: University of Chicago Press, 2010.

Karras, Ruth Mazo. *From Boys to Men: Formations of Masculinity in Late Medieval Europe*. Philadelphia: University of Pennsylvania Press, 2003.

Keller, John E., and Richard P. Kincade. *Iconography in Medieval Spanish Literature*. Lexington: University Press of Kentucky, 1984.

Kennedy, George. *Classical Rhetoric and Its Christian and Secular Tradition from Ancient to Modern Times*. Chapel Hill: University of North Carolina Press, 1980.

Kennedy, Kathleen E. *Medieval Hackers*. Brooklyn, NY: punctum books, 2015.

Kennerly, Michele. *Editorial Bodies: Perfection and Rejection in Ancient Rhetoric and Poetics*. Columbia: University of South Carolina Press, 2018.

Kim, Dorothy. "#medievaltwitter." *In the Middle*, January 7, 2014. http://www.inthemedievalmiddle.com/2014/01/medievaltwitter.html.

Kimball, Bruce A. *Orators and Philosophers: A History of the Idea of Liberal Education*. New York: Teachers College Press, 1986.

King, Gary, Benjamin Schneer, and Ariel White. "How the News Media Activate Public Expression and Influence National Agendas." *Science* 358, no. 6364 (2017): 776–80.

Kinsley, James. *Scottish Poetry. A Critical Survey*. London: Cassell, 1955.

Kirschenbaum, Matthew. *Mechanisms: New Media and the Forensic Imagination*. Cambridge, MA: MIT Press, 2008.

Kleinman, Sherryl, and Matthew B. Ezzell. "Opposing 'Both Sides': Rhetoric, Reproductive Rights, and Control of a Campus Women's Center." *Women's Studies International Forum*, no. 35 (2012): 403–14.

Knapp, Ethan. "Chaucer Criticism and Its Legacies." In *The Yale Companion to Chaucer*, edited by Seth Lerer, 324–56. New Haven, CT: Yale University Press, 2006.

Knoblauch, C. H. "Modern Composition Theory and the Rhetorical Tradition." *Freshman English News*, no. 9 (1980): 3–17.

Knoblauch, C. H., and Lil Brannon. *Critical Teaching and the Idea of Literacy*. Portsmouth, NH: Boynton/Cook, 1993.

Knoblauch, C. H., and Lil Brannon. *Rhetorical Traditions and the Teaching of Writing*. Upper Montclair, NJ: Boynton/Cook, 1984.

Knoblauch, C. H., and Lil Brannon. "Writing as Learning through the Curriculum." *College English*, no. 45 (1983): 465–74.

Koh, Adeline. "The Political Power of Play." *Hybrid Pedagogy*, April 3, 2014. http://hybridpedagogy.org/political-power-of-play/.

Konrad, Annika M. "Access Fatigue: The Rhetorical Work of Disability in Everyday Life." *College English* 83, no. 3 (2021): 179–99.

Kress, Gunther. *Multimodality: A Social Semiotic Approach to Contemporary Communication*. New York: Routledge, 2010.

Kristeller, Paul O. "Humanism and Scholasticism in the Italian Renaissance." *Byzantion*, no. 17 (1944–45): 346–74.

Lacan, Jacques. *Écrits: The First Complete Edition in English*. Translated by Bruce Fink. New York: W.W. Norton, 2006.

Lambert, Alex. *Intimacy and Friendship on Facebook*. London: Palgrave Macmillan, 2013.

Lanham, Carol Dana. *Salutatio Formulas in Latin Letters to 1200: Syntax, Style, and Theory*. 1975. Reprint, Eugene, OR: Wipf & Stock, 2004.

Latini, Brunetto. *La Rettorica*. Edited by F. Maggini. Florence: Felice le Monnier, 1968.

Latour, Bruno. *Reassembling the Social: An Introduction to Actor-Network-Theory*. Oxford: Oxford University Press, 2005.

Latour, Bruno. "Why Has Critique Run Out of Steam? From Matters of Fact to Matters of Concern." *Critical Inquiry* 30, no. 2 (2004): 225–48.

Lebègue, Raymond. *Etudes sur le théâtre français*. Vol. 1. Paris: Nizet, 1977.

LeClercq, Jean. "L'amitié dans les lettres au moyen âge." *Revue du moyen âge latin*, no. 1 (1945): 391–410.

Lecoy de la Marche. *La Chaire française au moyen âge*. Paris: Renouard, 1886.

Lemoine, M. "Le oeuvre de encyclopédique de Vincent de Beauvais." *Journal of World History*, no. 9 (1966): 571–79.

Lerer, Seth. *Children's Literature: A Reader's History, from Aesop to Harry Potter.* Chicago: University of Chicago Press, 2008.

Lerer, Seth. *Inventing English: A Portable History of the Language.* New York: Columbia University Press, 2007.

Lessig, Lawrence. *Remix: Making Art and Commerce Thrive in the Hybrid Economy.* New York: Penguin, 2005.

The Letters of Abelard and Heloise. Translated by Betty Radice. Rev. ed. Penguin: London, 2003.

Leuf, Bo, and Ward Cunningham. *The Wiki Way: Quick Collaboration on the Web.* Boston: Addison-Wesley, 2001.

Lim, Sook. "How and Why Do College Students Use *Wikipedia*?" *Journal of American Society for Information Science and Technology* 60, no. 11 (2009): 2189–202.

Liu, Alan. *The Laws of Cool: Knowledge Work and the Culture of Information.* Chicago: University of Chicago Press, 2004.

Liu, Andrew. *The Wikipedia Revolution: How a Bunch of Nobodies Created the World's Greatest Encyclopedia.* New York: Hyperion, 2009.

Lloyd-Jones, Richard. "Using the History of Rhetoric." In *Learning from the Histories of Rhetoric: Essays in Honor of Winifred Bryan Horner*, edited by Theresa Enos, 15–25. Carbondale: Southern Illinois University Press, 1993.

Locke, John. *An Essay Concerning Human Understanding.* London: Thomas Basset, 1690.

Lombard, Peter. *Sentences.* Edited by Ignatius Brady. 2 vols. Grottoferrata: Collegi S. Bonaventurae ad Claras Aquas, 1971–81.

Losh, Elizabeth. "Hacktivism and the Humanities: Programming Protest in the Era of the Digital University." In Gold, *Debates in the Digital Humanities*, 161–86.

Losh, Elizabeth. *Virtualpolitik: An Electronic History of Government Media-Making in a Time of War, Scandal, Disaster, Miscommunication, and Mistakes.* Cambridge, MA: MIT Press, 2009.

Losh, Elizabeth. *The War on Learning: Gaining Ground in the Digital University.* Cambridge, MA: MIT Press, 2014.

Losh, Elizabeth, Jacqueline Wernimont, Laura Wexler, and Hong-An Wu. "Putting the Human Back into the Digital Humanities: Feminism, Generosity, and Mess." In Gold and Klein, *Debates in the Digital Humanities 2016.* https://dhdebates.gc.cuny.edu/read/untitled/section/cfe1b125-6917-4095-9d56-20487aa0b867.

Lounsbury, Thomas R. "Compulsory Composition in Colleges." *Harper's Monthly Magazine*, November 1911, 866–80.

Lyall, R. J. "Books and Book Owners in Fifteenth-Century Scotland." In *Book Production and Publishing in Britain, 1375–1475*, edited by Jeremy Griffiths and Derek Pearsall, 239–56. Cambridge: Cambridge University Press, 1989.

Lynch, Jack. *You Could Look It Up: The Reference Shelf from Babylon to Wikipedia*. New York: Bloomsbury, 2016.

Macdougall, Norman. "Whitelaw, Archibald (1415/16–1498)." *Oxford Dictionary of National Biography*. Oxford: Oxford University Press, 2004. https://doi.org/10.1093/ref:odnb/54336.

Maierù, Alfonso. *University Training in Medieval Europe*. Translated by D. N. Pryds. Leiden: Brill, 1994.

Mak, Bonnie. *How the Page Matters*. Toronto: University of Toronto Press, 2011.

Manguel, Alberto. *A Reader on Reading*. New Haven, CT: Yale University Press, 2010.

Manly, John, and John Arthur Powell. *Better Business English*. Chicago: Frederick Drake, 1921.

Manly, John, and Edith Rickert, eds. *The Text of the Canterbury Tales*. 8 vols. Chicago: University of Chicago Press, 1940.

Manly, John, and Edith Rickert. *The Writing of English*. New York: Henry Holt, 1919.

Mann, Jill. *Feminizing Chaucer*. Chaucer Studies 30. Cambridge: D.S. Brewer, 2002.

Mann, Jill. *From Aesop to Reynard: Beast Literature in Medieval Britain*. Oxford: Oxford University Press, 2009.

Mapstone, Sally. "Robert Henryson." In *The Cambridge Companion to Medieval English Literature, 1100–1500*, edited by Larry Scanlon, 243–55. Cambridge: Cambridge University Press, 2009.

Marichal, Robert. "L'Écriture latine et la civilisation occidentale du Ier au XVIe siècle." In *L'Écriture et la psychologie des peoples*, edited by Marcel Cohen, 199–247. Paris: A. Colin, 1963.

Marie de France. *Fables*. Edited and translated by Harriet Spiegel. Toronto: University of Toronto Press, 1994.

Marie de France. *Marie de France: Poetry*. Translated by Dorothy Gilbert. New York: W.W. Norton, 2015.

Marenbon, John. *Later Medieval Philosophy (1150–1350): An Introduction*. New York: Routledge, 1987.

Marino, Mark C. "Why We Must Read the Code: The Science Wars, Episode IV." In Gold and Klein, *Debates in the Digital Humanities 2016.* http://dhdebates.gc.cuny.edu/debates/text/64.

Martinez, Aja Y. *Counterstory: The Rhetoric and Writing of Critical Race Theory.* Champaign, IL: NCTE, 2020.

Mazzota, Giuseppe. "Humanism and the Medieval Encyclopedic Tradition." In *Interpretations of Renaissance Humanism,* edited by Angelo Mazzocco, 113–24. Leiden: Brill, 2006.

Mbembe, Achille. *Necropolitics.* Translated by Steven Corcoran. Durham, NC: Duke University Press, 2019.

McCloud, Scott. *Understanding Comics: The Invisible Art.* New York: HarperCollins, 1993.

McCorkle, Ben. *Rhetorical Delivery as Technological Discourse: A Cross-Historical Study.* Carbondale: Southern Illinois University Press, 2012.

McLeod, Susan, and Elaine Maimon. "Clearing the Air: WAC Myths and Realities." *College English* 62, no. 5 (2000): 573–83.

McLuhan, Marshall. *Understanding New Media: The Extensions of Man.* New York: Gingko Press, 1964.

McPherson, Tara. *Feminist in a Software Lab: Difference + Design.* Cambridge, MA: Harvard University Press, 2018.

Meech, Sanford Brown. "An Early Treatise in English concerning Latin Grammar." In *Essays and Studies in English and Comparative Literature by Members of the English Department of the University of Michigan,* 81–125. Ann Arbor: University of Michigan Press, 1935.

Minnis, A. J., and A. B. Scott, eds. *Medieval Literary Theory and Criticism c. 1100–c. 1375: The Commentary Tradition.* Oxford: Clarendon, 1988.

Minnis, Alastair. *Medieval Theory of Authorship: Scholastic Literary Attitudes in the Later Middle Ages.* 2nd ed. Philadelphia: University of Pennsylvania Press, 2010.

Minnis, Alastair. "*Nolens Auctor Sed Compilator Reputari*: The Late-Medieval Discourse of Compilation." In *La métode critique au Moyen Âge,* edited by Mireille Chazan and Gilbert Dahan, 47–63. Turnhout: Brepols, 2008.

Miller, Richard E. *On the End of Privacy: Dissolving Boundaries in a Screen-Centric World.* Pittsburgh, PA: University of Pittsburgh Press, 2019.

Mitchell, W. J. T. *Picture Theory: Essays on Verbal and Visual Representation.* Chicago: University of Chicago Press, 1995.

Mol, Annemarie. *The Body Multiple: Ontology in Medical Practice.* Durham, NC: Duke University Press, 2002.

Montaigne, Michel de. "De l'amitié." *Essais*. Book I. Paris: Pléiade, 1959.

Morey, Sean. *Rhetorical Delivery and Digital Technologies: Networks, Affect, Electracy*. New York: Routledge, 2016.

Mueller, Alex. *Translating Troy: Provincial Politics in Alliterative Romance*. Columbus: Ohio State University Press, 2013.

Müller, Jan-Dirk. "The Body of the Book: The Media Transition from Manuscript to Print." In *Materialities of Communication*, edited by Hans Ulrich Gumbrecht and K. Ludwig Pfeiffer, translated by William Whobrey, 32–44. Stanford, CA: Stanford University Press, 1994.

Munimenta Alme Universitatis Glasguensis. Edinburgh: T. Constable, 1854.

Murphy, James J. *Rhetoric in the Middle Ages: A History of Rhetorical Theory from St. Augustine to the Renaissance*. Berkeley: University of California Press, 1974.

Murphy, James J. "Trends in Rhetorical Incunabula." *Rhetorica: A Journal of the History of Rhetoric* 18, no. 4 (2000): 389–97.

Murray, Alexander. *Reason and Society in the Middle Ages*. Oxford: Clarendon, 1978.

Nagel, Alexander, and Christopher S. Wood. *Anachronic Renaissance*. New York: Zone, 2010.

Nair, Meera. "Annotate the Plot: Using Annotation to Write Better Fiction." In *Digital Is*. National Writing Project, September 17, 2014. http://digitalis.nwp.org/resource/6179.

"National Council of Teachers of English College Section." *College English*, no. 3 (1942): 584–86.

Navas, Eduardo. *Remix Theory: The Aesthetics of Sampling*. Vienna: Springer, 2012.

Nederman, Cary. "Nature, Ethics, and the Doctrine of Habitus: Aristotelian Moral Psychology in the Twelfth Century." *Traditio*, no. 45 (1989–90): 87–110.

Neem, Johann. *What's the Point of College?: Seeking Purpose in an Age of Reform*. Baltimore, MD: Johns Hopkins University Press, 2019.

Newfield, Christopher. "Aftermath of the MOOC Wars: Can Commercial Vendors Support Higher Education?" *Learning and Teaching* 9, no. 2 (2016): 12–41.

Newfield, Christopher. "When Are Access and Inclusion Also Racist?" *Remaking the University*, June 28, 2020. https://utotherescue.blogspot.com/2020/06/when-are-access-and-inclusion-also.html.

Newman, Katherine. "Online Ed Key to Closing Racial, Class Gaps." *Common-

wealth, June 7, 2020. https://commonwealthmagazine.org/opinion/online-ed-key-to-closing-racial-class-gaps/.

Nichols, Stephen G. "Introduction: Philology in Manuscript Culture." *Speculum* 65, no. 1 (1990): 1–10.

Noble, Safiya Umoja. *Algorithms of Oppression: How Search Engines Reinforce Racism*. New York: New York University Press, 2018.

Norris, Sigrid. *Analyzing Multimodal Interaction: A Methodological Framework*. New York: Routledge, 2004.

Novikoff, Alex J. *Medieval Culture of Disputation: Pedagogy, Practice, and Performance*. Philadelphia: University of Pennsylvania Press, 2013.

Nowviskie, Bethany. "Alternate Futures/Usable Pasts." October 24, 2016. http://nowviskie.org/2016/alternate-futures-usable-pasts/.

Nunberg, Geoffrey. "The Place of Books in the Age of Electronic Reproduction." *Representations*, no. 42 (1993): 13–37.

O'Donnell, C. Oliver. "Erwin Panofsky's Neo-Kantian Humanism and the Purported Relation between Gothic Architecture and Scholasticism." In *Thinking of the Medieval: Midcentury Intellectuals and the Middle Ages*, edited by R. D. Perry and Benjamin A. Saltzman, 167–89. Cambridge: Cambridge University Press, 2023.

O'Neil, Mathieu. *Cyberchiefs: Autonomy and Authority in Online Tribes*. New York: Pluto, 2009.

O'Neil, Mathieu. "The Sociology of Critique in Wikipedia." *Critical Studies in Peer Production* 1, no. 2 (2011): 1–11.

Ong, Walter J. *Fighting for Life: Contest, Sexuality, and Consciousness*. Ithaca, NY: Cornell University Press, 1981.

Ong, Walter J. *Orality and Literacy: The Technologizing of the Word*. 1982. London: Routledge, 2002.

Ong, Walter J. *Ramus, Method, and the Decay of Dialogue*. Chicago: University of Chicago Press, 2004.

Ong, Walter J. *Rhetoric, Romance, and Technology: Studies in the Interaction and Expression of Culture*. Ithaca, NY: Cornell University Press, 1971.

Orme, Nicholas. "The Cathedral School before the Reformation." In *Hereford Cathedral: A History*, edited by Gerald Aylmer and John Tiller, 565–78. London: Hambledon, 2000.

Orme, Nicholas. *Education and Society in Medieval and Renaissance England*. London: Hambledon, 1989.

Orme, Nicholas. *English Schools in the Middle Ages*. London: Methuen, 1973.

Orme, Nicholas. *Medieval Schools from Roman Britain to Renaissance England*. New Haven, CT: Yale University Press, 2006.

Ovid. *Heroides, Amores*. Vol. 1. Translated by Grant Showerman. Revised by G. P. Goold. Cambridge, MA: Harvard University Press, 1977.

Panofsky, Erwin. *Architecture gothique et pensée scolastique: "Gothic architecture and scholasticism."* Preface by l'Abbé Suger de Saint-Denis. Translated and with a postface by Pierre Bourdieu. Paris: Éditions de Minuit, 1967.

Panofsky, Erwin. *Gothic Architecture and Scholasticism*. Latrobe, PA: Archabbey Press, 1951.

paperson, la. *A Third University Is Possible*. Minneapolis: University of Minnesota Press, 2017. https://manifold.umn.edu/projects/a-third-university-is-possible.

Parkes, Malcolm B. "The Influence of the Concepts of *Ordinatio* and *Compilatio* on the Development of the Book" (1976). In *Scribes, Scripts, and Readers: Studies in the Communication, Presentation, and Dissemination of Medieval Texts*, 35–70. London: Hambledon, 1991.

Parr, C. "Not Staying the Course: New Study of Low MOOC Completion Rates." *Inside Higher Ed*, May 10, 2013. http://www.insidehighered.com/news/2013/05/10/new-study-low-mooc-completion-rates.

Patterson, Annabel. *Fables of Power: Aesopian Writing and Political History*. Durham, NC: Duke University Press, 1991.

Pearsall, Derek. *The Nun's Priest's Tale*. Part 9 of *A Variorum Edition of the Works of Geoffrey Chaucer*, Vol. 2, *The Canterbury Tales*. Norman: University of Oklahoma Press, 1984.

Perrin, Porter G. "The Teaching of Rhetoric in American Colleges before 1750." PhD diss., University of Chicago, 1936.

Petrarch, Francesco. *De sui ipsius et multorum ignorantia*. Edited by Luigi Mario Capelli. Paris: H. Champion, 1906.

Petrarch, Francesco. *On His Own Ignorance and That of Many Others*. In *The Renaissance Philosophy of Man*, edited and translated by Ernest Cassirer, Paul Kristeller, and John Herman Randall Jr., 47–133. Chicago: University of Chicago Press, 1969.

Petrarch, Francesco. *Prose*. Edited by G. Martellotti, P.G. Ricci, E. Carrara, and E. Bianchi. La letteratura italiana, storia i testi 7. Milan: R. Ricciardi, 1955.

Petronius. *Petronii Arbitri Satyricon reliquiae*. Edited by Konrad Mueller. Stuttgart: Teubner, 1995.

Phillips, Whitney. "The Oxygen of Amplification: Better Practices for Reporting on Extremists, Antagonists, and Manipulators Online." *Data & Society*, May 22, 2018. https://datasociety.net/library/oxygen-of-amplification/.

Plato. *Phaedrus*. In *Plato: Complete Works*, translated by Alexander Nehamas and Paul Woodruff, edited by John M. Cooper, 506–56. Indianapolis, IN: Hackett, 1997.

Porter, James E. "Recovering Delivery for Digital Rhetoric." *Computers and Composition*, no. 26 (2009): 207–24.

Powell, Annette Harris. "Access(ing) Habits, Attitudes, and Engagements: Rethinking Access as Practice." *Computers and Composition*, no. 24 (2007): 16–35.

Powell, Marianne. *Fabula docet: Studies in the Background and Interpretation of Henryson's Morall Fabillis*. Odense University Studies in English 6. Odense: Odense University Press, 1983.

Price, Leah. "Introduction: Reading Matter." *PMLA* 121, no. 1 (2006): 9–16.

Progressive Education Association. *Language in General Education: A Report of the Committee on the Function of English in General Education*. New York: Appleton, 1940.

Quintillian. *The Orator's Education, Volume 1: Books 1–2*. Edited and translated by Donald A. Russell. Cambridge, MA: Harvard University Press, 2002.

Reagle, Joseph Michael, Jr. *Good Faith Collaboration: The Culture of Wikipedia*. Cambridge, MA: MIT Press, 2010.

Reydellet, Marc. "La Diffusion des *Origines* d'Isidore de Séville au Haut Moyen Age." *Ecole Française de Rome: Mélanges d'Archéologie et d'Histoire*, no. 88 (1966): 383–437.

Reynolds, L. D., and N. G. Wilson. *Scribes and Scholars: A Guide to the Transmission of Greek and Latin Literature*. Oxford: Clarendon, 1978.

Reynolds, Suzanne. *Medieval Reading: Grammar, Rhetoric, and Classical Text*. Cambridge: Cambridge University Press, 1996.

Richards, I. A. *The Philosophy of Rhetoric*. New York: Oxford University Press, 1936.

Rickert, Thomas. *Ambient Rhetoric: The Attunements of Rhetorical Being*. Pittsburgh, PA: University of Pittsburgh Press, 2013.

Ricoeur, Paul. *Freud and Philosophy: An Essay on Interpretation*. New Haven, CT: Yale University Press, 1970.

Ridolfo, Jim, and Dànielle Nicole DeVoss. "Composing for Recomposition: Rhetorical Velocity and Delivery." *Kairos: A Journal of Rhetoric, Technology, and Pedagogy* 13, no. 2 (2009). http://kairos.technorhetoric.net/13.2/topoi/ridolfo_devoss/index.html.

Ridolfo, Jim, and William Hart-Davidson, eds. *Rhetoric and the Digital Humanities*. Chicago: University of Chicago Press, 2014.

Rockinger, Ludwig. *Briefsteller un Formelbücher des eilften bis vierzehnten Jahrhunderts*. Quellen ud Erörterungen zur bayerischen und deutschen Geschichte 9. Munchen: Georg Franz, 1864.

Romele, Alberto, and Dario Rodighiero. "Digital Habitus or Personalization without Personality." *HUMANA.MENTE: Journal of Philosophical Studies*, 13, no. 37 (2020): 98–126.

Rose, Mike. "The Language of Exclusion: Writing Instruction at the University." *College English* 47, no. 4 (1985): 341–59.

Rosen, Christine. "More, But Not Merrier." *Wall Street Journal*, October 5, 2007. https://www.wsj.com/articles/SB119153630741849393.

Rosenblatt, Louise. *Literature as Exploration*. Rev. ed. New York: Noble and Noble, 1938/1968.

Rosenblatt, Louise. *The Reader, the Text, the Poem: The Transactional Theory of the Literary Work*. Carbondale: Southern Illinois University Press, 1978.

Roszak, Theodore. "Shakespeare Never Lost a Manuscript to a Computer Crash." *New York Times*, March 11, 1999.

Rouse, R. H., and M. A. Rouse. "*Ordinatio* and *Compilatio* Revisited." In *Ad Litteram: Authoritative Texts and Their Medieval Readers*, edited by Mark D. Jordan and Kent Emery Jr., 113–34. Notre Dame, IN: University of Notre Dame Press, 1992.

Rubin, Miri. "The Person in the Form: Medieval Challenges to Bodily 'Order.'" In *Framing Medieval Bodies*, edited by Sarah Kay and Miri Rubin, 100–122. Manchester: Manchester University Press, 1994.

Russell, David R. "Romantics on Writing: Liberal Culture and the Abolition of Composition Courses." *Rhetoric Review* 6, no. 2 (1988): 132–48.

Russell, David R. "A Technique for Teaching Exposition: Medieval and Modern." Meeting of the Oklahoma Council of Teachers of English. Stillwater, OK. April 16–17, 1982. https://files.eric.ed.gov/fulltext/ED218676.pdf.

Russell, David R. "Writing across the Curriculum and the Communications Movement: Some Lessons from the Past." *College Composition and Communication*, no. 38 (1987): 184–94.

Russell, David R. *Writing in the Academic Disciplines: A Curricular History*. 2nd ed. Carbondale: Southern Illinois University Press, 2002.

Saloman, David A. *An Introduction to the Glossa Ordinaria as Medieval Hypertext*. Cardiff: University of Wales Press, 2012.

Sanford, Eva Matthews. "Honorius, Presbyter, and Scholasticus." *Speculum*, no. 23 (1948): 397–425.

Sayers, Dorothy. *The Lost Tools of Learning: Paper Read at a Vacation Course in Education, Oxford, 1947.* London: Methuen, 1948.

Sayers, Jentery. "Dropping the Digital." In Gold and Klein, *Debates in the Digital Humanities 2016*. https://dhdebates.gc.cuny.edu/read/65be1a40-6473-4d9e-ba75-6380e5a72138/section/f29056aa-c434-4322-a185-009e0f7e3a9d#ch37.

Sayers, Jentery, ed. *Making Things and Drawing Boundaries*. Minneapolis: University of Minnesota Press, 2017.

Schacht, Paul. "Annotation." In *Digital Pedagogy in the Humanities: Concepts, Models, and Experiments*, edited by Rebecca Frost Davis, Matthew K. Gold, Katherine D. Harris, and Jentery Sayers. Modern Language Association Commons. https://digitalpedagogy.hcommons.org/keyword/Annotation.

Schumpeter, Joseph A. *Capitalism, Socialism, and Democracy*. 5th ed. London: Routledge, 1994.

Searson, J. W. "Determining a Language Program." *English Journal*, no. 13 (1924): 274–79.

Seneca, Lucius Annaeus. *Epistulae morales*. Edited by L. D. Reynolds. Oxford Classical Texts, Loeb Classical Library. London: Heinemann, 1953–62.

Seneca, Lucius Annaeus. *Seneca IV: Ad Lucilium Epistolae Morales, I*. Edited by G. P. Goold. Translated by Richard M. Gummere. Cambridge, MA: Harvard University Press, 1979.

Shipka, Jody. *Toward a Composition Made Whole*. Pittsburgh, PA: University of Pittsburgh Press, 2011.

Shirky, Clay. *Cognitive Surplus: Creativity and Generosity in a Connected Age*. New York: Penguin, 2010.

Shirky, Clay. *Here Comes Everybody: The Power of Organizing without Organizations*. New York: Penguin, 2008.

Shotter, John. *Cultural Politics of Everyday Life*. Milton Keynes: Open University Press, 1993.

Simone, Raffaele. "The Body of the Text." In *The Future of the Book*, edited by Geoffrey Nunberg, 239–51. Berkeley: University of California Press, 1996.

Singel, Ryan. "Veni, Vidi, Wiki." *Wired*, September 7, 2006. https://www.wired.com/2006/09/veni-vidi-wiki/.

Sir Gawain: Eleven Romances and Tales. Edited by Thomas Hahn. Kalamazoo, MI: Medieval Institute Publications, 1995.

Smith, D. Vance. "Africa Writes Back." *Aeon*, June 17, 2021. https://aeon.co/essays/africas-ancient-scripts-counter-european-ideas-of-literacy.

Smith, Ron. "The Composition Requirement Today: A Report on a Nationwide Survey of Four-Year Colleges and Universities." *College Composition and Communication* 25, no. 2 (1974): 138–48.

Spring, Joel. *The American School, 1642–1985*. New York: Longman, 1986.

Steiner, Emily. *John Trevisa's Information Age: Knowledge and the Pursuit of Literature, c. 1400*. Oxford: Oxford University Press, 2021.

Steiner, Emily. "Radical Historiography: Langland, Trevisa, and the *Polychronicon*." *Studies in the Age of Chaucer*, no. 27 (2005): 171–211.

Stettler, René. "Reframing Semiotic Telematic Knowledge Spaces, and the Anthropological Challenge to Designing Interhuman Relations." *Technoetic Arts: A Journal of Speculative Research* 6, no. 2 (2008): 163–70.

Stewart, Donald. "Some Facts Worth Knowing about the Origins of Freshman Composition." *CEA Critic*, no. 44 (May 1982): 2–11.

Struever, Nancy. "Rhetoric of Familiarity: A Pedagogy of Ethics." *Philosophy and Rhetoric*, no. 31 (1998): 91–106.

Taylor, Warner G. *A National Survey of Conditions in Freshman English*. Bull. no. 11. Madison: University of Wisconsin Press, 1929.

Temple, Olivia, and Robert Temple, trans. *Aesop: The Complete Fables*. New York: Penguin, 1998.

Thomson, David, ed. *An Edition of the Middle English Grammatical Texts*. New York: Garland, 1984.

Thoreau, Henry David. *Journal*. Edited by John C. Broderick, Elizabeth Hall Witherell, William L. Howarth, Robert Sattelmeyer, and Thomas Blanding. Vol. 1. Princeton, NJ: Princeton University Press, 1981.

Thrift, Nigel. *Spatial Formations*. London: Sage, 1996.

Thurber, Samuel. "English in the Secondary Schools: Some Considerations as to Its Aims and Needs." *School Review*, no. 2 (1894): 468–78.

Tkacz, Nathaniel. *Wikipedia and the Politics of Openness*. Chicago: University of Chicago Press, 2015.

Travis, Peter. "Aesop's Symposium of Animal Tongues." *Postmedieval: A Journal of Medieval Cultural Studies* 2, no. 1 (2011): 33–49.

Trevisa, John. *Trevisa's Dialogus inter Militem et Clericum; Sermon by FitzRalph; and þe Bygynnyng of þe World*. Edited by Aaron Jenkins Perry. Early English Text Society, Original Series, no. 167. London: Oxford University Press, 1925.

The Trials and Joys of Marriage. Edited by Eve Salisbury. Kalamazoo, MI: Medieval Institute Publications, 2002.

Trice, Michael. "Gamergate: Understanding the Tactics of Online Knowledge Disruptors." In *Rhet Ops: Rhetoric and Information Warfare*, edited by Jim Ridolfo and William Hart-Davidson, 105–22. Pittsburgh, PA: University of Pittsburgh Press, 2019.

Trimbur, John, and Karen Press. "When Was Multimodality? Modality and the Rhetoric of Transparency." In *Multimodality in Writing: The State of the Art in Theory, Methodology, and Pedagogy*, edited by Arlene Archer and Esther Breuer, 19–42. Leiden: Brill, 2015.

Turkle, Sherry. *Alone Together: Why We Expect More from Technology and Less from Each Other*. New York: Basic Books, 2011.

Turkle, Sherry. *Life on the Screen: Identity in the Age of the Internet*. New York: Simon & Schuster, 1995.

Turner, Henry. *The Corporate Commonwealth: Pluralism and Political Fictions in England, 1516–1651*. Chicago: University of Chicago Press, 2016.

Turner, Henry. "The Problem of the More-than-One: Friendship, Calculation, and Political Association in *The Merchant of Venice*." *Shakespeare Quarterly* 57, no. 4 (2006): 413–42.

Tyre, Peg. "The Writing Revolution." *Atlantic*, October 2012. http://www.theatlantic.com/magazine/archive/2012/10/the-writing-revolution/309090/.

Vaidhyanathan, Siva. *Anti-social Media: How Facebook Disconnects Us and Undermines Democracy*. Oxford: Oxford University Press, 2018.

Vaidhyanathan, Siva. *Copyrights and Copywrongs: The Rise of Intellectual Property and How It Threatens Creativity*. New York: New York University Press, 2003.

Vandendorpe, Christian. *From Papyrus to Hypertext: Toward the Universal Digital Library*. Translated by Phyllis Aronoff and Howard Scott. Urbana: University of Illinois Press, 2009.

Vecchi, G. *Il magistero delle "Artes" latine a Bologna nel medioevo*. Bologna: Patron, 1958.

Vee, Annette. *Coding Literacy: How Computer Programming Is Changing Writing*. Cambridge, MA: MIT Press, 2017.

Venturini, Tommaso, and Bruno Latour. "The Social Fabric: Digital Traces and Quali-quantitative Methods" (2010). https://medialab.sciencespo.fr/publications/Venturini_Latour-The_Social_Fabric.pdf.

Vickers, Brian. *In Defense of Rhetoric*. Oxford: Clarendon, 1988.

Villanueva, Victor. "The Politics of Literacy across the Curriculum." In *WAC for the New Millennium: Strategies for Continuing Writing-across-the-Curriculum Programs*, edited by Susan McLeod, Eric Miraglia, Margot Soven, and

Christopher Thaiss, 165–78. Urbana, IL: National Council of Teachers of English, 2001.

Vivian, Bradford. "In the Regard of the Image." *JAC: Rhetoric, Writing, Culture, Politics* 27, nos. 3/4 (2007): 471–504.

Wahlstrom, Billie, and Chris Scruton. "Constructing Texts/Understanding Texts: Lessons from Antiquity and the Middle Ages." *Computers and Composition*, no. 14 (1997): 311–28.

Wakelin, Daniel. *Humanism, Reading, and English Literature, 1430–1530*. Oxford: Oxford University Press, 2007.

Wakelin, Daniel. *Scribal Correction and Literary Craft: English Manuscripts, 1375–1510*. Cambridge: Cambridge University Press, 2014.

Waldron, Ronald. "John Trevisa and the Use of English." *Proceedings of the British Academy*, no. 74 (1988): 171–202.

Wallace, David. *Premodern Places: Calais to Surinam, Chaucer to Aphra Behn*. Malden, MA: Blackwell, 2004.

Weisheipl, J. A. "Curriculum of the Faculty of Arts at Oxford in the Early Fourteenth Century." *Mediaeval Studies*, no. 26 (1964): 143–85.

Welch, Kathleen. *Electric Rhetoric: Classical Rhetoric, Oralism, and a New Literacy*. Cambridge, MA: MIT Press, 1999.

Welzenbach, Rebecca. "Making the Most of Free Unrestricted Texts: A First Look at the Promise of the Text Creation Partnership." *Deep Blue*, November 20, 2011, 1–14. https://hdl.handle.net/2027.42/87997.

Wendell, Barrett. *English Composition: Eight Lectures Given at the Lowell Institute*. New York: Charles Scribner's Sons, 1891.

Wharton, Robin. "Digital Humanities, Copyright, and the Literary." *Digital Humanities Quarterly* 7, no. 1 (2013). http://www.digitalhumanities.org/dhq/vol/7/1/000147/000147.html.

Wheatley, Edward. "The Aesopic Corpus Divided against Itself: A Literary Body and Its Members." *Journal of the Early Book Society for the Study of Manuscripts and Printing History*, no. 2 (1999): 46–72.

Wheatley, Edward. "The 'Fabulae' of Walter of England, the Medieval Scholastic Tradition, and the British Vernacular Fable." PhD diss., University of Virginia, 1991.

Wheatley, Edward. *Mastering Aesop: Medieval Education, Chaucer, and His Followers*. Gainesville: University Press of Florida, 2000.

Whitelaw, Archibald [Whytelaw, A]. "Address to King Richard III, advocating the strengthening of peaceful ties between the English and the Scots."

Translated by D. Shotter. In *The North of England in the Age of Richard III*, edited by A. J. Pollard, 193–9. Stroud: Sutton, 1996.

Whitelaw, Archibald [Whytelaw, A]. "Oratio Scotorum ad regum Ricardum tertium." In *The Bannatyne Miscellany*, vol. 2, edited by D. Laing, 41–48. Edinburgh: Bannatyne Club, 1836.

Wilcox, Thomas. *A Comprehensive Survey of Undergraduate Programs in English in the United States*. ED 044 422. Office of Education, Washington, D.C., Bureau of Research. May 14, 1970. https://files.eric.ed.gov/fulltext/ED044422.pdf.

Wilhelm, James J. *The Romance of Arthur: An Anthology of Medieval Texts in Translation*. New expanded ed. New York: Garland, 1994.

Willinsky, John. *The Intellectual Properties of Learning: A Prehistory from Saint Jerome to John Locke*. Chicago: University of Chicago Press, 2017.

Wilson, Anna. "Immature Pleasures: Affective Reading in Margery Kempe, Petrarch, Chaucer, and Modern Fan Communities." PhD diss., University of Toronto, 2015.

Wilson, Anna. "The Role of Affect in Fan Fiction." In "The Classical Canon and/as Transformative Work," ed. Ika Willis, special issue, *Transformative Works and Cultures*, no. 21 (2016). http://dx.doi.org/10.3983/twc.2016.0684.

Winroth, Anders. *The Making of Gratian's Decretum*. Cambridge: Cambridge University Press, 2004.

Witt, Ronald G. "Medieval 'Ars Dictaminis' and the Beginnings of Humanism: A New Construction of the Problem." *Renaissance Quarterly* 35, no. 1 (Spring 1982): 1–35.

Witt, Ronald G. *The Two Latin Cultures and the Foundation of Renaissance Humanism in Medieval Italy*. Cambridge: Cambridge University Press, 2012.

Witte, Stephen P. *A National Survey of College and University Writing Program Directors*. Technical Report 2. Austin: University of Texas, 1981.

Wogan-Browne, Jocelyn, Nicholas Watson, Andrew Taylor, and Ruth Evans, eds. *The Idea of the Vernacular: An Anthology of Middle English Literary Theory, 1280–1520*. University Park: Pennsylvania State University Press, 1999.

Woods, Marjorie Curry. "Among Men—Not Boys: Histories of Rhetoric and the Exclusion of Pedagogy." *Rhetoric Society Quarterly* 22, no. 1 (Winter 1992): 18–26.

Woods, Marjorie Curry, ed. and trans. *An Early Commentary on the Poetria nova of Geoffrey of Vinsauf*. Garland Medieval Texts 12. New York: Garland, 1985.

Woods, Marjorie Curry. "Some Techniques of Teaching Rhetorical Poetics in the Schools of Medieval Europe." In *Learning from the Histories of Rhetoric:*

Essays in Honor of Winifred Bryan Horner, edited by Theresa Enos, 91–113. Carbondale: Southern Illinois University Press, 1993.

Woods, Marjorie Curry. "The Teaching of Writing in Medieval Europe." In *A Short History of Writing Instruction from Ancient Greece to Twentieth-Century America*, edited by James J. Murphy, 77–94. Davis, CA: Hermagoras Press, 1990.

Woods, Marjorie Curry. *Weeping for Dido: The Classics in the Medieval Classroom*. Princeton, NJ: Princeton University Press, 2019.

Wright, A. E. *"Hie lert uns der meister": Latin Commentary and the German Fable, 1350–1500*. Medieval and Renaissance Texts and Studies 218. Tempe: Arizona Center for Medieval and Renaissance Studies, 2001.

Wright, A. E. "Readers and Wolves: Late-Medieval Commentaries on 'De lupo et capite.'" *Journal of Medieval Latin*, no. 8 (1998): 72–79.

Wysocki, Anne Frances. "awaywithwords: On the Possibilities in Unavailable Designs." *Computers and Composition* 22, no. 1 (2005): 55–62.

Yancey, Kathleen Blake. "Made Not Only in Words: Composition in a New Key." *College Composition and Communication* 56, no. 2 (2004): 297–328.

Young, Katherine, ed. *Bodylore*. Knoxville: University of Tennessee Press, 1993.

Zumthor, Paul. *Essai de poétique médiévale*. Paris: Éditions du Seuil, 1972.

Zumthor, Paul. *La lettre et la voix: De la "littérature" médiévale*. Paris: Éditions du Seuil, 1987.

Index

Abelard, Peter, 27, 214; *Historia calamitatum*, 93, 96, 192
access, 5, 17, 81–82, 108, 152, 171, 175, 209–10, 215–16, 218–20, 225; accessibility and, 14, 21–23, 43–56, 58–62, 64–68, 69–72, 75–78, 88, 93, 190, 196, 200–4, 212–13. *See also* open access
Acontius, 109, 196
Actor-Network-Theory (ANT), 32–33. *See also* Latour, Bruno
Aeneid, 101, 198
Aesop, 18–21, 102–6, 167–80; and academic commentary, 131–46, 149–51, 223–26; and authorship, 3–4, 155; as a body and property, 157–65, 180–88; as a classroom author, 109, 117. *See also* Caxton, William; Chaucer, Geoffrey; Henryson, Robert; Marie de France
Aesop: The Complete Fables, 181–2
Aesopus moralizatus, 135–36, 149, 163–64
Agamben, Giorgio, 29–30, 151–52, 154, 200
algorithmic culture, 4–5, 7, 9, 36–38, 98; surveillance and, 14, 25–26, 123–24, 190, 195–96, 203, 210, 215–17, 224–26, 228

amicitia, 191, 197–201, 207–9. *See also* Cicero, Marcus Tullius
amplification, 29, 102, 123–54; Aesop's fables and, 131–45, 158–59, 169; *amplificatio* and, 18, 124–27, 143–45, 213–14; annotation and, 10–12, 17–20, 127–31, 146–51; as a habit, 151–54, 186, 220, 223–28; circulation and, 123–25, 209–10
appropriation, 3–4, 12, 14–16, 19–21, 40–42, 44, 67, 79, 96, 131–32, 213, 216–18; as a habit, 155–88, 220–22
Aquinas, Thomas, 30, 36
ars dictaminis, 22, 27–29, 37, 66, 191–201, 223. *See also ars dictandi*
ars dictandi, 13, 22, 29, 123–27, 195, 226–28. *See also ars dictaminis*
Arthur, King, 52–53, 95, 110–14, 121
Aristotle, 8, 13, 29, 87, 209–10, 213, 227; *hexis* and, 26–27, 36
artificial intelligence, 216–17
Augustine, 8, 96
authority, 4–5, 7, 21, 39–41, 222–24; amplification and, 124, 141–42, 146–49, 151–53; appropriation and, 156, 158, 165,

299

167–68, 175–80; *auctoritas*, 16, 29, 124, 151–53, 168–69, 175, 177, 187–88, 200–1; compilation and, 16–17, 70–72, 74–76, 79–87, 92, 219; disputation and, 94–96, 112–15, 120; salutation and, 201–2, 205, 219; translation and, 14–15, 43–54, 60–64, 219
auctoritas. *See* authority
Avianus, 20–21, 133–34, 165, 168, 187. *See also* Aesop

Bahr, Arthur, 15–16, 70, 82
Banks, Adam J., 5, 8–9, 224
Barthes, Roland, 145–46
Bassandyne, Thomas, 171–80
benevolentia, 188, 195
Benjamin, Ruha, 216–17, 224–25
Benjamin, Walter, 165, 177, 186
Bernard of Chartres, 98–101
Blau, Sheridan, 90–91
Boethius, 55, 101–2
Bolens, Guillemette, 160–61
Bolter, Jay David, 5–6, 77–79, 189
Bourdieu, Pierre, 13–14, 25–27, 30–41, 49, 82, 218, 222–23
boyd, danah, 190–91
Boyle, Casey, 216–18, 221–25
Boyle, Jen, 114–15, 182
Brannon, Lil, 60, 100–1
Breen, Katharine, 31, 153
Brock, Kevin, 98, 224–25
Brooke, Collin, 85–87, 210, 212
Bruni, Leonardo, 83–84
Burrows, Cedric, 14, 55, 180
Bush, Vannevar, 77–78, 226

Camargo, Martin, 8–9
Canterbury Tales, The. *See* Chaucer, Geoffrey
Carruthers, Mary, 8–9, 79–80, 84, 94, 155, 190, 211
Caxton, William, 16; Aesop and, 135, 157, 160–61, 174–75, 178–80, 184–85; *Mirrour of the World*, 69–70, 76–80, 88, 92
ChatGPT, 7, 73–74

Chaucer, Geoffrey, 4, 15, 22, 55, 85–86, 89, 101–2, 191, 193; Aesop and, 17, 94–95, 98, 104–8; *Canterbury Tales, The*, 17, 64–67, 71–72, 94–95, 98, 104–8, 112, 114, 118; *House of Fame, The*, 198–99; *Legend of Good Women, The*, 196–207, 212–14; *Troilus and Criseyde*, 102, 202
Chauntecleer, 105–8
Chrétien de Troyes, 52–53, 83
Chronicle of Walter of Guisborough, 73–75
Chuh, Kandice, 13–14, 41–42
Chun, Wendy Hui Kyong, 3, 13–14, 37–38, 93–94, 152–54, 215–16, 226–28
Cicero, Marcus Tullius, 51, 87, 184, 188; letter writing and, 22, 113, 191–93, 197–201; on friendship, 205–12; on *habitus*, 13, 27–29, 33–34, 36, 153
Colbert, Stephen, 16, 69, 85–87
Common Core State Standards Initiative, 89–92
Competency-Based Education (CBE), 49–50, 52
compilation, 12, 26, 34, 37, 67–68, 115, 134, 139, 149, 166, 169, 186, 213; as a habit, 15–16, 69–92, 219
Copeland, Rita, 8–9, 15
counterstory, 223–24, 226
COVID-19, 44–45, 47–48, 218–19
cursus, 197–99
Cydippe, 109, 196

data, 16, 19, 44; and data-driven culture, 35–36, 42, 124, 147, 152–53, 209–10, 215–17, 220, 229; storage, 70–71, 77–78, 182–85, 187, 190, 203–5, 212–13, 226
delivery, 23, 48–49, 78–79, 121–22; rhetoric and, 5, 8, 38–39, 94–95, 126–27, 131, 191–93, 209–14
Desmond, Marilynn, 197, 200–1
DeVoss, Dànielle Nicole, 8, 131
dictamen. *See ars dictaminis*
Dido, 111, 196–207, 212–14
Dinshaw, Carolyn, 72, 201
disputation, 12, 16–17, 30, 35, 37, 41–42, 53, 92, 222–25; as a habit, 93–122, 219–20

Douglas, Gavin, 22, 193, 197–201
Drucker, Johanna, 42, 129, 149–50, 205, 215–17, 225–28
Dunbar, William, 101–2

Early English Books Online (EEBO), 182–84, 187
encyclopedia, 64, 134, 177, 180; as a compilation, 15–17, 69–92, 97, 211–12, 221
Enders, Jody, 8–9, 94, 97, 109
English Language Arts (ELA), 90–1
epimythia, 133–34
epistolarity. *See* letter-writing
Erasmus, Desiderius, 196–97
Esposito, Roberto, 186–87
Eyman, Douglas, 8–9, 119

Facebook, 4, 18, 21, 36, 73, 89, 94, 97, 148, 218, 226; salutation and, 189–91, 194–96, 209–12, 220–21
fan fiction, 18, 94–95, 101, 104, 110–15
Fitzpatrick, Kathleen, 117–18, 166–67
Foys, Martin, 114–15, 145–46, 182
Fradenburg, Aranye, 67–68

Gawain, 112–13
Genius (website), 147–53, 220
Geoffrey of Monmouth, 52–53, 112
Geoffrey of Vinsauf, 9, 18, 22, 33, 37, 98–99, 217; *Documentum de modo et arte dictandi et versificandi*, 29, 123, 124–25, 143; *Poetria nova*, 101, 125–27, 153–54, 213–14, 226–28
Gerson, Jean, 193–94
Giovanni da Spira, 197–98, 207
Giovanni di Bonandrea, 9, 13, 22, 33, 36–37, 214, 217, 227; *Brevis introductio ad dictamen*, 27–29, 199–201, 221
Glenn, Cheryl, 8–9, 66
Google, 36, 73, 77–78, 80–81, 216–17, 224–25
Gossouin of Metz, 76–77
Gries, Laurie, 8, 127–28
Grosz, Elizabeth, 123, 228–29

habitus, 4, 9–23, 59, 215–18, 221–29; amplificatory, 123–25, 127–30, 138–40, 153–54; appropriative, 156–58, 161, 165, 180, 185–88; compilational, 69–72, 78–79, 81–83, 88–89, 91–92; digital, 218–21; disputational, 53, 93–94, 97–98, 102–3, 111, 113–15, 119–21; history of, 25–42; salutational, 190–91, 193–201, 203–14; translational, 45–50, 54–55, 61–64, 66–68
Hawhee, Debra, 9–10, 125
Hayles, N. Katherine, 6, 78–79
Héloïse, 96, 192–93, 214
Henryson, Robert, 98–99, 101–3; *Morall Fabillis*, 20, 102–3, 132, 143–46, 157–59, 167–80, 183–85, 187, 221; *Testament of Cresseid, The*, 101–2
Hercules, 16, 69, 83, 87–88, 221
Hermannus Alemannus, 25, 29, 217
hexis, 26–27, 36, 38. *See also* Aristotle
Higden, Ranulph, 14–15, 46, 50–51
hip hop, 148, 224
hive mind, 82–84, 210
homophily, 11–12, 22–23, 228
Honorius of Autun, 69, 76, 139, 166
House of Fame, The. See Chaucer, Geoffrey
Hugh of St. Victor, 210–11
hyper attention, 78–79

imago mundi, 16, 69, 75–81, 89
incunabule, 182, 187
Ingham, Patricia Clare, 20, 165
Instagram, 77, 123, 189–91, 226
internet, 9, 14, 16–17, 33, 72, 75, 79, 110, 147, 152, 191, 213, 218, 226; translation and, 45–46
Irvine, Martin, 81–83, 166–67, 185
Isidore of Seville, 16, 69–70, 75–78, 81–83, 87–88, 92, 221

Jenkins, Henry, 18, 104, 115–16
John of Garland, 9, 18, 124, 126–28, 210–12, 221–23, 227–28
John of Salisbury, 100–1

Kabyle, 40–41
Kairos (periodical), 116, 119
Karras, Ruth Mazo, 17, 97–98

Kirschenbaum, Matthew, 203–4
Knoblauch, C.H., 60, 100–1

Lacan, Jacques, 202, 205
Latour, Bruno, 13–14, 31–36, 82, 110. *See also* Actor-Network-Theory (ANT)
LeBlanc, Paul, 49–50
Legend of Good Women, The. See Chaucer, Geoffrey
letter writing, 4–5, 7–8, 13, 21–22, 66, 84, 91, 96, 109–10, 113–14, 124, 226–28; and epistolary style, 21, 196, 201–2; *habitus* and, 27–28, 33, 36–37; salutation and, 189–214. *See also ars dictaminis; ars dictandi*
Libyco-Berber, 40–41
Life of Aesop, 160–61, 171–75. *See also* Aesop
Liu, Alan, 19–20, 165
Longfellow, Henry Wadsworth, 155–56, 187
Losh, Elizabeth, 3, 7–9, 48–49, 97
Lounsbury, Thomas R., 58–61

Manguel, Alberto, 129–30, 147
manicule, 10, 132, 137, 146–48
Manly, John, 64–66
manuscript, 3–11, 13, 19, 30, 37–40, 51, 54, 65, 70, 72, 75–76, 78–85, 101, 111, 117–19, 124–27, 129, 131–43, 145–46, 151, 157–60, 164–71, 178–80, 203, 207–13, 215–17, 223; Aberdeen University Library MS 21, 237n27; Berlin, Staatsbibliothek, Preußischer Kulturbestiz, cod. Q 536, 139, 252n56; Biblioteca Universitaria di Bologna (BUB) Lat. MS 1 VIII, 260n30; BUB Lat. MS 313, 260n35; BUB Lat. MS 467, 260n30; BUB Lat. MS 1282, 260n30; BUB Lat. MS 1754, 260n35; BUB Lat. MS 2051, 260n30; BUB Lat. MS 2283, 260n30; BUB Lat. MS 2461, 28, 234n13, 260n35, 260n37, 262n14; Biblioteca Marciana MS 4018, 139; Boston Public Library, Griswold MS 835, 255n1; British Library MS Additional 11897, 163; British Library MS Additional 24194, 237n27; British Library MS Harley 3865, 169–77; British Library, MS Sloane 5, 247n33; Budapest, Magyar nemzeti múzeum, ms. lat. med. aev. 123, 140, 252n60; Cambridge, St. John's College MS 204, 237n27; Cambridge, Trinity College MS 0.5.4, 51; Carinthia, Stiftsbibliothek, Codex S. Pauli in Carinthia 255/4, 137–38, 251n48; Copenhagen, Kongelige Bibliotek, GKS 1905 4°, 138, 252n51; Erfurt, Stadtbücherei, Amplon.Q.21, 253n70; Huntington Library, MS 28561, 54; Lambeth Palace MS 431, 161; Liverpool Public Library MS f909 HIG, 237n27; Munich, Bayerische Staatsbibliothek, cgm 3974, 139–40, 252n59; Munich, Bayerische Staatsbibliothek, clm 391, 252n56; Munich, Bayerische Staatsbibliothek, clm 14703, 253n71; Prague, Universitní Knihovna, ms. 546, 140–41, 253n61; Princeton Univ. Library, MS Garrett 151, 237n27; St Andrews University Library MS PA6295.A2A00, 206–9, 258n70; Stiftsbibliothek Klosterneuburg, Codex Claustroneoburgensis 1093, 136–37; Venice, Biblioteca Nazionale Marciana Zanetti Lat. 541, 248n69; Venice, Biblioteca Nazionale Marciana Zanetti Lat. 4018, 139, 252n54; Vienna, Österreichische Nationalbibliothek, Codex Vindobonensis Palatinus 303, 133–34, 251n35, 253n71, 256n44; Vienna, Österreichische Nationalbibliothek, Codex Vindobonensis Palatinus 3235, 137, 251n47; Vienna, Österreichische Nationalbibliothek, Codex Vindobonensis Palatinus 15071, 252n56; Wolfenbüttel, Herzog August Bibliothek, Codex Guelf. 52 Gudian Lat. 2°, 248n70; Wrocław, Biblioteka Uniwersytecka, MS Codex IV.Q.126, 139, 252n55
Marichal, Robert, 30–31
Marie de France, 3–4, 104–5, 155, 187. *See also* Aesop
Martinez, Aja Y., 223–24
mash up, 19–21, 157–61, 165–67, 169–77, 185, 187–88, 220
Mbembe, Achille, 215–16, 226
McCloud, Scott, 227–28

McCorkle, Ben, 72–73, 191–92
McLuhan, Marshall, 6, 141–42
McPherson, Tara, 42, 225–26
media studies, 5–6
memory, 18, 123, 200–2; rhetoric and, 5, 8, 73–74, 94, 126–27, 155, 189–90, 209–14, 226–27; storage and, 77–79, 204–7
Minnis, Alastair, 126–27
Mirrour of the World. See Caxton, William
Mol, Annemarie, 13, 32–35
Montaigne, Michel de, 209–10, 213–14
MOOC (Massive Open Online Course), 48–49, 52
moralitas, 196, 201; Henryson and, 102–3, 143–46, 175; and moral instruction, 133–34, 138–39, 163–64
multimodality, 127–31, 146
Murphy, James J., 8–9

Nair, Meera, 147–48
Neem, Johann, 49–50
Netflix, 118, 148
Newfield, Christopher, 47–49
Newman, Katherine, 44–45, 47–48
Noble, Safiya Umoja, 224–25
Norris, Sigrid, 128–29

O'Neil, Mathieu, 17, 43, 81, 98
Obama Hope (meme), 123–24
Olson, Christa J., 9–10
open access, 69, 116–20, 182–84, 204–5
Ovid, 95, 109–10, 114, 196–207, 213
Oxford English Dictionary (OED), 87–88

pagina, 129–30
Panofsky, Erwin, 13, 30–32, 39–40, 222–23
paperson, la, 13–14, 41–42
Parkes, Malcolm, 70, 130–31
Peirce, C. S., 166–67
Pertelote, 105–8
Perusall, 147–48
petitio, 191, 195–97
Petrarch, Francesco, 125; encyclopedias and, 80–81, 83–84, 88; letter-writing and, 22, 113, 192–94, 197–98, 208–9
Plath, Sylvia, 148–50

Pliny the Elder, 75–77
Poe, Edgar Allan, 155–56, 187
Porter, James, 8, 212–13
posthumanism, 216–17, 221–22
Postmedieval: A Journal of Medieval Cultural Studies, 114–15, 117
promythia, 133–34
ProQuest, 182–83, 186

Quintillian, 8, 51, 125, 213
quodlibetal debate, 30–35, 93–94, 96–97, 108–9, 223. See also disputation

reflection, 23, 180–81, 221–23
repetition, 11, 134; as a rhetorical technique, 125–26, 152–54; *habitus* and, 27–28, 31, 123, 215–18, 221
Reynard, 102–3, 105–6
Rhetorica ad Herennium, 199–200, 210–11
Rickert, Edith, 64–66
Rickert, Thomas, 38–39
Ricoeur, Paul, 71, 109–10
Ridolfo, Jim, 7–8, 131
Rodighiero, Dario, 35–36, 228
Roman de Renart. See Reynard
Romele, Alberto, 35–36, 228
Romulus, elegiac, 102–3, 132–37, 157, 162–63, 167–68, 184–85. See also Aesop
Rosenblatt, Louise, 90–91

salutation, 12, 21–22, 28, 33, 36–37; as a habit, 189–214, 220–21, 226–28; *salutatio* and, 28, 195–96
SAT, 47, 91
Sayers, Jentery, 7, 84–85
Scholasticism, 76, 79, 81, 132, 139, 157; *habitus* and, 13–14; 25, 30–32, 37, 39–41, 95, 97, 108–9, 119–21, 222–23
Shirky, Clay, 18, 121
Shotter, John, 34–35
Snowden, Edward, 21, 71
social media, 4–5, 12, 17–18, 21, 97, 104, 124, 147–48, 217–18, 220–21; algorithmic culture and, 34–36, 88, 94, 152, 224, 226; salutation and, 190–91, 210–14. See also Facebook; Instagram; TikTok; Twitter

Index

Southern New Hampshire University (SNHU), 49–50, 52
St. Andrews, 102, 207
Steinhöwel, Heinrich, 134–35, 140–42, 162, 171–80. *See also* Aesop
Standard Written English (SWE), 54–55, 66–67

Temple, Olivia, 181–82
Temple, Robert, 181–82
Testament of Cresseid, The. See Henryson, Robert
Text Creation Partnership (TCP), 183–84
1381 Rising, 106–7
Thoreau, Henry, 89–90, 120–21
Thrift, Nigel, 13, 32, 34–35
TikTok, 123, 191, 209
translation, 12, 14–15, 29, 41, 83, 97, 107–8, 131, 134–35, 141, 168–69, 171, 181–82; as a habit, 43–68, 213, 219, 222; *translatio* and, 19–20, 141
Trevisa, John, 47, 67–68; *Dialogue between the Lord and the Clerk on Translation*, 14–15, 46, 50–54, 61–65, 92, 97
Troilus and Criseyde. See Chaucer, Geoffrey
Trump, Donald, 94, 122
Turkle, Sherry, 21, 116
Twitter, 3–4, 7, 10–12, 16–18, 21, 40, 94, 97, 104, 148, 218–21, 223–25; salutation and, 190–91, 195–96, 203–4, 209–12

University of California (UC), 47–48
University of Massachusetts Boston, 44–45

Vaidhyanathan, Siva, 157, 186–87, 196–96
Vee, Annette, 224–25
Venturini, Tommaso, 35–36
Vincent of Beauvais, 76, 80
Virgil, 69, 83, 101, 109, 197, 202
Vita Aesopi, 173–79. *See also* Aesop; Caxton, William; Steinhöwel, Heinrich

Wakelin, Daniel, 141–42
Walter of England, 20, 132, 165. *See also* Romulus, elegiac

Wedding of Sir Gawain and Dame Ragnelle, The, 112–13
Welch, Kathleen, 8–9, 94–95, 212–13
Western Governors University (WGU), 50, 52
Wheatley, Edward, 135–37
Whitelaw, Archibald, 193–94, 206–9, 212
Wikiality, 16, 85
WikiLeaks, 19–21, 70–72
Wikipedia, 3–4, 10–12, 15–18, 34–35, 39–40, 217, 223–24; amplification and, 139, 149, 151–52; compilation and, 69–92, 219; disputation and, 93–92, 97–98, 115, 121; salutation and, 211–12; translation and, 43, 45–46, 67
Woods, Marjorie Curry, 8, 100, 111
Writing Across the Curriculum (WAC), 47, 54–56, 59–61, 65–66
Wycliffe, John, 61–64

YouTube, 3–4, 37–38, 72, 123–24, 226

Zoom, 44–45
Zumthor, Paul, 141–42, 160